COATS & CLARK'S
SEWING BOOK
NEWEST METHODS A TO Z
ALTERATIONS   ZIPPERS

COATS & CLARK'S
SEWING BOOK
NEWEST METHODS A TO Z

ALTERATIONS   ZIPPERS

GOLDEN PRESS • NEW YORK
Western Publishing Company, Inc.
Racine, Wisconsin

PRINTED IN THE U.S.A. BY
WESTERN PUBLISHING COMPANY, INC.

LIBRARY OF CONGRESS CATALOG CARD NUMBER: 75-27185

GOLDEN and GOLDEN PRESS® ARE TRADEMARKS OF WESTERN PUBLISHING COMPANY, INC.

Contents

A Different Sewing Book

Different, because it answers your questions just as you ask them. Different, because the details of garment construction are arranged in alphabetical order, doing away with the usual hunt for the place where your particular problem may crop up. A glance at the table of contents will give you an idea of the range of subjects covered, and how they follow each other. If a detail is too small or too special to have a chapter of its own, you will find it listed in the index in the back of the book, which will direct you to the page you need. In addition, there are continual cross-references, so you can always have the benefit of the fullest information there is on any given subject.

This is, above all, a reference book, carefully planned to be of maximum use to you. It is meant to supplement your pattern guide sheet, not take its place.

The methods given are the most up-to-date, chosen in every case because they work, save time and error, and give beautiful results. Each one has been carefully tested by the staff of the Coats & Clark Educational Bureau, a body of highly-qualified home economists that for 40 years has been developing sewing techniques with a special concern for the ease with which they can be followed. In some cases, paying attention to every step we recommend might seem to slow you up, but before long you will find it paying dividends. One step properly handled makes the next step that much easier. When all the steps are properly dealt with, the result will be work of professional fit and finish. If you

- avoid the "I can't be bothered" attitude,
- read and follow all the directions,
- do all the measuring and marking called for,
- press wherever indicated,

you will find your sewing job completed, all details taken care of, when you think you're still in the middle of it. Suddenly, it's done. And done right.

1 Take your measurements—you will need help for some of them. Then decide on the size and type of pattern that is right for you.

See PATTERNS

2 Buy pattern, fabric, notions at the same time so you won't be held up. The pattern envelope tells you what you will need.

See FABRICS THREAD and NEEDLES INTERFACING UNDERLINING

6 Transfer the pattern markings to the garment sections—this is extremely important and must always be done with great care.

See MARKING

7 Look at the pattern guide sheet to see how your garment will be sewn together.

See ASSEMBLING A GARMENT

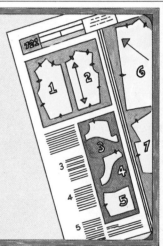

8 Get the sew machine ready— take out time to the stitch length tension, pressure balance on the you are using.

See MACHINE-STITCHING

11 Try on the garment, with side seams and waist seam (if any) basted. There should be very few adjustments, if any. Do not overfit!

See FITTING

12 Finish all machine-stitching and put in the zipper if you haven't done so before.

See ZIPPERS

3 Get organized— prepare a cutting surface, set up the ironing board and get out all the necessary equipment.

See EQUIPMENT

4 Study the pattern guide sheet—pick out the pattern pieces you will use and press them. Compare the pattern measurements with your own and make any necessary adjustments.

See PATTERNS, page 193

5 Cut out the garment —prepare the fabric if necessary, straightening ends and grain. Pin the pattern in place, following the cutting layout. Cut out.

See GRAIN
FABRIC
CUTTING

9 To baste or not to baste— let your judgment and experience be your guide; with an easy fabric and a simple pattern you may do very little basting but with a slippery fabric it may be better to baste.

See BASTING

10 Press as you sew— the pressing of seams as you finish each section is very important. You will hardly have any pressing to do at the end.

See PRESSING
and the various sewing techniques under individual headings.

3 Have someone mark your hemline— in most cases this is the best way.

See HEMS

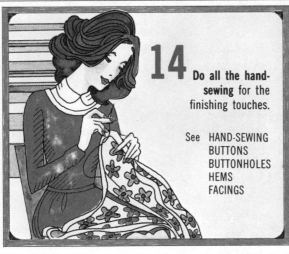

14 Do all the hand- sewing for the finishing touches.

See HAND-SEWING
BUTTONS
BUTTONHOLES
HEMS
FACINGS

15 A final pressing and you can wear it.

Words You May Wonder About

A number of terms used in sewing may be puzzling to you at first. The ones listed below are all defined in their proper places in the book (see the INDEX). In case you should come upon them without their explanation, however, here are some quick definitions.

Back-tack—A few stitches taken in reverse to secure a line of stitching.

Bar tack—A very short thread reinforcement for points of stress.

Baste-marking—Marking with hand- or machine-basting. Used to bring marks from one side of fabric to the other.

Clean-finishing—Edge of fabric turned under once and stitched. Used on edges of facings, hems, seams, etc.

Construction—The putting together of a garment (apart from preparation, decoration, and other finishing touches.

Construction stitching—Stitching, such as seams and darts, that shapes and holds a garment together (as distinct from stay-stitching, finishing, etc.).

Crocking—Color rubbing off.

Directional stitching—Stitching with the grain in woven fabrics. In knits, stitching all seams in the same direction.

Ease—The allowance added to a body measurement to make a garment wearable.

Ease, to (verb)—To attach a fabric edge to an edge that is slightly shorter. When ease-stitching, the longer edge is very slightly gathered.

Fashion fabric—The outer fabric in a garment.

Finger-pressing—Opening seam allowances with the thumbnail. Mostly used on fabrics that cannot be pressed.

Give—The degree of elasticity in a fabric or a thread.

Grading—Trimming each seam allowance to a different width to reduce bulk and avoid a ridge.

Hand—The feel and drape of a fabric.

Interlining—A layer of fabric added to a lining for warmth.

Miter—The diagonal fold made at the corner in an edge finish, such as a binding, hem, etc.

Nap—In actual fact, the raised, hairy or downy surface on fabrics such as flannel, etc. In patterns, however, "with nap" means any fabric surface that looks different when held up or down, such as pile, knits, one-way designs.

Non-woven fabric—A fabric not woven or knitted from thread or yarn. Non-woven fabrics include fake leather and suede, felt, various interfacings.

Notches—Markings on patterns used for matching. They are no longer notches but the opposite—they stand out from the cut edge. Notches cut into the seam allowance may weaken the seam.

Pivoting—Moving the fabric around with the machine needle in it and the presser foot up.

Pre-shrinking—Shrinking done before a fabric is used.

Self-fabric—The fabric from which the garment is made.

Sizing—A starch-like finish, added in the manufacture of some natural-fiber fabrics and rayon. It is water- and steam-soluble.

Stability—The degree to which a fabric resists pulling out of shape.

Stay—A tape added to a garment part to keep it in shape.

Stay-stitching—Stitching done inside the seam allowance, before construction, to stabilize curved or slanted edges. Usually done on a single thickness, but also used to attach interfacing or underlining.

Stitching-in-the-ditch—Stitching on the right side through a seam ("in the ditch"), to fasten something underneath.

Test seam—A seam done on a scrap of the garment fabric to test the machine stitch.

Topstitching—Hand- or machine-stitching, either functional or decorative, that shows on the outside of a garment.

Understitching—A line of stitching along the edge of a facing or undercollar to keep it from rolling to the outside.

Alterations
on Finished Garments

An alteration is an adjustment made in one detail of a garment, either ready-made or home-sewn, that is otherwise satisfactory (more than one alteration may be needed, of course). An alteration should not be confused with a make-over, which involves design.

Except in the matter of hemlines, alterations are generally made for fit. They are often necessary in ready-to-wear (which does not mean that, if a garment you like is not available in your size, you can alter an entirely wrong size to fit!). Alterations may also become necessary in your existing wardrobe, either because you have gained or lost weight, or because of a change in style, usually hemlines.

To check STANDARDS OF GOOD FIT, see page 102; also look at the adjustments on the pages that follow. These adjustments refer to a garment being sewn, but you may be able to adapt some solutions to your problems.

WHAT CAN AND WHAT CANNOT BE ALTERED

The general principle here is that you can almost always **take in,** that is, make a garment smaller or shorter; **letting out** a garment in order to make it wider or longer may present serious problems.

For instance, you can usually
 raise a hemline,
 raise a waistline,
 take in waist and hips,
 shorten sleeves,
 take in a plain faced neck,
 let out seams or hems if there is enough fabric and it is not permanently creased, clipped, faded, or stitch-marked,
  makes pants legs narrower,
  make crotch deeper,
  lengthen or shorten regular cuffed pants.

But you cannot
 lower a waistline (there isn't enough seam allowance),
 add width to shoulders or sleeve-caps, to a back cut in one piece, or to the seat of pants,
 let out seams or darts in fabrics that mark, (permanent press, tricot, taffeta, pile fabrics, etc.), because original seamlines will always show,
 let out seams whose allowance is not wide enough or has been clipped through; or darts that are slashed, or punctured at the point,
 let down a hem when outside fabric has faded or hemline fold has left a permanent mark,
 raise or lower the waistline of a fitted garment that has no waistline seam (one-piece).

Certain alterations, while possible, are inadvisable. You would find it extremely involved to
 alter an armhole with a sleeve,
 alter shoulders and neckline where there is a collar.

WHEN YOU ARE READY TO ALTER

If you have no one to help you with pinning and marking, you can do the job alone by pinning as seems necessary and trying on repeatedly. But it is both easier and safer with some help.

If the zipper is not in a seam you are altering, so much the better. The presence of a zipper, however, should not discourage you; remove it and press the opening allowances smooth. When your new seamline is established, proceed as directed in ZIPPERS. If the seam has been let out, widen seam allowance with seam binding (see p. 264).

The alterations that follow are the ones most often needed. When more than one is necessary (for instance, changing both hemline and side seams), study the steps in the instructions and combine them.

ALTERATIONS IN LENGTH

Alterations in length are usually made at the garment hem, the sleeve hem or the cuff. They are also made at the waistline, within the limits described under WHAT CAN AND WHAT CANNOT BE ALTERED.

HEMLINE TOO LONG, SHORT, OR UNEVEN

Changing a hemline is the simplest and most common alteration. It can be made to **straighten,** to **raise,** or to **lower** the hemline. When you buy a garment, the store will sometimes mark a hem alteration for you.

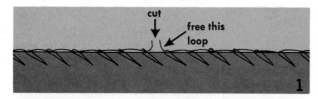

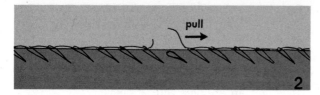

For any change in the hemline:

Take out the old hem. In a manufactured garment, this may be chainstitched. To take out stitching, cut through one stitch (1), free one loop—be sure it is on the side shown, and pull the thread-end (2). Press hem open. Then follow directions on page 120. When lowering a hemline, it is sometimes necessary to make a faced hem (see p. 126).

CUFFED SLEEVE TOO LONG

This often occurs in men's shirts. Remove cuff by taking out stitching. Trim raw sleeve bottom as needed. Replace cuff. The placket slit will now be shorter, but this is not a noticeable detail.

BODICE TOO LONG

This can be corrected by raising the waistline, which is not as difficult as you may think. To determine the right place for the waistline, put on the dress. Tie a string around the waist. Have someone mark correct waistline with pins along string.

Take off dress. Even out pin-line, then replace it with a line of baste-marking. If center front and back, side seams, darts, etc. on skirt do not match corresponding points on bodice, be sure to thread-mark their position. Remove zipper, if any, or just bottom half to clear the waistline. Take out waistline seam, or just the part of it that is to be altered. Press to remove creases.

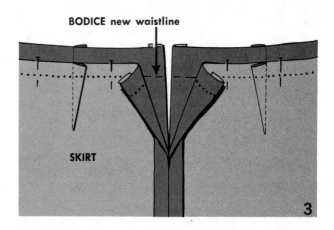

With skirt and bodice right sides together, match old waistline on skirt to new waistline on bodice and pin together (3), first at center front and center back; then work toward side seam, matching marked points between. Because of the tapering of seams and darts, bodice may now be wider than skirt. Depending on fabric and design, you may be able to ease or gather bodice to skirt, or you may have to take in darts and side seams.

After adjusting bodice to fit, pin again as described, baste and try on. Then stitch new waistline seam and trim away excess bodice fabric even with skirt seam allowance. Press. Replace all construction details (zipper, facing, hooks and eyes, buttons, etc.) as they were before.

ALTERATIONS IN WIDTH

An armhole-through-hips alteration in the width of a dress is simple, especially if the dress does not have a waistline and the zipper is at center back (if there is a waistline seam, take out waist seam at points of alteration). If you take in or let out a fraction of an inch at each side seam and each dart or in-between seam (ignoring center front and back), it will add up to a sizeable change. For carrying through this alteration on a skirt, see next heading.

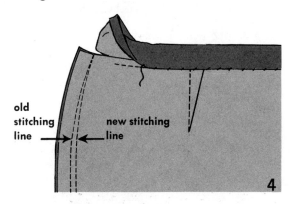

old stitching line   new stitching line

4

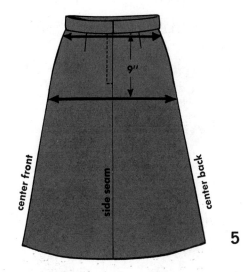

center front   side seam   9"   center back

5

SKIRT TOO LOOSE

This is normally corrected at side seams. Put on garment. Have someone pin side seams deeper (taking in zipper, if any) from waist down, so that skirt fits comfortably and smoothly and hangs straight. Then sit down to make sure there is enough ease. Check fit of waistband.

Take off garment. Turn inside out. Transfer pin-markings to one thickness of fabric on wrong side. Remove stitching in hem for a few inches at each side seam. Remove zipper if it is in a side seam. Waistband need not necessarily be entirely removed (or waist seam entirely opened). If it fits, remove the stitching as needed to release side seams (4). Press seam allowances together. Mark new seamlines with chalk, tapering from hip to waist and parallel to old lines (use yardstick) from hips through hem.

Stitch new seams (4). Take out old stitching. Trim seams, finish as needed, and press open.

Replace zipper and refinish hem. When replacing waistband, change position of closing as necessary.

SKIRT TOO TIGHT

There are two ways of widening a skirt.

WIDENING BY LETTING OUT SEAMS—If fabric does not show old marks and seam allowances are wide enough, this method is suitable for any skirt. It is the only possible one for a straight skirt. It is usually done at side seams, but if there are more seams, distribute the amount to be let out equally among them.

Measure your hips at fullest part—generally 7" to 9" below waist; add 2½"–3" for ease. Measure your waist, adding ½"–1" for ease.

Measure the skirt at the same distance from the waist; since the front and back are not of the same width, fold skirt lengthwise along center back and center front, side seams together as shown (5). The difference between the skirt measurements and your own plus ease, will be the amount of the alteration.

If alteration extends to waist, remove waistband or take out waist seam. Remove zipper if it is in a seam to be altered. Remove stitching in hem for a few inches at seams to be let out. Press seam allowances together, leaving seams stitched.

Using chalk and yardstick, mark new seamlines, going all the way through hem and either tapering to waistline if waistline is not altered, or carrying the alteration through as necessary. Amount to add at each seam will be:

. . . One-fourth of total alteration if only side seams are involved.

. . . Otherwise, one-half of total alteration divided by number of seams.

Stitch new seamlines. Remove old stitching. Press seams open.

Replace zipper, adding seam binding to widen seam allowance if needed (see p. 264). Refinish hem. If a waistband is included in alteration, lengthen it by adding a piece of fabric at end that will lap under. Replace and press.

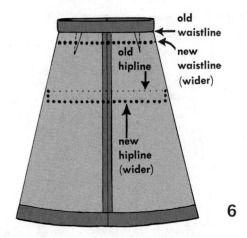

6

WIDENING BY RAISING AT WAIST—A gored, flared, or A-line skirt that is long enough can be widened at waist and hips by raising it at the waistline (6).

Put on skirt. Raise it around waistline (opening zipper as necessary) until hips are fitted comfortably. Tie string snugly around waist and adjust skirt evenly. Have someone mark new waistline with pins along string.

Take off skirt. Even out pin-marked line; replace it with line of baste-marking. Remove waistband or open waist seam. Remove zipper (if any). Press. Trim away top of skirt ⅝" above new waistline marking.

Lengthen darts because they have been made shorter. Re-fit waistline since it has become larger. If larger waist fits, adjust bodice waistline at seams and/or darts; or lengthen waistband with a piece of fabric at the underlay.

If waistline is now too large, either ease it to the bodice or waistband, or deepen the seams and/or darts to fit. Replace zipper, opening the seam at bottom to fit; replace waistband or restitch the waist seam; press.

MISCELLANEOUS ALTERATIONS

GAPING NECKLINES

Unless you are an expert, and know how to re-cut a collar to fit, we do not advise this alteration except in the case of a plain, faced neck. On such a neck, remove facing and see directions under GAPING NECKLINE, page 104.

UNDERARM BAGGINESS

If this occurs in a one-piece dress (no waistline seam), it is usually due to snugness at the hips. Letting out the side seams a bit will take care of it.

In a garment with a waistline seam, you deepen the bust dart, which shortens the side seams. It also adds a little fullness to the bust.

Try on garment. Tie a string around waist. Have someone check if the back needs shortening; if so, mark correct waistline with pins. Pin bust darts deeper to take in excess fullness, tapering to nothing at points (don't worry about tucks made in the back—they will come out). Take off garment.

Open waistline seam across back to about 2" beyond side seams. Open side seams to within 1" of armhole. Take out zipper, if any. Press opened seams. Transfer pin-markings on darts to wrong side. Mark new stitching line with ruler and chalk.

Restitch darts and press. Restitch side seams, except zipper opening, if any. Press seams open. Front will now be shorter than back.

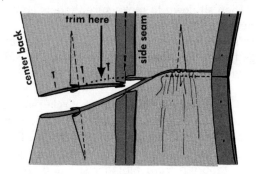

7

Fold bodice, still wrong-side-out, in half along center back line and pin side seams and bottom edge together as shown (7). Cutting through both thicknesses, trim off excess fabric in back—tapering as shown if back length is all right as is, or across entire back if it needs shortening. Pin and re-stitch waistline seam. Replace zipper, etc. Press.

ALTERATIONS ON PANTS

Alterations on pants should be approached with caution. Where the crotch seam is involved, any adjustment possible is minimal, and not very helpful. Certain other adjustments (plain hems, waist, hips) are similar to those in a skirt.

LENGTH WRONG

This is generally an easy alteration. For plain bottoms, see skirt hemline correction, page 12. For cuffed bottoms, see below:

CUFFED BOTTOMS, LENGTHENING—If you do not care about preserving the cuff, simply folding it down will usually give you the length you need.

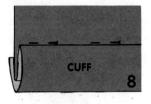 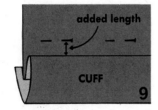

Otherwise, make a mock cuff, as follows:

On pants, mark location of top edge of cuff (8). Take out hem stitching and open out hem and cuff. Preserving the top and bottom creases of the cuff, move the cuff down from the mark as much as needed, making a new fold in the pants fabric **underneath** (9). Pin cuff in place all around. On inside of leg, stitch hem edge down where it falls. Press. Tack cuff to side seams. If you wish, you can attach top edge of cuff to pants leg, either visibly, by topstitching around ¼″ from edge, or invisibly by blindstitching by hand inside fold.

CUFFED BOTTOMS, SHORTENING—With fabrics on which the crease can be pressed out, you can take up the cuff, making it deeper, but by no more than ½″. Otherwise, and if you need more of an adjustment, shorten cuffs as follows:

On pants, mark new place for top edge of cuff. Take out hem stitching and open out hem and cuff. Preserving the top and bottom creases of cuff, move cuff up to the mark. Pin in place all around. The fold in the pants fabric will now extend below the bottom fold of cuff. Trim off the pants fold (not the cuff fold) to ¼″ above the cuff fold (10). Stitch the two cut edges together. Fold hem into leg and stitch down where it falls. Press. Tack cuff to side seams. If you wish, attach cuff to pants (see LENGTHENING, above).

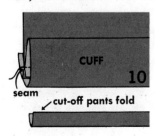

WAIST OR HIPS TIGHT OR LOOSE

See ALTERATIONS IN WIDTH, page 12.

LEGS TOO WIDE OR TOO NARROW

Side seams and in-seams can be slightly taken in or let out, but be sure to do it in the same amount on both leg seams so that the crease-line remains the same.

BAGGY SEAT

Put on the pants and, since the fitting must be done in the back, get someone to help you. The problem may be too much fabric in the length, or in the width, or both. The only way to find out is to pinch up fabric and pin until you are satisfied. **Be sure,** however, before stitching any alteration, to sit down, bend over, etc. Some ease must be allowed for movement.

Begin with the **length.** In back, just below the waistband, pinch up and pin in a tuck, tapering to the sides (11). If this eliminates the bagginess, detach that part of the waistband by taking out the stitching, and re-pin it along a new waistline. Try on the pants again. If they fit, re-stitch the waistband as pinned.

If there is too much **width** pin up the seams at the sides or at the crotch or both (12). If this does the trick, re-stitch the seams as pinned. This may involve taking out the zipper in part or entirely.

On occasion, taking in fabric in both length and width may be necessary.

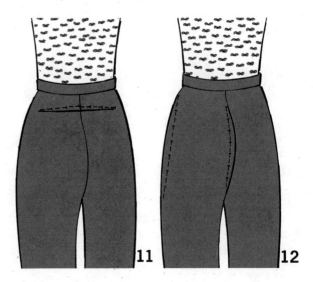

Appliqué

Appliqué is decoration consisting of a piece or pieces of fabric attached to the background fabric, either with hand- or machine-sewing, or by fusing. The design may be of any kind, from bands, straight or bias, to free-form motifs; and it may be purchased for the purpose, or copied from a model, or made up by yourself. Often, it is a motif in a printed fabric, cut out for application to another fabric. The fabric in every case should be chosen to conform to the properties of the background (whether washable or dry-cleanable, for instance).

For raised appliqués, add lamb's wool padding (with dry-cleanable fabric) or polyester fiberfill (with washable fabric). Leaving a small opening at edge, push padding under appliqué—do not overstuff. A fused appliqué cannot be raised.

TRACING THE MOTIF

Use a sharp pencil. Trace the outline of motif on the appliqué fabric, on the wrong side for a hand appliqué, on the right side for a machine-stitched or fused applique. Needless to say, tracing is unnecessary for a motif to be lifted from a print.

HAND APPLIQUÉ

Make a line of machine-stitching just outside the motif outline. Cut out, ⅛" to ¼" (depending on size of motif) outside the stitched line (1). Clip curves as shown. Pin motif in place.

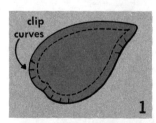
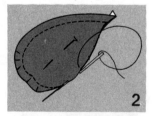

Attach the edges with invisible slip-stitching (see p. 122), turning them under on machine-stitched line as you go along (2). If you prefer to finish the edges with small blanket stitch (see p. 254), trim off the seam allowance close to stitched line.

Appliqués of felt, which do not ravel, are cut out on the outline itself and tacked on invisibly.

MACHINE APPLIQUÉ

Cut out the motif, leaving a seam allowance of about 1" all around. Pin in place.

Attach in place with a line of straight stitching just outside the motif outline. Trim away seam allowance carefully, close to stitching (3).

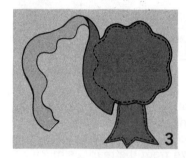
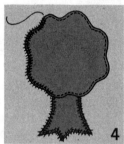

For the decorative stitching covering the edges (4), the thread should match either the appliqué, making appliqué look larger, or the background, making appliqué look smaller. (Contrasting thread shows up stitching imperfections.) For satin stitch, use the pattern-stitching foot. Other stitch patterns may be used as well.

Set the stitch width to ½ the fullest width on the machine. Make a test sample and adjust the stitch length and width if necessary: the narrower the width, the easier it is to control the stitching.

Stitch at slow speed. If the appliqué consists of several pieces, do not stitch any edge that will be covered by another piece—the machine may jam when going over a previous stitching, and this stitching would show as a ridge when pressed. At the end of each stitched line, pull thread to wrong side, tie off and clip before continuing.

ON STRETCHY KNITS, the area to be appliquéd must be backed with a lightweight, heavily-sized fabric with a low thread-count, such as starched lawn or cheap organdy. Cut a piece of any shape, larger than the appliqué plus seam allowance. Pin or baste it to the wrong side of the garment, and stitch through it when straight-stitching the motif in place. **Do not trim this backing** until after the zigzag stitching is completed.

FUSED APPLIQUÉ

Pin appliqué design to a piece of fusible web and cut out the two layers together. A pre-cut appliqué is used as a pattern for the web. Heat-baste and fuse (see p. 107).

fusible web

5

APPLIQUÉ BANDS

Appliqué bands may be flat bias tubing (see p. 29), ready-made bias tape, embroidered ribbons, or just a band of contrasting fabric. They can be applied by hand; or by machine with either straight or decorative (zigzag) stitching; or by fusing.

Assembling a Garment

Assembling the pieces of a garment should be a simple, logical procedure based on good work organization. The procedure generally followed by pattern guide sheets is called Unit Construction. A unit is any section of a garment on which work is to be done, and the idea is to do as much of that work as possible before joining the unit to another unit. Look at the illustrated sequence below. As you see, a unit may consist of one or several pieces, and small units go into making larger units.

The system is efficient because
it reduces handling and so keeps the garment looking fresh,
it eliminates waste motion,
it allows you to complete a garment unit (and take advantage of short work periods) while the rest of the work remains undisturbed.

In Unit Construction, however, any basic adjustments in the pattern must be made in advance (which is the right way to make them, anyway). In other words, you must be sure that the pattern fits, with darts in the right place, neckline right, sleeve-length correct, etc. Certain small alterations can be made when joining units (see FITTING A GARMENT, p. 101).

After cutting and marking, sort the cut pieces into a pile, units together and the pieces to be used first on top. If you complete the small units (sleeves, collar, patch pockets) first, the work on the large ones (skirt, bodice, jacket) can proceed without interruption. Keep the garment fresh by hanging up the larger units as they are sewn (a top when shoulder seams are in) and laying away the small ones. Unfinished sections can be pinned to a hanger.

Here is an example of efficient procedure with a bodice unit:
Collar and sleeves may be prepared first, if desired.
Stitch the darts on both front and back sections.
Attach interfacing and make bound buttonholes, if any (worked buttonholes are made later).
Press all darts and other stitching. Join seams; press.
Join seam; press.
Add facing, and prepared collar and sleeves.
Stitching as many darts and seams as possible before stopping to press them eliminates waste motion. Remember, however, that except when basting or fitting, you never catch a dart in a seam or cross a seam with another one, without first pressing it.

UNIT 1 SKIRT FRONT
UNIT 2 SKIRT BACK
UNIT 3 FRONT and BACK joined
UNIT 4 small pieces COLLAR, CUFFS FACING
UNIT 5 SLEEVES
UNIT 6 BODICE BACK
UNIT 7 BODICE FRONT
UNIT 8 FRONT and BACK joined at shoulders
UNIT 9 COLLAR and FACING added
UNIT 10 SLEEVES joined to BODICE
LAST UNIT BODICE and SKIRT joined; PLACKET; HEM

Basting

Essentially, basting means temporary sewing, done with long, loose stitches that are removed after a job is completed. Nowadays, it is often done by machine. Very often, however, the main purpose of basting—i.e., holding layers of fabric together preparatory to stitching—can be taken care of by pinning, and so we have pin-basting.

Thread-basting is also used for MARKING—see that chapter.

When thread-basting is a necessary part of the construction process, it is indicated in the pattern directions. Otherwise, the extent to which you do or do not baste, and whether you do it with pins or with thread, will depend on your skill and experience. The very safest way is first to pin-, then thread-baste. In general, basting is called for . . .

. . . where there are more than two layers of fabric, as in applying collars and cuffs,

. . . where seams contain fullness, such as ease, gathers, or pleats,

. . . when setting in sleeves,

. . . when matching plaids and stripes,

. . . with slippery fabrics, such as satin, velvet, etc.

. . . when a garment is to be tried on,

. . . in preparing a seam for a conventional zipper application.

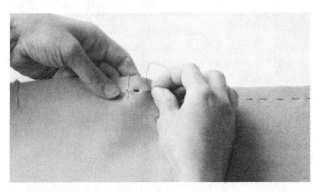

PIN-BASTING

When a fabric shows pin-marks, be sure to keep pins within the seam allowance. The way the pins are placed depends on whether the pinning is a preparation for stitching (or thread-basting), or for trying on (fitting) a garment.

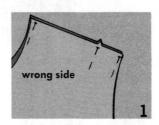

Pin-basting for stitching (or thread-basting). Pins are placed **crosswise** to fabric edge and so that they are on top when stitching. With raw edges even first pin seam-ends and notches (1), and any other matching points. Then add pins in between, as close together as necessary to hold seam securely (2). Remove pins as you stitch.

Pin-basting for fitting is done on right side of garment to allow pins to be moved while trying on. Pins are placed **parallel** to fabric edges (3), on seamline. If the seamline is altered by fitting, mark the new seamline on wrong side afterwards. Then remove pins and baste on wrong side.

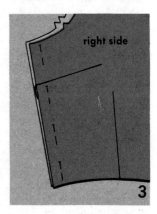

THREAD-BASTING BY HAND OR MACHINE

Machine-basting is quicker than hand-basting, of course. Whether you use one or the other will depend not only on your experience and skill, but on your fabric and preference.

Thread-basting for fitting is done on wrong side of garment. Clip basting as needed for alterations.

Basting of seams is done close to the seamline but within the seam allowance, to keep clear of final stitching.

To remove basting, clip thread every few stitches before drawing it out. This will avoid pulling the fabric out of shape. Use tweezers to remove any thread caught in stitching.

HAND-BASTING

Use a good quality needle, suitable for your fabric (see p. 251). There is special basting thread, but any light-colored sewing thread will do.

Even basting, the kind most generally used, is done with stitches about ¼″ long and ¼″ apart (4). As a rule, you do it flat, on the table (see photograph on opposite page). When one layer of fabric is to be eased to the other, you baste over the hand (5), with layer to be eased on top.

Uneven basting is used for marking and for holding one layer of fabric to the other where there is no strain, as in a hem. It is done with long stitches on top and short stitches through fabric (6).

Slip-basting is done on right side of fabric to match a fabric design at a seam. Use matching thread, since it will be exactly on the seamline and you may not be able to remove all of it after stitching.

On one edge, fold seam allowance under, baste or press. Working flat on the table, place this fold along seamline on the right side of the corresponding section. Pin in place, matching the design. At right-hand end of seam, bring needle and thread out through fold of upper section. Put needle into seamline of under section, at point precisely opposite where it came out of fold, and bring it out ¼″ ahead. Put needle into fold again at precisely the same point, take a ¼″ stitch through fold, running needle inside fold. Repeat. This actually makes a plain seam with even basting (7).

Diagonal basting serves to hold together areas of fabric rather than edges. It is used in the preparation of pleats (8) and in TAILORING (p. 233). Stitches are diagonal on top, straight underneath. They are left in until just before the final pressing, when they must come out, as they would mark the fabric.

MACHINE-BASTING

This requires some preliminary pin-basting. Then set machine at longest stitch, and use thread to match fabric, as the basting may be left in where seams are not to be pressed open. To remove basting, clip stitches every few inches and draw out. Some machines have a feature called speed basting, making stitches up to 1″ long or even more (see p. 152).

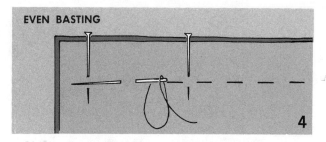
EVEN BASTING — 4

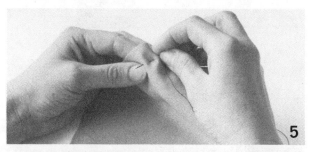
5

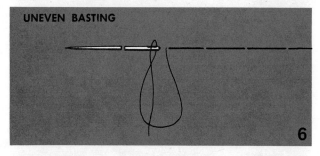
UNEVEN BASTING — 6

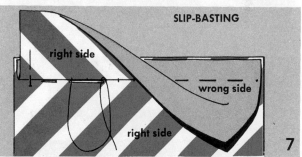
SLIP-BASTING — 7

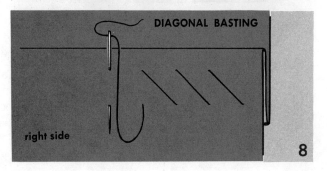
DIAGONAL BASTING — 8

Belts, Loops, Buckles

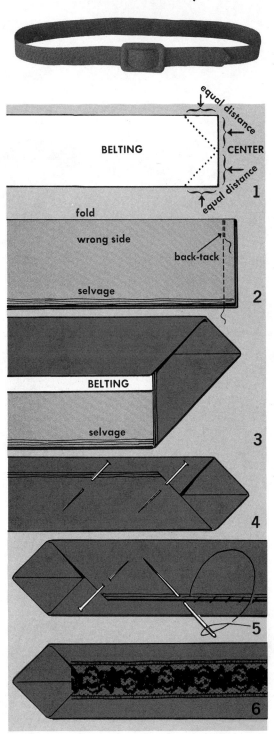

Ready-made belts are sold in a great variety of materials, widths, colors, and styles. You can easily make your own, however. You will find here directions for several kinds; also how to attach buckles and make belt loops.

COVERED BELT, SEWED OR FUSED

This can be made of practically any fabric, stitched or fused over a length of belting. Fusing is very neat and smooth—see directions below.

Belting, which can be washable, is sold by the yard, in widths ranging from ½″ to 3″ (see NOTIONS, p. 184). Buy it the desired width of the finished belt.

Cut belting to waist measurement plus 6″. At one end, carefully measure and cut a point, as shown (1).

Along a selvage edge, cut a strip of fabric to:

twice the width of the belting plus ½″;
length of waist measurement plus 6¾″.

(If you have no selvage edge, add ¼″ to the width; turn one edge ¼″ under, stitch, and use as "selvage edge.")

a. Fold one end of the fabric strip in half lengthwise, wrong side out. Stitch as shown (2). Press the seam open; trim to ⅛″.

b. Turn the stitched end to the right side, opening out the strip to form a point with the seam in center. Push out the point carefully; place the pointed end of belting inside point of fabric; press. Fold long **cut** fabric edge over belting, keeping the belting well centered (3). Press.

Fold the selvage edge over the other and press, with the fabric snug over the belting. Pin it down; keeping it snug (4).

c. At the straight end of belt, trim away the fabric ¼″ beyond end of belting. Sew free edges down (5). If desired, topstitch around edges.

Fused version—See the directions above, but cut the fabric strip to just twice the belting width. After preparing the point and inserting belting point as shown, press edges over to meet (not overlap) at center, and fuse in place (see p. 107). Finish by fusing a length of stretch lace over the raw edges (6).

For attaching a buckle, see page 23.

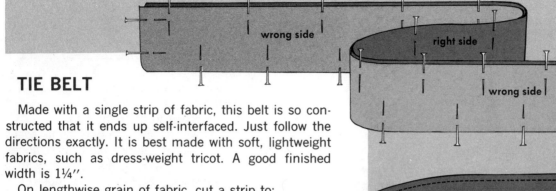

TIE BELT

Made with a single strip of fabric, this belt is so constructed that it ends up self-interfaced. Just follow the directions exactly. It is best made with soft, lightweight fabrics, such as dress-weight tricot. A good finished width is 1¼".

On lengthwise grain of fabric, cut a strip to:

   3 times the finished belt width plus 1";
   length of waist measurement plus 24" for hanging ends; 36" if ends are to be tied in a bow (piece if necessary).

a. Fold fabric into even thirds lengthwise, as shown. **Note the manner of folding:** if fabric has a right and a wrong side, the folded strip will show both sides. Pin the folded and raw edges together all around (7).

b. Place the strip on the machine **wrong** side of fabric up. Starting at about center of **raw edge,** stitch all around, ⅛" from edges. Leave a 3" opening for turning (8).

c. Turn the belt right side out. Slipstitch the opening closed. Press.

CORD BELT

Made of corded or self-filled tubing out of any fabric, woven or knit, this belt can be tied, or looped as shown. See instructions for CORDED TUBING, page 29. For cording, buy fluffy upholstery cord of desired thickness.

For the belt shown, prepare a length of corded tubing twice your waist measurement plus 1½ yards.

Fold cord in half, with the seam facing you. Keep the seam on the same side (inside) throughout. About 2" from the fold, tack cord together, forming a loop (9). Sew a hook on the end of the loop, as shown.

Put on the belt, pulling both ends through loop. Place a pin (for the eye) at the point opposite the hook. Mark the desired length of hanging cord-ends with pins. Take off the belt. At the pin-mark for the eye, tack the cords together on inside. On the outside, make a thread loop (see p. 252), or attach a straight eye. To finish the cord-ends, you can either knot each into a Chinese ball button (see p. 44), attach a tassel, or make a simple knot.

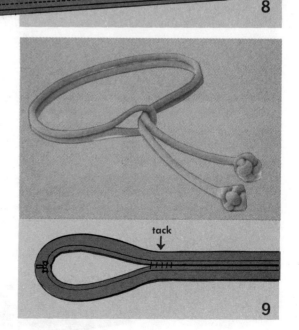

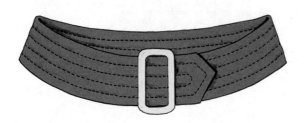

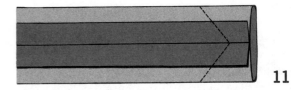

CONTOUR BELT

For knit fabrics only, with lightweight, nonwoven interfacing, all bias or one-way stretch. The belt is cut straight and the layers fused together. After the belt is stitched, it is steam-pressed to the desired curve. Width should be 2″ or less.

On crosswise grain of fabric (the direction of greatest stretch in knits), cut a strip to:

twice the finished width of belt plus 1″
length of waist measurement plus 6″.

Cut the interfacing and fusible web to twice the finished belt-width only (interfacing is not caught in seam), and the same length as the fabric strip.

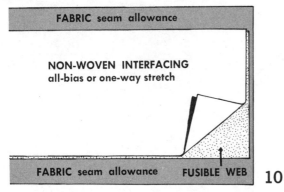

a. With fusible web in between, center interfacing on wrong side of the fabric strip (10) and fuse, following directions on page 107.

b. Fold the prepared strip in half lengthwise, wrong side out; stitch a ½″ seam. Do not trim the seam, but press it open. Fold belt so the seam is at center (11).

Measure, mark, and stitch, either a point (11), a rounded end, or a diagonal line. Trim the end seam to ⅛″ and turn the belt to the right side.

c. Topstitching, which can be done along edges alone or repeated over the entire width, is optional.

d. Shape the belt by **swirling** (see p. 26) with a steam iron. Work on right side, and do not try to complete the shaping in one step. Starting at point of belt, press while stretching the lower edge of the belt and easing the upper edge until the desired curve is obtained (12).

For attaching a buckle, see next page.

BELT LOOPS

Belt loops, or belt carriers, are necessary for any belt that is not at the natural waistline; or for keeping a narrow belt in place over a wider waistband. They also serve to keep belts from getting separated from garments, particularly coats, bathrobes, etc. Made in various widths and shapes, they may also serve for decoration or style. The loop described here is simply functional. How many loops are needed depends on the garment—the smallest number is two, one on each side seam.

Thread loops—On dresses, belt loops are usually made of thread, see page 252.

Fabric loops—Prepare the number of loops you need in a single strip. The length needed for one loop is equal to the width of the belt plus 1″ (plus a little extra if the belt is very thick).

Cut the strip along a fabric selvage. Unless your pattern calls for a specific width, make the strip three times the desired finished width (for loops ¼″ wide, cut the strip ¾″) and the total length of the loops.

Fold long raw edge one-third to inside; press (13). Fold the selvage edge over it; press. Fuse with fusible web or topstitch along both edges. Cut the strip into single loop lengths.

Mark the placement—width of belt centered over the belt line, one half above, one half below. When attaching the loops, make sure there is enough slack—the belt must slide through easily. Fold each end of loop ¼″ under and sew to garment, either by hand (14), or with machine-stitching, straight (15) or zigzag.

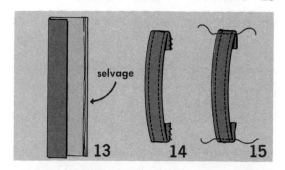

BUCKLES

When the belt closure is **not** a buckle, but a simulated tie or a simulated button closure (with a sewed-on bow or decorative buttons, etc.), it is fastened with large snaps or strong hooks and eyes.

Belt buckles of wood, metal, and plastic are available at notion stores and counters. Buckles covered with garment fabric can be made with a kit sold for the purpose, or ordered from the notions store, though that may take time.

ATTACHING BUCKLE TO BELT

BUCKLE WITHOUT PRONG (16)—Fold raw belt-end over the bar and sew down (17). To hold point of belt in place, attach a hook and eye or a piece of nylon tape fastener.

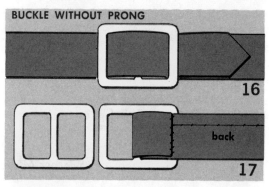

BUCKLE WITH PRONG (18)—1½″ from raw (straight) end of belt, make a small machine buttonhole; or cut a ½″ slit and overcast the edges (19).

For a **whole buckle,** fold the straight belt-end over the bar with the prong through the slit. Sew down (20).

For a **half-buckle** (21), make a fabric loop (see above), long enough to be folded around the belt and overlap ¼″. Sew the ends together on the wrong side of the belt without catching the stitches to the belt. Fold the straight belt-end over the buckle bar with prong through the slit. Slide the loop close to the buckle, fold the belt-end over it, sew down (22).

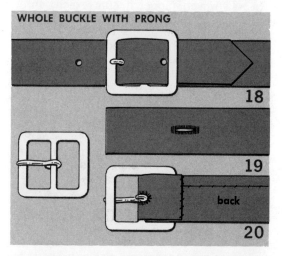

EYELETS can be made with a metal eyelet kit, by machine, or by punching holes through the belt and finishing them with buttonhole stitch. For placing the eyelets, try on the belt. Mark the point where the prong should come through. You will need three eyelets—one at the marked point and 1″ to each side of it.

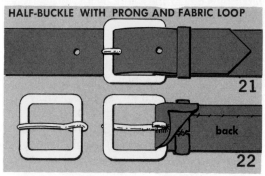

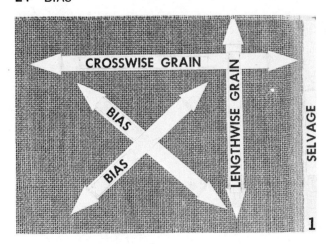

CROSSWISE GRAIN

LENGTHWISE GRAIN

BIAS

BIAS

SELVAGE

1

Bias

Bias is the corner-to-corner (45 degree) diagonal across a square of fabric. In woven fabric, it cuts exactly through the right angle formed by the lengthwise and crosswise grains (1), and is the direction in which the fabric has the greatest elasticity, flexibility, and "give". A close-fitting garment with the center line on the bias will cling to the body. A strip of bias-cut fabric can be stitched along a curve without a wrinkle—hence the wide use of bias strips in trimming and finishing. For the use of bias in knits, see FABRICS, page 81.

Please note: A diagonal line at any other angle is not bias; it is merely a slanted line.

GARMENTS CUT ON THE BIAS

A bias cut allows for graceful fitting and draping while bias-cut stripes and plaids, properly joined or placed, make attractive designs.

On the pattern, arrows indicating the straight grain automatically make the bias fall where it should. Be sure to follow these indications exactly.

A bias seam (two bias edges stitched together) may tend to stretch or sag, especially in loosely woven fabrics. A short stitch—about 20 to the inch—will stabilize such a seam. Better still, place a length of regular (straight grain) seam-binding over the seamline and stitch the seam through it.

BIAS STRIPS

Bias strips may be prepared by yourself (hand-cut) or bought ready-made. **The hand-cut bias strip,** which can be made from any fabric, to match or contrast, and in any width, is suitable for trimming or finishing any garment. Ready-made, or **packaged bias strips** (tape, piping, facing) come in polyester/cotton and rayon, with the edges pre-folded (see page 184 for listing of widths). With their wide choice of colors, they provide time-saving finishes for casual clothes. They are also much used for the inside finish of better garments.

Under the headings, BIAS BINDING, TUBING, PIPING, in this chapter, you will find directions for using the bias strip in trimming and finishing. For its use as a facing see page 96.

The **width and length** of a strip vary with its use.

For the **width,** see instructions later in this chapter under the heading describing its intended use. "Cut Width" means the width from raw edge to raw edge. "Finished Width" is the width that will show on the garment (right side or wrong side). It is also the diameter of round tubing. "Packaged Width" is the width of a packaged strip with the edges folded in, ready for application.

To determine the **length** needed, use a tape measure to measure the place of application. For separate pieces of trimming, such as frogs, make a sample out of tape or cord, then open out and measure it.

PREPARING THE HAND-CUT STRIP

The length of a single bias strip is limited by the width of the fabric: the bias cut being about one-third longer than the straight grain (2). When the strip needed is longer than what can be cut from the fabric, strips are joined end-to-end—needless to say, the longer the strips, the fewer the joinings. If you want to avoid joinings at conspicuous places, measure each length so that it meets the next one at places such as center back, side seams, under a belt, etc. Add 1″ for every joining. If the beginning and end of a strip are to be joined after application (as in a neckline), add at least 4″ to its total length.

For a very long strip in which it is not important where the joinings fall (a Hong Kong finish for hems or seams, for instance, see p. 125), you can pro-

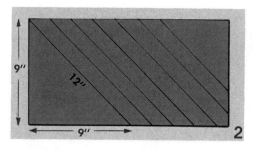

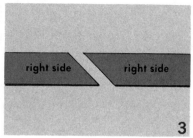

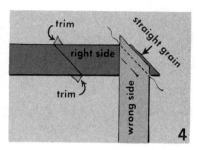

ceed like the manufacturers of ready-made bias strips, and join the fabric edges before cutting the strip—see CONTINUOUS BIAS STRIP, below.

LOCATING THE TRUE BIAS

Lay out a fabric end. To make sure that the lengthwise and crosswise grains are at a right angle, place an open newspaper over the fabric, one edge even with the selvage or with an edge cut parallel to the selvage. Trim the crosswise edge of fabric even with the other edge of the paper.

Mark off equal distances along the two fabric edges and, using a yardstick and chalk, draw a line between the two points (2). This is your bias.

SINGLE BIAS STRIPS—cut and joined

From the basic bias line marked, measure and mark the width of a strip—at several points if the strip is long—and draw another line. If the strip is intended for tubing, see STRETCHING, page 26. Repeat for as many strips as you need (2). Cut along the marked lines.

While strip-ends are diagonal in relation to the strip, they are on the straight grain. Two ends to

be joined must be parallel to each other (3). If necessary, trim one end to match the other.

To join, place two ends right sides together, at a right angle to each other, as shown (4); with the straight-grain edges even, but points extending so that the long edges cross at the seamline, forming small angles. Stitch on the straight grain, beginning and ending at angle centers. Press seam open and trim to a scant ¼". Trim off extending points.

CONTINUOUS BIAS STRIP

On a square or rectangular piece of fabric, mark a basic bias line (5); cut along line. Join straight edge **a** to straight edge **b**, in a ¼" seam, right sides together. Press seam open (6).

From one bias edge, on wrong side of fabric, measure the width of a strip, mark with yardstick and chalk. Repeat for as many strips as will come out of the fabric. **Trim off any excess along the last line.**

Bring straight-grain edge **c** to **d**, right sides together, carefully matching **x's**; one width of bias will extend at both top and bottom. Pin and stitch ¼" seam (7); press open.

Cut along marked lines for one continuous bias strip (8).

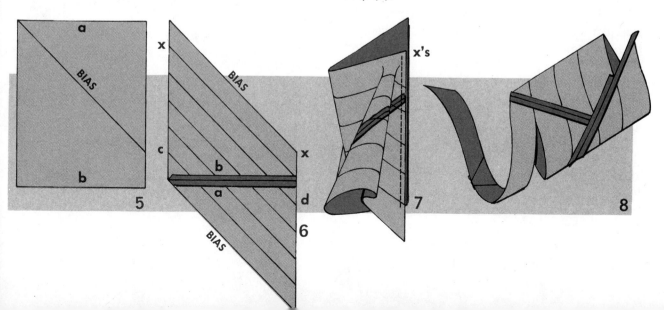

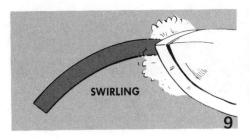
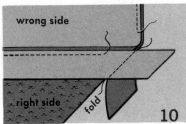
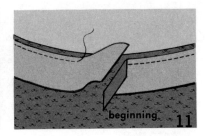

STRETCHING AND SWIRLING

Stretching a bias strip before using it is good practice, especially if the strip is intended for tubing, in which the stitching (which has no "give") may break while the tubing is turned to the right side. To stretch a strip, steam-press it firmly while stretching it with the other hand. Depending on the fabric and degree of stretch, the strip may become narrower in the process. If this happens (stretch a trial strip of bias before cutting the rest), cut the strips a little wider. (Packaged bias strips come prestretched.)

Swirling means shaping a bias strip to go around a curve (9), and should be done with both hand-cut and packaged strips. Steam-press firmly, stretching one edge and easing the other, as shown.

JOINING BEGINNING AND END OF A BIAS STRIP

There are two ways of joining: by seaming, which is the correct way, and by lapping, which is a quick way. Always start the application of the strip at an inconspicuous spot.

Seamed Joining—At the starting point, leave an extra 2″ of the strip free. When, after stitching the strip on, you are about to reach that point again, stop just short of it; cut the strip off 2″ beyond it. Fold the garment (10) so that the strips are at right angles as for any joining (when using packaged bias strip, open out folds). Seam ends together on the straight grain, close to fold of garment (10). Trim seam; press open. Finish stitching strip to garment, across the joining.

Lapped Joining—Before beginning to stitch, fold that end of the bias strip ½″ to wrong side on the straight grain. When completing the stitching, cut the second end on the straight grain to lap over the first for about ½″ (11). Stitch across.

BASTING

A bias strip should be pinned in place before stitching, especially around curves. On a close curve, basting is definitely necessary.

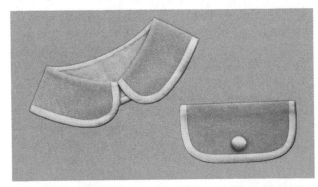

BIAS BINDING

A bias binding is a decorative finish that encases an edge. Its finished width varies.

On the edge to be bound, make a line of stay-stitching ¾″ from raw edge. Carefully trim away the entire ⅝″ seam allowance—no longer needed, since the edge is to be covered. If the edge is curved, shape the strip accordingly (see SWIRLING at left). For BINDING CORNERS (Mitering) see page 28.

HAND-CUT BIAS STRIP

Regular application

Cut strip 4 times as wide as the finished width desired.

Pre-crease the strip for easy application. Fold it in half lengthwise, right side out; steam-press firmly; fold in half again, press (12).

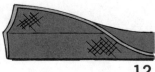

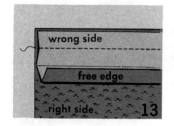
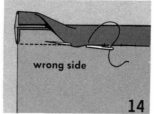
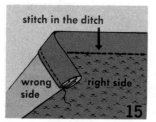
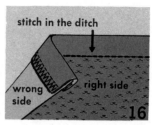

Pin or baste right side of opened-out strip to right side of garment, with raw edges even (be sure free edge of strip creases upward); if ends are to be joined, see at left before starting. Stitch along first crease (13). Fold strip up and to wrong side over cut fabric edges.

For a hand-finish, turn the free edge under on the crease. Slipstitch to line of stitching (14).

For a concealed machine-finish, "stitch in the ditch"; roll the underside of the strip so the free creased edge reaches slightly beyond the line of stitching. With right side of garment up, "stitch in the ditch"—that is, on garment fabric but closely alongside the binding, so as to catch the creased edge underneath (15). Thread color, well matched to garment fabric, is important here.

For a Hong Kong finish as an edge trimming where the inside will not show, cut strips a little narrower; do not pre-crease. Finish one edge with zigzag stitch. Stitch other edge to garment edge, right sides together. Fold strips to wrong side and "stitch in the ditch" on the right side (16) as described above.

QUICK TOPSTITCHED

This can be done with a sewing-machine attachment called a binder. Follow the directions that come with the attachment.

FRENCH BINDING

This is suitable only in sheer or very lightweight fabrics. Cut strips 6 times as wide as finished width desired.

Fold the strip in half lengthwise, right side out. Press. Pin or baste raw edges of folded strip to right side of garment, all edges even; if beginning and end are to be joined, see page 26 before starting, but leave 3" free at ends and when joining, open out the strip completely. Stitch at a

distance from the edge exactly equal to the finished width. Press the strip up; fold to wrong side over all raw edges.

For a hand-finish, slipstitch folded edge to stitching line (17).

For a concealed machine-finish, see directions under "Regular application" (15).

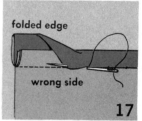

PACKAGED BIAS STRIPS

Regular application

¼" finished width, using ½" Single Fold Bias Tape. Apply in the same way as the HAND-CUT BIAS STRIP, page 26, with one fold opened out; on a packaged strip both creases turn upward, (18). For a concealed machine-finish, do your first stitching within the seam allowance, close to crease. Otherwise, stitch on the crease.

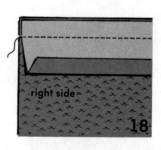

¼" finished width, using Double Fold Bias Tape. This is pre-folded with one side slightly wider than the other. Apply in the same way as the HAND-CUT BIAS STRIP, page 26, being sure to have the narrower side on top.

½" finished width, using 1" Single Fold Bias Tape (Wide Bias Tape). On right side of garment, mark a line ¼" from raw edge. Open out one fold of bias tape and pin or baste to the garment, right sides together, matching the raw edge of tape to the marked line. Then follow directions for HAND-CUT BIAS STRIP, page 26.

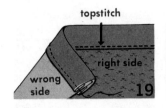

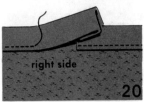

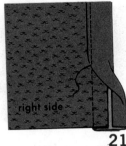

QUICK TOPSTITCHED

¼'' finished width, using Double Fold Bias Tape. With garment right side up, insert raw edge between creased edges of tape, narrower fold of tape on top. Topstitch (19). If ends must be joined, lap them (20).

½'' finished width, using 1'' Single Fold Bias Tape (Wide Bias Tape). Make it into a double fold by folding it in half length-wise with one side slightly wider than the other; press. Follow directions in preceding paragraph.

REGULAR TOPSTITCHED

Use ½'' or 1'' single fold tape, depending on finished width desired. Follow directions for Regular Application, but stitch tape first to wrong side of garment, then fold it over garment edge to right side, and topstitch in place (21).

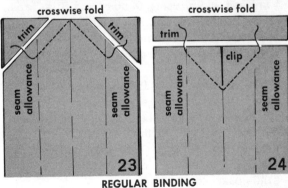

REGULAR BINDING

BINDING CORNERS (MITERING)

When a binding goes around a corner—either an outside corner, as on a pointed collar, or an inside corner, as in a square neck—the diagonal fold made in the binding is called a **miter.** A neat miter, while not difficult, takes a bit of care. It can be either stitched (for wider bindings) or folded.

A STITCHED MITER makes a firm, flat corner, but you must first determine exactly where it will fall. Fold the bias strip in half, lengthwise. With the fold matched to the garment edge, pin the strip along the edge to be bound. At corners, fold in the miters neatly (22a, 22b). Steam-press firmly, using the point of iron only. Unpin the bias strip, open out.

Where miters have been press-marked, fold the bias crosswise, as shown (23 and 24). Using a well sharpened chalk-pencil, draw lines over the creases outlining the point. Stitch the point, but leave seam allowances free. Trim ⅛'' beyond the stitching (23a and 23b, 24a and 24b); on an inside corner also clip into the corner (23b, 24b). Turn to right side.

When applying the binding, carefully match miters to corners. **On outside corners,** stitch with binding on top; when you reach the miter stitching, stop, fold miter out of the way, pivot on needle, and stitch along other edge of corner. **On inside corners,** stitch with garment on top, pivoting at corner and being careful not to let an unwanted pleat form at miter.

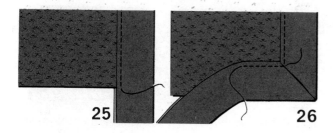

25 26

A FOLDED MITER is used in a quick topstitched application.

On outside corners, stitch to edge of fabric, as shown (25). Cut off thread, form the miter, and start stitching again from miter-fold (26). Afterwards, bring thread-ends to wrong side and fasten. Slipstitch miter fold if binding is wide.

On inside corners, carefully clip about ⅛″ into the garment corner. When applying the binding, stitch beyond corner to the width of binding. 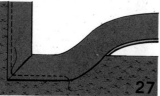 Cut off thread, form the miter, and start stitching again from corner of miter (27). Bring all thread-ends to wrong side; fasten. Secure miter in place with a few hand-stitches on wrong side.

TUBING

Tubing is made by stitching the edges of a bias strip together to form a tube, which is then turned inside out. It is used either flat or round. Flat tubing is suitable for ties and appliquéd decorations; round tubing (filled with its own seam allowance or with cord) for loops, buttons, ties, belts, frogs, and decorations. Tubing is usually made from hand-cut bias strips, since this allows for a choice of fabric. Joinings, which cause lumps, should be avoided. Packaged bias tape, however, can be used if the width from raw edge to raw edge is right. Tubing is turned with a loop turner or a bobby pin.

FLAT TUBING

Cut bias strip 3 times as wide as the finished width desired. Fold the strip in half lengthwise, wrong side out. Seam edges together, taking a seam allowance of a scant ⅓ of the width of the strip (as folded). Stretch the strip as you stitch.

Press the seam open lightly with tip of iron (if necessary, insert a pencil or rod into the tube to avoid creasing).

Turning with a loop turner: Insert loop turner into tubing, gathering up the fabric until the hook comes out at the other end. Catch hook securely through fabric at seam. Pull turner back through tube, turning tube inside out. Keep seam allowances open. Press tubing flat with seam at center.

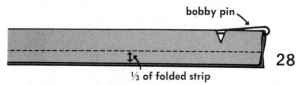

bobby pin

⅓ of folded strip 28

Turning with a bobby pin: Cut a notch at the fold ½″ from one end; slip a bobby pin over this end and insert through notch as shown (28). Push bobby pin through, turning the tube inside out. Keep seam allowances open. Press tubing flat with seam at center.

ROUND TUBING—self-filled

The diameter of self-filled tubing depends on the bulk of the fabric used—finished organdy tubing should be no more than ⅛″ wide; satin no more than ¼″; other fabrics in proportion to their weight.

Cut bias strips 5 times as wide as desired finished width.

Fold strip in half lengthwise, wrong side out. Stitch midway between fold and cut edges, stretching the strip as you stitch. For turning, see directions for FLAT TUBING, but do not press.

ROUND TUBING—corded

Cable cord for filling tubing comes in thicknesses from threadlike to ½″ plus. Select by eye (size designations vary). Remember that the tubing may compress a large, fluffy cord to a smaller size.

To determine width of bias strip, fold a corner of fabric over cord to be used; with a pin, fasten the two layers of fabric together so that the cord is tightly enclosed. Cut ½″ beyond pin (29). Open out the piece—the width between the two parallel edges will be the width of strip needed.

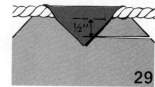

29

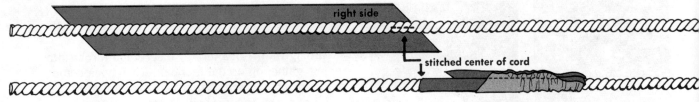

right side

stitched center of cord

Cut a length of cord twice the length of your bias strip. Attach center of cord to right side of one end of the bias strip with a few machine- or hand-stitches (30).

Fold strip over cord, raw edges even. Starting at attached end, stitch with a zipper foot close to cord, stretching the strip as you go. Trim seam allowance to ¼″.

Turning—Starting at free edge of tubing, push fabric over cord toward center of cord; ease tubing over stitched end (31). Continue until entire tubing has been reversed over cord. Keep seam allowances open for smoothness. Cut off excess cording.

If ends are to be finished, pull out cording slightly and cut it ¼″ shorter than tubing. Pull tubing back over cording, turn in raw edges and slipstitch.

PIPING

Piping is a folded bias strip, either plain or corded. Its purpose is always decorative. You can prepare it yourself or buy it packaged. Whether it is placed on an edge or on the body of a garment it is always caught in a seam.

CORDED PIPING

To make corded piping—Determine width of bias strip, see corded TUBING (29), but cut fabric ⅝″ below pin, for a regular seam allowance.

Fold strip in half lengthwise over cording, right side out. Stitch close to cord, using a zipper foot (32).

To apply corded piping—Piping is stitched to a sin-

gle garment section before the two garment sections are seamed together. Pin or baste piping to right side of section, raw edges even. Clip seam allowance of piping if necessary (33).

Stitch with zipper foot over stitching on piping. Pin or baste the two garment sections together, wrong sides out, raw edges even. With zipper foot, stitch alongside former stitching, closer to cord (34).

Packaged corded piping comes in only one width and has a seam allowance of about ¼″.

On right side of one garment section, mark a line ⅜″ from raw edge. Pin or baste piping in place, with raw edges even with this line. Apply as for corded piping (33, 34).

PLAIN PIPING (uncorded)

For width, add ⅝″ to desired finished width and cut strips double that measurement.

Fold strip in half lengthwise, right side out. Press. Stitch at finished width from fold.

Follow directions under "To apply corded piping" but use regular presser foot.

JOINING ENDS OF A PIPING

At the beginning, start in an inconspicuous place, leaving ½″ of piping free. **At the end,** stop 1″ from beginning stitches. Cut off piping even with beginning stitches. If piping is corded, remove a few stitches at the end and cut off ½″ of cord. Fold raw end ¼″ in and wrap around beginning (35).

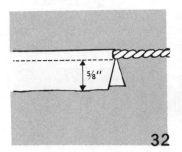
⅝″
32

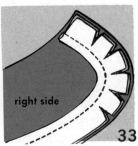
right side
33

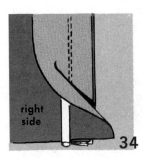
right side
34

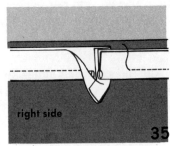
right side
35

Buttonholes

Buttonholes are basically slits cut through the fabric. The raw edges of a slit may be finished with fabric (bound buttonhole), or may be worked over with thread by machine or by hand (worked buttonhole).

Buttonholes are usually horizontal or vertical; now and then, to carry out a design, they may be diagonal. The making of either bound or hand-worked buttonholes undeniably requires care, precision, and time; also, practice. If you do not wish to spend the necessary time on such a project (and machine-worked buttonholes do not suit your purpose), select a pattern that does not call for buttonholes at all, or fake them by placing buttons on top of snaps.

FOR SUCCESSFUL BUTTONHOLE-MAKING

Good buttonholes should be exactly on grain and exactly the same size if they are in a row.

Use good scissors with very sharp blades and points.

Other equipment needed is: a 6″ ruler, a longer ruler or yardstick, and a contrast-colored pencil, not too hard and very sharp.

Have on hand the actual buttons for which you are making buttonholes, to make sure of correct measurements.

Interface any edge that is to have buttonholes, whether the pattern specifies it or not. That edge will always have extra wear. Avoid loose-woven or ravelly interfacing fabrics.

Reinforce ravelly or stretchy garment fabric by stabilizing the buttonhole area on the wrong side with a piece of lightweight interfacing fused in place.

Possible re-spacing—If you have altered the length of your pattern, the buttonholes may need re-spacing. As a general principle, the top and bottom buttonholes should be placed at their original distance from the top and bottom edges of the garment. The buttonholes between are then re-spaced to be at equal distance from each other.

Length of buttonhole—Buttonhole markings on a pattern indicate the buttonhole position. They do not indicate the buttonhole length, which is determined by the button.

DIAMETER **+** THICKNESS **=** LENGTH OF BUTTONHOLE

Measure diameter and thickness of your button: as a general rule, the two added together equal the necessary buttonhole length. (For instance, a button ⅞″ in diameter and ⅛″ thick needs a 1″ buttonhole.)

As an additional check, especially for buttons that are fabric covered, dome-shaped, ball-shaped or of some unusual shape, cut a slit in a swatch of your fabric, and try the button in the slit. Lengthen the slit, if necessary, until the button slides through easily. The length arrived at is the one you will mark on the interfacing.

Always make a test buttonhole before starting the buttonholes on the garment; then you will know how your fabric and interfacing handle. Follow the buttonhole directions exactly.

BOUND BUTTONHOLE

MACHINE-WORKED BUTTONHOLE

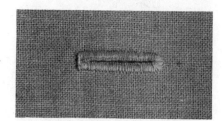

HAND-WORKED BUTTONHOLE

KEYHOLE BUTTONHOLE

MARKING

Here we need accuracy. Lines must not only be correct as to placement, but also exactly on grain if the grain is clearly visible. Markings for buttonholes must be on the outside of garment, since that is where the greater part of the buttonhole is made. Since dressmaker's tracing paper leaves permanent marks, the marking is done in two steps, the first one on the interfacing, the second by basting through to the right side.

MARKING THE INTERFACING (1, 2)—Using dressmaker's tracing paper and a rule, transfer center lines and buttonhole markings to the interfacing (if interfacing is woven, make sure the center line is on grain).

Using pencil and yardstick, add the following lines to ensure correct and uniform buttonhole length:

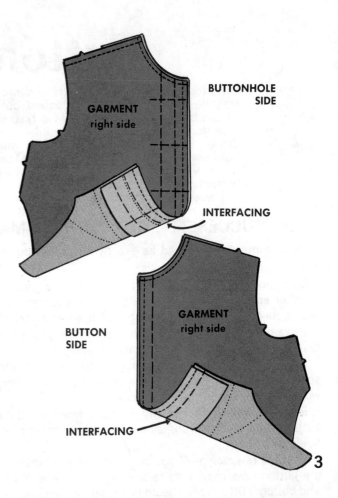

BUTTONHOLE SIDE

GARMENT right side

INTERFACING

BUTTON SIDE

GARMENT right side

INTERFACING

3

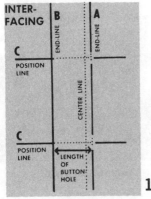

HORIZONTAL BUTTONHOLES

1

For horizontal buttonholes (1), draw lines A, B, and C, extending them **at least 1″** beyond existing markings.

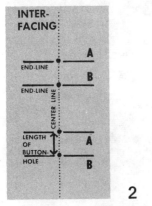

VERTICAL BUTTONHOLES

2

For vertical buttonholes (2) draw lines A and B (endlines) 1″ to each side of center (position) line.

Pin marked interfacings to wrong side of corresponding garment sections, matching edges exactly.

MARKING THE GARMENT SECTION (3)—Many fabrics can be marked with machine-basting. Others (taffeta, polished cotton, certain treated fabrics) which show needle marks, must be hand-basted with a fine needle. Women's garments have the buttonholes on the right-hand side of a front opening; men's garments have them on the left. On the side where the buttons will be, baste-mark the **center line only.** On the buttonhole side, disregard the center line except in the case of vertical buttonholes.

If the fabric grain is not noticeable, baste-mark by going over the lines from the interfacing side through to outside.

If the garment fabric has a noticeable grain, put a pin through from the interfacing side to the outside at the ends of all marked lines. Machine- or hand-baste on outside, starting at pins and following a thread in the grain.

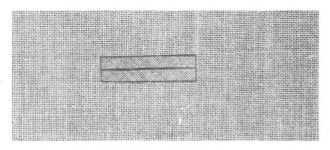

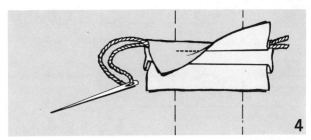

THE BOUND BUTTONHOLE

The bound buttonhole is generally finished with self-fabric, the possible exception being trimming fabric. This buttonhole is good in all garments except where the fabric is unsuitable, such as:

    sheer, embroidered, or nubby fabrics,
    ravelly weaves (which, however, can be stabilized with fused interfacing).

There are several gadgets sold at notions counters designed to help in making bound buttonholes. They come with their own directions, which must be followed precisely.

Bound buttonholes are made after the interfacing is attached to a garment section, but before the section is seamed to any others. There are various ways of making these buttonholes. We give you here three tried and true methods:

    ONE-PIECE FOLDED BUTTONHOLE
    FIVE-LINE BUTTONHOLE
    PATCH BUTTONHOLE

Lips can be corded for more body if they are cut on the bias. The directions indicate at what point this is done. Soft cord of suitable thickness, soft twine (single or doubled), doubled knitting worsted or Wintuk yarn can be used for cording. Draw short lengths of cord or yarn through the lips with a tubing turner or a tapestry needle (4); cut cord-ends off even with fabric.

Do not try to make a bound buttonhole less than ⅞″ long, unless you are an expert. To fit a smaller button, a buttonhole may be shortened after it is finished by slipstitching the lips together invisibly on the wrong side, at far end from garment edge.

Press finished buttonholes with a steam iron—do this lightly, as the added thickness may mark the outer fabric.

For uniformity of buttonholes in a row and for efficiency in making them, do not complete each buttonhole separately, but do one step on all, then the next step on all, etc. Try to complete the job in one work session.

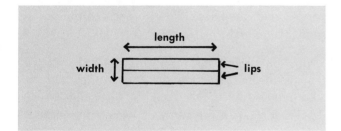

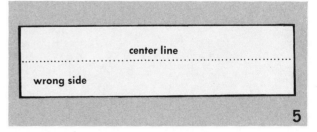

A good bound buttonhole should have:
    lips even in width,
    corners square and not ravelly,
    no visible stitching.
Lips are best cut on the bias; they may, however, be cut on the straight grain. Their overall width should be about ¼″, a little less if the fabric is light, a little more if the fabric is heavy.

PREPARING THE BUTTONHOLE LIPS—Cut one bias strip for all the buttonhole lips, according to measurements given with each bound buttonhole (it will be cut apart later). On the wrong side of the strip, carefully mark the entire lengthwise center (5). Baste-marking by machine or hand is the most accurate. If you are marking with a colored pencil, make dashes rather than a continuous line.

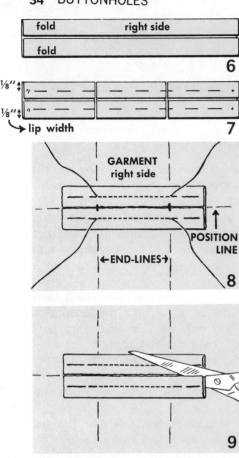

ONE-PIECE FOLDED BUTTONHOLE

A good buttonhole for light and medium-weight fabrics.

a. Cut one bias strip for all the buttonhole lips, measured as follows: WIDTH—1″
LENGTH—Add 1″ to your buttonhole length and multiply this figure by the number of buttonholes.

b. Mark center of strip (see preceding page, ill. 5). Fold both edges to center line and press (6). Baste-mark ⅛″ from each fold (half-way between fold and center), going through both thicknesses (7). The two basted lines must be ¼″ apart. Now cut the strip into individual sections (length of buttonhole plus 1″) for each buttonhole.

c. On outside of garment section, pin a strip-section over a buttonhole position, with center marking of strip matching position line, ends of strip extending ½″ beyond end-lines, as shown (8). Baste along center line. Re-connect end-line markings across strip.

d. Set the machine stitch at 20 to the inch. Stitch over basting lines at each side of center, starting and finishing at end-lines, as shown (8); leave thread-ends of about 3″. Check stitched lines on both the outside and the interfacing: they must be on grain, ¼″ apart, and extend exactly to end-lines (if necessary, use a needle to correct the length of line—draw out a stitch or two or put a thread-end into the needle to add an extra stitch). If the stitching is not perfect, remove it carefully and stitch again. Draw thread-ends to interfacing side and tie but do not trim off. Remove center basting from strip.

For a corded buttonhole, insert cording at this point (see p. 33).

e. Cut the strip in two through the center line (9). Be careful not to cut into the garment.

f. Working from the interfacing side, cut the buttonhole through interfacing and garment fabric opening: starting at center, cut toward each end, stopping ⅜″ from end-lines. Clip into each corner as far as possible without clipping stitches (10); be very careful not to cut into the strips on other side.

Put strips gently through opening to interfacing side (11). Flatten strips and see that lips meet. On wrong side, secure lips with diagonal basting (to be removed only after the garment is finished).

g. Place garment section on machine, right side up. Fold one edge back as far as buttonhole-end, exposing the strip-ends with a tiny triangle lying on top. Holding thread-ends taut (be careful not to pull a soft fabric out of shape), stitch back and forth across the triangle base at end-line (12). Repeat on the other end of buttonhole. Trim off thread-ends. Remove all baste-markings on the garment section. Press the buttonholes.

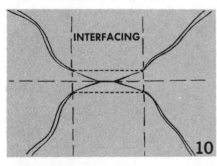

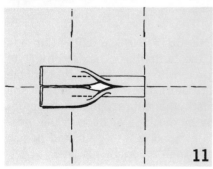

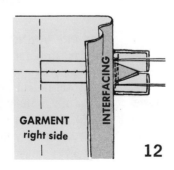

FIVE-LINE BUTTONHOLE

This buttonhole is suitable only for fabrics that do not show needle marks, because all marking here is done with machine-basting.

a. Cut one bias strip for all the buttonhole lips, measured as follows:
WIDTH—2″
LENGTH—Add 1″ to your buttonhole length and multiply this figure by the number of buttonholes.

b. Mark center of strip (see page 33, ill. 5) with machine basting. Cut the strip into individual sections (length of buttonhole plus 1″) for each buttonhole.

c. On outside of garment section, pin strip-section over a buttonhole position, right sides together, center marking of strip matching position line, ends of strip extending ½″ beyond end-lines, as shown (13). Machine-baste in place over center line, across the entire strip. Make two more lines of machine-basting, ¼″ to each side of the first line, again across the entire strip-section (13).

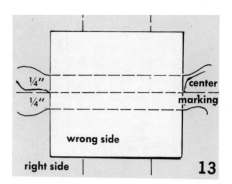

13

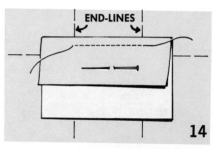

14

d. Press down one free edge of the strip, folding on the outer basting line; pin in place. Set the machine stitch at 20 to the inch. Stitch ⅛″ from pressed fold, starting and finishing at end-lines, as shown (14). Leave thread-ends of about 3″. Remove pin. Repeat on the other edge.

On the interfacing side, check to make sure that all 5 lines of the buttonhole are parallel and ⅛″ apart, and start and end at the end-lines (15). If the stitching is not perfect, remove it carefully and stitch again. Draw thread-ends to interfacing side and tie but do not trim off. Remove all machine-basting from the strip.

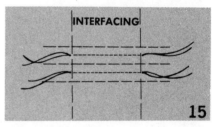

15

For a corded buttonhole, insert cording at this point (see p. 33).

e. Cut the strip in two through the center line (opposite page, ill. 9). Be careful not to cut into the garment.

f. Working from the interfacing side, cut the buttonhole opening, through interfacing and garment fabric: starting at center, cut toward each end, stopping ⅜″ from end-lines. Clip into each corner as far as possible without clipping stitches (opposite page, ill. 10); be very careful not to cut into strips on the other side.

Put strips gently through opening to interfacing side (16). Flatten strips and see that lips meet. On wrong side, secure lips with diagonal basting (to be removed only after garment is finished).

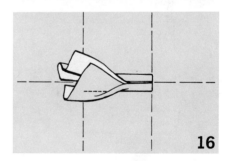

16

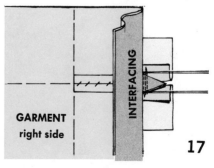

17

g. Place garment section on machine, right side up. Fold one edge back as far as buttonhole-end, exposing the strip-ends with a tiny triangle lying on top. Holding thread-ends taut, stitch back and forth across the triangle base at end-line (17). Repeat on the other end of buttonhole. Trim off thread-ends. Remove all baste-markings on the garment section. Press the buttonholes.

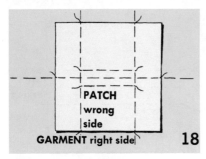

18

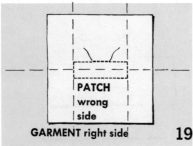

19

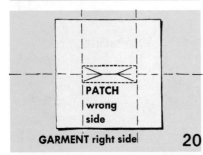

20

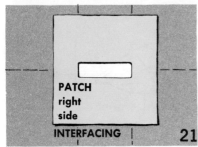

21

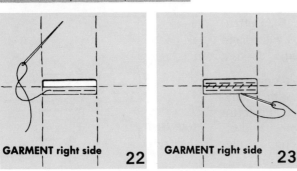

22

23

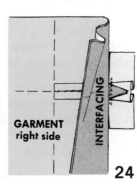

24

PATCH BUTTONHOLE

This is a good buttonhole for all fabrics.

a. Cut one bias strip for all the buttonhole patches (lips), measured as follows: WIDTH—2"

LENGTH—Add 1" to your buttonhole length and multiply this figure by the number of buttonholes.

b. Mark center of strip (see page 33, ill. 5). Cut the strip into individual patches (length of buttonhole plus 1") for each buttonhole.

c. On the outside of the garment section, pin a patch over a buttonhole position, right sides together, center marking of patch matching position line, ends of patch extending ½" beyond end-lines, as shown (18). Re-connect end-line markings across patch. Draw or baste-mark two lines parallel to center line, ⅛" to each side of it (18). The rectangle formed outlines the buttonhole.

d. Set the machine stitch at 20 per inch. Stitch slowly over the outlined rectangle: start at center of one long side; at corner, pivot on needle; count stitches across end; pivot and continue, counting off the same number of stitches across other end. To finish, stitch over the beginning stitches (19). Check the stitching on outside of garment. If it is not perfectly on grain, remove it carefully and stitch again.

e. Cut the buttonhole through all thicknesses (20): starting at center, cut toward each end, stopping ⅜" from end-lines. Then clip into each corner as far as possible without clipping stitching (20). Remove basting from the patch and put the patch gently through opening to interfacing side. Smooth out the patch to make the opening a perfect rectangle (21). Press lightly to flatten edges.

f. Working from the right side (22), bring a fold of patch even with center marking, as shown, forming a ⅛" lip (keep seam allowance out of lip). Baste through center of lip, as shown. Repeat to form second lip. Hold lips together with diagonal basting (to be removed only after garment is finished). Secure lips in position with hand-backstitching hidden in the seam (23).

If you want a corded buttonhole, remove bastings from center of lips and insert cording at this point (see p. 33).

g. Place garment section on machine right side up. Fold one edge back as far as buttonhole-end, exposing the patch-end with a tiny triangle lying on top. Stitch back and forth across the triangle base at end-line (24). Repeat on the other end of buttonhole. Remove all baste-markings on the garment section. Press the buttonholes.

BUTTONHOLES IN HEAVY INTERFACING

The heavier interfacings used in tailoring are often too bulky to be part of the buttonholes. In such a case, the buttonholes are made before interfacing is applied; openings are then cut in the interfacing to accommodate buttonhole patches.

If there is an underlining, it is sufficient interfacing. Otherwise, each buttonhole is individually interfaced with a patch of light interfacing fabric, such as organdy; or with lightweight interfacing fused in place if garment fabric allows it.

a. Cut a piece of lightweight interfacing 1″ wide and 1″ longer than buttonhole. Baste or fuse to wrong side of buttonhole location.

b. Make buttonholes and then apply interfacing.

c. Put a pin through each end of the buttonhole from right side through to interfacing. Measure about ⅜″ out from pins and using a pencil, mark out a rectangle as shown (25).

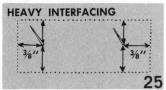

d. Cut out the rectangle, slightly rounding corners. Slip the buttonhole patch through the opening (26) and catchstitch edges loosely to interfacing all around.

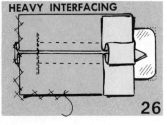

FINISHING THE FACING SIDE

You may use one of the three methods that follow. The first two are done after the facing has been applied. If you have backed the buttonhole area of the garment fabric with fusible interfacing to prevent fraying (p. 31), do the same on the facing. Secure facing with pins all around buttonholes.

Two-cornered finish (27). The easiest method. From outside of garment, stick a pin through each end of buttonhole. On facing side, cut between pins, following the fabric grain. Remove pins and cut ⅛″ more at each end. Turn both raw edges under and hem.

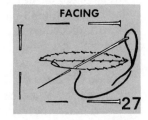

Rectangular finish (28). Good for garments that may be worn open. From outside of garment, stick a pin through each corner of the buttonhole. On the facing, cut through center of buttonhole and into corners (as on the buttonhole itself). Turn in raw edges; hem.

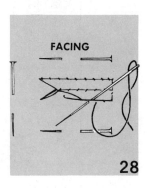

Rectangular finish, faced with lightweight fabric. Very neat and durable. Excellent for garments that may be worn open, and for heavy fabrics. It is done before the facing is entirely applied.

a. For each buttonhole, cut a patch 1½″ wide and 1″ longer than buttonhole, of lightweight fabric in matching color (organdy is excellent; underlining or lining fabric may be right if it does not fray).

b. Center patch under buttonhole and pin it to the **facing only.** From outside of garment, stick a pin through each corner of buttonhole. On the patch, mark location of these pins with a dot in contrasting pencil. Remove the marking pins. Open out the facing, keeping the patch firmly pinned in place. Using pencil and ruler, connect corner dots in an even rectangle (29).

c. Following the directions for PATCH BUTTONHOLE, stitch around marking; cut through center and diagonally into each corner; push the patch through the opening to wrong side; press flat.

After facing is finished, slipstitch edges of openings to buttonholes. Press lightly.

For a quick finish in knits, see page 81.

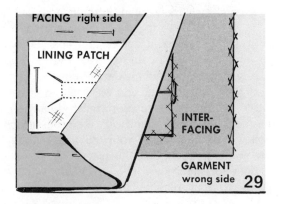

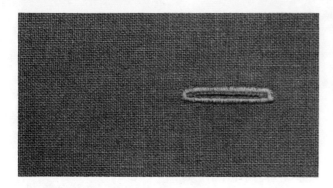
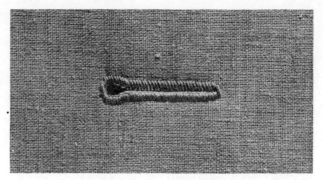

THE WORKED BUTTONHOLE

In a worked buttonhole, whether made by hand or by machine, the raw edges are worked over with thread. Suitable for any garment and fabric it is a must in sheers, where the seam allowances of a bound buttonhole would show.

Worked buttonholes are made on the outside of a garment after the facing has been applied (for marking, see p. 32). Secure the facing in place with pins or basting near buttonhole markings until the buttonhole slit has been reinforced and cut. Always make a test buttonhole.

A buttonhole which is never closed (such as the top buttonhole of a shirtwaist or the top buttonhole of a 3-button jacket) can be made from the facing side because this is what will show.

MACHINE-WORKED BUTTONHOLE

The machine-worked buttonhole is always suitable in casual and children's clothes, which are washed frequently. A carefully-made machine buttonhole, however, can serve in other garments as well.

A good machine-worked buttonhole should have
stitches close together, forming a satin stitch, stitches even in depth, and lips just a thread apart so they do not fray when cut open.

Any zigzag machine makes buttonholes, but with a straight-stitch machine you will need an attachment. Keyhole buttonholes, used in tailored garments, can be made on the machine with a special attachment. Follow the directions in your machine manual. Here are some additional helpful hints.

Color of interfacing should be close to color of garment, as it will show at buttonhole edges.

For a stronger, better-looking buttonhole, stitch around a second time. On a machine where you can control the length of the buttonhole do this second stitching after slitting the buttonhole (hold lips a hair's-breadth apart).

When slitting a buttonhole open, first run the point of the scissors or seam ripper backward between the lips; this will help to separate the threads before slashing.

Place a straight pin across each end of the buttonhole. This will protect the ends from being cut. If you are using scissors, start in the center and cut to each end; with a seam ripper, start at each end and cut to the center.

When using an attachment, thick, napped or lustrous fabric may snag on it. Protect the fabric by covering the buttonhole area with a piece of clear plastic when sliding the garment into stitching position; remove the plastic; make the buttonhole and then replace the plastic again before sliding the garment out.

HAND-WORKED BUTTONHOLES

The regular hand-worked buttonhole provides a more careful finish in many cases where a machine-worked one might do.

The keyhole buttonhole, generally corded, is used in tailored garments (see p. 175).

The thread you use should be waxed to prevent curling and knotting, but this must be done sparingly to avoid staining the fabric.

A good hand-worked buttonhole has
stitches worked close together,
stitches of even depth.

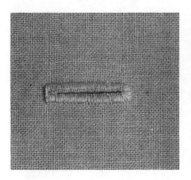 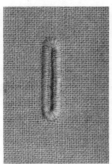  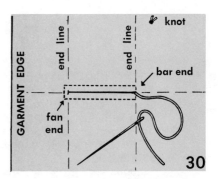

Regular hand-worked buttonhole

The regular buttonhole may be

horizontal, with a rounded fan-end near the garment edge (where the button rests), and a bar tack at the other end; or **vertical,** with the same finish at both ends, either fans or bar tacks.

The thread you use (waxed) depends on your fabric. It may be regular sewing thread, single (for a 1″ buttonhole, cut a 30″ length), or double (cut 65″ and double), or buttonhole twist (cut 36″).

a. For this buttonhole, the slit is cut before the edges are worked over. **Before** cutting the slit, however, reinforce the edges: either make a line of straight machine-stitching (20 stitches to the inch) 1/16″ to each side of the position line; or work a narrow machine-buttonhole over the position. Then cut the slit between the end-lines (30).

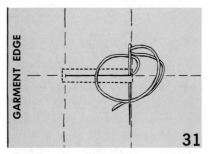

b. Start at bar end. With a knot at thread-end, insert needle into right side of fabric about ½″ from bar end, and bring it out through the slit at that end (30). (The knot will be removed later.) Cover edges with buttonhole stitch (see below), making a fan or a bar tack at ends.

c. Finish off thread-ends carefully. Clip off the thread used for starting, and pull out the knot.

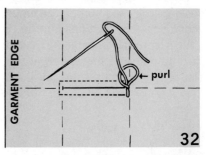

Buttonhole stitch is worked from right to left, with the needle pointing toward you. Use the machine stitching as a guide for stitch depth (except at fan end). Loop the thread as shown (31) and insert needle into slit, bringing it out just below stitching **with eye and point over the looped thread.** Draw up needle away from you so that the purl (32) is formed at edge of slit. Do not draw up the thread too tight.

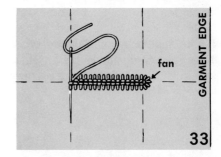

The fan is worked around the end as shown. Keep stitch-depth even and turn the work gradually (33).

The bar tack is made by taking two stitches at buttonhole end, across both rows, and then working over these threads with blanket stitch without catching the fabric. Use the needle eye-first, as shown (34). Then put the needle through to wrong side.

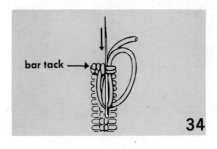

Button Loops

Button loops, extending beyond the finished edge of a garment, often take the place of buttonholes. Any buttons can be used with fabric loops, but the ones most often seen are ball buttons or Chinese ball buttons (see p. 44) made of the same cord as the loops.

Loops vary greatly in thickness and size, depending on fabric, button, location, etc. Their size must be carefully established. If too loose, a loop will come off a ball button by itself. Loops can be either decorative or concealed.

As a decorative fastening, loops are made of fabric tubing, self-filled or corded, or of round braid. They are used on dressmaker suits, on a close-fitting long sleeve or bodice, and on coats and jackets. While a row of loops is definitely part of the garment design, frogs will furnish an important bit of extra decoration (see that heading on next page).

As a concealed fastening, a loop, usually single, may be made of thread (as at the neck corner of a blouse), or of fabric (as at the neck corner of a man's sport shirt or a coat underlap).

ROW OF LOOPS

Use round tubing (⅛″ or narrower), self-filled or corded (see p. 29), or round braid.

On an edge to be faced, loops may be applied before the facing is stitched on. In this case, the tubing or cord should be at least three times the length of the opening, but it need not be in one piece.

a. Cut a piece of sturdy paper about 2″ wide and as long as the opening. On one long edge, mark off the seam allowance. Determine size of loop needed for size of button. Measure and mark size of loops on paper (1), without or with intervals (2 or 3).

b. Place one end of paper and one end of cord under presser foot (always keep seam of cord, if any, turned up; see 2 or 3), and anchor the cord with the needle on marked seam line. Form the first loop; stitch on seam line. Continue, forming loops as you go, until all loops are attached to the paper.

c. Pin the paper to right side of garment, loops facing away from the edge, as shown (4). Stitch on top of the stitching which holds the loops. Tear off paper. Apply facing. Trim seam allowances and loop-ends to ¼″. Finish the opening (5).

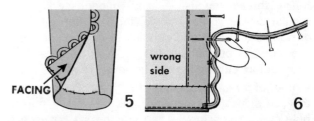

On a finished edge, cord should be about twice the length of the opening and must be in one piece.

Determine size of loop needed. On garment edge, measure and mark placement of loops with pins (6). On cord, measure and mark size of loops. Beginning at first mark and matching pins, attach cord to edge with small stitches, sliding the needle to the next mark through fold of garment. Keep seam of cord (if any) on wrong side.

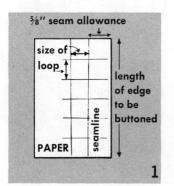

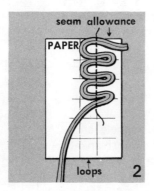

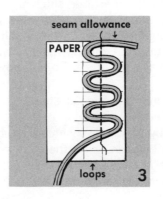

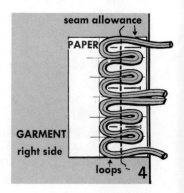

 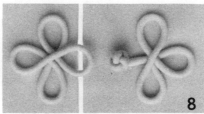 

SINGLE LOOPS

Use round tubing, either self-filled or corded (see p. 29) of a size in keeping with the size of the button and the weight of the fabric. Single loops are always applied to a faced edge, before the facing is stitched on.

With seam of tubing up, pin the tubing to right side of garment, forming a loop as shown, large enough to accommodate the button (7). Stitch to garment on seamline, as shown. Stitch facing to garment.

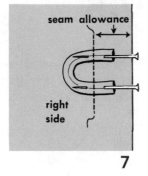

FROGS

Frogs, shown here in two designs, are decorative button loops that can be used on any finished front opening. They vary greatly in size, and can be used in pairs (8), or singly (9). The button can be a Chinese ball button (see p. 44) made with the same cord as the frog, or any ball button.

Use tubing, self-filled or corded (see p. 29), or braid. The length needed depends on the design. Determine the size of loop needed for your button. Draw outline of frog on a piece of sturdy paper (10 or 11). The frog will be constructed on this paper right side down, which means that the seams on the tubing, stitches, and cord-ends will all face up as it is made.

Made from one piece of cord. Starting at the center, baste cord to paper, following the outline (10). Sew the cord together at crossings. Secure ends.

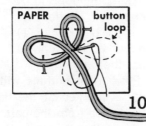

Made from two pieces of cord. Begin by stitching together a small, tight spiral, making sure that the cord-end and stitches all face you. When the spiral is the right size, repeat in contrary direction with other end of cord, to fit the design (11). Cut off cord-end in center of spiral. Finish the end. Baste to paper. Form loops with a separate piece of cord, basting to outline and joining at center. Sew the two parts together at crossing.

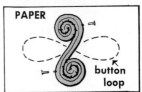

Remove the frog from the paper; take more stitches if needed. Sew to garment right side up. The button loop extends beyond edge. If frogs are made in a pair, sew button securely to "button loop" or start with a Chinese ball button and use the rest of the cord to form the frog (8).

CONCEALED FASTENINGS

THREAD LOOP—Made after the garment is finished (12). See page 252.

FABRIC LOOP—Can be bias or straight-grain, and is usually made from garment fabric (13). It is applied before the facing is attached—see SINGLE LOOPS above.

Bias Loop—Made of tubing, either flat or self-filled (p. 29). Size depends on garment.

Straight-grain Loop—Cut a strip on the straight grain, about ½″ × 2¼″. Turn in long edges, fold in half lengthwise, and topstitch (14).

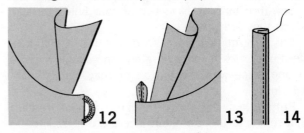

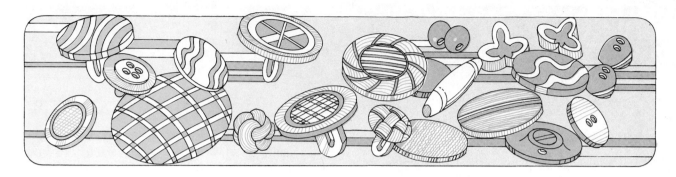

Buttons

Buttons, with their companion button-holes, generally serve as fastenings. They are also, with or without buttonholes, used as decoration—often as counterparts to "working" buttons (as in most double-breasted garments), or for simulating a button closure.

Buttons must be carefully chosen, wherever they are placed and even where they are not visible (in a fly closure, the buttons must be flat, of the right size and color, and of good quality). In the usual front closure, buttons can make or mar a garment. If you cannot get the buttons you would like, your best bet, when the garment fabric is suitable, is fabric-covered buttons, which never look out of place.

TYPES AND SIZES OF BUTTONS

Buttons may be made of almost any material—wood, metal, plastic, mother-of-pearl, glass, fabric, crochet cotton, etc.—and in many shapes; they may be plain or fancy. From the standpoint of sewing on the button, however, they fall into just two categories:

Sew-thru buttons have two or four holes through which they are sewed on.

Shank buttons have a solid top and a shank or stem underneath for sewing on. The shank may be in one piece with the button or may consist of a wire loop.

Buttons are sized by line (or ligne), a measurement that refers to the diameter. There are forty lines to the inch. The smallest button made is line 18, or ⅜ of an inch. Many patterns indicate the recommended button size by drawings on the pattern tissue.

⅜″–LINE 18	1⅛″–LINE 45
½″–LINE 20	1⅜″–LINE 55
⅝″–LINE 24	1½″–LINE 60
¾″–LINE 30	1¾″–LINE 70
⅞″–LINE 36	2″–LINE 80
1″–LINE 40	

POSITION OF BUTTONS

The position of **buttons in a closure** is marked after the garment is completed. Lap the opening of the garment as it will be worn, with neck, waistline and/or hem evenly lined up. Through the but-tonhole, place a pin at exact spot where the button is to be sewn, picking up a small amount of fabric: on a horizontal buttonhole, near the outer edge (1); on a vertical buttonhole, near the top end.

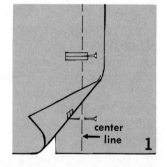

Position of **buttons without buttonholes** (decorative) is marked at the time that all markings are transferred from the pattern.

REINFORCING BUTTON POSITION

Buttons need a firm backing. In closures, they usually fall on a faced and interfaced part of the garment, but even a decorative button should not be sewn to a single thickness of fabric. When such a button falls on a single-thickness area, or when the existing backing of a "working" button does not seem strong enough for the strain to which it will be subjected, reinforcing is necessary. This is done in one of the three ways below.

For light and medium-weight fabrics—Cut a circle of fusible interfacing a little smaller than the button. Before sewing on the button, press the circle to wrong side of button position (if possible, between garment and facing).

For any fabric—Place a small square of doubled fabric to wrong side of button location and stitch through it as you sew on the button.

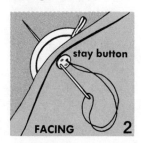

On heavy or tailored garments—Hold a small, flat "stay-button" to wrong (facing) side of garment and stitch through it as you sew on the button (2).

CHOICE OF THREAD

Be sure to choose the right thread for the fabric to which the button is sewn (see p. 251). Use the thread single or doubled, depending on the fabric; if the thread is doubled, be careful to draw it up evenly with each stitch. For smoothness in handling, and extra strength, it is helpful to draw the thread over a piece of beeswax.

SEWING ON BUTTONS

The smooth fit of a buttonhole and whether a button stays on or not, both depend on the way a button is sewn on. Buttons come off for only two reasons: the thread has either not been fastened securely, or has worn through. This may be due to rough edges on the holes or shank of a button, which should be watched for.

A "working" button always needs a shank, to allow the buttonhole to fit smoothly under it. For a sew-thru button, a shank is made out of thread (see below). The length of the shank is determined by the thickness of the fabric: a sheer fabric needs a very short one, while with a heavy fabric it may be necessary to extend even the stem of a shank button.

A decorative button needs no shank; omit bobby pin (or whatever you use) in the instructions below.

Start sewing on right side of garment (thread-knot, if any, will be covered by the button). Take a small stitch at the button position, picking up all fabric thicknesses, but, in the case of a jacket or a coat, being careful not to let the stitch show through on the facing. Take a second small stitch at the same place.

 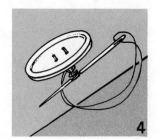

SEW-THRU BUTTON—Bring the thread up through one hole in the button. Centering the button over the stitch, place a bobby pin, matchstick, or toothpick (depending on length of shank desired) between the button and the fabric (3), and take three or four stitches through each pair of holes. Bring needle and thread out between button and fabric, remove bobby pin, and wind the thread a number of times around the attaching thread, to form a shank. Take a small stitch in the fabric (4). Finish off the thread securely. Cut, do not break the thread.

SHANK BUTTON—If the length of the shank is sufficient, take 6 to 8 stitches (less if thread is doubled) through shank and finish off like a sew-thru button, above. If the shank needs lengthening, take a first stitch through the shank, then place a bobby pin underneath and proceed as for a sew-thru button.

MAKING FABRIC BUTTONS

Whether you have fabric buttons made commercially or make them yourself, have them ready before you make the buttonholes. To attach, catch the fabric (or cord) underneath and handle like a shank button.

COVERED BUTTONS are made (covered) with your own fabric. You may:

. . . order them from a notions store or counter;

. . . make them yourself, using a kit sold for the purpose (directions with package);

. . . make them yourself, using bone or plastic rings as a base (5) as follows: Cut fabric circles twice the diameter of rings (6). Gather the edge, using doubled thread (7). Draw up over the ring (8), and fasten securely (9). To trim, use matching or contrasting thread and take stitches inside the ring (10). More stitching can be added (5).

Optional: Cover the back with a small circle of fabric (11).

CHINESE BALL BUTTONS (12) are made with a length of round cord, which may be either purchased braid or bias tubing, corded or self-filled (see p. 29). Here is an estimated amount needed for each:

for a ⅜″ button:	use ⅛″ cord	6″ length
for a ½″ button:	use ³⁄₁₆″ cord	8″ length
for a ⅞″ button:	use ¼″ cord	10″ length
for a 1″ button:	use ⅜″ cord	12″ length
for a 1⅜″ button:	use ⅜″ cord	36″ length*

*fold in half and double

Loop the cord as shown in diagrams 13 to 15 (colored section indicates the part looped in previous steps), keeping loops open while working. Then draw them together, easing, kneading, and shaping them into a smooth ball, while keeping the two ends firmly together underneath. Trim off the ends and sew flat to underside of button (16).

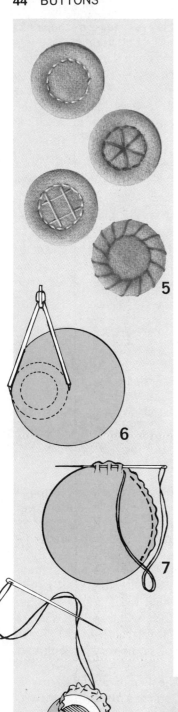

5

6

7

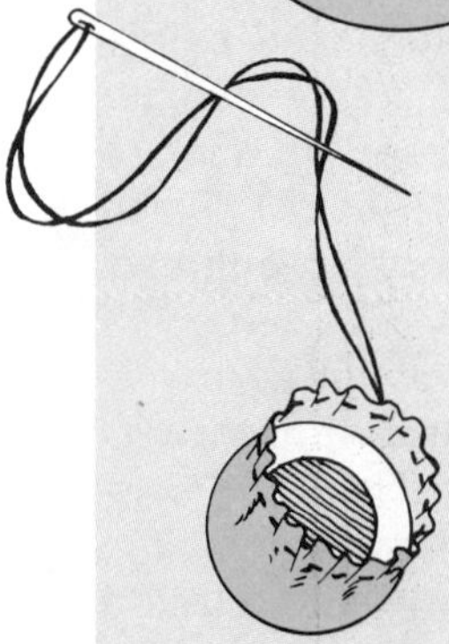

8 9 10 11

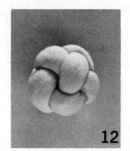

12

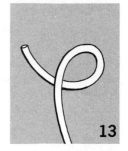

13

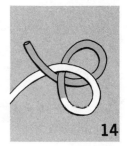

14

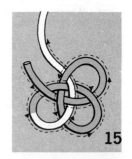

15

16

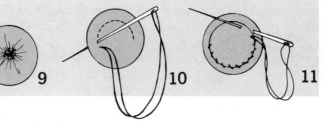

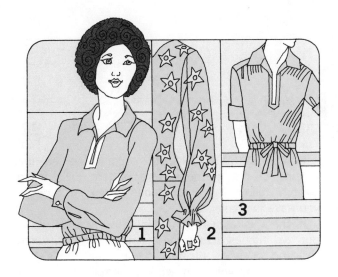

Casings

The purpose of a casing is to hold an elastic or a drawstring. It may be formed by a **hem** (1,2) or, as an **applied casing** (2,3) it may be a separate strip stitched to the garment.

A casing with a heading—an extension forming a ruffle when the casing is drawn up (2)—can be made either way: Both casing and heading (double) can be part of the hem. Or the casing can be applied as a separate strip, with the heading extending in a single thickness, finished with a narrow hem.

MAKING A CASING

Finished width of casing: Width of the elastic or drawstring plus ⅛″ (more if elastic or drawstring is bulky).

Opening in casings: Before proceeding to stitch the casing, read the instructions under this heading on the next page.

APPLIED CASING—for any location other than an edge.

The strip used may be straight-grain, bias, or shaped. Usually, it is placed on the inside of a garment. When it is on the outside, it is part of the garment design and generally cut to match the garment grain. Packaged bias tape or stretch lace of the nearest suitable width make inside casings with quick and easy application. If you hand-cut your strip, add ½″ to the finished width you need; turn edges under ¼″ and press.

For a waistline casing, put the garment on and tie a string around the waist to find the correct location. Mark at the side seams and at the center front and back. Pin strip along markings. Stitch along both edges (4).

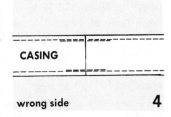

CASING IN A TURNED-UP HEM—for straight edges. Turn in ¼″ at edge; press. Turn in hem to desired depth (width of casing; or casing plus heading). Pin and machine-stitch. On a casing without a heading (5), a second line of stitching close to the fold is optional. On a casing with a heading (6), make a second line of stitching to form the casing.

CASING IN A FACED HEM—for curved edges. Follow directions for FACED HEM (see p. 126), using a bias strip the width of the casing alone or of casing plus heading (plus seam allowances). After turning the facing to the wrong side, machine-stitch edge of facing in place. On a casing without a heading (7), make a second line of stitching close to fold as shown. On a casing with a heading (8), make a second line of stitching to form casing.

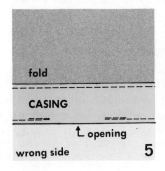

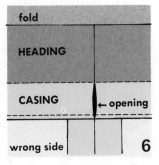

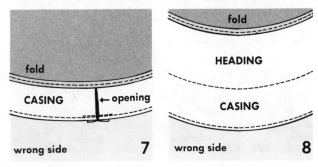

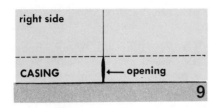

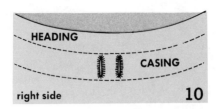

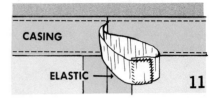

OPENING IN A CASING

FOR AN ELASTIC, the opening is on the inside of the garment.

In a turned-up hem, you may either leave a 1″ opening when stitching the hem, in which case you back-tack at beginning and end for reinforcement (5); or you can take out stitches in a seam that crosses the casing (6).

In an applied casing or a faced hem, fold strip-ends under ½″ at beginning and end (see ill. 4 and 7 on preceding page). Have folds meet and run the stitching across both ends, as shown.

FOR A DRAWSTRING, the opening is on the outside of the garment. If a pattern calls for a casing, follow the instructions given. Otherwise, you have two choices:

If there is a seam at a suitable location, take out the stitches across the casing (9) and reinforce the end or ends of the opening; or, make two **hand-worked eyelets or worked buttonholes** in the outside fabric (single thickness) of the casing (10).

TO INSERT ELASTIC OR DRAWSTRING, use a bodkin or a safety pin. Be sure not to let the elastic twist. Keep the two ends out; overlap and whip-stitch them together before letting them go into the casing (11).

Children's Clothes

Sewing for children is tackled much more readily than sewing for adults, and with good reason. Children's clothes are more casual and generally made with simpler techniques. Children are also easier to fit. Once the right pattern size has been found, fitting sessions, if needed at all, can be short.

The one real problem in sewing for children is their constant change and growth. This, however, mainly concerns height, because children will grow a great many inches while, as they lose their baby fat, their width stays the same. There are ways of preparing for changes in both height and width, however—see THE PROBLEM OF GROWTH, later in this chapter.

TO BEAR IN MIND

For safety (important with small fry)

Bright colors to make wearers visible to motorists— and to you.

Hats and hoods that will not cut out vision.

Flame-retardant fabric for sleepwear.

No cuffs on pants—feet get caught in them.

For durability

Good fabrics—children wear clothes hard, especially playclothes.

On pants, knees reinforced by **inside** patches **before** pants are worn.

Built-in growth allowance—see later in this chapter.

For comfort and enjoyment

Roomy sleeves, such as raglan, on coats and jackets.

Pockets big and deep enough to hold things.

Openings that allow doing for oneself; which means front openings wherever possible, large buttons and zipper pulls; also elastic waists for easy on and off.

PATTERNS

Sizes in children's patterns can be misleading. Although, in a way, they indicate age groups, they cannot be used in selecting a pattern. Decide on the pattern size by the chest measurement, which is shown in the pattern catalogue, and which you should take around the fullest part of a child's chest (for pants, take the hip measurement).

After you have bought the pattern, according to chest (or hip) measurement, compare its other measurements with those of the child. Waist size, and back waist length are only necessary in a garment with a waist seam. Both these measurements, and the garment length, can be taken from a garment that is **currently** of good fit. Never forget that a child's measurements must be constantly up-dated.

For pattern adjustments, use the same methods as for adults (see p. 193).

There are, however, different categories of patterns designed for children of different builds.

TODDLERS' patterns have a diaper allowance, and dresses are shorter than **Children's** dresses of the same size.

Breast or chest	19″	20″	21″	22″	23″
Finished Dress Length	14″	15″	16″	17″	18″
Size	½	1	2	3	4

CHILDREN'S patterns are proportionately longer than **Toddlers'** of the same given size.

Chest	20″	21″	22″	23″	24″	25″	25½″
Approx. Height	31″	34″	37″	40″	43″	46″	48″
Size	1	2	3	4	5	6	6X

GIRLS' patterns are designed for the girl who has not yet begun to mature.

Breast	26″	27″	28½″	30″	32″
Approx. Height	50″	52″	56″	58½″	61″
Size	7	8	10	12	14

CHUBBIES patterns are for girls of more than average weight for their height.

Breast	30″	31½″	33″	34½″
Approx. Height	52″	56″	58½″	61″
Size	8½C	10½C	12½C	14½C

BOYS' patterns

Chest	26″	27″	28″	30″
Height	48″	50″	54″	58″
Size	7	8	10	12

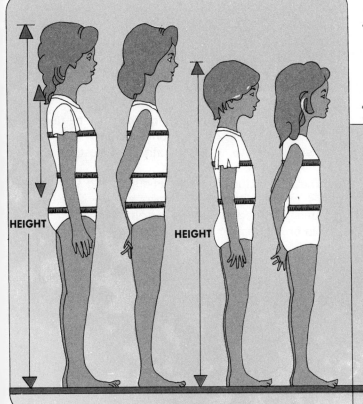

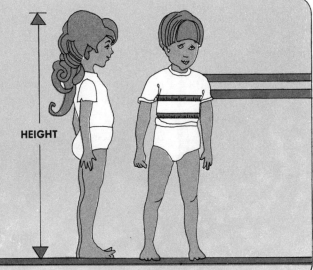

FITTING

This should be brief, and not too fussy.

Check the following areas (1):

Width of shoulder and fit of neck.

Fit of waist—width and length—where there is a waist seam.

Length.

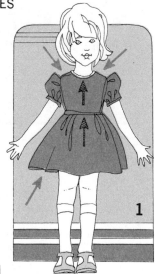

CONSTRUCTION

Some children's garments—a winter coat, for instance—require the same care, precision, and attention to detail as an adult's, and are made in the same way. With the great majority of children's clothes, however, you can have a more relaxed attitude. Use short cuts, and when there is a choice of techniques, choose the simpler one. Just use your judgment. In play-clothes, fit and finish are not particularly relevant, while in a party dress durability is not a consideration.

Here are a couple of useful simplifications that may not have been included in the pattern guide sheet.

Facings on a collarless, sleeveless garment may be given as separate pieces for the neck and the armhole (2). If this is the case, combine them into one (3), which you will find easier to handle (see COMBINED ARMHOLE-AND-NECK FACING, p. 97).

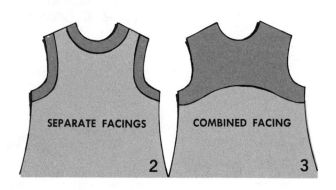

SEPARATE FACINGS

COMBINED FACING

Flat construction makes for easier handling and eliminates the difficulty of sewing sleeves into small armholes. It also makes it easier to let out side seams if the wearer grows in width.

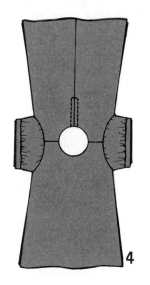

Stitch the shoulder seams; finish neckline, including putting in zipper, attaching collar, if any, etc. While the garment is still flat, sew the sleeves in (4). **Then,** stitch the side and sleeve seams in one operation (5). Hem sleeves and bottom edge.

THE PROBLEM OF GROWTH

Growth allowance stitched into a garment can serve two purposes: to be built into a garment against future growth; to take in a garment (often necessary with hand-me-downs), and perhaps to be let out later.

In any case, it means stitching that may be taken out later. For this, use a longer stitch, which is easier to remove, or chain stitch (easiest of all), if your machine has it.

The main difficulty about let-outs is old stitching lines or fold lines that remain visible. The only solution is to cover them with trimming—rick rack, braid or contrasting bias tape.

GROWTH IN LENGTH

The more obvious ways of meeting this are known to every sewing mother: deep hems (add 2″ to the regular hem depth) on dresses and pants, to be let down when needed; long shoulder straps on jumpers, overalls, etc. on which buttons can be adjusted. Here are a few more ideas for allowing for growth.

ON A DRESS WITH A BODICE, add 1½'' to the bodice when cutting it from the pattern. Complete the dress, taking a regular ⅝'' seam at the waist. On the inside, take up the extra length in a ¾'' tuck; stitch just below the waistline seam so it will not show on the outside (6). Let out the tuck when the waistline needs lengthening.

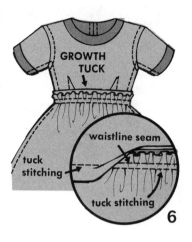

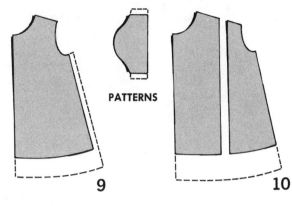

PATTERNS

9   10

ON ANY DRESS, there are special ways of storing extra depth in a hem, because only a straight-cut, full skirt can take a very deep hem without spoiling its appearance. On an A-line garment, growth allowance can be built in by means of tucks, either on the outside or the inside. Begin by adding the extra length as you cut out the garment.

GROWTH IN WIDTH

Gain in width is slow, and an inch added will make a big difference in a garment size.

TO ADD THE GROWTH ALLOWANCE when cutting out a garment, you can either

a) add an extra ¼'' at each side seam and sleeve seam (9), or

b) slash the pattern from mid-shoulder to hem and spread it ½'' (10).

With method a), take the regular seam allowance when stitching side and sleeve seams, then make a second line of stitching ¼'' from the first. Use a long stitch or chain stitch and take out when needed.

With method b), after the garment is completed, take a ¼'' tuck across the shoulder seam, from the inside, as shown (11) to be taken out when needed. Stitch it parallel to the armhole about half-way down the armhole, back and front.

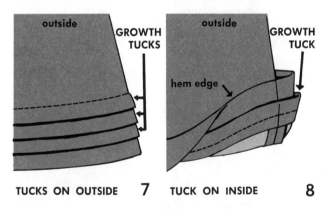

TUCKS ON OUTSIDE   **7**   TUCK ON INSIDE   **8**

On the outside, one or several tucks (of any depth, but ½'' is good) can be made above the hem (7), to be let out as needed while the hem remains untouched (until it too is needed).

On the inside, the tuck is placed within the hem (8). Before sewing in the hem, make a tuck (of any depth, but ½'' is good) about ½'' from the edge you are about to sew down. When additional length is needed, let out the tuck; the garment simply acquires a new and lower fold line, until the hem too is needed.

WAISTBANDS ON SKIRTS AND PANTS—Make a little looser than necessary, but stitch a piece of elastic into the band (stretching the elastic as you stitch) to hold it securely until the extra width is needed. This can also be done at the back of a dress with a fitted waistline.

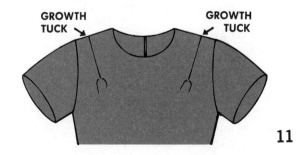

11

MAKE-OVERS IN LENGTH, WIDTH
Use gay, contrasting fabric. A ruffle goes on at the edge, but a band should go higher up, as an insertion; for style, always add something of the same fabric elsewhere, whether necessary or unnecessary. Think of adding rick rack along edges, a bow at the neck.

ADDING LENGTH   ADDING WIDTH

Collars

A good collar is one that fits well, lies down or stands up as it was designed to do. At the edges, seams should roll to the underside. All this can be achieved by special attention to basic details during construction. These details are generally the same for all collars, whether pointed or rounded, in one part or two, attached or unattached, or even cut as part of the garment body. Tailored collars (see p. 240) and collars in menswear (see p. 173) have their own rules.

In their construction, collars fall into two categories: two-piece (separate facing or undercollar), and one-piece (folded in half along the edge).

On either one, after you have transferred pattern markings to fabric, make a small clip-mark or notch at the center of the neck edge to make sure of placing it accurately later.

TWO-PIECE COLLAR

A collar with a separate facing or undercollar is almost always shaped (not cut as a straight band). It may be in one part or two.

INTERFACING—Preparation

Collars generally need an interfacing. You have a choice of:
standard interfacing sewn in,
standard interfacing attached with fusible web,
fusible interfacing, or
fusible web alone (see p. 108).

If interfacing is not specified in the pattern, cut it from the collar pattern.

To obtain a perfectly even finished edge, mark seam lines on interfacing. To reduce bulk, trim away any outside corners (see illustrations below).

Attaching Interfacing

By machine—Stay-stitch interfacing, marked-side-up, to wrong side of upper (outside) collar, ½'' from edge. This, giving a double thickness to the upper collar, will prevent seam allowances from showing on the finished collar.

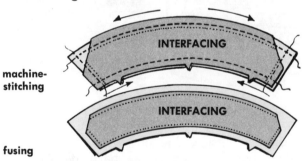

machine-stitching

INTERFACING

INTERFACING

fusing

By fusing (see p. 107)—Trim away ½'' from all edges of interfacing.

If appearance of garment fabric is not affected by fusing (try it on a fabric scrap), fuse interfacing, marked-side-up, to wrong side of upper collar. Otherwise fuse interfacing to wrong side of undercollar.

In either case, stay-stitch the remaining (uninterfaced) collar section, and proceed with construction steps as shown on next page.

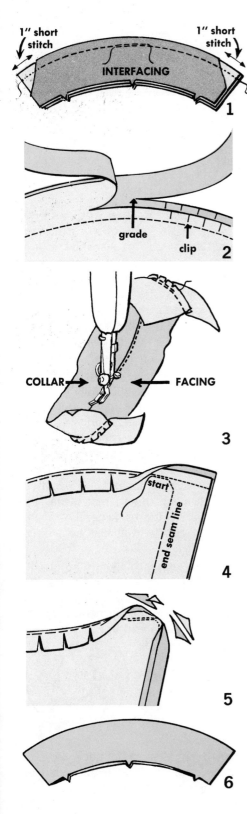

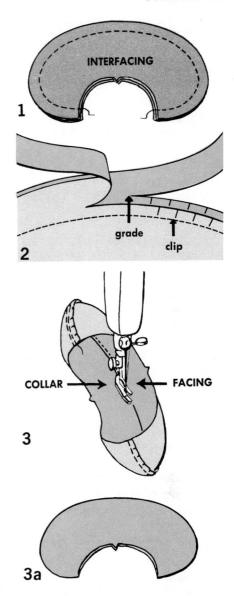

SEWING A COLLAR

1. Pin collar sections together, wrong sides out. With interfacing on top, stitch outer edge on marked seamline. On collar with corners, stitch from end to end of fabric, as shown, reinforcing corners by shortening stitches to 20 to the inch at beginning and end; do not stitch collar ends.

NOTE: If your fabric is slippery or otherwise difficult, stitch from the center to each end, overlapping about three stitches in the middle.

(To avoid confusion, staystitching and interfacing are not shown in the drawings after this step.)

2. Grade and clip seam allowances (see p. 94).

3. Understitch the seam (see p. 94). On a rounded-edge collar, understitch the entire seam. On a collar with corners, start and stop understitching 1½″ from ends.

3a. Rounded-edge collar is now finished. Turn to right side and press.

4. On collar with corners, stitch end-seams, reinforcing corner as follows: Starting ½″ from end-seamline, stitch with shortened stitch on top of previous stitches almost to the seamline. Pivot, take two stitches diagonally across the corner, pivot again and stitch for about an inch; return to regular stitch length and complete end-seam. Trim corners.

5. Press end-seams open with point of iron. Grade end-seam allowances, taper corners.

6. Turn collar to right side, pulling out corners carefully. Press. For attaching a collar, see next page.

ONE-PIECE COLLAR

A collar cut in one piece with its facing, with a fold instead of a seam along its edge, is always an entirely straight band. It may have square or pointed corners, and it may be a stand-up (mandarin) collar, as shown here (7), or a wider collar folded down (shirtwaist, man's shirt, etc.). Interfacing may be standard or fusible. In either case, cut interfacing exactly like the outer fabric. Mark seam lines and fold line.

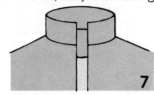

Standard interfacing—Use a very lightweight fabric. Pin to wrong side of collar, marked side up. Along fold line, catch interfacing to collar with tiny stitches, about ½″ apart and invisible on right side (8). Start and end stitches about 1″ in from outer edges.

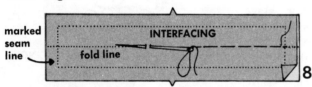

Stay-stitch ½″ from outer edge. (To avoid confusion, stay-stitching and interfacing are not shown in drawings after this step.)

Fold collar in half lengthwise, interfaced side out. Stitch ends, reinforcing corners by shortening the stitch (9). Trim corners. Press end-seams open with point of iron.

Grade, and taper seams toward corners.

Turn collar to right side. Press.

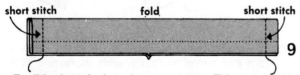

Fusible interfacing (see p. 108)—Trim away ½″ from all edges of interfacing.

If appearance of garment fabric is not affected by fusing (try it on a fabric scrap), fuse interfacing to wrong side of entire collar; otherwise cut interfacing off at fold line, fuse it to the half of the collar which will become the undercollar. Continue as for regular interfacing above (ill. 9—"Fold collar in half, etc.").

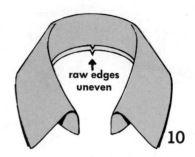

ATTACHING A COLLAR

A collar can be attached to a garment in different ways, depending on the style of the garment. Its neck edge may be caught in a shaped facing all around, or in a shaped facing at front of garment only; or the neck edge may be finished with a bias strip. The pattern instruction sheet will tell you which method applies to your garment.

Here, however, are some useful pointers:

IMPORTANT—After a collar is turned, the raw edges at the neck are no longer even. The upper collar will be smaller because it has been brought slightly over the outer edge by understitching. **Do not try to make these raw edges match** but keep them in this position by machine basting ½″ from the undercollar raw edge. If your collar has a roll, accentuate this difference before stitching by folding the collar over your hand as it will be on the garment; then pin the layers together (10). When stitching the collar to the garment, match the raw edge of the undercollar to the neckline. The seam allowance on the upper collar will just be a little narrower.

Always stay-stitch garment neckline, so you can safely clip the seam allowance before attaching the collar.

When stitching the collar to the garment, begin at center and stitch toward each end to avoid slippage.

A two-part collar must be anchored together before attaching, to prevent it from spreading. Overlap ends so that edges meet at neck seam line; baste across by hand or machine (11).

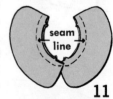

After collar has been stitched to neck edge of garment, grade, clip, and understitch this seam as you would any facing seam (see p. 94).

MAKING A COLLAR DETACHABLE

A collar can be made detachable by means of an extension cut from the garment neck-facing pattern. This is then slipped inside the garment neck edge and attached with snaps (12).

Pin the back and front neck-facing patterns together at shoulder seam line, making one continuous pattern (13). From lining or collar fabric, cut two entire neck facings.

Stay-stitch neck edges of collar and of each facing piece, ½″ from edge.

With collar sandwiched between the two facing pieces, (these wrong-side-out), pin or baste all neck edges together. To make stitching easier, clip neck edge of facing to stay-stitching line, as needed (14). Stitch ends of facing and neck edge in one operation, pivoting on needle at corners (14). Turn facing to right side.

Stitch facing down through all thicknesses, close to neck seam. Stitch raw edges of facing together. Finish with pinking or with bias binding.

Sew a hook and eye at collar opening. Snaps are placed at shoulder seam on garment and at matching points on collar facing (for comfort, when wearing the garment without the collar, attach the socket-half to the garment and the ball-half to the collar).

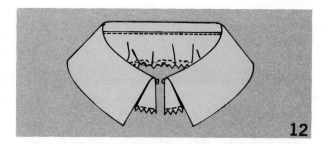

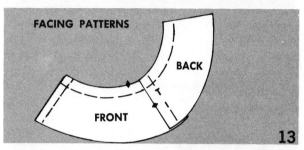

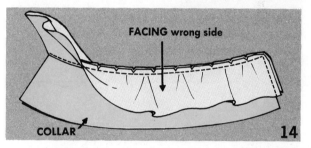

Cuffs

Cuffs vary a great deal in design and construction. They fall into two categories
—cut in one with the garment (sleeve or pants legs)
—made separately and stitched on.

CUFF CUT IN ONE WITH GARMENT

Used on sleeves or pants legs (1,2). Interfacing is generally not needed.

A turned-back cuff is simply a very deep hem partly folded up on the right side. Beyond the finished (folded-up) length, you need two times the depth of cuff plus 1″.

Mark as shown (3). Turn cut edge to wrong side on fold line; stitch hem. Fold cuff to right side.

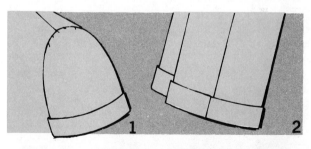

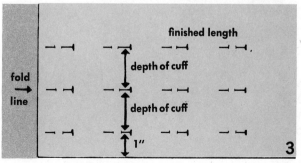

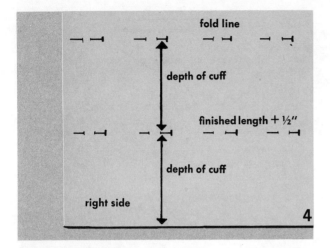

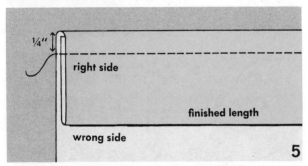

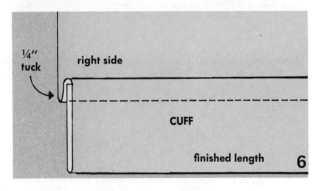

A mock cuff is made by forming a tuck which, while securing the hem, simulates the upper edge of a regular, topstitched cuff. It saves fabric since it requires only one depth of cuff plus ½″ for the tuck.

Mark as shown (4). Remove the pins used for marking the finished length.

Turn cut edge to wrong side on finished length line. Fold a second time to wrong side on fold line, so that raw edge is inside fold. Stitch ¼″ from this second fold, as shown (5).

Fold cuff down and press (6).

CUFF MADE SEPARATELY

A cuff made separately may be
    closed, stitched to a closed sleeve (7,8)
    open, stitched to a closed sleeve (9)
    open, stitched to a sleeve with a placket (10),
      or without a placket (14).
(see the chapter on PLACKETS.)

Like a collar, such a cuff generally needs interfacing, and its edges should be smooth and flat. See directions for collars, page 50, substituting the word "cuff" for "collar" throughout.

A cuff can be made detachable by encasing the unfinished wrist edge in double-fold bias tape. This edge then can be attached inside the finished sleeve edge by means of basting or small snaps.

ATTACHING CUFFS

Cuffs can be attached to a garment in different ways, depending on the style of the garment. Follow your pattern instruction sheet. Here, however, are some additional pointers.

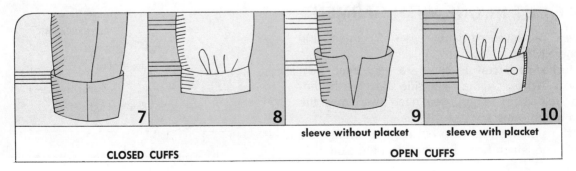

CLOSED CUFFS   sleeve without placket   sleeve with placket   OPEN CUFFS

To prevent an open-end cuff from spreading as it is being stitched to a closed sleeve, overlap the ends so that the edges meet at the seam line, and baste across by hand or machine (11).

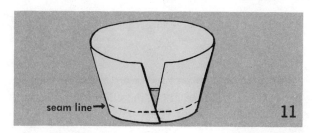

When attaching a cuff to a gathered sleeve, stitch with the gathered side (not the cuff side) up. This allows you to control the gathers.

To avoid hand-hemming on the inside when attaching the cuff to a sleeve, "stitch in the ditch": Make sure the folded edge on the inside reaches at least ⅛" beyond the first stitching line, covering it. Pin the fold in place from right side. **From right side** of sleeve, stitch around as closely as possible to the cuff, catching the fold underneath.

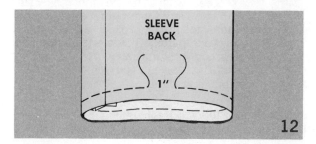

QUICK METHODS FOR ATTACHING CUFFS

An open-end cuff can be attached to a sleeve without a placket opening in knits and lightweight fabrics, as follows.

Do not make a placket opening even if your pattern calls for it. If sleeve is to be gathered into cuff, make a line of machine-stitching (longer stitch) along bottom seam line, leaving 1" unstitched toward back of sleeve (12).

Pin cuff to right side of sleeve, all raw edges even, matching ends of cuff to ends of stitching; draw up gathers.

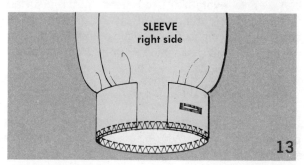

Stitch on seam line; trim seam allowance to ¼", finish raw edges with zig zag (13). If your machine has an overlock stitch, trim seam allowance, then stitch.

Turn cuff down; seam allowance will fold up into sleeve. Topstitch the free 1" space close to fold. When the cuff is buttoned, the free area will look like a placket (14).

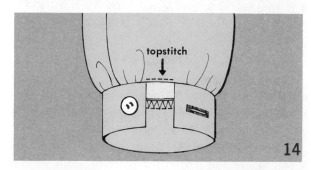

A closed, turned-up cuff can be attached with the raw edges concealed in the fold of the cuff.

Pin cuff to sleeve, raw edges even, outside of cuff to wrong side of sleeve and seams matched, as shown.

Stitch around on seam line. Make another line of stitching (straight or zigzag) in seam allowance. Trim (15). Turn to right side and turn cuff up, over seam.

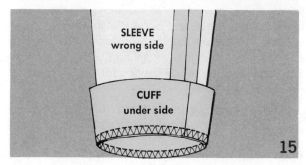

Cutting

A mistake in cutting cannot be taken out like a badly-sewn seam. In expensive fabric, it can be costly. The thing to do is to proceed without haste and make sure you have everything right before putting scissors to fabric. Follow all directions, study your pattern guide sheet, and take into account all indications on the pattern pieces themselves. You will find below a reliable procedure.

Be sure your fabric is straightened and pre-shrunk, if necessary—PREPARING FABRIC FOR USE, page 74.

Assemble everything you need: cutting surface (large table or cutting board), fabric, pattern, sharp shears, tape measure, yardstick and small ruler, pencil, pins and pincushion, iron and ironing board.

PREPARATION

Pick out the pattern pieces you will use (depending on what "View" of garment you have selected on envelope). Smooth out the pieces with a warm, dry iron, placing each new one on top of the pressed pile. Make pattern alterations, if any (see p. 193).

Small pieces, if printed together, are cut apart.

Grain line marks, to serve their purpose properly, should extend the entire length of pattern pieces; using a yardstick and pencil, extend grain line arrows on printed patterns.

Selecting your pattern layout—On the pattern guide sheet, locate and circle your pattern layout for the **selected view** of your garment, for your **pattern size, fabric width,** and fabric either **"with nap"** or **"without nap"** (see next page). See page 73 for the fabrics that are classified "with nap" and why (there are many besides actual napped fabrics). If in doubt, cut "with nap".

Fabrics "without nap" have no up or down direction in design, weave, or texture, and may be cut with the pattern pieces placed in either direction, as long as they are on grain (1).

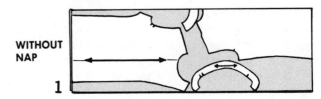

Fabrics **"with nap"** must be cut with the tops of all the pattern pieces going in the same direction (2, 3, 4 and 5).

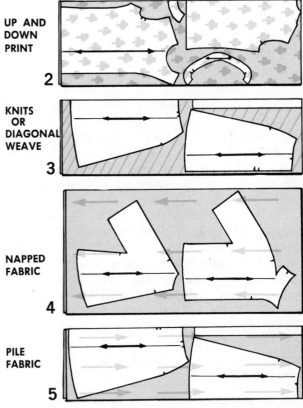

A true napped fabric (wool broadcloth, flannel, camel's hair, etc.) looks best with the nap running toward the hem of a garment (4).

A pile fabric (velvet, corduroy, etc.) has a richer color with the pile running toward the top of a garment (5). Fake fur varies; long hair generally runs down—for short hair, hold it up both ways and decide.

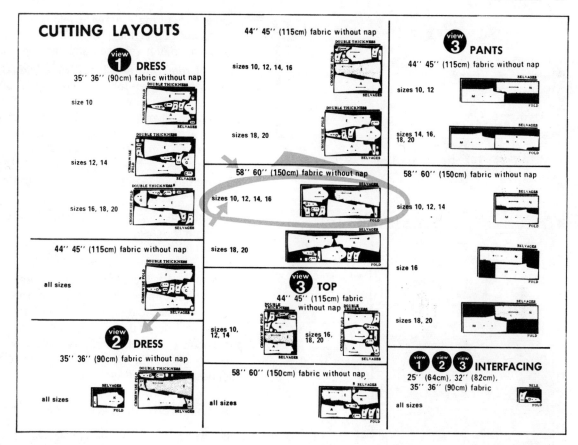

CUTTING LAYOUTS

view **1** DRESS
35'' 36'' (90cm) fabric without nap
size 10
sizes 12, 14
sizes 16, 18, 20

44'' 45'' (115cm) fabric without nap
all sizes

view **2** DRESS
35'' 36'' (90cm) fabric without nap
all sizes

44'' 45'' (115cm) fabric without nap
sizes 10, 12, 14, 16
sizes 18, 20

58'' 60'' (150cm) fabric without nap
sizes 10, 12, 14, 16
sizes 18, 20

view **3** TOP
44'' 45'' (115cm) fabric without nap
sizes 10, 12, 14
sizes 16, 18, 20

58'' 60'' (150cm) fabric without nap
all sizes

view **3** PANTS
44'' 45'' (115cm) fabric without nap
sizes 10, 12
sizes 14, 16, 18, 20

58'' 60'' (150cm) fabric without nap
sizes 10, 12, 14
size 16
sizes 18, 20

view **1** view **2** view **3** INTERFACING
25'' (64cm), 32'' (82cm), 35'' 36'' (90cm) fabric
all sizes

THE FOLD IN THE FABRIC

You have already straightened and pre-shrunk your fabric, if necessary (see p. 74). Press out any wrinkles. Press out the center fold to make sure it does not leave a mark. If the fold cannot be pressed out, you will have to avoid it as you lay out the pieces. See A TRIAL LAYOUT, page 61. Carefully refold the fabric for cutting, following the grain.

Fabric is usually folded right sides together for cutting. The only time it is cut right side out is if it has a design that must be taken into account and that does not show through to the wrong side (printed corduroy, bonded fabrics).

Fold the fabric as shown in the cutting layout on the pattern guide sheet. Keep in mind that excess fabric hanging over the edge of the cutting surface may pull the fabric you are using out of shape.

Layout using regular lengthwise fold (A)
Match the selvages and pin them together in a few places (A-a).

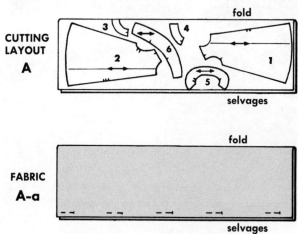

CUTTING LAYOUT A

FABRIC A-a

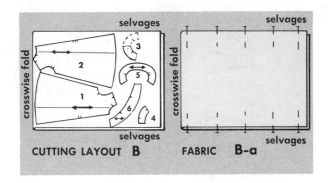

CUTTING LAYOUT **B**

FABRIC **B-a**

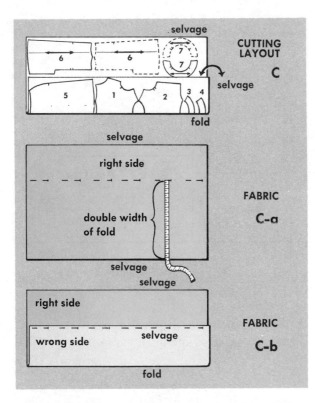

CUTTING LAYOUT **C**

FABRIC **C-a**

double width of fold

FABRIC **C-b**

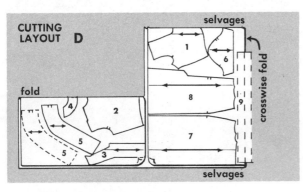

CUTTING LAYOUT **D**

Layout requiring crosswise fold (B)

Press out center fold. Fold fabric across the width, as shown; match selvages and pin together (B-a).

Layout requiring new lengthwise fold (C)

Press out center fold. On cutting layout, identify the pattern piece which determines the width of the fold (in layout C, piece 5). Pick out the actual pattern piece and measure its width. On the fabric, spread out singly, measure double this width from the selvage and mark with pins (C-a). Fold the fabric, bringing the selvage to the pin-line; smooth out, and pin selvage along line (C-b).

Layout requiring a combination of folds (D)

In such a case, you position only the pattern pieces requiring a certain fold. Cut these out, then make the new fold.

EXAMPLE: In layout D, two different folds are needed. You would first cut out pieces 2, 3, 4, 5 with lengthwise fold; then press out the fold on remaining fabric and fold the fabric crosswise. Cut out pieces 1, 6, 7, 8, 9, placed as shown. For piece 9 (belt) open out the fold and cut on a single thickness.

ARRANGING PATTERN PIECES

If you have bought the correct yardage, as given on the pattern envelope, a trial layout will not be necessary (see page 61 for cases requiring a trial layout). Just be guided exactly by the layout you have circled.

When, on a layout, a pattern piece is shown extending beyond a fold line (piece 9 on layout D), cut out the other pieces, then open out the remaining fabric to cut this one.

When a pattern piece is drawn with a broken line (second piece 6 on layout C), it means that after other pieces are cut you either:

fold remaining fabric (here, crosswise) and cut piece out through both thicknesses; or

cut piece through a single thickness, then reverse the pattern (printed side down) and cut the piece out a second time.

When half of a pattern piece is drawn with a broken line (piece 3 in layout B), it means that the piece is a half-pattern, to be cut on a fold. Cut out all other pieces as laid out, then re-fold fabric to cut each of these pattern pieces.

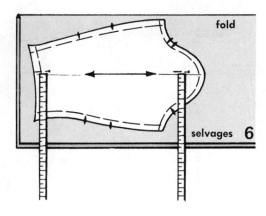

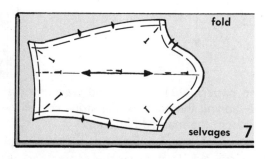

Place the first pattern piece (largest piece located at one end of layout) on fabric. To position the grain line, measure the distance from one end of extended grain line to selvage; pin pattern through grain line. Pin through other end of grain line at the same distance from selvage (6); then through center of line.

Smooth pattern out from grain line and pin at opposite corners, then at opposite sides (7). Keep the pins inside the cutting line of the pattern and don't use too many—they can distort the cutting line.

Repeating the same steps for each, pin in place all the pattern pieces that require the same fold in the fabric. When pattern pieces are close together, overlap margins to the cutting line (8).

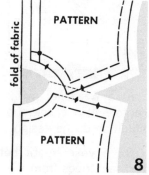

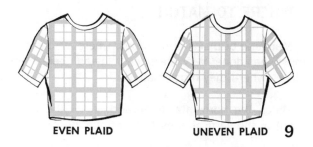

PLAIDS AND STRIPES

For a garment to look well-made, plaids, stripes, or other designs forming bands must be matched at closures and important seams. This means having the lines meet so as not to interrupt the design. In bias seams, it means joining the lines in a chevron pattern (10). All of these designs may come in an even (symmetrical) or in an uneven repeat (9). Uneven plaids, stripes, or bands require more care in matching.

Since some fabric is wasted in the process of matching, it means buying extra yardage. In matching a large pattern there is more fabric loss than in matching a small one.

The pattern should have few seams, and preferably be designed for plaids or stripes. If it calls for a chevroned seam (10), be sure you have an even plaid or stripe—an uneven design cannot be matched in that manner.

With even plaids and stripes the fabric may be folded for cutting. Fold it carefully, with edges pinned together so that the corresponding lines are matched. At various points in the rest of the fabric, pin the two layers together, checking on the other side to make sure that the lines match.

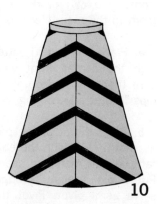

Uneven plaids and stripes must be cut singly (see p. 61) and "with nap"—that is, with the tops of the pattern pieces all facing the same way.

WHERE TO MATCH

Matching of plaids and stripes, wherever possible, must be done very carefully. Listed below are places where they must match.

Match the horizontal lines and check the placement of the vertical lines for continuation of design at:

center front and center back when there are seams or openings;

side seams, from the notch (below the underarm dart) on down;

front armhole notch (the back cannot generally be matched).

Match the vertical lines and check the placement of the horizontal lines for continuation of design at:

waist seam, at center front and center back;

collar and yoke, where they meet the bodice.

Match both the horizontal and vertical lines on:

patch pockets, flaps and welts, unless they are cut on a bias.

HOW TO MATCH

The fact that most pattern paper is transparent allows you to do a perfect job of matching a design. Once you have established the position of your main pattern piece (usually the bodice or skirt front), you can mark the other pieces, matching them to the main piece as follows:

a. Place the main pattern piece on the fabric with the center front where you want it. Make sure that any horizontal stripe across the bust or hips falls at a becoming level. Pin in place.

b. Place the adjoining pattern piece on the fabric as shown (11); with the edge lapped over front pattern so that matching seam lines cross at notches. Put a pin straight through the crossing point to serve as a pivot. Pivot the second pattern piece until the straight-grain marking is in the correct position (even with a vertical stripe). Pin to hold in place. Trace the lines to be matched (horizontal, vertical or both) in three different places on the

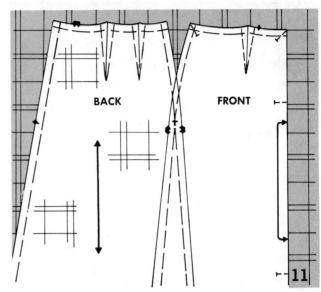

BACK FRONT

11

second pattern (11); use colored crayons or a soft pencil, adding the name of the stripe color if necessary. Unpin the marked pattern.

c. Move the pattern to the fabric area where it will be cut out. First place the center back where you want it, then move the pattern up or down until the marked lines match the fabric stripes. Pin in place.

On a sleeve and armhole, match seam lines at notch in the same way, marking only the horizontal stripes on the sleeve pattern (12). When moving it to the fabric for cutting out, have the strongest vertical line fall at sleeve center.

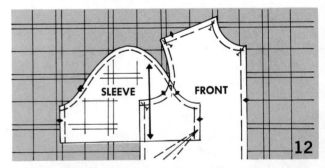

SLEEVE FRONT

12

At a waistline, match the vertical stripe at the center. Also check the horizontal stripe for continuation of the design.

On a yoke, mark both the horizontal and the vertical stripes from the center out.

On pockets, flaps, etc., place the pattern on top of the garment pattern and mark both the horizontal and the vertical lines.

LARGE PRINTED DESIGN

The pattern should call for few seams. Buy extra yardage, because some fabric will be lost in placing the motifs attractively. To decide where these should fall, hold the fabric up against you in front of a mirror. Then place the pattern pieces on the fabric accordingly. Try to match the motifs at seams wherever possible in the same manner you match plaids and stripes.

A TRIAL LAYOUT

This may be necessary

. . . if your fabric is of a width not indicated on the pattern guide sheet;

. . . if your fabric is "with nap" (see p. 73) and there is not a cutting layout "with nap";

. . . if you have been unable to press out the fold in your fabric and need to avoid it;

. . . if your fabric has a plaid or other design that must be matched.

To make a trial layout, select the cutting layout that seems closest to what you need and place all pattern pieces in position, with one or two pins in each. When you have made sure that you have sufficient fabric, proceed as directed on pages 57–59, folding the fabric as necessary and checking each piece for grain position.

CUTTING

Cutting lines on patterns are indicated with either a single or a double line. Cut exactly outside the single line; or between the two lines.

For cutting out pieces, use bent-handled shears; never use pinking shears, because they do not make a reliable cut line.

Keep fabric and pattern flat on table. Never draw fabric toward you to reach a piece.

Cut with long strokes. When cutting into a corner, open shears only wide enough to have points of blades reach end of cut.

Wipe lint from blades of shears frequently, especially when working with synthetics.

Notches are important pattern markings, and absolutely reliable matching points. They are not really notches any longer, although they have kept the name. A notch is cut **out** from the pattern, adding a point to the seam allowance. Two or more notches are cut in a block (13).

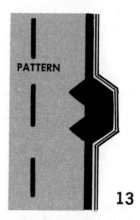

13

In sections that are at center front or center back of garment, mark center points, top and bottom, with a notch or a small clip in the seam allowance.

Do not remove pattern pieces from section cut. You will need them for the next step, marking.

CUTTING A SINGLE THICKNESS

Some fabrics require that they be cut through a single thickness at a time.

When a pattern is to be cut on a fold (usually at center front or center back), trim the pattern margin from fold edge. Pin the pattern in place on the fabric. Place a pin across the fold line, at top and bottom, so that you will not inadvertently cut into the "fold" line. With chalk or pins, mark the fabric at top and bottom of "fold" edge of the pattern piece. Cut around the pattern piece except for "fold" edge. Unpin the pattern and reverse it, matching "fold" edge to chalk marks. Re-pin and cut out the second half (14). When cutting two corresponding sections, such as sleeves, from a single thickness, reverse the pattern for the second section.

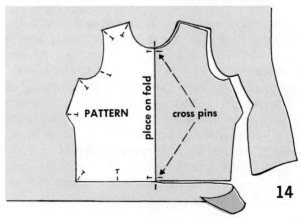

14

Darts

Darts are stitched, pointed tucks that shape the fabric to fit the body. They are a very important part of garment construction, even though certain garments (loose-fitting or cut on the bias, for instance), may be designed without them.

Standard darts (1) may be straight or curved, vertical, horizontal, or at a slight angle. French darts (2) are diagonal, going from side seam at waist or hip to point of bust. Darts are clearly indicated on patterns. Since their exact length, depth, and placement have a great bearing on the fit of a garment, they may need adjustment (see PATTERN ADJUSTMENTS, p. 193).

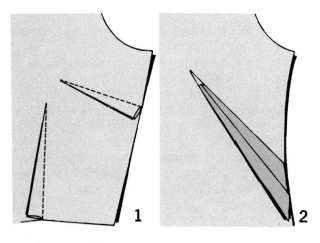

MARKING

Deep darts may be given on the pattern with the center cut out. On uncut darts, a center line is usually given. If it is not, carefully measure and mark center of dart at widest point, and draw a line to point of dart. Carefully transfer center line (on uncut darts), stitching lines, and matching dots to fabric (see the chapter on MARKING). If you are using a tracing wheel and dressmaker's tracing paper, make short crosslines (3) to mark point of dart and matching-dots (omit this if it would show on the right side). If you are making tailor's tacks, place tacks at dots and at intervals along the center line.

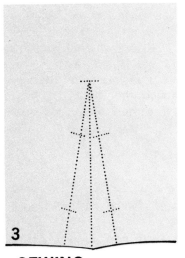
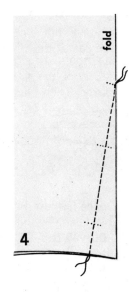

SEWING

Fold dart on center line (for cut-out darts, match edges) and be sure the stitching lines and markings are matched; pin or thread-baste.

Start stitching either at point or at wide end. To make sure that the point will taper to nothing gradually (as it **must**), take two stitches at the point, along the fold, as close to the fold as possible (4). Tie thread-ends at point.

On double-pointed darts, reinforce the stitching at the center; clip at widest part (5).

When stitching straight darts it is helpful to use a paper guide: Lower machine needle into fabric on stitching line. Place a firm piece of paper (such as an envelope) along the stitching line, one end against the machine needle, the other against the pin at other end of dart. Lower machine foot and stitch along the guide, removing any pins as you go along.

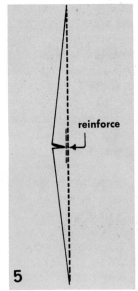
reinforce

FINISHING

BEFORE DARTS ARE PRESSED, some require the following treatment:

Deep dart—If uncut, slash to within ½″ of point (6). Overcast edges if the fabric requires it.

Heavy fabric—Slash to within ½″ of point (6). Overcast if necessary.

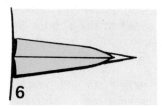
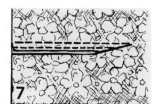

Lace or sheers, unbacked—Make a second line of stitching ⅛″ from first; trim (7).

Curved dart—Trim to ⅝″; clip at curve; reinforce stitching. Overcast if necessary.

AFTER SEAMS ARE STITCHED, trim the wide end of any dart diagonally, to reduce bulk in the seam allowances (8).

PRESSING

Press darts only when you are sure of fit.

First press the line of stitching as is, but be careful not to put a crease into the fabric beyond the point. Then open out the garment; to maintain the shaping, complete the pressing over a pressing ham, the end of an ironing board, or a sleeve board. Trimmed or slashed darts are pressed open like a seam (6). Vertical uncut darts are pressed toward the center of a garment (1). Horizontal and diagonal darts are pressed downward (1). If the fabric marks easily, slip a piece of paper between the dart and the fabric.

A FEW SPECIAL CASES

DART IN UNDERLINED GARMENT—In order to keep the two layers of fabric together at the fold, machine-baste (on the underlining side) through center line before folding and stitching the dart.

DART IN INTERFACING—see TAILORING, p. 236.

DART IN VERY SHEER FABRIC—"BOBBIN-STITCHING" will avoid a knot at the point, where it might show through.

For regular machines: Thread machine as usual, and turn the wheel to bring the needle and take-up lever to the highest point. Then:

a. Draw out about 20″ of bobbin thread through the hole in the throat plate.

b. Remove upper thread from machine needle. Thread the bobbin thread through the needle, in the opposite direction.

c. Knot the bobbin and spool thread together (9). Wind the spool, drawing bobbin thread through needle and onto the spool (10). Bobbin thread is now continuous from spool to bobbin.

d. Stitch the dart, **starting at point.** The machine must be re-threaded for each dart.

For machines with self-winding bobbins, wind bobbin with enough thread to make one dart. Do not cut this continuous thread. Stitch dart, starting at point. Re-wind the bobbin for each dart.

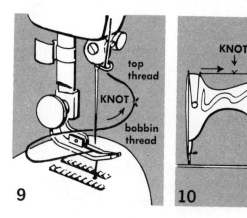

RELEASED DARTS release fullness at one or both ends. Mark and pin or baste as for regular darts. Starting at the fold, stitch across to marking; pivot the fabric on the needle; stitch along marking to edge of garment (11), or pivot again and stitch across to the fold (12). Press toward the center of garment.

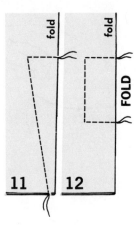

Easing

Easing is what you do when a fabric edge is slightly longer than the edge or area to which you are joining it. In a seam, the purpose is subtle shaping. A smooth sleeve cap is always eased to the armhole. The back edge of a shoulder seam may be eased to the front. The hem in a skirt must often be eased (see p. 121).

Ideally, easing should be invisible after pressing. Fabrics treated for easy care, however, resist easing and can never be pressed entirely smooth. This is particularly true of permanent press fabrics.

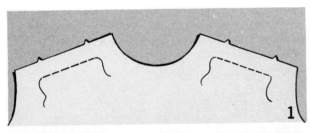

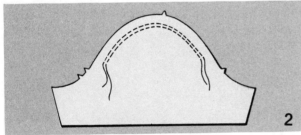

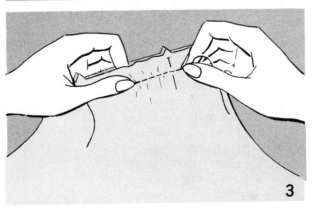

EASING IN SEAMS

Easing in seams occurs between dots or other pattern markings. In woven and stable-knit fabrics, **the longer edge is always eased to the shorter** (in other words, do not try to stretch the shorter edge). For very stretchy knits, see FABRICS, page 81.

As the first sewing step (when stay-stitching, if the piece is stay-stitched), make a row of stitching on the seamline with a stitch slightly longer than usual (1). For perfect evenness, make a second row in seam allowance, ⅛″ from the first (optional).

When you are ready to join sections, pin at notches and other marks. Draw up one end of easing thread(s) until edges match. Holding edge as shown (3), work fabric along the easing thread with thumb and forefinger until the fullness is distributed smoothly and evenly, with no suggestion of tucks. Draw up first one half of the edge, then the other half. For easing a sleeve cap, see p. 228.

Stitch seam with eased edge on top, for better control.

With edge of iron, press the stitched line as is (with seam closed), before continuing with your sewing or, as needed, pressing the seam open.

In some fabrics, especially wool, steam-pressing will entirely shrink out the ease. Work over a pressing ham or a sleeve board, so that the area is molded as intended. With a **steam iron,** hold iron over eased area, and allow steam to penetrate fabric, then lower iron and apply light pressure until ease has disappeared. With a **dry iron,** use a dampened press cloth and touch lightly with the iron.

Other fabrics are handled in the same way, but will not really shrink, although untreated natural fibers may do so to a slight extent. The important thing here is to press the seam only, using the point of the iron, as putting the iron down flat may make creases out of the slight indication of gathers.

Equipment

 It is possible, of course, to accomplish wonders with an old sewing machine and not much else. Good equipment, however, goes a long way in making work easier (and more fun!) and in assuring good results. We can't recommend it too strongly. Buy the best you can afford—you don't need to get it all at once—and care for it with the respect that good tools deserve.

The articles marked √ in the listing that follows are the ones you really should have. You can acquire the rest as you go along. A full-length mirror, while it cannot be listed as sewing equipment, is of immense help, not only in checking on an individual garment, but in keeping you aware of what looks well on you and what does not.

There are scores of additional sewing aids on the market, impossible to list here. New ones are being introduced all the time—some excellent, others merely gadgets. Look around for whatever answers your particular needs.

SEWING MACHINE

√ Your sewing machine is your major investment, even if the machine is second-hand. And you are not likely to buy another one soon. Therefore, shop around carefully. See what the different brands and models will do, and how well they function (go over the check list below). If your budget is limited, don't worry about a cabinet—you can always get that later. Most portables are standard machine-heads that will fit into a cabinet or folding table. If you prefer a portable, make sure you can lift it without strain. Depending on the kind of work you do, you may like a free-arm machine, which allows you to get into places such as cuffs. As for prices, they vary greatly, depending on brand, model and a variety of considerations.

Machines fall into four categories:

1. Straight stitch—forward, reverse, and darning. Will make good buttonholes with an attachment, bought separately.

2. Basic zigzag—The most practical machine. Besides regulation straight stitch, it overcasts edges, makes buttonholes, sews on buttons and appliqués, and does even-width satin-stitch.

3. Design-stitching, forward motion—Same as No. 2, but can also be set to working in patterns.

4. Design-stitching, forward and reverse motion—Its biggest plus is the stretch stitch, excellent for knits and stretch fabrics. It will also stitch a straight seam while overcasting the edge; and has a repertory of fancy stitches. For further details, see MACHINE STITCHING.

CHECK-LIST FOR ALL BRANDS

1. On a zigzag machine, does the straight stitching come out smooth and even? How good a buttonhole does it make?

2. Does the machine satisfactorily sew various weights of fabrics?

3. Does the foot or knee control work smoothly?

4. Is the machine quiet and free from vibration at all speeds?

5. Does the light shine directly on the work area?

6. Is the bobbin easily accessible? Can cover plates be easily removed and all parts made accessible for cleaning?

7. Are upper and lower tensions easy to adjust? Does the manual explain this clearly?

8. How much of a guarantee comes with the machine? You should have one, in writing, from both the manufacturer **and** the dealer. Is service available?

9. Are lessons on the use and care of the machine included?

When you buy your machine, you will do well to add a supply of **extra bobbins.** Also, be sure you have a **zipper foot.** You may find an even feed or roller foot useful for stitching fabrics difficult to handle.

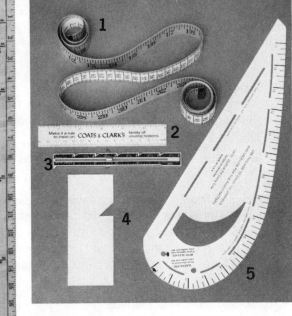

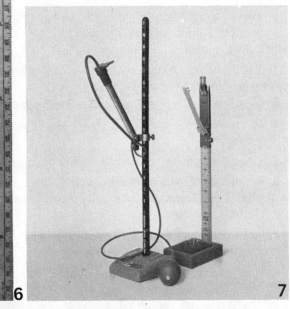

Buying a used or re-conditioned machine—A perfectly good machine can be purchased second-hand, but before doing so it is essential that you sew on the machine to see if it is in good operating condition. Then, in addition to the information above about sewing machines, check the following: Has it been well cared for; are there any dents or scratches? Is there an instruction book for the machine? Are parts readily available?

FOR MEASURING

Where possible, buy equipment marked with both inches and centimeters.

√ **Tape measure** (1)—Usually 60″ long, with metal ends. A good tape measure must not stretch, and has measurements clearly marked on both sides, starting at opposite ends.

√ **Short ruler** for marking hem depth, buttonholes, etc. Either a plain 6″ ruler (2), or a hem gauge (3), which combines a ruler with a movable indicator. You can make a hem gauge using a piece of cardboard, notched at the desired mark (4).

√ **Yardstick** (6)—Indispensable for marking straight long lines; often used for marking hemlines from the floor. Should be firm and straight, with smooth edges and clear markings.

French curve (5)—For re-drawing curved lines when a pattern is adjusted, and to use as a guide when transferring curved lines with tracing paper and tracing wheel.

Skirt hem marker (7)—For marking a hem when trying on a garment. There are various models. Some, using powdered chalk and a bulb, allow you to do the job alone; one attaches to a door at any height. The one using pins is the most accurate, but requires a helper.

FOR MARKING

√ **Dressmaker's tracing paper and tracing wheel** (8)—For transferring pattern markings to fabric. Paper comes in several colors, to contrast with your fabric. Wheels come with teeth, for general use, or smooth, for hard-to-mark and delicate fabrics.

√ **Tailor's chalk** (9)—For transferring pattern markings to fabric. Clay chalk comes in several colors, in squares or in pencil form.

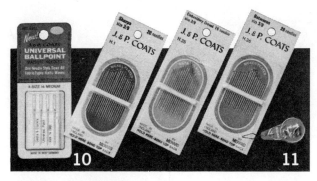

10   11

FOR SEWING

√**Needles** (10)—For hand- and machine-sewing. Buy quality brands only, and be sure to have on hand a variety of sizes and types (see p. 250).

Needle-threader (11)—If you have trouble threading needles.

√**Straight pins** (12)—Use quality brand rust-proof pins, size 17 for general use. Available with plain or plastic heads. Also come extra-thin, extra-long, and in magnetic wire. There are also magnetic pins available but they tend to stick together and to any metal surface.

√**Pincushion** (13)—To avoid scattering pins. A wrist pincushion, attached to a bracelet (14) is handiest. You can buy one; or make one by sewing a pincushion to a bracelet of elastic. There are many kinds, including a magnetic one to use with steel pins.

Emery bag (15)—Used to sharpen and remove rust from needles. Do not leave needles in emery as it can damage the needle finish.

√**Thimble** (16)—For faster, easier hand-sewing, learn to use a thimble. Whether it is of metal or of plastic, make sure it fits the middle finger of your sewing hand.

FOR CUTTING

Good scissors and shears make all the difference, and with care last a lifetime. Avoid dropping them, or using them on heavy paper or cardboard, and have another pair for household chores. Keep your scissors sharp too—for sharpening, check with your local hardware store or sewing machine repair shop. Or write to the manufacturer.

√**Dressmaker shears** (17)—Shears for cutting out fabric. Bent handles allow the fabric to remain flat on the table. A 7″ or 8″ overall length is good, and left-hand models are available. Blades may be plain or serrated—the latter good for cutting synthetic fabrics.

Electric scissors (18)—take the strain out of cutting out fabric. Available in a variety of models.

Light trimmers (19)—Shears for general use, trimming seams, clipping threads, etc. A 6″ or 7″ overall length is recommended.

√**Sewing and embroidery scissors** (20)—For cutting buttonholes, clipping, and other precise work. Equipped with two sharp points. Most useful in a 4″ or 5″ overall length.

Pinking and scalloping shears (21)—For finishing seam (**not** to be used for cutting out fabric). A 7½″ overall length is good. Left-hand models are available.

√**Cutting surface**—Should be at least 30″ wide and 48″ long. A folding cutting board will protect or enlarge a table top and can be used on floor or bed. Made of special cardboard, it has markings to help keep fabric straight, and will take pins, which is especially useful with knits.

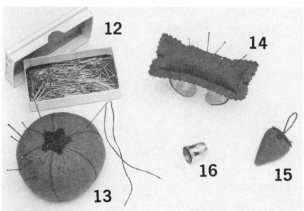

12   14   16   15   13

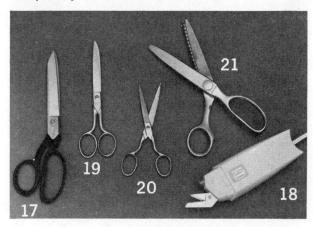

21   19   20   17   18

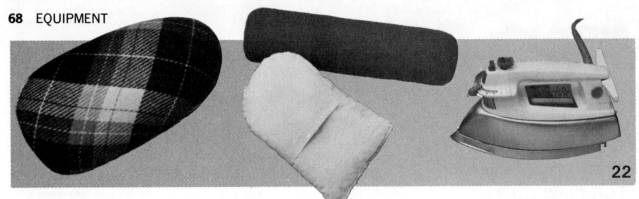

22

FOR PRESSING

Here you draw on your household equipment.

√ **A good iron** must be on hand, set up, and ready for use throughout any dressmaking. A combination steam/dry iron is the most satisfactory. There are many models available; pick one that gives a good amount of steam.

√ **Press cloth**—Recommended because most fabrics tend to shine if they come in direct contact with iron. Cloth can be dampened to provide the moisture for more steam. You can buy a specially-treated cloth; or use a piece of unbleached muslin, about 14″ × 30″, thoroughly washed to remove sizing. For dark woolens, use a dark wool press cloth with a steam iron.

Slipcover for iron—Used in place of a press cloth. Slipped over bottom of iron, it allows a complete view of what you are pressing. Can be purchased or made.

√ **Ironing board** should be firm and well-padded, its cover clean at all times.

√ **Sleeve-board**—Useful for pressing seams in sleeves and other narrow spaces; the ends are good for darts and curved edges. It should be well-padded (add padding as necessary, using an old blanket).

Dressmaker's ham, seam roll, pressing mitt (22), —Important pressing aids for hard-to-reach areas, shaped seams and darts. Can be purchased or made.

A point-presser (23), for pressing open seams of points in collars and lapels. **Pounding block** (clapper or beater), very useful for tailoring. Some point pressers have a bottom designed to be used as a clapper (23). **Needle board**—A luxury item for pressing velvet and other pile fabrics.

MISCELLANEOUS

Dress form—A form to your specific measurements can be extremely useful, especially if you have no one to lend a hand in fitting, or you are hard to fit, or both. A number of kinds are available, varying greatly in price.

The following smaller sewing aids are particularly helpful: **Loop-turner** (24)—for turning bias binding and inserting cord into tubing. **Bodkins** (25)—for inserting elastic or ribbon into casings. **Thread clipper** (26)—handy to have at the sewing machine. **Magnetic seam guide**—Very helpful in stitching an even seam line. **Seam ripper** (27)—also used for cutting machine worked buttonholes. **Beeswax**—helpful when sewing on buttons. **Magnet**—for picking up pins from the floor.

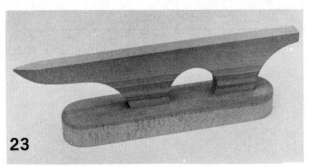

23

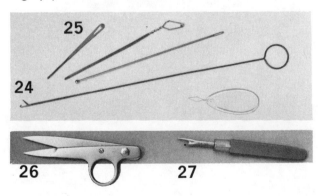

25

24

26   27

Fabrics

Today's fabrics, in their ever-increasing variety, call for a whole new set of guidelines. And new fabrics turn up with every season. For the user, the two developments of the greatest interest in the fabric field are probably: The importance of the descriptive label, since the most expert buyer can no longer identify fibers by look or by feel, let alone blends, and the tremendous popularity of knits.

In what follows, we shall try to help you identify the different types of fabrics and give you the information you need to handle them successfully (see HANDLING THE DIFFERENT FABRICS, starting on page 75).

Fabrics are what they are because of:
- the materials, or **fibers,** from which they are made.
- their **construction,** or the way the fibers are assembled.
- their **finishes,** added to improve performance.

FIBERS

The fibers in a fabric may be natural, man-made or blended.

NATURAL FIBERS

By these are meant the old standbys furnished directly by nature. They are still very much with us, but nowadays are seldom sold without some treatment or finish (indicated on the label) that improves their performance.

Cotton still accounts for the majority of all the fabrics used in the world. It is spun from the ball of white fluff, or "boll", of the cotton plant. Cottons, being washable, are now almost always treated for shrink-resistance; unless absorbency is required, as in terry cloth, they are usually also treated for wrinkle resistance and no-iron performance.

Wool, the warmest and most absorbent of fabrics, is made from the hair of animals, usually sheep, and occasionally camel, alpaca, vicuna and others. The following

terms commonly describe wool: **Virgin wool,** as it comes from the animal, is the best and performs the best; it has never been processed before its manufacture into the finished product. **Re-processed wool** is re-spun from scraps of new fabrics made of previously unused wool. **Re-used wool,** obtained from used rags and worn clothing, is usually blended with new wool before it is re-spun.

Good quality woolens, especially the better domestic ones, are now almost always pre-shrunk, and have considerable natural crease-resistance. They are sometimes washable. Worsted (not to be confused with knitting worsted) is a long-staple wool, spun to a hard, smooth twist.

Linen, the most ancient of spun fibers, comes from the stems of the flax plant. It is cool, strong and washable, but, in its natural state, extremely crushable. Nowadays it is almost always treated for crease-resistance, either by blending or with a finish.

Silk, produced by the silk worm, is the most expensive, strongest, lightest and finest of the natural fibers. While its performance varies with its quality, it has, at its best, natural crease-resistance. It is often washable. It requires ironing, however, and so far has been given no new treatment or finish. It is sometimes used to add quality to blends.

MAN-MADE FIBERS

The confusion that surrounds man-made fibers stems largely from the fact that, having been created to simulate a natural fiber, no man-made fiber has a recognizable appearance of its own. As an example, rayon, the oldest one, first called artificial silk, now also imitates successfully linen ("butcher linen" is rayon), cotton, and even wool. Nylon is most admired when it is most like silk, but it can imitate other fibers too. The public has come to rely very much on trade names in identifying fabrics of man-made fibers, but the label will give the generic or descriptive terms, and it is well to know what they mean.

Man-made fibers are of two kinds:

- **Rayons and acetates,** processed from cellulose, which is derived mainly from wood pulp and cotton linters.
- **Synthetics,** produced in the laboratory from complex chemical compounds.

RAYONS AND ACETATES

These fibers have the advantage of not producing static electricity.

Rayon, the first marketed man-made fiber, is much used for linings and underwear. It is sold under trade names such as Avril, Bemberg, Cupioni and others. It is also used as a blend to add softness and reduce cost.

Acetate is used in reproducing the various silk weaves, such as taffeta, foulard, georgette, etc. Trade names are Celanese Acetate, Avisco, Estron, among others.

Triacetate is a modification of acetate for crease-resistance. Arnel is a trade name.

SYNTHETICS

The synthetic fibers are the ones that make up the bulk of the washable, quick-drying, crease-resistant, long-wearing, no-care fabrics of today.

Nylon, the first synthetic fiber made, is still being experimented with to reduce the static electricity it produces and to increase the opacity of its knits. Among the trade names under which nylon fabrics are sold are Antron, Blue C, Caprolan and Qiana.

Polyester, similar to nylon but more resilient, is the most popular of the synthetics, in both woven and knit fabrics. It is also very common in blends. Dacron, Fortrel, Kodel, Trevira are some trade names.

Acrylic is the fiber that most often imitates wool. Acrilan, Creslan, Orlon, Zefran are a few of the trade names for acrylics.

Modacrylic is used in the making of fake fur, usually with a backing of some other fiber. Dynel is one of the modacrylic trade names.

Ban-Lon, often referred to as though it were a fiber, is really a label applied to various fabrics that have met quality control standards by the manufacturer.

PLEASE NOTE that the foregoing are only the terms you will encounter most often. As new fibers emerge from the test tube, new terms appear. A number are already around, labelling certain newer fabrics. What matters to you is not so much their names, but their properties and care, about which the label is required to inform you.

BLENDS

Blends come in so many combinations—of two or more natural fibers, of different synthetics, of naturals with synthetics or rayons—and in so many different proportions, that it would be impossible to enumerate even part of them. The best way to learn about a blend is to examine the label on the bolt of the fabric.

FABRIC CONSTRUCTION

The great majority of fabrics are **woven** or **knitted** from fibers spun into yarn. In a few fabrics, classed as **non-woven,** the fibers are simply matted by various processes.

Fabrics come in many **weights.** Weight in fabric means its thickness, not its actual weight. In woven and knitted fabrics, weight is determined by several factors: not only the thickness or fineness of the yarn used, but also the type of construction, the closeness or looseness of the weave or knit, the presence of a nap or pile, etc. It can vary all the way from sheer to blanket weight.

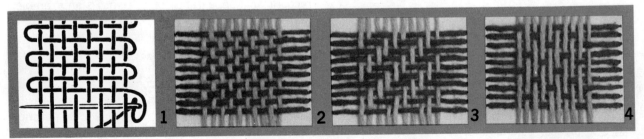

PLAIN WEAVE   TWILL WEAVE   SATIN WEAVE

The **hand** of the fabric, or how it feels and drapes, is determined by the fiber content, the fabric construction, and the finish used.

Color can be added before or after the construction of the fabric. When put in before construction, it is described as yarn dyed; a pattern may be woven in with the pre-dyed yarns. After construction, the whole piece may be dyed or a design may be printed on the fabric.

WOVEN FABRICS

All woven fabric is made from threads interwoven at right angles to each other (1). The lengthwise threads are called the warp, and the crosswise threads are called the filling or weft. The lengthwise and crosswise directions of a woven fabric are called its **grain.** When such a fabric comes from the loom, before it is processed with a finish, it is "grain-perfect", which means that the two directions are at true right angles to each other. (Read the chapter on GRAIN—it is very important in sewing.)

While the direction of the threads never changes, all kinds of textures are achieved by varying the pattern according to which the threads cross. The three basic weaves are the **plain** weave (2), the **twill** (diagonal) weave (3), and the **satin** weave (4). In all weaves, the two finished edges, or selvages, are reinforced by a doubling of warp threads.

A **nap** fabric is created by brushing up the natural fuzziness of certain fibers. In a **pile** fabric, the "stand-up" threads are added to the basic weave, which may be made from a different fiber. In both nap and pile fabrics, the plain basic weave can be seen on the wrong side. Fake fur is a special deep-pile fabric.

Woven fabrics, which have been with us since the loom was invented, are made from all the fibers and in an immense variety of weaves.

KNITTED FABRICS

The properties that make knitted fabrics so popular—stretch, pliability, crease-resistance—are due to the fact that they are constructed out of loops instead of straight threads. Knitting machines, which began by simply imitating hand knitting, now turn out fabrics in which the interlocking of stitches not only creates texture, but furnishes a degree of control and recovery (return to shape after stretching) that has eliminated the problems associated with early knits. In addition, the use of synthetic fibers has made a great many knits not only machine-washable, but no-iron and non-crushable. Knit fabrics are made from any fiber. However, the great majority of knits sold by the yard are now synthetics.

There are weft knits and warp knits. Weft knits are worked crosswise, exactly the way hand knitting is, and may be sold either tubular, or flat with selvages. Warp knits are worked lengthwise and are always flat.

Jersey (5), a weft single knit, reproduces a stockinette stitch. It is light, soft and comfortable. It is often bonded to another fabric to prevent too much stretching.

Double-knit (6), also a weft knit, has greater stability and weight, as it is worked in two interlocking layers. Unless a pattern in color is involved, it looks much the same on both sides. It is an extremely popular fabric, easy to handle and comfortable to wear.

Tricot (7) is a simple warp knit, mostly used for lingerie but also for shirts and dresses.

Raschel (8), a more complex and heavier warp knit, comes in many textures often simulating crochet lace and others. It is used in all kinds of clothing.

Sweater knit, made from bulkier yarn, simulates a hand-knit effect. Worked either as a weft or a warp knit, it may have considerable stretch. It includes knit velour, which has a nap.

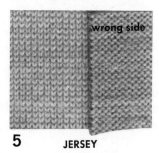

5 JERSEY

6 DOUBLE-KNIT

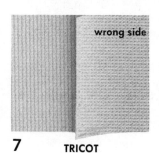

7 TRICOT

8 RASCHEL

LACE and NET

Lace and net are openwork fabrics made by various processes, some very intricate.

Lace, consisting of a pattern of decorative motifs, ranges in weight from sturdy to filmy. Heavy lace (crochet-look raschel) is generally of cotton or a cotton blend. The finer varieties, which imitate the costly hand-made laces (needlepoint, bobbin, and others), may be of any fiber or blend.

Net, the most transparent of fabrics, is cotton, rayon, or synthetic thread worked in a uniform honeycomb pattern. Very fine net is called tulle.

NON-WOVEN FABRICS

Having no grain, these fabrics can usually be cut in any direction, do not ravel, and do not curl at the edges—which means they often do not need to be hemmed or otherwise edge-finished. The ones sold by the yard are felt, suede- and leather-look fabrics and certain interfacing fabrics.

Felt is made of wool fibers matted and steam-pressed. It lends itself well to steaming and shaping.

Suede-look (fake suede) is a synthetic fabric, in certain brands nearly unbelievable in its imitation, made by a highly sophisticated chemical process.

Leather-look describes simulated leather fabrics, generally known as vinyl, crinkle patent, or polyurethane. They are usually bonded to a woven or knitted backing.

Non-woven interfacings, made of synthetic fibers bonded by chemicals, come in a number of weights, under various trade names. Some, called "all-bias", stretch in all directions. Others stretch only in one direction (this must be taken into account when cutting).

BONDED FABRICS

Two fabrics, often of different construction, are fused together for better performance. Sometimes a thin layer of foam is bonded between the two fabrics, adding body and a certain amount of insulation.

FINISHES

Very few fabrics (such as unbleached and unsized cotton, raw silk) are put on the market as they come from the loom. A great many others are bleached, dyed, or printed with a color pattern. They may also be treated for glazing or for nap-raising. These processes, however, are not called finishes.

Finishes are added to give a fabric a better "hand" (meaning feel and drapability) or better performance. They may often pull the crosswise threads off grain (9). With a **temporary finish,** this condition can and should be corrected. With a **permanent finish,** it cannot.

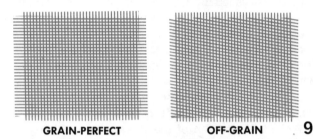

GRAIN-PERFECT   **OFF-GRAIN**   **9**

Temporary finishes, which are not mentioned on the label, are water and steam-soluble. Consisting of some kind of sizing (in silk, weighting), they are used only on the natural fibers and rayon, mostly the imported ones. Their use is diminishing. For removing a temporary finish, see PREPARING FABRIC FOR USE, page 74.

Permanent finishes, added to improve performance, are mentioned on the label and are in to stay. **Pre-shrinking** (indicated by the terms Pre-shrunk, Shrink-resistant, and Sanforized), and **flame-retardance,** very important in children's sleepwear, do not affect grain. **Crease-resistance** (indicated by terms such as Permanent Press or Durable Press) and **stain-resistance** do affect grain, because in the process the fabric is treated with a chemical and then cured (heat-set), locking the weft threads in whatever position they take as they are processed. Progress is constantly being made toward keeping the grain straighter. Fabrics so treated also take on a stiffer "hand". There are other finishes applied for various reasons. One is an insulating finish, used in linings, such as Milium. There is even talk of an anti-perspirant finish in preparation for lining fabrics.

BUYING FABRIC

A choice of fabrics and the amount you will need are indicated on the envelope of the pattern you have selected.

FABRIC CHOICE

A list of suitable fabrics is given on the back of the envelope. In addition, there will often be a more specific directive on the front, such as "For stretchable, unbonded knits," "Suitable for knits," or "Not suitable for diagonals," etc. For checking on fiber contents and fabric properties see next column.

AMOUNT

The amount needed is always specified "without nap" or "with nap".

"With nap", please note carefully, means **not only** fabrics that actually have a nap or pile, but all fabrics that are "one-directional", which means that for one reason or another (texture or pattern) they look different when held up or down. These take a little more yardage because the pattern pieces will all have to be laid out in the same direction, that is, with all top edges facing the same way (see p. 56).

(see p. 56)

> Use the "with nap" yardage figure for:
> Nap and pile fabrics.
> Fabrics with the design (print or texture) going in one direction.
> Fabrics in which the construction reflects the light differently up and down. This includes all knits, all diagonal weaves, satin and sateen.

When in doubt, figure "with nap."

You will also need additional yardage when a design (plaid or other) is to be matched at the seams; the larger the design, the greater the allowance necessary. This is also true with large irregular designs, such as florals, which may not need to be matched but must be placed carefully.

The pattern envelope gives the yardage needed in several widths, but there is an even greater range of fabric widths available. Here, for your convenience, is a yardage conversion chart that should take care of all possibilities.

YARDAGE CONVERSION CHART

	FABRIC WIDTHS							
	35"-36"	39"	41"	44"-45"	50"	52"-54"	58"-60"	66"
YARDAGE	1¾	1½	1½	1⅜	1¼	1⅛	1	⅞
	2	1¾	1¾	1⅝	1½	1⅜	1¼	1⅛
	2¼	2	2	1¾	1⅝	1½	1⅜	1¼
	2½	2¼	2¼	2⅛	1¾	1¾	1⅝	1½
	2⅞	2½	2½	2¼	2	1⅞	1¾	1⅝
	3⅛	2¾	2¾	2½	2¼	2	1⅞	1¾
	3⅜	3	2⅞	2¾	2⅜	2¼	2	1⅞
	3¾	3¼	3⅛	2⅞	2⅝	2⅜	2¼	2⅛
	4¼	3½	3⅜	3⅛	2¾	2⅝	2⅜	2¼
	4½	3¾	3⅝	3⅜	3	2¾	2⅝	2½
	4¾	4	3⅞	3⅝	3¼	2⅞	2¾	2⅝
	5	4¼	4⅛	3⅞	3⅜	3⅛	2⅞	2¾

Courtesy of COOPERATIVE EXTENSION SERVICE
Rutgers University—The State University of New Jersey

READ THE LABEL

For facts about the fiber content and fabric properties we now depend on consumer protection laws requiring that the label tell all. On a label, a hangtag, or the end of the bolt (10), you should find:

Fiber content (for example: 100% wool; or 50% cotton and 50% polyester; or 65% triacetate and 35% polyester; etc.)

Fabric properties, such as "Pre-shrunk", "Sanforized", "Crease-resistant".

Permanent care labeling, which tells you whether the fabric is washable, and how; whether it can stand bleach; whether it is "dry-clean only"; in short, exactly how to care for it. And please note that permanent care labeling extends beyond the bolt. If you buy such yardage, you are entitled to a label to take with you. Ask for it.

NOTE: As a general rule, exact and complete labeling can be found only in the big, regular fabric departments and stores. In the many small stores where beautiful fabrics are often sold, the label information may be present only in part or not at all. Here you will have to trust your judgment, or go by whatever information you may obtain from a salesperson.

crosswise fold

fold

selvages

11

CHECK A DESIGN

In the case of a regular design such as plaids, geometrics, or even floral prints arranged in rows, examine the fabric to make sure the design is at right angles to the selvage; otherwise it will not be possible to match it or have it hang properly. If such a fabric has a permanent finish other than shrink resistance, check as follows before ordering the yardage cut: Unroll about a yard from the bolt; fold back half a yard, matching selvages (11). The design should be even with the fold; if it is not, it is wiser not to buy. On fabric with a lengthwise center fold, check the second layer by looking **inside** the fold as well.

PREPARING FABRIC FOR USE

There are various things you may have to do to your fabric before cutting it out. Depending on the fabric, you may have to straighten the ends, straighten grain and/or pre-shrink it.

Washable fabrics—It is a good idea to wash the fabric before cutting it out. This will take care of possible shrinkage, remove excess finishing solution which may cause skipped stitches, and relax fabric which may have been stretched on the bolt.

If you plan to wash the finished garment, wash the fabric in the same manner as you will care for the finished garment. Even if you plan to dry-clean the finished garment (because of inner construction, for example) wash the fabric first.

NOTE: Some fabrics, especially inexpensive ones, may loose their crispness after washing; in this case you may want to underline the garment or choose a different pattern style that is suited for a softer fabric. In any case, you are better off finding this out before the garment is made.

Dry the fabric in the same way you plan to dry the finished garment, either flat or in the machine, unless the grain must be straightened; in that case, dry flat as explained under STRAIGHTENING THE GRAIN.

Dry-cleanable fabrics—Unless the fabric has been marked pre-shrunk or "needle ready" by the manufacturer, pre-shrink woolens, cottons, and linens, since steam-pressing may shrink these fabrics. Use the London shrinkage method on the next page.

STRAIGHTENING THE ENDS—This is necessary with fabrics where the grain can be straightened and other fabrics that will be dried flat.

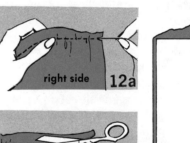

right side **12a**

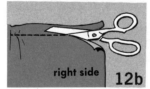

right side **12b**

PAPER

FABRIC **13**

For woven fabrics that can be straightened, trim one cut end along a crosswise thread; if the grain is not clearly visible, draw up a thread (12a) and cut along the pucker (12b).

For woven fabrics that cannot be straightened, and for knits, cut the ends at right angles to the selvage, using the square corner of a large sheet of paper as a pattern (13).

STRAIGHTENING THE GRAIN—This may be necessary with untreated woven woolens, cottons, linens, silks or rayons.

Fold the fabric lengthwise, selvages even. If the two halves of the trimmed ends do not match, the fabric needs straightening.

If fabric has been pre-washed or pre-shrunk, straightening can be done when the damp fabric is laid out flat to dry. Carefully smooth out fabric so ends are at right angles to the selvages.

If the fabric is not to be dampened, the fabric can be straightened by grasping the two selvage edges and pulling on the bias (two people will be needed if the fabric is wide). Repeat at several points until the ends are even.

PRE-SHRINKING is necessary for any fabric that may shrink during washing. It is also necessary with woolens, cottons and linens, even if they are to be dry-cleaned, since steam-pressing may shrink these fabrics.

Washable fabrics should be treated as the finished garment will be treated later.

Hand-washables—First straighten fabric ends; then fold the fabric and immerse it in warm or hot water for at least a half hour. (To make fabric easier to handle, edges may be basted together, as described under dry-cleanable fabrics, to the right.) Squeeze out water (do not wring) and dry flat, smoothing out the fabric so ends are at right angles to the selvages.

Machine-washables—Put the fabric through the washer and dryer at a setting suitable for the fabric. If, however, the grain needs straightening, first straighten fabric ends, then fold fabric smoothly in half lengthwise and hand- or machine-baste the selvages and ends together before washing. Dry flat, smoothing out the fabric so ends are at right angles to the selvages.

For dry-cleanable fabrics—Use the "London shrinkage" method. Straighten fabric ends. Fold fabric smoothly in half lengthwise and hand- or machine-baste the selvages together, clipping them every 5" or 6". Baste the ends together. Spread on a damp sheet (either as it comes out of the washer after spinning; or dunked and wrung out well). Fold fabric and sheet together and leave overnight. Dry flat, smoothing out the fabric so ends are at right angles to the selvages. Press lightly with a steam iron.

HANDLING THE DIFFERENT FABRICS

We don't have to tell you that chiffon requires a more delicate touch than denim. Any fabric, however, even the sturdiest, is better off for being handled as lightly and as little as possible. Our sewing techniques are carefully planned for minimum handling.

The directions throughout this book apply to standard fabrics in standard weights. Certain fabrics, however, require special handling. In the pages that follow, you will find a special section for each of these in alphabetical order. Any detail not mentioned can be handled in the standard manner. The fabrics covered are BONDED FABRICS, FAKE FUR, KNITS, LACE, LEATHER AND SUEDE, LEATHER LOOK, PERMANENT PRESS, PILE FABRICS, SHEERS, SUEDE LOOK.

NOTE: If you are working with a very expensive fabric, or a fabric where changes will leave marks, it may be a good idea to make a trial garment in order to be sure of the fit (see p. 205).

BONDED FABRICS

Bonded fabrics are two fabrics fused together. The face-fabric, of any fiber content, may be woven or knitted. The backing is usually acetate or nylon tricot, but may also be a woven or non-woven fabric. Sometimes a thin layer of foam is bonded between the two fabrics, adding body and a certain amount of insulation. Weights vary from medium-light to heavy.

Bonded fabrics are firm, easy to work with and do not ravel at the edges. They are practically never washable. In dry-cleaning, it is safest to have the work done professionally, as the cleaning agent used in coin-operated machines may dissolve the bonding chemical.

No preparation is needed before the fabric is cut out and sewn.

Choice of notions, sewing details, etc. are the same as for any fabric of the same weight and "hand", with the following facts to remember.

INTERFACING is seldom needed, as the backing fabric generally gives sufficient firmness. If more is desired, add interfacing in the usual way.

LINING is optional. Underlining is practically never used.

CUTTING should be done with the face-fabric up, so you can place the pattern according to the lengthwise grain or a design to be matched.

FACINGS, where they do not show, may be placed, for greater comfort, with the backing-fabric up (toward the skin). With heavy fabric, reduce the bulk by using lining fabric for facings.

SEAM ALLOWANCES need not be finished.

WHEN HEMMING, catch stitches to the backing fabric only.

WHEN PRESSING, set the iron to suit the fiber on the side you are pressing. Test first on a scrap of fabric.

FAKE FUR

Sewing fake fur presents no real problems. The short-pile varieties are handled like any pile fabric. The longer ones demand a little extra attention in cutting and marking, but can be stitched on any sewing machine. And fur has a way of concealing stitching mistakes.

The fur, or pile, is usually synthetic, varying from the very short (pony, zebra) to the long (fox, bear, etc.), with several depths in between (seal, rabbit, shearling, mink, jaguar, etc.). There are also the "fun furs", which come in a variety of patterns, finishes, and colors—even jewel tones.

The backing, knit or woven, may be of cotton or some synthetic fiber.

There are also fabrics with fur on one side and a garment fabric on the other, which can be worn with the fur on the inside as a lining.

The care required varies—some fake furs are washable, some dry-cleanable, still others may need to be cleaned like real fur. It will all be on the label.

Certain **patterns** are specially recommended for fake fur. Otherwise, any pattern of suitable style will do, but fitted styles are best—unless you are looking for a bulky look.

Yardage is, naturally, figured "with nap". If the fur has markings (not only such definite ones as in zebra and jaguar, but shadings such as lynx), be sure to allow extra fabric for matching at the seams. If the fabric is not to be used at once, hang it up or roll it to avoid creasing the pile.

Lining may or may not be needed, depending on the garment. Underlining and interfacing are hardly ever necessary.

Facings, unless they are to show, should be made of lining fabric. In a lined garment, you can avoid inside facings by extending the lining to the garment edge (see p. 144).

As for **notions,** you may want to get frogs, or large, thread-covered hooks-and-eyes in order to avoid buttonholes and zippers (see CLOSURES on next page). For stitching, you will need a #14 or #16 machine needle. For hand-sewing, a #7 needle. You will also need extra long pins, such as the ones with glass or plastic heads.

THE PATTERN—For accurate cutting, trim away the pattern margins (**not** the seam allowances). If the pattern needs adjusting, do it with particular care, especially around the shoulders which should fit closely. To reduce bulk, eliminate any straight-grain seams by pinning the pattern pieces together and cutting the fabric in one piece. For example, a stitched-on facing at a straight-grain front opening can be replaced by an extended one as shown (14).

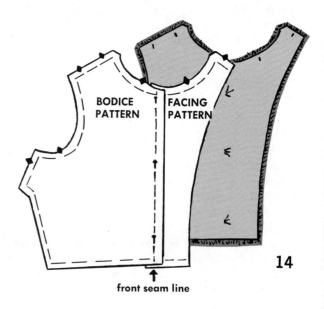

BODICE PATTERN FACING PATTERN

front seam line

14

CUTTING is done through a single thickness, with wrong side up (any markings in the fur will show on the wrong side). Use the pattern layout "with nap". Long pile should run down; short pile may go up or down so long as it is all in the same direction. See page 61 for how to handle the pattern when cutting through a single thickness. Pin the pattern in place securely. Using only the point of the scissors, cut only the backing, while sliding the **down** scissor-point through the pile on the other side. Do not cut notches, but mark their places clearly in the seam allowance.

MARKING—use pins, chalk, pen or tailor's tacks. The tracing wheel will not mark accurately here. Mark each section before removing the pattern to cut the next piece.

STITCHING—On two thicknesses of fake fur scraps, check the pressure and tension of your sewing machine, and test the seams described below. The stitching may be either straight or zigzag. Thick pile may cause a shortening of the stitches. You may have trouble getting the two thicknesses under the machine foot, but **don't forget to lower the foot** before stitching. With the point of scissors or a darning needle, push the pile in (toward the garment), away from the seam. Stitch slowly, in the direction the pile goes, and keep pushing in the pile. After you have stitched the seams, use a long needle or a fine comb to work out, from the right side, any pile caught in seams.

SEAMS may be plain or narrow, depending on where they are placed.

Plain seams are satisfactory almost everywhere. Set the machine for straight stitching, at 8–10 stitches per inch. Stabilize shoulder seams by including seam binding in the stitching. Stitch all the seams necessary for fitting the garment; where a seam is to cross another one, shear the pile from the seam allowances on the first one, using sharp scissors and cutting as close to the backing as possible. Once you are sure that the seams will not be changed, work out the pile on the right side as described above. Finger-press seams open; to flatten them properly, catch seam allowance edges to fabric backing. On unlined garments, finish raw edges if the fabric ravels.

Narrow seams, with either zigzag or straight stitch, can be used anywhere, but are necessary in areas where you want to reduce bulk, such as a collar or a lapel.

Zigzag—set the machine at 12–14 stitches per inch and almost the widest width. Trim seam allowances close to stitching.

Straight stitch—stitch on seam line (8–10 stitches per inch); make a second line of stitching ⅛"–¼" from the first. Trim seam allowances close to stitching.

The pile on all seam allowances may be sheared if the seam appears bulky. This, however, is seldom necessary.

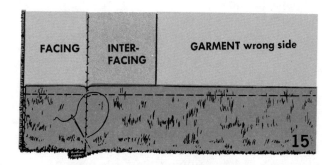

FACINGS of fake fur are not understitched. To keep a facing from rolling to the outside, pin it down (pins placed lengthwise) ½" from edge seam, then fold the facing back on the pin-line and catch it to the garment (15).

DARTS are slashed after stitching and finished like a plain seam.

PRESSING—some fake furs cannot be pressed because of their fiber content, but you don't want a crisp, pressed look in fur anyway. Finger-press seams by opening them with your thumbnail. If you must use an iron, never do so without first testing it on a scrap of the fabric. Press on the wrong side, with a needle-board or a piece of the same fabric, pile up, underneath.

CLOSURES are best kept as simple as possible.

Loops, frogs, buckles and other decorative closures allow you to avoid zippers or buttonholes. For concealed closings, you can use furrier hooks, coat hooks or covered snaps (see p. 100).

Zippers are not very common in fake fur garments. However, if you want to insert a zipper, first cover the seam allowances at the opening with grosgrain ribbon and shear off the pile underneath.

Machine-worked buttonholes are not recommended. Home sewing machines are not equipped to make buttonholes in deep-pile fabric.

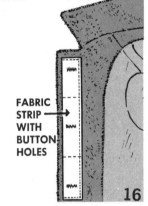

For a hidden button closure, machine-worked buttonholes can be made on a doubled strip of plain fabric. Sew strip by hand to underside of right front as shown (16).

FABRIC STRIP WITH BUTTON- HOLES

16

Bound buttonholes on short-pile fabrics may be made with 1″-wide grosgrain ribbon. Mark placement of buttonholes (see p. 32). For each buttonhole, cut two strips of ribbon, 1″ longer than the buttonhole. Pin or baste the two ribbons to right side of garment, with edges touching the baste-marking, as shown. Stitch ⅛″ or more from adjoining edges of ribbon for the length of the buttonhole (17), leaving thread-ends of about 3″. Complete buttonhole, following steps **f** and **g** under ONE-PIECE FOLDED BUTTON-HOLE on page 34. Sew seam allowances of buttonhole to back of garment. Sew edge of ribbon to back of garment.

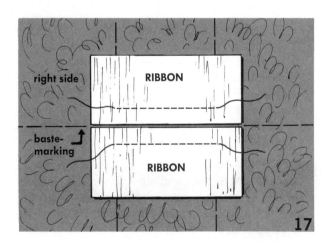

right side

RIBBON

baste-marking

RIBBON

17

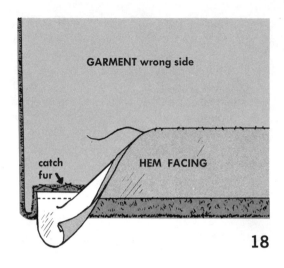

GARMENT wrong side

catch fur

HEM FACING

18

HEMS in **short-pile fabrics** are handled like hems in any heavy fabric. To eliminate bulk in **deep-pile fabrics,** allow only 1″ for the hem when cutting, and use a hem facing of lining fabric, about 3″ wide. After stitching the strip of facing to the bottom edge of the garment, turn the edge up on the hemline and catch-stitch the edge of the fur fabric to the backing, which will keep the edge flat (18). Then hem the free edge of the facing to the backing, as shown.

FAKE FUR AS A LINING—Choose a coat style that is not closely fitted. Use the lining pattern to cut the fur lining, but eliminate the pleat in center back and omit the sleeves. Sleeves should be made of lining fabric for ease in slipping the coat on. After assembling the lining, sew it in as usual.

KNITS

Exactly what knits are—their construction, fiber content, and general properties—was explained under KNITTED FABRICS, on page 71. (In addition to the information given here, if you are using tricot, also look up the chapter on LINGERIE). There are several factors which must be considered in handling any knit.

First among these is the fabric's **degree of stretch** (and recovery). After you have picked out a knit you like, you must make sure that its stretchability is suited to the pattern you have selected. This factor is now so generally recognized that the big pattern companies provide gauges on which the stretch of knits can be measured and classified. Sometimes the gauge is even printed on a pattern envelope. The gauge is not standard, however, and you would do well to use the one put out by the company whose pattern you are using. From the point of view of handling the fabric, knits fall into the categories of **stable, moderately stretchy** and **very stretchy.** Don't judge the stretchability by looks alone; stretch the fabric with your hands to test.

A stable knit has very little stretch, keeps its shape and can be used wherever knits are listed among the choice of fabrics on the pattern envelope. It can generally be handled like a woven fabric except that it does not ravel at the edges. Most double-knits are stable knits.

A moderately stretchy knit is softer and more clingy, suitable for draping and for soft fullness. Make sure that the weight and hand of the fabric are what you want.

Very stretchy knits are the only ones that should be used with patterns specifying "For stretchable, unbonded knits", or "Stretchable knits only", because such patterns often provide for no darts or other shaping. Some lightweight knits, however, such as tricot, can have considerable stretch and yet be suitable for regular patterns also, provided the fabric has good recovery.

Generally, stretch is tested crosswise, on a fold of fabric about 2″ from a cut edge. While the gauge will indicate the stretch category, there is no actual measure for recovery, but it can easily be seen; after stretching, the fabric should instantly spring back to its former width.

If you happen to have bought the fabric first, be sure to establish its stretch category before buying the pattern. In either case, whichever one comes first, just bear in mind that fabric and pattern must be suited to each other from that particular standpoint of stretch.

YARDAGE should be figured "with nap", because knits reflect light differently up and down (see BUYING FABRIC, p. 73).

Lining is used only with the heavier stable knits; tricot is a good choice. Underlining is practically never used.

Interfacing may be necessary to stabilize an area, such as around buttonholes. See the chapter on INTERFACINGS for choice.

Facings, when the fabric is bulky or spongy, may be made of lining fabric unless they show.

Pre-made bandings, ribbings, turtlenecks are available to match some sweater knits.

PREPARATION—Read PREPARING FABRIC FOR USE on page 74; it also applies to knits. Cotton knits tend to have progressive shrinkage, and you would do well to wash and dry them more than once before cutting them out. Synthetic knits should be run through the washing machine to remove any excess finish, which often causes skipped stitches in seams. Adding a fabric softener to the water will reduce static electricity. Unless it has been washed, a knit should be allowed to lie flat for at least 24 hours to let the fabric relax.

CUTTING—If the fabric comes in tubular form, cut one fold open, but follow a **rib,** not the fold. In this case, and also if the fabric comes folded through the center, try to press out the fold and refold the fabric along a rib, as a guide for the "Straight Grain" marking on the pattern. If the fold will not press out, arrange the pattern to avoid it (see TRIAL LAYOUT, p. 61).

A straight-grain center back seam can be eliminated by cutting the back on a fold; if an opening is needed here, it can be slashed for an exposed zipper (see p. 272).

Use the "with nap" pattern layout. Work on a large, flat surface. Do not let the fabric hang over the table edge, as this will pull a knit out of shape. Use very sharp pins and shears. Wipe the blades of the shears often to remove lint.

MARKING—Use any method that will not show through or mark the right side of the fabric. Pins and chalk, or tailor's tacks, are good. A tracing wheel and tracing paper should be tried out before use, as the wheel might mar the fabric.

STITCHING can be done with either straight stitch or with zigzag. A zigzag attachment, however, is not recommended. An even feed or roller foot may help avoid puckered seams.

Thread and needle—For strength and elasticity, use polyester core thread in regular size or, for very lightweight fabrics, extra fine. The needle should be a # 11 or a # 14 Universal Ballpoint, depending on the fabric weight. Change your needle often—a blunt or burred needle can damage your fabric and thread.

Make a test seam to make sure of a balanced stitch (see p. 149). The tension should generally be loose, but both the tension and the pressure needed vary with the type of knit.

Lightweight knits—Be sure the tension is very loose (though balanced!) and the pressure rather heavy. When stitching, hold the fabric taut, slightly stretching it—this will put more thread in the seams and reduce puckers. To avoid bunching under the foot, lower the needle by hand when starting, and hold both thread-ends; **never back-tack.** When straight-stitching with a zigzag machine, use the small-hole throat-plate to prevent the fabric being drawn into the hole; or, if your machine has an adjustable needle position, move the needle either to the left or the right—just make sure you maintain your seam allowance width (see p. 88, ill. 43, 44).

Very stretchy knits—Tension should generally be loose. The pressure to use will vary with the thickness and sponginess of the fabric, which should not be allowed to stretch as you stitch. Certain seams, such as shoulders and waistlines, should be stabilized by including pre-shrunk seam binding in the stitching. When stitching very bulky stretchy knits, flatten the fabric in front of the presser foot with a small ruler or anything suitable.

All knits should be stay-stitched at the usual edges (neck, other curved seams) where control is necessary to avoid stretching, or where edges will be clipped.

SEAMS may be plain and pressed open or narrow, generally double-stitched. No seam finish is needed on stable knits, which do not ravel. On stretchy knits of any weight, where the seam allowances tend to roll, make narrow, double-stitched seams.

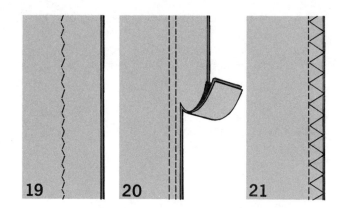

Plain seams—Either set the machine for a straight stitch (10–12 stitches per inch) or for the narrowest zigzag (14–16 stitches per inch); the slight zigzag will give elasticity to a seam by adding more thread (19). If your machine has a straight stretch stitch, you may want to use it for extra strength.

Narrow seams—Make a plain seam as above and make a second line of stitching ⅛″–¼″ away. The second line may be either like the first (20) or a wide zigzag stitch (21). Trim seam allowances close to stitching. If your machine has a stitch that seams and overcasts in one operation, you may want to use it for narrow seams.

Topstitching is fine on double-knits and other stable knits. It can also be done on moderately stretchy knits that have been interfaced. Make a test first.

CLOSURES must be chosen according to the type of knit.

Zippers—For most knits you can use any zipper in any application; for very lightweight knits, however, you may want to use a coil zipper.

Buttonholes—In all knits, the buttonhole area must be stabilized, meaning interfaced (see p. 132 for suitable fabrics).

Stable knits will take corded bound buttonholes and machine-worked buttonholes.

Moderately stretchy knits will take corded bound buttonholes; machine-worked buttonholes can also be made in such knits, but only in the direction of greater stability, which generally means with the rib—even interfacing will not prevent bunching and stretching in the crosswise direction.

In bulky sweater knits, machine-worked buttonholes should be made in the direction of the rib and preferably be corded. If your machine allows the adjustment, have the stitches not too close together.

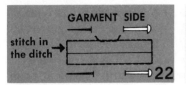 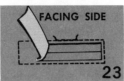

A time-saving facing-finish for bound buttonholes can be used on stable knits: After the buttonholes are made and the facing is attached, place pins around each buttonhole, holding the facing in place. With right side up, "stitch-in-the-ditch" around each buttonhole, pivoting at corners (22). Then carefully cut away the facing fabric within each stitched rectangle (23).

HEMS should be turned up after the garment has been allowed to hang for 24 hours.

A machine hemming stitch will incorporate the most stretch into the hem (see your machine manual).

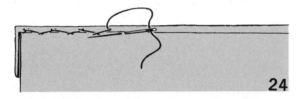

A tailor's hem, sewn with a loose catch stitch (p. 123) is very good for knits (24). For a twice-stitched hem in heavy fabrics see page 124. If the fabric ravels, first overcast the edge by hand or machine.

Stretch lace used as seam binding is also good. Hem loosely.

Fusing (see p. 108) works well on most knits, except for the very spongy ones. Test it first.

PRESSING must be done carefully to avoid stretching the fabric. Set the iron for the proper fiber and do not push the iron back and forth as you press. Sweater knits should be lightly steamed.

MISCELLANEOUS POINTERS

Binding—Medium and heavy stable knits can be bound with self-fabric or fold-over knit braid. Very lightweight stable and moderate stretch knits should be self-edged with French binding (see p. 27), the strips being cut on the cross-grain for greatest stretch.

Banding—Unless ready-made banding is used, very stretchy knits can be banded with self-fabric cut on the cross-grain.

Edge-stitching the crease in pants is sometimes desired to retain a pressed crease in knits. Before finishing top and bottom, lay the pants on the ironing board, right side out. Match lengthwise seams carefully and pin. Press firmly the folds formed down the front and back. Edge-stitch carefully along front crease only—the depth will depend on the thickness of fabric; try it out first. Pleats in skirts may also be stitched in this manner.

Set-in sleeves in very stretchy knits—Use the flat construction method: Do not stitch side seams in garment or underarm seam in sleeve. Do not ease-stitch in the sleeve cap. Pin the sleeve cap to the armhole, right sides together, matching edges and markings (25). Stitch with the armhole (garment) side up, gently stretching the edge to match the sleeve cap. Then stitch the garment side seam and sleeve seam in one operation.

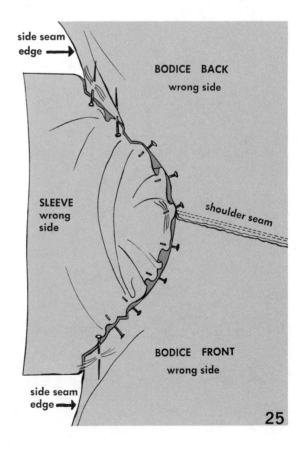

LACE

Lace that is unbacked, or backed only with net, needs special handling. Lace backed with an opaque fabric ceases to be lacy and is handled like any other fabric of comparable weight. The sturdy laces such as crochet-look or raschel, however, are treated as lace.

Lace fabric often has one decorative edge that can take the place of a hem.

PATTERN and YARDAGE—Choose a simple style with few seams, in order to avoid cutting up the lace design. Consider lace as a patterned fabric and allow extra yardage for matching large design repeats.

In laying out the pattern, your first consideration should be how the design falls. Heavy or heavily-embroidered lace may need to be cut out singly (see page 61).

FACINGS and INTERFACINGS—Avoid facings if possible. Where they are necessary, as on collars and cuffs, place interfacing of a suitable kind between the two layers of lace. Elsewhere, a bias strip of suitable material can take the place of a facing. See EDGE-FINISHES in the next column.

MARKING should be done with tailor's tacks or basting.

STITCHING—For very sheer lace, use polyester core thread, extra fine, and a Universal Ballpoint needle #11 or #14. Use a new needle to avoid damaging the fabric. Set the machine at 12–14 stitches per inch for sheer lace, 10–12 stitches for heavier.

On very open lace, a reinforced zigzag stitch may be useful: Stitch over a thread as for gathering on page 110; omit drawing up the thread.

If the lace catches in the feed dog, place strips of tissue paper under the seam while stitching. Afterwards, tear away the tissue.

DARTS should be double-stitched (26a) and trimmed (26b) or bobbin-stitched (see p. 63).

SEAMS—It may be necessary to baste seams. As a rule, make narrow, double-stitched seams (see p. 224). With fairly opaque lace, make plain seams, pressed open.

EDGE FINISHES—These may include hems. A facing strip of tulle (fine net) makes a practically invisible edge finish on lace. Cut a strip 2½″ wide on the crossgrain; piece as needed. Fold strip in half lengthwise; pin and stitch to the right side of the garment edge, all raw edges even. Add a second line of stitching and trim away fabric close to it. Turn the strip to the wrong side and slipstitch the folded edge to the lace (27).

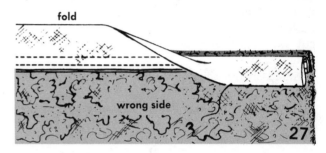

A French binding in a different fabric also makes an attractive edge finish (p. 27). So do various ready-made bindings in suitable fabrics.

CLOSURES will vary a great deal according to the kind of lace you are working with. Buttonholes in general should be avoided. Heavily embroidered lace will not take buttonholes of any kind; in other laces you might have machine-worked ones, or hand-worked with buttonhole twist or a strand of embroidery floss. When a zipper is not suitable, the pattern may suggest using snaps instead. If you do use a zipper, it should be a coil zipper, and you may want to do the outside stitching by hand (see p. 276). Buttons with loops are often a solution (see p. 40). Remember, however, whenever buttons or snaps are used, there should be at least one extra layer of fabric—a facing and/or interfacing.

HEMS—See EDGE FINISHES above. If you wish a hem-edge to have more body, finish it with horse-hair braid—see page 127.

PRESSING should always be done on the wrong side. With heavily embroidered lace, cover the ironing board with a piece of terry cloth.

LEATHER and SUEDE

While leather is not a fabric, it is sold in fabric stores and made into clothes; you may want to know how to handle it. As for care, it should be cleaned only by a cleaner qualified to do so.

Leather is a general term for all tanned animal skins, and includes **smooth leather, suede** and **splits.** Suede has been given a soft nap on the right side. Splits are rough on both sides, quite sturdy, and less expensive than suede.

Ready-to-wear leather garments will give you ideas on style as well as pointers as to sewing and details such as closures and finishing. Since leather does not ravel, it will depend on the thickness of the leather, the style of the garment and your own preference whether or not you will turn edges under.

Leather is sold in skins of various sizes and weights. The price may or may not be an indication of quality: you had best shop around and compare weight, size and quality in relation to price. Do not buy, however, before making quite sure of what you need, and for this you must depend on your pattern. One important difference between working with real leather and working with imitation is that in real leather the size of the cut pieces is limited by the size and shape of the skins.

The PATTERN and the SKINS—Prepare your pattern with particular care: Trim off the margins (not the seam allowances); make fitting adjustments very precisely; trace and cut out a duplicate of each piece marked "cut 2" and mark the pieces "right" and "left"; make a folded duplicate of pieces marked "cut on fold"; and decide if you will need self-facings (used only on coats and jackets and to finish the top of skirts and pants).

Take the entire prepared pattern with you when you go to buy a skin or skins: You will have to measure the pattern pieces against the leather. If you need more than one skin, select the ones most uniform in weight and color. Plan to use the best-matched skins on the front and sleeves.

Suede has a nap, and in smooth leather the faint creases have a direction. With both these leathers, the pattern pieces should be placed "with nap"—the top edges toward the neck, the bottoms toward the

tail. Splits, which include cowhide, have no direction and can be cut out any way. In all leathers, the crosswise direction has more give than the lengthwise.

When a pattern piece is too large for the leather available, it can often be cut apart at a suitable place, so the leather can be pieced: A jacket, skirt or pants can be made with a yoke; or a seam can be added at a center back, etc. If you make such changes, remember to add a seam allowance on both pieces to be joined.

LINING is often advisable, to prevent the color from crocking and the garment from clinging. Inside facings can often be eliminated by extending a lining all the way to the edge (except a hem edge, which should hang free). **Underlining** and **interfacing** are not necessary.

SPECIAL EQUIPMENT
Magic transparent tape to replace pins, which leave holes in leather.

An even feed or roller foot to facilitate stitching. A glover's needle for hand-sewing. (There is a wedge-shaped needle for machine-stitching leather, but it is not really necessary.)

A mallet, small hammer or pounding block for flattening seams, and a wooden block or piece of board to hammer on.

Rubber cement for "basting" (see SEAMS, on the next page) and for gluing down edges.

CUTTING and MARKING—Spread out the leather in a single layer right side up so that unsightly marks can be avoided. Arrange the pattern pieces according to the type of leather (see above).

NOTE: If your leather is heavy, take some of the ease out of a sleeve cap by folding a short vertical dart, ¼" deep in the pattern, and redrawing the cutting line between ease markings (notches), ¼" in from the existing line.

Tape the pattern pieces to the skin. Cut out singly. After cutting, place them on the wrong side for marking. Use a ballpoint pen (no more than absolutely necessary) or a pencil. If the right side must be marked, as for buttonholes and pockets, use magic transparent tape.

STITCHING—Use polyester core thread; for needles use the Universal Ballpoint machine needle #11 for lightweight leather, #14 for heavier. Set the machine for 8 stitches per inch and watch the stitching to make sure the stitches do not come out smaller—small stitches may cut through the leather.

Make a test seam for correct tension, balance and pressure (see pp. 148, 149).

Never back-tack, because it may tear the leather; just tie threads on the wrong side.

Topstitching is good on leather, and often serves for holding down faced edges and seam allowances. Done with buttonhole twist on top (use a #16 needle) or double thread (see TOPSTITCHING, p. 151), it can be definitely decorative. Parallel rows of topstitching must, however, always be stitched in the same direction. An even feed or roller foot may be helpful here. If, however, the leather sticks to the feed dog or the presser foot, place strips of tissue paper under or on top of the seam while stitching; afterwards tear away the paper.

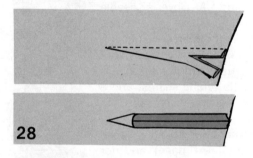

DARTS—Stitch dart; trim; glue open (28).

SEAMS—Instead of basting or pinning, hold seam edges together with paper clips, bobby pins or tape. Where an edge must be eased to another, as in a sleeve cap, "baste" the two edges together with rubber cement, as follows: Dab a few spots of rubber cement on the seam allowances (only) to be joined; allow the cement to dry slightly, then place the two edges together, matching markings and pinching in any ease with your fingers. If an alteration is needed, the surfaces can be carefully pulled apart and re-glued. The seam can then be stitched. Seams are flattened, not by pressing (not recommended on leather), but by hammering, and then gluing or stitching.

A plain seam is hammered open and the seam allowances glued down as just described.

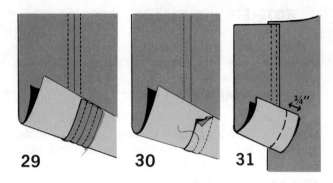

29   **30**   **31**

In a double topstitched seam (29) the seam allowances are held down by topstitching done from the right side.

In a welt seam (30) both seam allowances are hammered to one side; one is trimmed close to the stitching, and the wider one is then topstitched from the right side.

A lapped seam (31), where one edge is lapped flat over the other, is particularly well-suited to heavy leather: Trim ½″ from the edge to go on top. On the wrong side of the same edge, mark a line ¾″ from the edge. Bring the lower edge to that line (this will match the original seam lines) and tape in place. From the right side, topstitch close to the cut edge, and again ¼″ or more away. (If you have a zipper in this seam, first see the application on the following page.)

FACINGS—Leather facings are generally used only where at least part of them will show, as in coats and jackets. Where they will not show, as in a jumper, you may want to substitute fabric for the facings on light to medium-weight leathers. Where there is a lining, it can sometimes be extended to the edge to replace facings (see p. 144).

In light to medium-weight leather, facings are attached and handled like any other facings, except that they are not understitched. Instead, they are topstitched along the edges, or glued down, or both.

In heavy leather, facings can be attached with the edges left raw: Trim the seam allowances from facing and garment edges (actually, this should have been planned at the pattern stage). Matching raw edges, glue and topstitch the facing to the garment, either on the wrong side, or on the right, as part of the design.

For attaching a lining to a garment with leather facings, see ATTACHING A LINING, page 86).

EDGE FINISHES—These may include hems. Leather of a certain weight may need no finish at all, or just a line or two of top-stitching. Medium and lighter weight leather may be turned under, clipped as necessary, glued and top-stitched (32).

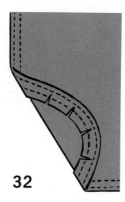

32

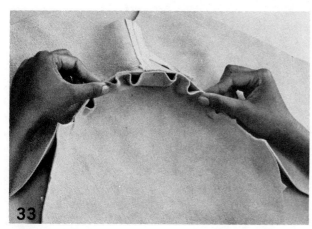

33

SLEEVES are attached with the flat construction method, before stitching the garment side seams or the sleeve underarm seams. Do not ease-stitch the sleeve-cap, but glue-baste it in place (33) as described under SEAMS, on the preceding page. Then stitch with the sleeve side up. Stitch garment and sleeve underarm in one operation.

ZIPPERS—The choice of application depends largely on the weight of the leather.

In lightweight leather, where seams are stitched as in fabric, you may use either an invisible zipper (see p. 270) or a conventional zipper in a centered application (see p. 268).

• For a centered application, test the leather: If a fine needle leaves no permanent marks, close the opening with hand-basting; otherwise, hammer the seam allowances down and tape the opening firmly together on the right side.

• After an invisible zipper application, glue down the seam allowances.

In medium-weight and heavy leather, the cut edges are usually left raw. In the following applications, a zipper can be inserted in a lapped seam or in a slash.

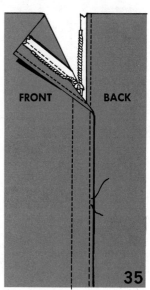

34

35

Zipper in a lapped seam (35)—Sew in zipper before the seam is sewn. On the two edges of the open seam, mark bottom of zipper opening.

a. Back seam allowance—Trim ½″ off the seam allowance for the length of the zipper opening. Place trimmed edge along zipper coil or teeth. Using zipper foot, edge-stitch (34), starting across the bottom, pivoting, and stitching to the top.

b. Front seam allowance—As instructed under SEAMS on the preceding page, trim ½″ from the entire seam allowance. Edge-stitch this single layer for the length of the zipper opening only. On the wrong side, mark a line ¾″ from the trimmed edge.

c. Lap seam below zipper as follows: With wrong sides up, match raw edge of back section to the ¾″ line on the front and tape securely in place. At zipper area, since zipper tape extends beyond the ¾″ line, mark a new line parallel to the other one; match and securely tape edge of zipper in place.

d. From the right side, stitch with a zipper foot about ½″ from the edge, from top of zipper to end of seam.

e. Finish seam by stitching edge of lap from bottom of zipper to hem (35).

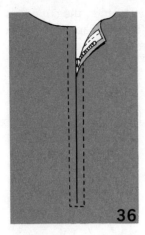

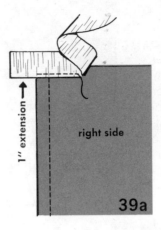

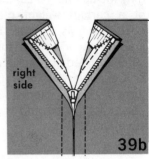

WAISTLINE FINISH in SKIRTS or PANTS (39a, b)—Here you can reduce bulk by using ½″ to ¾″ grosgrain ribbon instead of a leather facing (see WAISTBANDS, p. 261.)

Zipper in a slash—covered (36)—Make a straight slash the length of the zipper. On the wrong side, tape the zipper face-down over the slash, being careful to keep the edges of the leather together. From right side top-stitch along both edges of the slash, beginning each row at the bottom and stitching ¼″ from the center.

Zipper in a slash—exposed (37)—In the garment, carefully cut an opening ¼″ wide and the length of the zipper. Position the zipper under the opening and tape it in place on the wrong side. From right side topstitch close to the edges, beginning each row at the bottom.

OTHER CLOSURES—All kinds of closures can be used on leather, including loops, frogs, gripper snaps and laces going through punched holes or grommets. In medium and lightweight leather, buttons can be self-covered, and bound buttonholes made, but make a trial buttonhole first and don't shorten your machine-stitch.

In heavy leather, an easy buttonhole can be made by double-stitching through garment and facing, along both sides and ends of the button-hole position and then carefully cutting out a tiny strip between the stitching (38).

Machine-worked buttonholes are possible if you can adjust the stitches so they are not too close together—this would tear the leather.

HEMS—See EDGE FINISHES, page 85. If you don't want to topstitch, but want a turned-up hem, keep it not more than 1″ wide; turn it up and glue it in place, easing in any extra fullness. In heavy leather, the hem edge can be just a cut edge.

ATTACHING A LINING—The lining may be stitched in by machine in the usual way (see p. 144), but the bottom edge may be allowed to hang free. A lining can also be sewed in by hand, but since leather may be hard to stitch through, leather facings should be prepared beforehand: Along the free edge, stitch a folded bias strip, raw edges matching (40). Then slip-stitch the lining to the strip, as shown. A smooth braid might be used instead of the bias.

PRESSING is not recommended. If you must press leather, try it first on a scrap and be very careful.

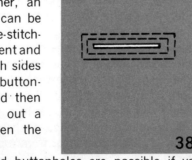

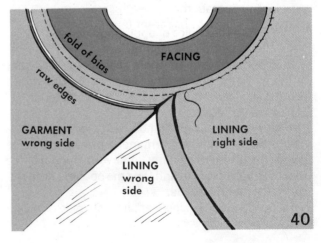

LEATHER-LOOK FABRICS

(Please note that this section does not include suede-look fabrics, which are found on p. 91). Popularly known as vinyl, crinkle patent and polyurethane, simulated leather fabrics usually have a backing of woven or knitted cotton or nylon. A knitted backing has more elasticity than a woven one.

The care of these fabrics varies, even though they look and feel alike. Read the hang-tags and labels with particular care. They should all be rolled instead of folded when bought, as they tend to take on permanent creases.

LINING, if one is added, should have the same cleaning requirements as the garment fabric. **Interfacing** may be needed with knit-back polyurethane. The more stable, woven-back fabrics may require interfacing only in buttonhole areas.

THE PATTERN—Look at ready-to-wear, leather-look garments for ideas. Select a simple style. Set-in sleeves work best with knit-back fabric; for woven-back fabric, raglan sleeves are a better choice. Pattern alterations should be made carefully, before cutting, because stitching marks will remain in the fabric. Straight-grain seams should be eliminated wherever possible—see the PATTERN paragraph for fake fur, page 76.

CUTTING—For accuracy in cutting, trim off the pattern margins (not seam allowances). Lay out the pattern on a single layer of fabric (see p. 61), wrong side up for ease in marking unless the fabric has a design that has to be taken into account. Place pins in seam allowances only, as they leave holes, or attach the pattern with Magic transparent tape or masking tape.

MARKING—Mark on the wrong side, with pen, pencil, marking pencil or tailor's chalk. If the right side must be marked, as for buttonholes and pockets, use tape.

STITCHING—See this heading for LEATHER, page 84.

DARTS and SEAMS—Seams may be **plain, welt** or **double-topstitched.** See SEAMS, page 84. Slash darts open. Both seams and darts can be finger-pressed open (pressing is seldom possible with these fabrics—consult the label) and seam allowances can be glued down with fabric glue, if desired.

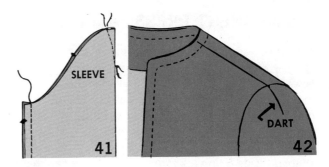

FACINGS are never understitched; they are held in place by topstitching or gluing. Free edges are lightly caught to the backing, or glued down.

SET-IN SLEEVES—Since some of these fabrics are difficult to ease, you may want to make a curved dart at the center of the sleeve cap to reduce fullness (41). The dart should be lined up with the shoulder seam, 2½″ long and not deeper than ⅜″ (42).

EDGE FINISHES—Even when these fabrics do not ravel, their cut edges cannot be left raw because the backing would show. Turn them under and glue or topstitch.

CLOSURES—See ZIPPERS IN LIGHTWEIGHT LEATHER, page 85 and OTHER CLOSURES, page 86. Of course you substitute finger-pressing for hammering. Bear in mind also that when a fabric has a contrasting-colored backing, you should avoid details in which cut edges would show.

HEMS—Catch the hem to the backing only. Or trim it to a 1″ depth and glue in place.

PRESSING—Consult the label. Some of the fabrics are "pressable". Even so, protect any right-side surfaces (such as seam allowances) with a dry press cloth and use a light touch. Test the iron on a scrap of fabric. Otherwise, finger-press seams and edges, creasing with a fingernail. A crisp, pressed look is not necessary in these fabrics.

ATTACHING A LINING—See this paragraph for LEATHER, on the preceding page.

VINYL as a TRIM—Scraps of vinyl can make attractive trimming on garments of other fabrics, provided they have the same cleaning requirements. To apply, just turn the edges under and edge-stitch with straight machine stitch.

PERMANENT PRESS FABRICS

The tremendous popularity of these fabrics is due to their easy-care qualities. The very characteristics, however, that give permanent press fabrics their virtues create certain difficulties in sewing them. Because the surface is smoother and harder, the fabric is less pliable and more resistant to handling, to scissors, and to pins and needles. They cannot be shrunk or shaped by steaming (as for easing a sleeve cap to an armhole), and they may have a springiness that resists a sharp crease or a flat seam. They also tend to pucker at the seams if your sewing machine is not properly adjusted. The answer to all this is simply to learn how to cope with the characteristics of these fabrics.

The term permanent press is generally applied only to woven fabrics made of cotton, synthetics, or a blend of the two. Their care is, of course, very simple, as the label will show.

THE PATTERN—Choose an uncomplicated design, not broken by too many seams. Avoid long zippers in straight-grain seams. The tendency of these fabrics to pucker is greatest on lengthwise straight-grain seams. Eliminate such seams wherever possible as described under THE PATTERN for fake fur on page 76.

Carefully make all fitting adjustments on the pattern. Seams and darts cannot be adjusted later, as stitch marks stay in.

LINING, if used, should also be permanent press. **Interfacing,** if any, should have permanent-press qualities; self-fabric can often be used.

NOTIONS should have the same care requirements as the fabric. It is a good idea to pre-shrink seam binding to remove any possibility of future shrinkage. For a hem finish, use stretch lace. A zipper should be a coil zipper (no pre-shrinking is needed if zipper tape is 100% polyester).

PREPARATION—Put the fabric through your washer and dryer at the setting you expect to use for the finished garment. If the fabric comes folded through the center, open it out and try to press out the fold after washing. If the fold cannot be pressed out, you will have to arrange the pattern to avoid it. See TRIAL LAYOUT, page 61.

CUTTING—Whether or not the crosswise grain is straight, its position is permanent and will not affect the hang of the garment. Lay the straight-grain marking on the lengthwise grain as usual, and disregard the crosswise grain. If, however, you have a fabric with an off-grain plaid or other regular repeat, you will have to follow the design in laying out the pattern.

Use the finest, sharpest pins you can find. Place the pins in seam allowances only, as pin marks will remain.

MARKING—Use dressmaker's tracing paper and a tracing wheel, but be sure not to use a color in direct contrast to the fabric. It does not wash out, and may come through to the right side. Or use pins or tailor's tacks.

STITCHING—The key to success in stitching permanent press fabrics lies in the correct use of your sewing machine. Turn to page 148 and adjust the pressure, tension, and balance with particular care. On some machines, the presser foot pressure or the bobbin tension cannot be adjusted. In this case, make whatever adjustments are possible to achieve unpuckered seams.

Do not omit a test seam, it is **absolutely necessary.** Use a needle of the finest size your thread can take without becoming frayed—a heavy needle will mark the fabric. Change your needle often—a blunt or burred needle can damage your fabric and thread. Set the machine for a medium-to-long stitch, or 10 to 12 per inch.

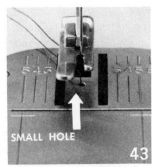

SMALL HOLE 43

WIDE HOLE use right or left needle position 44

When straight-stitching with a zigzag machine, use the small-hole throat-plate (43)—this prevents the fabric being drawn into the hole which causes puckers; or, if your machine has an adjustable needle position, move the needle either to the left or the right (44)—just make sure you maintain your seam allowance width.

Topstitching is not recommended, as it usually produces puckers.

PRESSING—Use steam at a permanent press or a low synthetic setting. Don't forget that a crease, once pressed, stays in; do not press any seam until you are sure it is right.

FACINGS and SEAM FINISHES—The springiness of permanent press fabrics and their tendency to ravel make certain techniques specially important. See BEFORE TURNING THE FACING on page 93. See the SEAM FINISHES on page 224. A particularly neat facing finish **for washable garments** will be found in INTERFACINGS, page 134.

PILE FABRICS

The three major pile fabrics are corduroy, velveteen and velvet—all woven fabrics. (Knit velour is not a pile fabric; it is stretchy and is handled like a very stretchy knit.) Fake fur, a deep pile fabric, takes special handling—see that heading.

Corduroy, usually cotton, is also available in blends with a permanent press finish. It is usually washable —check the label. Corduroy has wales (ribs), ranging from narrow (pinwale) to wide, running in the lengthwise direction. Other variations include narrow-wide combinations, ribless and waffle-weave corduroy. It also comes in prints.

Velveteen, a short-pile fabric with a smooth surface resembling velvet, is usually made of cotton. It is available in solid colors and prints.

Velvet, distinguished by its lustrous surface, was originally made of silk. Now the less expensive grades are rayon, the better ones synthetic. The synthetics have a denser and more beautiful pile. Velvet requires more special handling than the other pile fabrics because it tends to shift while being stitched. There are, however, variations of velvet such as crushed velvet, panne, and cut velvet for which the only special requirement is that they be cut "with nap".

THE PATTERN—Choose a pattern with simple lines and not too many seams.

FABRIC—Your choice will depend, as usual, on the type of garment you are planning. Remember that it is easier to work details on pinwale and ribless corduroy than on wide-wale. Yardage will of course be figured "with nap".

LINING, UNDERLINING, INTERFACING, FACINGS —Whether or not a garment is **lined** will depend on its kind and style. **Underlining** is often used with velvet for body and elegance. **Interfacing** should be chosen and used as usual (see that chapter); fusibles may be used on ribless or pinwale corduroy. **Facings** of lining fabric may be substituted for facings of self-fabric where they don't show.

CUTTING—Follow the pattern layout "with nap". To determine the way the pile runs, brush hand over fabric surface: The smoother feel gives the direction of the pile. Whether the nap runs up or down is a matter of preference. In all these fabrics, the color is richer with the nap running up, but corduroy wears better with the nap running down—a point to remember with children's playclothes. Never use a layout with a crosswise fold, as it will result with the pile running in different directions on matching pieces.

MARKING—Any method will do on corduroy. On velvet or velveteen, use pins or tailor's tacks.

STITCHING—Use thread and needle according to weight of fabric. Set machine for 10 to 12 stitches per inch. Make a test seam and check the tension, balance and pressure of the machine (see pp. 148, 149). Pressure is particularly important: If it is too light, the fabric will not feed properly; if it is too heavy, the presser foot may mark the pile.

Corduroy and velveteen can be pin-basted in the usual way for stitching. Velvet, with its tendency to pucker and shift, needs to have its edges held more firmly. Try one of the following methods and, when stitching, hold the fabric taut to avoid puckers:

• Hand-baste with small stitches, taking a backstitch every few stitches.
• Pin along the seamline with pins parallel to the edge, taking up small amounts of fabric with each pin. Have pin-heads toward you as you stitch—holding fabric taut—and remove pins as you stitch.

• Although we do not usually recommend stitching over pins, the following method can be used if the others do not seem to prevent shifting: If you have a hinged zipper foot, place pins at right angles to the edge, not more than 1″ apart. To stitch, turn your work over so the pins are on the bottom. Stitch slowly over the pins. Change your machine needle as it becomes scratched.

• You may also wish to try a roller foot.

Topstitching may be done on corduroy, but not on velvet or velveteen.

SEAMS and SEAM FINISHES—Corduroy can take a flat felled seam and a welt seam, excellent for sturdy wear. Plain seams are best for velvet and velveteen. If the fabric frays and the garment is not to be lined, finish the seam allowances with straight stitch, zigzag stitch, hand overcast or binding (regular or Hong Kong). For all these techniques see the chapter on SEAMS AND SEAM FINISHES.

DARTS should be slashed and pressed open.

PRESSING is a problem with all pile fabrics—smooth velvet being the most difficult. Here are a few pointers:

• Always use steam.

• Never touch the iron to the right side of fabric.

• To open seams, press with the point of iron only. Never let the iron "sit" on the fabric.

• If you do not have a needle board or a velvet board, spread a piece of your pile fabric, face up, under the area you are pressing.

• When pressing seams or hems in corduroy or velveteen, avoid press marks on the outside by placing a strip of brown paper between an edge and the garment (45).

• On all pile fabrics, let the iron down very lightly and raise it again—sliding it along will flatten the pile.

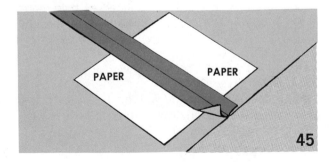

CLOSURES—Practically all types of closures can be used in pile fabrics, depending on the garment.

Zippers—Use a coil or a metal zipper. An invisible zipper can be used on velveteen and pinwale and medium wale corduroys. In velvet, finger-press the seam open to avoid a permanent crease from pressing and, to avoid topstotching, do at least the last step of the application by hand (see p. 276).

Buttonholes—Machine-worked buttonholes will do well in corduroy and velveteen. In velvet, outline the buttonhole with light zigzag stitch over cording (a heavy thread), and finish with hand buttonhole stitch (see p. 38), using buttonhole twist.

For bound buttonholes, cut the lips on the bias (see p. 33). In velvet, add cording. Make a test buttonhole with your fabric first.

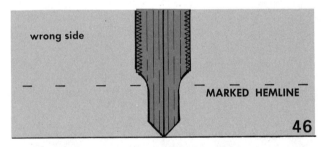

HEMS—Reduce bulk by trimming seam allowances inside the hem (46). To finish hems, use nylon stretch lace, seam binding or a Hong Kong finish (see p. 125).

SHEERS

Sheers are the semi-transparent lightweight woven fabrics—organdy, voile, chiffon, dotted Swiss, georgette—that used to be of fine cotton or silk and are now mostly rayon, acetate or synthetics. This often makes them "easy-care", but in sewing them we still have the old problem of neat finishes where everything shows through.

When a sheer is underlined, either with an opaque fabric or with self-fabric, it ceases to be sheer and is handled like any other fabric. The details that follow are only for sheers that are **not underlined**.

THE PATTERN—Designs with soft fullness are best for sheer fabrics—check the list of fabrics on the envelope.

FACINGS and INTERFACING—Use lightweight interfacing in collars, cuffs and where there are buttons and buttonholes. The thing to avoid, if possible, is facings with a free edge that would show through: Instead, you might cut a whole bodice double, and finish the neck edge on a collar with a bias strip rather than a facing. Neck and sleeve edges may be finished with narrow French binding (see p. 27) or faced with a bias strip.

CUTTING—Sheers have a way of shifting around on the cutting surface. This is where a cutting board, to which you can pin the fabric, is useful. Use the finest, sharpest pins you can find.

MARKING—Mark with tailor's tacks; other marks will show on the right side, and pins may slip out.

STITCHING—Soft sheers may require hand-basting before stitching. For very fine sheers, use polyester core thread, extra-fine and a Universal Ballpoint machine needle #11. Insert a fresh needle in your machine to avoid damaging the fabric. Set stitches at 12 to 14 per inch. **Make a test seam.** When straight-stitching with a zigzag machine, use the small-hole throat plate—this prevents the fabric being drawn into the hole which causes puckers; or, if your machine has an adjustable needle position, move the needle either to the right or the left (see p. 88, ill. 43, 44)—just make sure you maintain your seam allowance width.

If sheer fabric catches in the feed dog, place strips of tissue paper under seams. After stitching, tear away the paper.

SEAMS must be narrow and neat. **French seams** and **double-stitched seams** are both good (pp. 224 and 226).

DARTS should be double-stitched or bobbin-stitched (see p. 63).

CLOSURES will depend on location and fabric. The pattern may suggest snaps instead of a zipper. Otherwise, use a coil zipper. In the last step, hand-stitching may look better than machine stitching (p. 276).

If buttonholes or loops are to be made, the area should be reinforced with lightweight interfacing. Bound buttonholes should be small, with narrow, corded lips. Machine-worked buttonholes may be right in certain garments, while others may require that the buttonholes be finished by hand with one or two strands of embroidery floss (see p. 38). Button loops (see p. 40) may be corded or uncorded. Other possible closures include covered or plastic snaps, hooks and eyes (see p. 99), or tiny buttons and thread loops (see p. 252).

HEMS—In a straight, full skirt, the hem may be anywhere from 3″ to 8″ wide. A circular skirt may have either a ROLLED HEM, an EDGE-STITCHED HEM, a narrow HORSEHAIR-FACED HEM or a TUCKED HEM (see pp. 126, 127).

PRESSING—Use caution. Some sheers cannot be steamed. Others require a low or synthetic setting.

SUEDE-LOOK FABRICS

Fabrics simulating suede vary greatly in quality, appearance and weight—not to mention price. Some look like suede on both sides, others have a woven fabric back. Some are soft, others stiff. They come in different widths. They have, however, certain properties and requirements in common (as usual, examine the label):

• Practically all are synthetic and washable. Some are machine-washable. They do not shrink. They are easy to handle.

• They do not fray at the edges. On some, cut edges can often be left raw, as on real leather.

• They are rather difficult to hand-sew. But, since they can be pressed, they can be fused (see p. 107). Wherever machine-sewing is not possible or advisable, attach edges with fusible web.

• For machine-stitching, an even feed or roller foot may be helpful.

THE PATTERN should be chosen to go with the weight and hand of the fabric, as usual.

YARDAGE should be bought "with nap".

LINING is optional, but in a coat or jacket it makes it easier to slip the garment on and off. **Underlining** is not needed. **Interfacing** should be washable.

NOTIONS should be washable if you plan to wash the garment. Any tapes or seam binding should be pre-shrunk.

PREPARATION is necessary only with woven-back fabric, which should be machine-washed to get rid of any excess finish.

CUTTING can be done through a double thickness. Use the "with nap" layout. Even the fabric that looks like suede on both sides has a right and a wrong side and should be cut accordingly. Pinning should be done in the seam allowances, as pin marks remain.

MARKING may be done lightly with pencil or tailor's chalk. Avoid other methods as they may leave marks on the right side.

STITCHING—Start work with a new needle, size 14 or 16 depending on fabric weight. Set the machine for 8 to 10 stitches per inch. Make a test seam to be sure of the right tension and pressure (see p. 149). With woven-back fabrics, watch your needle in case the resin finish should leave a deposit on it—if so, change the needle or clean it.

Topstitching can be done with regular polyester core thread. Silk twist is not recommended, as it shrinks. (If you want to use it on a garment that is not to be washed, use a size 16 needle.) Any parallel lines of topstitching should be made in the same direction.

DARTS—To avoid a bubble, start stitching darts at the point.

SEAMS—All the seams recommended for leather are good (see p. 84), except that you do no hammering and use fusible web to attach seam allowances instead of glue.

EDGE FINISHES—If an edge, including a hem, is to be turned up, attach it with fusible web. Otherwise, edges need no finish.

SET-IN SLEEVES should be attached with the flat construction method, as with leather (see p. 85). They can be pin-basted in the seam allowances, however, instead of glue-basted.

ZIPPERS—See this heading for leather, page 85; just omit hammering down folded edges.

OTHER CLOSURES—See this heading for leather, page 86.

HEMS—See EDGE FINISHES, above. Do not make hems more than 1″ deep.

PRESSING—Use a steam iron with synthetic setting. Press on the wrong side of fabric.

Facings

A facing is a piece of fabric of a certain width, placed on the inside of a garment edge. Its purpose is to finish the edge and, usually with the addition of interfacing, give body to the area. Sometimes, as in a lapel, the facing is partly folded to the outside. While facings are generally of the same fabric as the garment, they may be made of other fabrics in order to reduce bulk, or because there is not enough garment fabric, or for comfort, if the garment fabric is rough-textured. As a design feature, a facing may be made to contrast the garment in color or texture.

A well-applied facing has a sharp, clean edge and corners, and a smooth, flat-lying surface. There are three kinds of facings:

The shaped or fitted facing (1) is a separate piece of fabric, cut to match the garment section and on the same grain. Shaped facings (generally with interfacing) are used at front and back openings, at neck and sleeveless armhole edges, and as the underside of shaped collars and cuffs.

The extended facing (2) is cut in one piece with the garment section, from a single pattern piece, and is folded back along the garment edge. Extended facings (generally with interfacing) are used at front and back openings, and form the underside of straight collars and cuffs.

The bias facing is a bias strip, and is never interfaced. It can be used on gently-curved edges, such as hems, open necklines and sleeveless armholes.

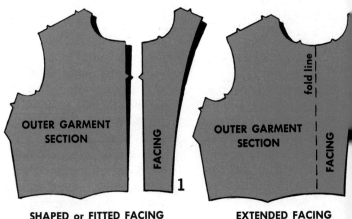

SHAPED or FITTED FACING   EXTENDED FACING

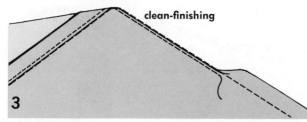

3

SHAPED and EXTENDED FACINGS

PREPARING THE FACING

Stay-stitch curved and slanted edges to be seamed. Join pieces if there are more than one. Trim seams to ⅜″ and press open.

If the free (unnotched) edge is not to be covered by a lining, it may require a finish, depending upon the fabric weight and the garment style:

On fabrics which do not ravel or roll, such as firm knits, leather and suede (real or fake), no finish is needed.

On light or medium-weight fabrics, make a line of stitching ¼″ from edge and **clean-finish,** that is, fold the edge under on the line of stitching and top-stitch close to the fold (3) with straight or zigzag stitches.

On heavy fabrics, make a line of stitching ¼″ from edge and pink the edge (4). On heavy fabrics that ravel, overcast the raw edge, either by hand after making a line of stitching (5), or by machine with plain or multi-stitch zigzag (6).

On any fabric, a very neat finish consists of binding the raw edge with bias binding (see p. 26) or with stretch lace. It is particularly good for the inside of an unlined garment that may be worn open—a jacket, for instance.

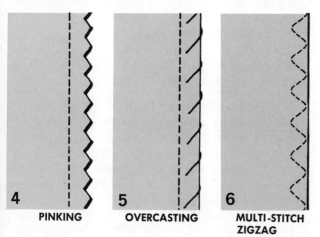

4 **PINKING**   5 **OVERCASTING**   6 **MULTI-STITCH ZIGZAG**

Another very neat finish, special to washable garments with worked buttonholes, involves the interfacing (see p. 134).

ATTACHING A SHAPED FACING

Pin or baste the facing to the corresponding garment section, right sides together, edges and construction marks carefully matched.

As a general rule, stitch with the facing on top for better control (7). Be careful to keep the seam even, as any irregularity along the edge will show after the facing is turned; use a seam gauge or, better still, measure and mark the seam line.

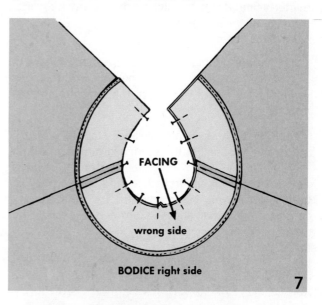

FACING

wrong side

BODICE right side

7

BEFORE TURNING THE FACING

Before turning a shaped facing, a few things must be done to smooth down and flatten the seam that will form the edge. These details, simple as they are, make all the difference in the way the facing lies and fits. Not all of them are needed everywhere.

All edge seams are **graded.** Almost all are **understitched.**

Inside curves are **clipped.**

Outside curves on light fabrics are **clipped.** On heavy fabrics they are **notched.**

Inside corners and outside corners take special handling. See these headings on page 95.

All the above techniques are explained on the following pages.

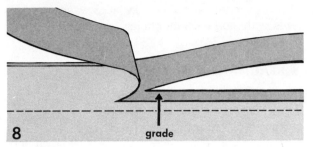

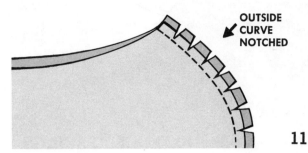

GRADING, (8) done to eliminate bulk, means trimming each seam allowance to a different width, so that the cut edges are graduated. Trim the seam allowances as follows:

Interfacing, if any, to stitching or stay-stitching line;
Facing seam allowance to ⅛″;
Garment seam allowance to ¼″.

If there are additional layers, trim them to graduated widths but always leave the garment seam allowance the widest, to keep the outside surface smooth.

CLIPPING allows seam allowances to lie flat. A clip is a straight cut across the seam allowances to within a thread of the line of stitching. A **straight seam** is clipped only when understitched, and takes few clips. **Curves,** as shown, take many (9, 10). The more pronounced the curve and the firmer the fabric, the more clips are needed to make the seam lie flat. They may have to be as close as ¼″. To reduce the strain on the seam, clip the seam allowances at alternating points, as shown, not at the same spot. For **inside corners,** see the next page.

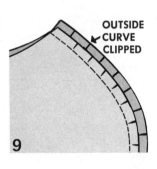

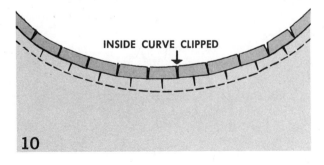

NOTCHING (11) removes uneven bulkiness on outside curves, a notch being a small wedge of fabric cut out from the seam allowance. It is used in heavy fabrics, or when a fabric is too ravelly to be closely graded.

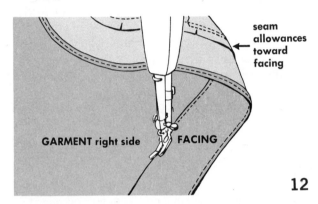

UNDERSTITCHING insures that the facing will not roll to the outside. It is done on all facing edge-seams except the very short ones, such as the ends of a straight collar, or where the stitching would show, as on a lapel.

Place the work on the machine right side up, with the facing opened out (12). Turn all seam allowances (graded, clipped) to lie smoothly under the facing. Stitch on the facing, as shown, very close to the seam, through all thicknesses.

For a facing on a lapel, stop just short of the point where the lapel is folded to the outside. At an outside corner, stop about 1″ short of the corner.

Edge seams that cannot be understitched, such as the short seams and lapel seams just mentioned, should be pressed open before they are graded in order to get a sharp edge in the final pressing. Place the opened seam over a point presser (13), or over a pencil wrapped in cloth (14), and press it with the point of the iron only.

13

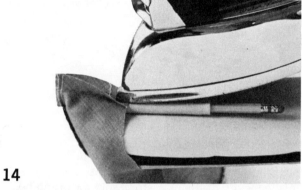

14

INSIDE CORNERS, to lie flat, need to be clipped, and therefore must be reinforced. As you stitch the corner, shorten the stitch to 20 per inch, as shown (15). After grading the seam allowances, clip into the corner to within a thread of the line of stitching (16).

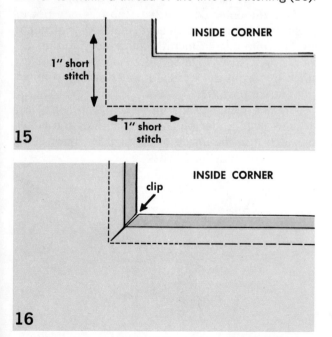

INSIDE CORNER

1″ short stitch

1″ short stitch

15

INSIDE CORNER

clip

16

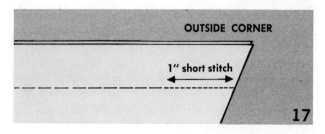

OUTSIDE CORNER

1″ short stitch

17

OUTSIDE CORNERS must be flat and sharp. To achieve this, you reinforce the seam and remove as much as possible of the seam allowance.

The corner is stitched in two operations. Stitch the longer edge first, shortening the stitch to 20 per inch as you approach the corner. Stitch all the way to the cut edge (17). Grade and clip this seam. Understitch, stopping 1″ short of the corner.

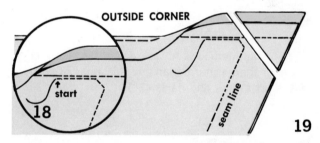

OUTSIDE CORNER

start

seam line

18   **19**

To stitch the second side of the corner, start with shortened stitch on top of the seam just completed, ½″ from corner point (18). At corner, pivot on the needle, take two stitches diagonally across the corner, pivot again and stitch the seam for about an inch, then return to regular stitch-length to complete the seam. **Trim off the point** close to stitching (19). Press the seam allowances open and grade them. Then **taper the corner** by snipping off more seam allowance (20).

AFTER THE FACING HAS BEEN TURNED, press all edges carefully.

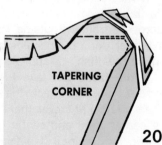

TAPERING CORNER

20

FASTENING THE FREE EDGE

The free edge of a shaped or extended facing is never entirely caught to the inside of a garment. After the garment is otherwise completed and before the lining, if any, is sewn in, you just fasten the facing in place here and there where it will not show on the outside. You can do it in different ways:

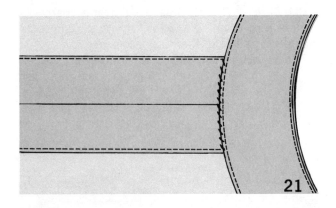

21

The usual method is to **tack down** the facing edge wherever there is more than one thickness of fabric—that is, at seams and darts (21).

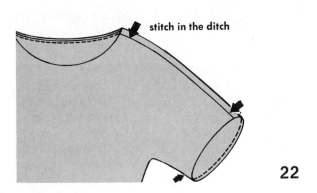

stitch in the ditch

22

If the fabric is springy, or if the facing does not lie flat for some other reason, anchor it by stitching across it, from the outside, through cross-seams (22). Whether done by machine or by hand, this "stitching-in-the-ditch" disappears into the seam.

If the fabric can take fusing (experiment with a scrap), you can attach the facing with fusible web (see p. 107) wherever there is a garment seam and at center front and center back on a neckline. It is particularly helpful if a facing tends to roll to the outside at the point of a V neckline. Place short, narrow strips of fusible web between facing and garment (23). Press as directed under APPLYING MAGIC POLYWEB, page 107.

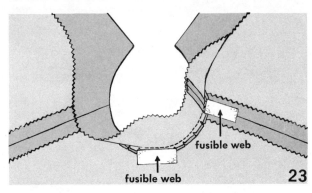

fusible web

fusible web

23

BIAS FACING

A bias facing consists of a bias strip of even width with both edges attached. Note that a wide facing will not lie smoothly on a close curve; the 2″ finished width of the bias strips sold for facing hems would not do for a neckline. The closer the curve, the narrower a bias facing must be.

Join the cut strips as necessary (see p. 25). If the facing is to be applied to a curve, steam-press or "swirl" the entire strip to fit (see p. 26).

Along the outer edge of the strip (the one not to be seamed to the garment edge) make a line of stitching ¼″ from edge. Stitch the other edge to the garment, right sides together. Grade, clip, and understitch the seam as described under BEFORE TURNING THE FACING, page 93.

Turn the facing to the inside on seam line. Turn the raw edge under on the stitched line and either slipstitch it to the inside of garment as shown (24), or baste and topstitch. Press.

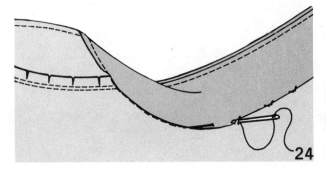

24

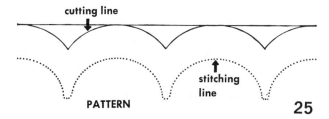

cutting line

PATTERN

stitching line

25

FACING A SCALLOPED EDGE

When cutting the edge to be scalloped, do not cut out the scallops on pattern, garment, or facing, but leave the edge straight along the scallop tops, as shown (25). Cut a strip of tissue paper the same width and length as the facing, and trace the entire stitching line of the scallops on that.

Join the facing lengths and finish the free edge, if necessary (see PREPARING THE FACING, p. 93). Pin to the garment edge, right sides together. Pin the tissue strip over the facing, matching the edges.

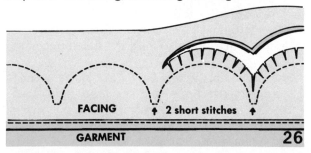

FACING   2 short stitches

GARMENT   **26**

Using a short stitch, stitch slowly through the paper, along the scallop stitching line. At the points between scallops, pivot and take two short stitches (26). When finished, tear away the tissue paper.

Cut out the scallops, leaving a seam allowance of ¼″ to ⅛″, depending on your fabric. Clip into the seam allowance around scallops and into the points between (26). Turn the facing, carefully bringing the seam to the edge. Press.

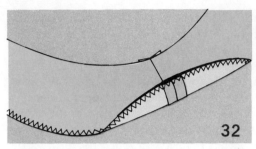

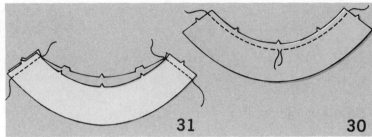

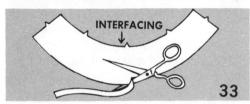

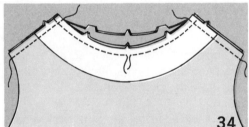

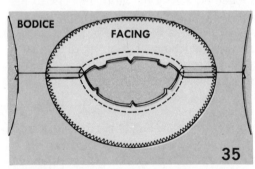

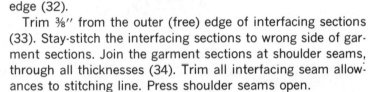

A STEP-BY-STEP DEMONSTRATION

This page gives you a complete picture of a facing application, with the details in their natural sequence. The shaped neck facing, with or without a collar, is present in practically every garment. The one we use here as illustration is for a plain round neck, and is interfaced.

Stay-stitch the neck edge of facing pieces ½″ from the edge (30). NOTE: To avoid confusion, the stay-stitching will not be shown in the drawings after this one.

Join the back and front facing pieces (31). Press seams open. Trim the seam allowances to ⅜″. Finish the free (unnotched) edge (32).

Trim ⅜″ from the outer (free) edge of interfacing sections (33). Stay-stitch the interfacing sections to wrong side of garment sections. Join the garment sections at shoulder seams, through all thicknesses (34). Trim all interfacing seam allowances to stitching line. Press shoulder seams open.

Pin the facing to the garment, right sides together, shoulder seams and notches matched. Stitch around the neck edge (35).

Grade and clip seam allowances (36). Understitch (37).

Turn facing to inside (38). Press. Catch the facing to the interfacing. Tack or anchor the facing at seams.

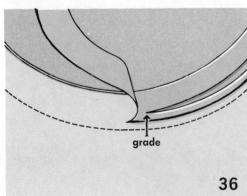

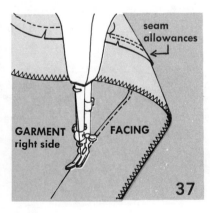

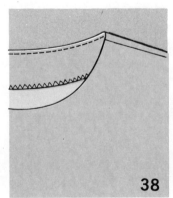

Fasteners

Fasteners that are not buttons or zippers (which you will find in their own chapters) are usually snaps or hooks and eyes. Fasteners are generally concealed, but they can also be visible, even decorative. The kind of fastener you use depends on the type and style of the garment, and on how much strain is to be put on the opening.

Since fasteners are placed only at openings, they automatically fall on a part of the garment that is not only faced, but usually interfaced. In any case, a fastener is never attached to a single thickness of fabric.

SNAPS

Snaps consist of a ball-half and a socket-half. Some snaps are sewed on, others are hammered on.

SEW-ON SNAPS are concealed, and generally used where there is little strain. They are preferable to hooks and eyes on knits and other fabrics that may snag. Snaps are made of metal or nylon, and come in different sizes. To sew them in place, use over-and-over stitches or buttonhole stitches. The following are different ways of using sew-on snaps.

The regular snap (1) is used where one garment edge laps over the other.

Secure the thread at the snap position on underside of overlap, being careful to catch only the facing and interfacing fabric. Place the ball-half of the snap over it and take 4 or 5 stitches through each hole,

never stitching through to the right side of garment. Fasten the thread securely and cut.

To mark the place of the socket-half, pin the opening together. If there is a hole through the ball, push the threaded needle (no knot in thread) from the right side of garment through the hole into the underlay; slip the ball-half off the needle and thread. Make a knot; draw up. Center the socket over the knot and sew it on (1). If the ball has no hole through center, rub chalk on it and press it firmly against underlay. Center the socket over the mark and sew on through all thicknesses.

The extended snap (2) is used where two edges meet, as at the top of a zipper in a centered application.

Sew ball-half to one edge, using only one hole, as shown. Mark place for socket-half on the underneath side of the other edge, being sure that fabric edges meet. Sew on as directed for the regular snap.

The hanging snap (3) is another way of holding two edges together when they just meet. It is especially good at the top of an invisible zipper application.

Sew socket-half on the underneath side of one edge. Snap ball-half into socket. Starting at the corresponding point on the opposite edge and going through one hole in the snapped-in ball-half, make a thread-loop (see p. 252) over 3 threads, and finish off securely. Make the loop short to hold the two edges close together.

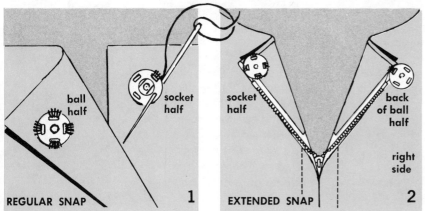

ball half · socket half
REGULAR SNAP 1

socket half · back of ball half · right side
EXTENDED SNAP 2

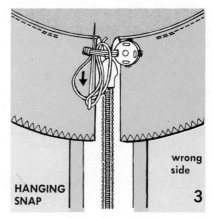

HANGING SNAP · wrong side 3

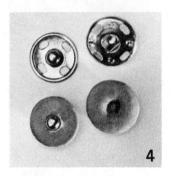

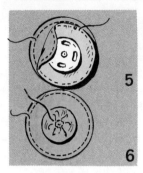

5

6

4

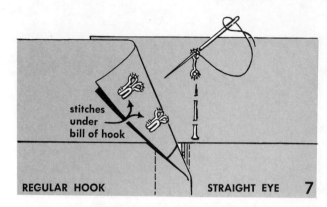

stitches
under
bill of hook

REGULAR HOOK · · STRAIGHT EYE **7**

The covered snap (4) is used in a garment opening where the snap may be seen (a jacket or coat, for instance). Use lightweight fabric (lining or underlining), as close to garment color as possible.

Cut two circles of fabric a little more than twice the diameter of the snap. Run a gathering thread around the edge of each circle. Pierce a tiny hole through the center of **both** circles, and pull **both** of them over the ball of the snap. Snap the ball into the socket-half, with the two thicknesses of fabric between (5). Draw up each circle over its snap-half and secure thread on underside (6). Open the snap and sew on as usual.

HAMMER-ON SNAPS are visible, as they are put through from the right side of a garment, and can stand considerable strain. They are generally used on children's clothes, work clothes, and sportswear. They are sold packaged in various types, sizes and colors, with complete instructions for attaching.

HOOKS AND EYES

Since hooks and eyes form a strong closure, they are used at waist seams and in waistbands, but can serve at neck and other edges as well. Made of metal or plastic, they come in several styles and many sizes. While they are almost always concealed, occasionally a large, decorative hook and eye is worn on the outside. Whatever the type, they are sewn on with over-and-over stitches or buttonhole stitches.

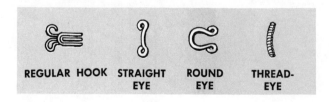

REGULAR HOOK · STRAIGHT EYE · ROUND EYE · THREAD-EYE

REGULAR HOOK (7)—A hook is placed about ⅛" in from the edge, on the underside of an overlap. In sewing it on, be careful to catch only the facing and interfacing fabrics and not stitch through to the right side of the garment. After securing the thread at the position, take a few stitches under the bill to secure the hook in place. Then pass the needle through the fabric to the hook eyelets and sew them down. Fasten thread and cut.

With the opening pinned together, mark the place for the eye with a pin in the underlay. Sew the eye (7) in place, stitching through all thicknesses. There are three kinds of eyes:

Straight eye—Used where there is an overlap as on a skirt waistband.

Round eye—Used where two edges meet (8), as at a waist stay.

Thread-eye—The most inconspicuous eye, used in place of the straight eye where there is little strain, as at the top of a neck zipper opening. For directions, see page 253.

COAT HOOK

ROUND EYE **8**

9

LARGE HOOKS—
These are generally coat hooks (9) or flat hooks (10). Place the hook and eye like a regular hook and eye, and sew them on through the holes. There are also hammer-on hooks and eyes.

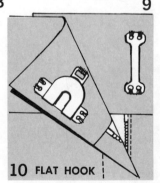

10 FLAT HOOK

NYLON TAPE FASTENER (Velcro)

Velcro (11) consists of two pieces—one with tiny hooks and one with tiny loops. When pressed together they mesh and hold. This closure can only be used where there is an underlay.

Pin the loop piece on the underside of the overlap, and the hook piece in matching position on the underlay, machine- or hand-stitch the edges (11).

For information on BUTTONS, BUTTONHOLES, BUTTON LOOPS, and ZIPPERS, see those chapters.

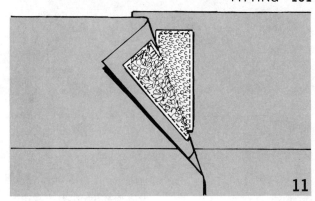

11

Fitting a Garment

Fitting is making adjustments while trying on an incompleted garment (for alterations on finished garments, see that chapter). Adjustments made in the process of fitting should be small ones—any major change, and even minor ones that you **know are necessary,** should have been taken care of on the pattern (see PATTERNS). In fact, if the same adjustment turns up in fitting more than one garment, you can take it as a hint to make the change in future patterns, and so catch the trouble at the root.

Whether or not fittings are needed, and how many, will depend on how well the pattern is adapted to your figure and how much shaping there is in the garment. Children's clothes, once the proper size is established, are most often completed without fittings. So are loose garments such as capes, caftans, robes, etc. For something carefully shaped, however, at least one fitting is needed, except perhaps when you have first made a trial muslin (see MAKING A MUSLIN, p. 205). And it is generally necessary to try on an otherwise completed garment for length and for evenness of hem (see HEMS, p. 120).

Vertical and horizontal direction lines are extremely helpful in judging the hang of a garment. After cutting out garment, mark vertical lines at center front, center back and sleeves; horizontal lines at bust, back, sleeve cap and hips. These will be grain lines on straight-cut garments, but direction lines on bias-cut garments. Use baste-marking (see p. 159).

WHEN TO FIT

At what point you first try on your garment will depend on what, if any, you consider your special problem to be.

As a rule, fitting is done when all the construction seams are stitched except side seams, waistline and armhole seams (sleeves); these should be thread- or pin-basted. The neckline is unfinished, but a collar (preferably finished) can be pinned to it after the neck has been checked. On skirts or pants, pin or baste the waistband in place; if the waist is an elasticized pull-on, see the next page.

If, however, you want to check certain points, such as neckline or dart placement before going further, try on that garment section as soon as the necessary stitching is done; in a bodice or one-piece dress, this would mean darts and shoulder seams. Pin-baste side seams (since many adjustments can be made there). And if you want to be very careful indeed, baste the whole garment and try it on before stitching anything.

HOW FITTING SHOULD BE DONE

• Have someone help you, unless you anticipate no changes: Adjustments are hard to make on one-self. Besides, a second opinion is good to have. A full-length mirror is a great help, too.

• Wear the same underthings and heels of the same height as those you will wear with the finished garment.

• Try on the garment right side out: Right and left should be where they belong, and one side may need an adjustment the other side does not (the human body is seldom quite symmetrical). In any case, fit cannot be judged from the wrong side.

• If there are shoulder pads, pin them in for fitting. Pin up garment opening, one edge folded under, center lines or closure lines matched. Anchor center front to undergarment with a pin. If there is a belt, put it on.

• It may be necessary to clip an unstitched seam allowance, such as armholes or a high, round neckline (1), so the area can lie flat for fitting. In such a case, there should always be stay-stitching to protect the seam line.

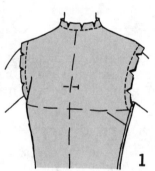

1

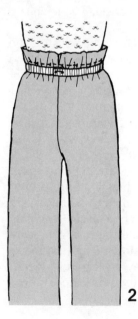

2

• For pull-on pants or skirts with an elasticized waist, pin the elastic around the waist, over the garment. Draw the fabric up until the entire hip-and-crotch area fits smoothly—especially the crotch should be well positioned, neither too high nor too low. Mark the fabric along the upper edge of elastic; this will be the casing fold-line (2). Be sure there is enough fullness for getting in and out of the garment.

• If there is a lining, it makes for better final fit to have it assembled and in the garment for fitting. Needless to say, any but the smallest corrections must be made in the lining as well.

• See the next headings for the standards of good fit and the adjustments to make. In making corrections, remember the cardinal rule: DO NOT OVERFIT. The only part of a garment that should be snug is the waistline of a skirt or pants.

• Make the corrections on the outside of the garment as follows:

To take in a seam, pinch up the seam line, taking in all thicknesses, and form a new one with pins parallel to the body.

To let out a seam, take out pins or stitching and pin a new seam line with allowances on the outside.

After taking off the garment, transfer corrected lines to the inside of the garment with chalk or pins, re-pin seams and baste new seam lines. Try on again for fit. If letting out has made seam allowances too narrow, widen them with seam binding, especially if the fabric tends to ravel. Stitch seams, press, etc.

Be sure to adjust any related piece (facing, collar, etc.) that might be affected by an alteration.

STANDARDS OF GOOD FIT

Garment lines change with fashion; standards of good fit do not. Good fit consists mainly of the relationship between the body and the garment, which should fit smoothly, hang straight (vertical and horizontal grain in place) and, above all, be comfortable, neither too tight nor too loose. When you are standing upright with arms at the sides, it should be free from wrinkles. Except for folds called for in the design, the only thing like a fold should be a vertical looseness between the outer edge of the shoulder and the point of the bust in women's garments; this is **meant to be there** and should not be fitted out.

As a guide, keep before you the picture on the pattern envelope. You will notice that in these fashion drawings and photographs no garment ever fits tightly, no matter how "fitted" it is in style. The lines follow the lines of the body without tightness (except sweaters, of course). Darts and seams are there to shape, not to make tight. To repeat, DO NOT OVERFIT! This is particularly important for the large figure, whose problem is greatly accentuated by a tight fit. (Conversely, a skinny figure will only look skinnier in clothes that are too loose.) Overfitting also points up any lack of symmetry in the two sides of the body—a fault that most of us have to some degree. By fitting one side loosely, you can often create an appearance of symmetry.

LOOK OVER YOUR GARMENT and check the following points. For correcting what is wrong, see AD-JUSTMENTS, which begin in the next column.

Ease means just enough looseness for comfort as you walk, sit and bend, and for freedom of movement across the back as you bring your arms forward. It does not mean bagginess.

Vertical lines, such as center lines, should hang perpendicular to the floor, dividing the body into two equal halves. Side seams and pleats (basted together at this stage) should also hang straight. For an easy way to check this, use a plumb line (see page 206).

Horizontal lines (bust, waist, hip) should be parallel to the floor, without dipping.

Shoulder seams should go evenly across center of shoulders from neck base to top of arm.

The neckline should lie smoothly where it belongs, neither gaping nor too snug. The seam line on a high, round neckline should just fit the curve at the base of the neck.

Darts in a bodice front should point toward points of bust, underarm darts stopping ½″ to 1″ short of point of bust.

A waistline seam should encircle the figure evenly, at the level designed. At normal waistline or hips it should be snug, but not look or feel tight.

Sleeves should hang straight from the shoulders, without wrinkles when your arms are hanging down. Any grain lines should be vertical or horizontal.
- Sleeve cap (unless designed otherwise) should follow the normal shoulder curve.
- Armholes should be comfortable, allowing freedom of movement—raise your arms above your head.
- Darts or other ease in long sleeves should fall at the elbow when arm is bent. With two darts, the space between should be at the elbow.
- Check the sleeve length.

The crotch in pants should fit smoothly and be placed right, neither hiked up nor sagging. It should be comfortable without bagginess.

Check placement of any pockets, flaps, half-belts, buttonholes.

ADJUSTMENTS

It must be understood that what follows are all small adjustments, involving only fabric that can be taken out of seam allowances (or added to them). Anything larger should have been corrected in the pattern.

A correction made on one side only, because of body unevenness, must be a compromise between fitting the garment and playing down the fault. Go easy. Center lines or pleats out of plumb are indications that such a correction is needed. The same is true for horizontal lines that dip at one side.

Poor fit in other areas simply means that your figure is not exactly like the one for which the pattern was drafted.

SHOULDER ADJUSTMENTS

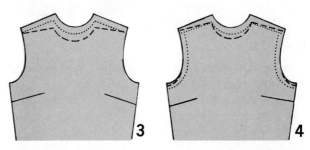

Wrinkles from top of armholes across front and back (square shoulders).

There are two ways to solve this problem:
. . . Deepen shoulder seam allowances at neck, tapering to the original width at armhole (3). Adjust the neckline (see next page) to fit neck and collar, if any. Bodice will have been slightly shortened.
. . . Remove sleeves and open the shoulder seams. Re-pin, letting out seams at armhole as necessary and tapering to the original width at neck (4). When replacing the sleeves, raise the seam line (reduce seam allowance) at bottom of armhole the same amount as the shoulder. Sleeve seam allowance stays the same.

Folds from bottom of armholes, pointing toward the neck (sloping shoulders).

Try shoulder pads. If they do not work, re-move the sleeves; deep-en the shoulder seams at armhole and taper to the original width at neck edge. Lower the armhole seam line at underarm the same amount (5).

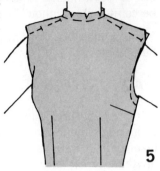

Armhole seams falling off the shoulders (narrow shoulders).

Open the armhole seam at sleeve cap, be-tween notches. Re-set the sleeve cap, keeping the same seam allow-ance width in the sleeve, but taking a deeper one in the armhole; taper to the original seam line at bottom of armhole (6).

Tightness across shoulders and top of sleeves (broad shoulders).

Open the armhole seam at sleeve cap, between notches. Re-set the sleeve cap, keeping the same seam allowance width in the sleeve, but taking a narrower one in the armhole; taper to the original seam line at the bottom of the armhole.

Bodice back pulls up at waistline and has wrinkles at armholes (round shoulders).

There are two ways to solve this problem:

. . . Open the shoulder seams from neck to arm-hole seam line. Re-pin, leaving front seam allowance the same width, but letting out the back seam allow-ance, tapering it to the original width at armhole. If the back still pulls, let out the waist seam at center back and taper to side seams (7).

. . . Remove sleeves and open the shoulder seams. Deepen the shoulder darts. When replacing the sleeves, reduce the armhole seam allowance of the back sec-tion accordingly, joining the original seamline at un-derarm. If the back still pulls, let out the waist seam at center back and taper to side seams (8).

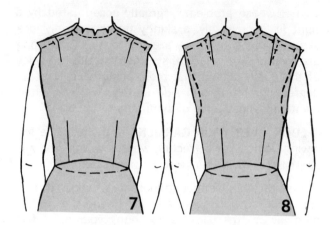

NECKLINE ADJUSTMENTS

Neckline too tight, riding up on the neck, even af-ter the seam allowance has been clipped.

Clip **very carefully** through stay-stitching until the neck lies flat. Mark the new neckline. Immediately upon removing the garment, make a new line of stay-stitching.

Neckline a little too wide.

Mark the new neckline in seam allowance, remov-ing the stay-stitching as necessary. When stitching on the facing, take a smaller seam allowance.

Neckline gaping in front.

Open the shoulder seams. Re-pin, raising the bodice front and deepening the seam allowance at the neck; taper to original seamline at armhole edge (back seam allowance stays the same). If the fabric can be eased, cut the facing slightly smaller and ease the garment to it.

ADJUSTMENTS at BUST

Darts too low or too high.

Remove stitching and re-pin darts, parallel to the old location, so they point toward the bust.

NOTE ABOUT DARTS: As you fit darts, you may want to shape them slightly, curving them in or out for better fit. This applies to skirt darts too.

Tightness across front and back; waist may ride up at sides (large bust).

Open side and waistline seams. Pin deeper darts, checking the direction and length at the same time. Re-pin sides and waist seam with smaller seam allow-ances. Let out sleeve seams to correspond.

Too much fullness at the bustline (small bust).

Open side seams and waist seam. Re-pin side seams to fit, continuing into the sleeve seam as necessary. Re-pin waist seam, shortening bodice to fit. If necessary re-pin smaller darts, checking the direction and length at the same time.

ARMHOLE and SLEEVE ADJUSTMENTS

Sleeveless armholes too tight.

Treat the same as you would a tight neckline.

Gaping sleeveless armholes.

This may have various causes. First make sure that shoulders fit and there is not too much ease across bust. If these areas fit, make the same correction as for a gaping neckline. With a very large bust, it may be necessary to take a small dart into the armhole (9).

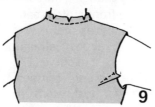

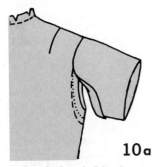 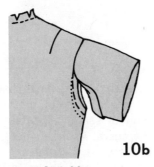

Armholes (with sleeves) uncomfortable.

Remember that the armhole seam will be trimmed at the underarm after it is stitched. If the seam is about 1″ below the armpit, it should be comfortable. A sleeve set in lower at the underarm will have less, not more, freedom of movement.

Open the armhole seam at the underarm between the notches. Keeping sleeve seam allowance the same, re-pin, taking a deeper or a narrower seam allowance in the bodice, as needed (10 a, b).

Tightness of sleeve across upper arm; arm cannot swing freely.

Open side seam to waist and underarm sleeve seam from armhole to elbow. Re-pin both, tapering allowances to as little as ¼″ at armhole.

Diagonal wrinkles in sleeve cap (distribution of ease is not right for you).

Open the armhole seam at sleeve cap, between notches. Re-pin, shifting ease toward front or back as needed for a smooth fit (11). Re-baste sleeve and check fit.

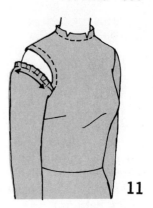

Elbow darts in the wrong place.

Remove stitching; re-pin the darts in the right place, parallel to the old location.

ADJUSTMENTS at WAIST and HIPS

Garment too tight or too loose at waist.

Let out or take in side seams. If this is not sufficient, let out or take in darts in bodice and skirt (distribute the amount among darts on both sides of center).

Waistline too low.

Open waist seam and bodice side seams at waist. Tie a string around waist and mark a new seam line with pins (12). Re-fit darts, if necessary. Re-pin and check fit. (In a fitted one-piece dress this adjustment should be made on the pattern.)

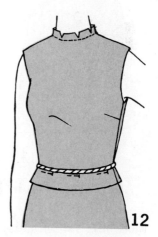

Garment too tight or too loose across hips.

Let out or take in side seams equally on both sides, continuing the adjustment to the hem. (Seam allowances can be as narrow as ¼″, if necessary.) Taper to original seam line at waist.

Wrinkles or excess fabric in back, above or below waistline.

Open waist seam across the back and take up excess fabric in skirt and/or bodice, tapering to side seams (13). Re-fit darts, if necessary. (In a fitted one-piece dress, this adjustment should be made on the pattern.)

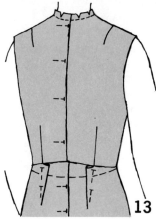

Skirt dips to one side (14), with center line out of plumb (body unevenness).

Open waist seam and re-pin (either to bodice or to waistband), lowering one side and raising the other until center line is straight and hem is parallel to the floor (15). Re-fit darts.

ADJUSTMENTS in PANTS

The fit of pants is a very individual matter, for which it is difficult to lay down general guide lines. Waist and upper hip adjustments are the same as in skirts. For problems of the seat and crotch, try to determine the cause; an adjustment at the inner leg seam will often be all you need. Corrections do not always have to be made in both the front and the back of the pants.

Tightness in the crotch area, indicated by horizontal wrinkles and pulling at the sides; the crotch seam may pull down at the waist.

Let out inner leg seams. If necessary, let out waist at center, tapering to original seam line at sides (16). Re-fit darts, if necessary.

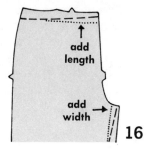

Bagginess at crotch in front.

Try changing the curve of the front crotch seam. Re-draw it as shown, with a line almost straight from waist to curve (17). If necessary, compensate for lost width by letting out side seams.

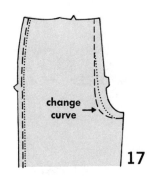

Bagginess at crotch in back (flat buttocks).

Open and re-baste back crotch seam, taking a narrower seam at the bottom and tapering to the original seam line after the curve. At the center of the waist, take a deeper seam and taper to the original seam line at sides (18). Re-fit darts if necessary.

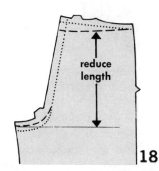

While not too tight, pants are uncomfortable to sit in and pull down at waist in back.

On back crotch seam, change the curve as for bagginess at crotch in front, above (17). Let out waist at center back, tapering to original seam line at sides. If necessary, let out side seams and re-fit the darts.

Fusibles

The term "fusibles" includes both fabrics applied with an iron and the separate fusing agent (web) by means of which two fabrics can be bonded together. Fusing can eliminate quite a bit of sewing. Used on the fabrics that are suitable for them, fusibles are fast and easy to apply, and often add welcome body to a fabric. The fusing survives normal wear, washing and dry-cleaning.

FUSIBLE FABRICS are fabrics backed with a fusing substance or agent. They fall into two categories.

Iron-on patches, which come in various sizes, weights and colors, are applied simply with a hot iron (no steam). They are mainly used for mending (see p. 160), appliqués or for reinforcing and stabilizing points of stress, such as buttons (see p. 42).

Fusible interfacing fabrics require both heat and steam, and can be used only with fabrics that are not adversely affected by steam. Their main use is for interfacing (see that chapter, and chapters on garment areas to be interfaced), but they are also used to reinforce points of stress such as buttonholes (see p. 31) or corners of gussets (see p. 115).

FUSIBLE WEB is a gossamer-fine web that, when placed between two layers of fabric and steampressed, will bond them together. It comes pre-packaged in handy strips ¾″ to 2″ wide and in pieces up to 9″ × 36″, or by the yard. It can be used with any fabric that can take the amount of steam needed for fusing. The web is particularly useful for hems (see the next page), especially if thread color is a problem, as in a large contrasting-color print. You will find many other uses for it too—including appliqués and trimmings (see p. 17), patching (see p. 166), and anchoring facings (see p. 96).

Fusible web is available under different brand names. Each brand has its own directions for use, which should be **read and followed carefully.** By and large, however, the methods can be exemplified by the one given for the popular product known as Magic Polyweb® .

APPLYING MAGIC POLYWEB

Test the web on a piece of your fabric, large enough to fuse only part of it. This will show you how the fabric reacts to steam, if the fused part looks different from the rest, or if too much of a ridge appears for hemming. Use the web only if you are satisfied with the results.

The steps for fusing are as follows:

a. Set the iron to STEAM, at the temperature appropriate for your fabric (1).

b. Cut the web to the size needed and place it between the two layers of fabric. Pin, if desired (2).

c. Heat-baste by pressing lightly with the point of iron between pins (3) to hold all the layers in place; remove pins.

d. Cover fabric with a wet press-cloth. Steampress for 10 seconds, or until press-cloth dries (4). DO NOT MOVE IRON BACK AND FORTH and do not press heavily: heat and steam, rather than pressure, are what cause the fusing. As you place the iron on a new area, slightly overlap the area already fused.

Keep the iron from direct contact with the web. Always keep the same side of the press-cloth up, as the underside may pick up some of the web, which would then stick to the iron.

Once the fusing has been completed, let the fabric cool before further handling.

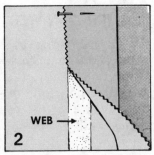

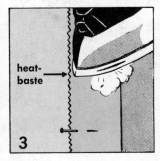

Never wash or iron any fusible product before application. Fusibles need no pre-shrinking or other treatment; use them as they come from the package or bolt.

FUSING A HEM

Use a ¾″ strip of the web.

a. Turn up hem and pin or baste as usual (see HEMS p. 120). A pinked edge will show less on the outside than a straight-cut one.

Do all the steps that follow in one area (the width of the ironing board), then move the garment and continue.

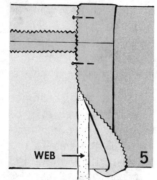

b. Slip the strip of web between the two layers, just below the cut edge. Be careful not to stretch the web. Pin if you wish (5). Heat-baste, remove any pins and fuse as directed on the preceding page.

c. In a curved hem, fusing helps to ease in the extra fullness. On a very curved hem, you may want to make a line of ease-stitching (see HEMS p. 121) to control the fullness before putting the web in place; in that case, place the web below the ease-stitching.

FUSING UNDER TOPSTITCHING

Patch pockets can be held securely in place for topstitching:

After pinning the prepared pocket to the garment, slip ⅜″-wide strips of the web under the bottom and side edges (6) and fuse in place; then topstitch. This same technique can be used for other details to be topstitched to a garment, such as a belt.

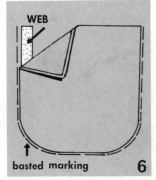

FUSIBLE WEB USED AS INTERFACING

Fusible web can sometimes be used alone, in the place of interfacing—this works particularly well with polyester double-knits. There are two ways of using the web: Stitching it in with the facing, or slipping it in after the facing is stitched. (If, however, you want to use fusible web with a lightweight interfacing, see INTERFACING.)

STITCHED-IN WEB

a. To cut the web, use the pattern for the garment section you want to interface (collar, facing, cuff, pocket edge or flap, etc.). For a collar, trim away the entire seam allowance from the web at the neck edge. For a facing, trim away ⅛″ from the web at the free (unnotched) edge. (On a facing, the free fabric edge needs no finish or just pinking—the web will prevent raveling.)

b. Place the web on the wrong side of the outer section; then pin and stitch the web as you would any interfacing (7). Grade, clip and understitch, as usual.

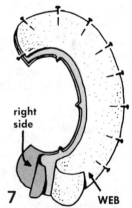

c. BE SURE NEVER TO DO ANY PRESSING UNTIL THE PIECE IS TURNED AND THE WEB IS SAFELY BETWEEN TWO LAYERS OF FABRIC. Be particularly careful to have edges smooth and even, corners pushed out, etc. Flatten edges and pin every few inches.

d. Heat-baste, remove pins and press as directed on the preceding page.

SLIPPED-IN WEB

a. Apply facing as usual, omitting interfacing. Trim, grade and clip seam allowances. Press facing to wrong side.

b. Cut the web from garment pattern (collar, facing, etc.), and trim off **all** seam allowances; on a straight edge you may use a 2″-wide strip of web.

c. Slip the web between garment and facing (8), heat-baste and fuse, following directions on page 107.

NOTE: Since it fuses the facing to the garment fabric, fusible web **cannot** be used where there are bound buttonholes. These are made only through garment fabric and interfacing, with the facing finished separately.

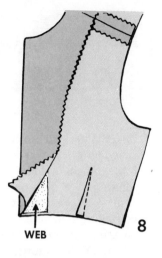

WEB 8

SEPARATING FUSED FABRICS

If this becomes necessary, simply press again with a steam iron and a wet press cloth and peel the layers apart while they are still warm. To remove web from fabric, place an old, wet cloth over it and press; repeat until the cloth has absorbed the web.

PRACTICAL TIPS

● Do not stretch the web as you place it between fabrics; after it is applied, it will then be able to stretch and recover with the fabric.

● If it is necessary to piece the web, simply lay the pieces edge to edge or overlap them slightly.

● Fusible web disappears when used with enough steam. It even becomes invisible between two layers of sheer lace.

● With heavy fabrics, especially where a seam may furnish an extra thickness, allow extra fusing time.

● Arnel triacetate may not absorb the web, causing a hem to come down after laundering or dry-cleaning. If this happens, simply renew the bond by steam-pressing again.

● Save scraps of fusible web—every little piece can be used.

● To clean an iron that has inadvertently come into contact with fusible web, use a commercial hot iron cleaner or a steel wool soap pad. Glide cleaned iron over waxed paper to restore smoothness.

Gathers and Shirring

Gathers are formed by fabric drawn up on a line of stitching. They are part of the design of a garment, supplying a soft fullness where needed (1). Shirring, a decorative use of gathers, consists of several (three or more) rows of gathers (2) and is often done with elastic thread.

The fullness of the gathers, or the amount of fabric each pattern allows for gathering, depends upon the design of the garment. If you are not using a pattern, you can generally allow about 1½ to 2 times the finished length for gathering.

In both gathering and shirring, the stitching can be done with a hand running stitch (see p. 118), but is faster and more even when done by machine, with the machine set for a longer stitch (the heavier the fabric, the longer the stitch).

When stitching a gathered or shirred edge to a flat edge, do it with the gathered side up. Stitch on the seam line, then make a second line of stitching within the seam allowance.

Never press a gathered or shirred area flat; work only the point of the iron into the gathers.

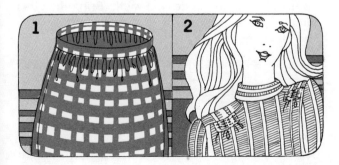

1 2

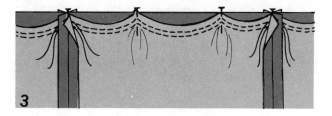

GATHERS

Gathers can be made either with straight stitch or with zigzag stitch. To fall evenly, gathers should be drawn up on a double line of stitching. This means that with straight stitch you make two lines of stitching, while zigzag automatically takes stitches at two levels.

If the edge to be gathered is long (as in a skirt top), divide it into equal sections, each to be stitched and drawn up separately (3). If the fabric is heavy, stop short of seams, going **under** the seam allowances, as shown.

STRAIGHT STITCH—The stitching is done on the right side; the gathers will then be drawn up by the bobbin thread. Generally, the first line of stitching is made on the seam line, the second one ¼″ above, in the seam allowance. If, however, your fabric does not mark, you will get better control if you have one line of stitching ½″ and the second line ¾″ from the cut edge. The seam will fall between the two lines, and you can then remove the lower (visible) one after the final stitching.

Before drawing up the gathers, pin the edge (4) to the shorter edge to which it is to be attached (waistband, bodice, or other), matching and pinning at notches, ends, centers, etc. Grasp the two bobbin threads at one end, draw up one half of the gathers to match the flat edge, and fasten the thread-ends by winding them around a pin (4). Repeat with the other end of the bobbin threads. Distribute and straighten gathers evenly. Put in additional pins, no more than 2″ apart.

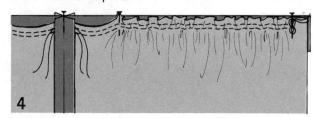

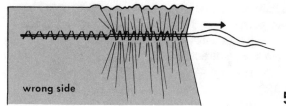

ZIGZAG STITCH is worked so as to straddle a doubled length of thread, which is then drawn up (5). Set the machine for a medium stitch width and a medium stitch length. Place the fabric under the presser foot, wrong side up. Turn the hand wheel once, taking one stitch through the fabric where you want the gathering to begin. Pull the bobbin thread up, through the fabric. Bring both threads toward you, until they cover the distance to be gathered. Lay the threads within the ⅝″ seam allowance near the seam line; zigzag over them, being careful not to catch the threads in the stitching.

Proceed as for the straight stitch, at left, beginning with "Before drawing up the gathers". Then pull the threads to gather the fabric.

SHIRRING

Shirring may be done with regular thread or with elastic thread. In both cases, the stitching is done on the right side.

WITH REGULAR THREAD, make the first line of stitching on the seam line and the second line ¼″ above in the seam allowance. Since the additional rows will remain visible, stitch them very carefully, even and parallel, an equal distance apart. After the stitching is done, bring all the thread-ends **at one end** to the wrong side. Tie the ends of each row separately and clip ends. At the other end of the stitched lines, hold the bobbin threads (6) and draw up the shirring to the desired width. Bring the other thread-ends to the wrong side, tie each row separately and clip ends.

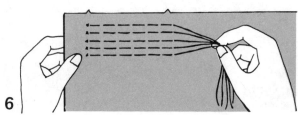

ELASTIC THREAD is particularly useful when the shirring is to fit snugly, as at the waist or wrist.

The elastic thread will be on the wrong side. Hand-wind it on the bobbin in the same direction the machine would wind it. Set the machine for the longest stitch. Before starting to stitch, tie the end of the elastic thread to a pencil. Hold this behind the presser foot as you stitch, stretching the fabric. As you start each new row, tie the bobbin (elastic) thread again to the pencil, leaving the old thread on. Be careful to make all the rows even and parallel, an equal distance apart. If, after the stitching has been completed, you want tighter gathers, pull up the elastic threads and distribute the extra fullness

evenly. Bring all thread-ends to the wrong side and tie each row separately. Clip thread-ends.

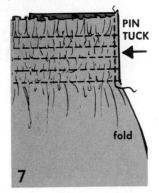

WHEN AN END OF A SHIRRED SECTION is not caught in a seam, make a neat, strong, inconspicuous finish by folding the fabric on the wrong side and stitching a pin-tuck across the ends, as shown (7), catching in the ends of the gathering threads.

Grain in Fabric

All woven or knitted fabric has grain, or direction, established by the position of the yarn out of which the fabric is made. The only grainless fabrics are the relatively few that are made, not from yarns, but from pulped fibers, such as felt, fake suede or non-woven interfacings.

In the fabrics we generally use, grain may be invisible, as in satin, for example, or it may appear as interlaced loops, as in knits —but it is always there, running lengthwise and crosswise in the yardage. Patterns never fail to take it into account. Grain is of prime importance in the fit and hang of a garment.

GRAIN in WOVEN FABRIC

Woven fabric has three directions:

LENGTHWISE—the direction of the **warp,** the yarns that run the whole length of the bolt. It is the direction of greatest strength, straightest hang, and least give. "Straight grain" on a pattern means lengthwise grain.

CROSSWISE—the direction of the **woof** or **filling yarn,** running over and under the warp, back and forth, from selvage to selvage.

These two sets of yarn, forming the lengthwise grain and the crosswise grain, are always at right

angles to each other, no matter what the surface texture of the fabric may be. So-called diagonal weaves, or any other variations in weave texture, are established, not by changing the direction of the yarn, but by varying the over-and-under pattern of the crossing threads, as you see in "Twill Weave" (1).

BIAS—running diagonally across the weave, at the intersection of the lengthwise and crosswise yarns (2). While this is a direction, and a very important one (see the chapter BIAS), it is not a grain, but cuts through the grain. Bias is the direction of greatest give and elasticity in woven fabric.

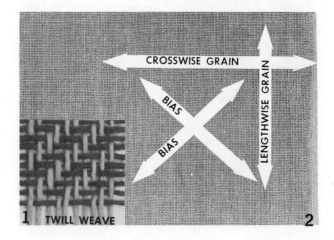

1 TWILL WEAVE

CROSSWISE GRAIN

BIAS

BIAS

LENGTHWISE GRAIN

2

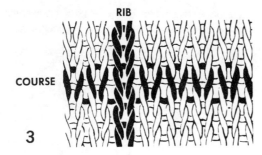

3

GRAIN in KNITS

For all practical purposes, knits have only two grain directions (3):

LENGTHWISE—indicated by the ribs running with the yardage. As a general rule, this direction does not have much give.

CROSSWISE—the course running at right angles to the lengthwise grain. This direction can have considerable elasticity and is used where bias would be used in a woven fabric.

GRAIN and the HUMAN FIGURE

The relationship of fabric to figure is simple and direct. The grain is established down center front,

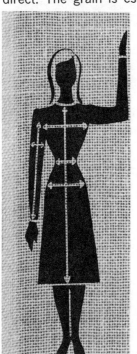

center back, and sleeve centers (4): In all the work done thereafter to shape the fabric to the body—seams, darts and gathers, steaming, pressing—this grain direction must be constantly maintained. This is a basic rule of dressmaking, which no one can disregard without sad consequences for fit and hang. (In practice, you follow the rule by following the pattern markings faithfully).

In almost all garments made or bought, the lengthwise grain corresponds to the up-and-down or lengthwise direction of the figure.

4

On occasion, fabric design may make it necessary to reverse these directions: in a border-printed fabric, for instance, the border runs lengthwise in the fabric, but may run crosswise (along the hem) on the figure.

In a garment cut on the bias, the center lines (front, back, sleeves) will be on the true bias.

GRAIN and FABRIC FINISHES

Fabric as it comes from the loom is grain-perfect, which means that the lengthwise and crosswise yarns cross exactly at right angles (5). The various finishes with which fabrics are treated, however, very often cause the crosswise (weaker) grain to be pulled out of line, making the weave off-grain (6). This situation can or cannot be corrected, depending on whether a finish is permanent or temporary.

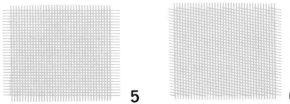

5   6

A permanent finish locks the grain in position. All synthetic fabrics and blends of natural and synthetic fibers have a permanent finish. So have the natural-fiber and rayon fabrics labeled "Permanent Press", "Crease-Resistant", etc. In any case, a permanent finish is always mentioned on the label, as it is a selling point. (The shrink-resistance process does not affect the grain). Bonded fabrics (two fabrics fused together) also have the grain locked in position.

A temporary finish is one that is water- or steam-soluble. Sizing is the most common. If the finish of a fabric is not mentioned on the bolt, you can assume that it is temporary. The use of such finishes is diminishing; nowadays they are found mostly in woolens and in imported cottons and silks. A temporary finish will come out later in washing or dry-cleaning a garment. If the finish has pulled the fabric out of line, it must be removed from the fabric before cutting, so the yarns can return to their natural position. This is particularly important when matching plaids and stripes. See FABRICS, page 74, for how to remove a temporary finish.

GRAIN in MAKING a GARMENT

Patterns are designed and marked with careful attention to grain as it relates to the figure. The double-headed arrow marked "lengthwise grain" or "straight of goods" (which mean the same thing) is the most important marking on your pattern. Be sure to place it exactly right, and never overlook the grain marking on even the smallest pattern piece (see CUTTING). The marking "lay on fold" also means "lay on the lengthwise or straight grain". In a bias-cut garment, straight grain is still straight grain—place the arrow correctly and the bias will fall where it belongs.

Permanent-finish fabrics—Just make sure that the straight-grain mark on your pattern falls correctly on the lengthwise grain of your fabric. If the cross-wise grain is crooked, it will remain so, without impairing the hang of the garment, because the grain is locked in position.

Temporary-finish fabrics—Any deviation in grain must be corrected before a garment is cut out (see PREPARING FABRIC FOR USE, p. 74). Since the finish is soluble, the yarn in the fabric will eventually return to its straight position, and if this happens **after** a garment is finished, you can't expect it to retain its shape. In general, take care not to pull the fabric out of shape. For more on taking grain into account, see CUTTING, and MACHINE-STITCHING.

Gussets

A gusset is a triangular or diamond-shaped piece set into a slash in the fabric or into a seam. It is most often added at the underarm curve of a kimono sleeve to provide ease.

Since a set-in piece looks difficult, you may be afraid to tackle a gusset. If you take one step at a time, however, it is not really difficult. But, take no short cuts!

The instructions for reinforcing the slash apply to any other corner in a garment with a set-in piece or to any slash.

THE GUSSET PATTERN

Diamond-shaped gussets can be either in one piece (sometimes with a dart to remove bulk) or in two pieces, with a curved seam that is stitched before insertion (1), also to remove bulk. A diamond-shaped gusset has four corners and is inserted after the underarm seam is stitched.

Combination gussets are part of a garment section, such as a side-panel (2) or the underarm section of a sleeve (3).

Triangular gussets are cut in two pieces. These are the easiest to handle, as they are inserted before the underarm seam is stitched (4).

DIAMOND-SHAPED GUSSET
1

one-piece (with or without dart)

two-piece (with seam)

gusset part

bodice part

2 COMBINATION GUSSET

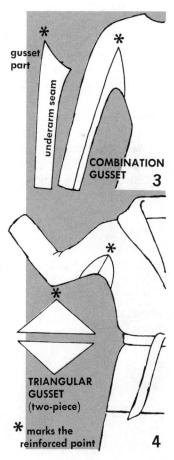

gusset part

underarm seam

COMBINATION GUSSET 3

TRIANGULAR GUSSET (two-piece)

* marks the reinforced point

4

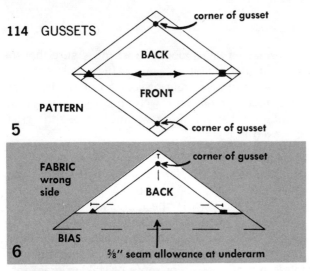

MAKING TWO TRIANGLES OUT OF A DIAMOND

If you have a one-piece diamond-shaped gusset, convert the pattern into two triangles which are easier to insert.

On pattern pieces for front and back of bodice, compare markings (dots, triangles, etc.) at underarm slash with matching markings on the gusset pattern. Mark the gusset corners for FRONT and BACK. With a ruler, draw a line between the **other** two corners (5). Cut gusset pattern in half on this line.

Pin each triangle to fabric doubled on the bias, adding ⅝″ along the bias edge for seam allowance—this will be the underarm seam (6). Cut out the triangles. Cut through the bias. Transfer **all** pattern markings, including seam lines, to **all** gusset pieces.

Follow the instructions on the following pages for reinforcing the slash and inserting the gusset.

ADDING A GUSSET TO A PATTERN

It sometimes happens that, for the sake of simplicity, a pattern omits a gusset where it would be safer and more comfortable to have one. Unfortunately, the need for a gusset is seldom discovered until a kimono sleeve tears under the arm; nothing can be done then, because the tear is not in the direction a slash would be. In general, a gusset is needed with a kimono sleeve if the underarm curve is cut rather close to the body; if the sleeve is narrow and long; if you have a heavy upper arm or if you like plenty of ease in your clothes.

To slash a pattern and add a gusset, proceed as follows:

a. To determine the direction of the slash, fold the pattern as shown, from underarm to neck edge near the shoulder seam (7). Along that crease, measure 4¼″ up from the underarm edge and ½″ to each side of crease at underarm. Connect these points with a slightly curved line, as shown—this will be the stitching line for the slash (8).

b. To make the gusset pattern, draw a rectangle on tissue or other paper as shown (9). Draw a triangle in it as shown. Cut out.

You will note that the two edges to be stitched to the slash have ½″ seam allowances, while the bottom edge, which will be part of the underarm seam, has a regulation ⅝″ seam allowance. When cutting out the gussets (two triangles for each sleeve), place this bottom edge on the bias of fabric.

Follow the instructions on the following pages for reinforcing the slash and inserting the gusset.

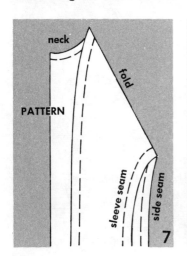

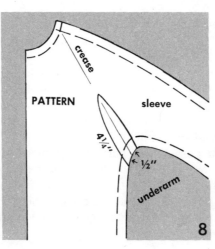

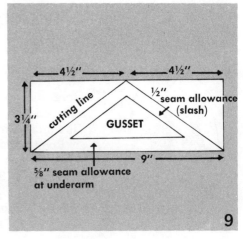

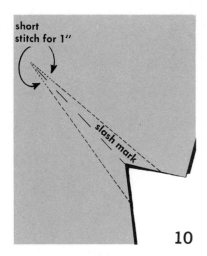

short stitch for 1"

slash mark

10

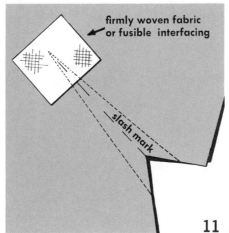

firmly woven fabric or fusible interfacing

slash mark

11

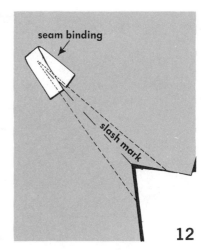

seam binding

slash mark

12

REINFORCING THE SLASH

The point or end of an underarm slash is subjected to considerable strain. Since there is no seam allowance there, the gusset may easily pull out. Before inserting any gusset, it is extremely important to reinforce the slash, either at the **point only** or by **facing the entire slash.**

REINFORCING THE POINT can be done in one of several ways, always before cutting the slash.

Machine-stitching (10) at the point with short stitches may be sufficient with very firmly woven fabrics. Starting at the fabric edge, stitch over the marked seam line of the slash. About an inch before the point, shorten the stitch to 20–25 per inch. Stitch to the point; pivot and **take one or two stitches across the point;** pivot again and stitch for an inch; change to regular stitch and continue to the edge as shown.

A patch of thin, firmly woven fabric may be added (11). Cut it 1½" square, on the bias. Place it over the point on wrong side of garment, marking the point with a pin. Stitch as described in the preceding paragraph.

Lightweight fusible interfacing (11) is good for very ravelly fabrics. Before using it, test it by ironing a piece to the wrong side of a scrap of your fabric, following manufacturer's instructions. If the results are satisfactory, press a 1½" square over point of slash. Mark the point and machine-stitch as described before.

Seam binding (12). Fold a 4" piece of seam binding in a V and place it over the point as shown. Mark the point with a pin. Machine-stitch as described before.

NOTE: The cut corner of a garment where a panel will be added should be reinforced in the same way as the point of a slash.

FACING THE ENTIRE SLASH allows for a quick, topstitched insertion of the gusset later.

Cut a strip of lining or underlining fabric on the bias, 1" wider and ½" longer than the slash marking. Transfer the marking to the wrong side of the strip. With right sides together, place the strip over the slash mark on the garment, matching the markings. Stitch (13) as instructed for **machine-stitching** in the preceding column. Slash to the point and turn facing to wrong side. Roll seam slightly to wrong side and press.

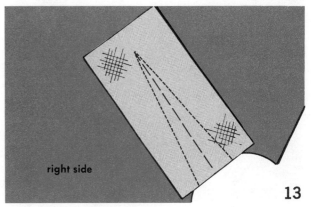

right side

13

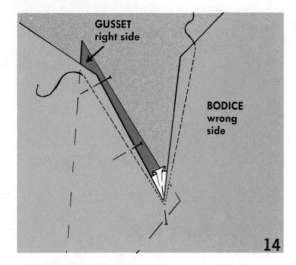

GUSSET
right side

BODICE
wrong
side

14

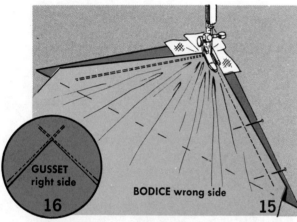

GUSSET
right side

16

BODICE wrong side

15

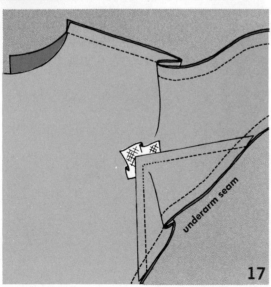

underarm seam

17

INSERTING A GUSSET

Inside stitching in a slash with reinforced corners.

NOTE: The technique shown here on a triangular gusset can also be used to insert a diamond-shaped gusset or even a gusset that is part of a garment section. Stitch any darts or seams that may be in the gusset and follow your pattern guide to stitch all the necessary seams before inserting the gusset.

a. Cut slash as far into the point as possible without clipping the stitching.

b. To attach the first edge of the gusset, pin one edge of slash over one edge of gusset as shown: Right sides together, matching point of slash to corner of gusset and stitched line of slash to seam line on gusset (14). With garment side up, stitch over the stitched line, going toward the point; about an inch before reaching the point, shorten stitches to 20–25 per inch. At the point, **leave the needle down** in the fabric.

c. To attach the second edge, pivot free edges of slash and gusset forward around the needle, then match and pin as before (15). Stitch with shortened stitch, returning to a regular stitch after an inch.

Optional: Reinforce the seam by topstitching through all thicknesses close to seam (16), again shortening the stitch before reaching the point. At the point, continue for 3 stitches beyond, then backstitch to the point. Pivot the work, backstitch 3 stitches along the direction of the next seam, then stitch forward, changing back to a regular stitch after an inch.

d. Repeat with the second triangle; stitch underarm seams, as shown (17).

Quick topstitching, with a faced slash.

Pin or baste the gusset triangle under the faced slash, faced edges even with the seam line on the triangle. Edge-stitch (18) along both sides, pivoting at the point.

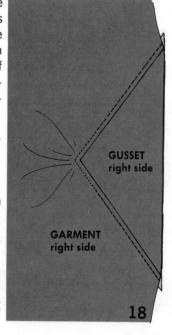

GUSSET
right side

GARMENT
right side

18

Hand-Sewing

Hand-sewing may no longer be needed for "sewing a fine seam", but it still has its place in dressmaking—see the list below. In addition, you can often give a garment the careful look of luxury by doing some of the finishing by hand—the outside stitching on a zipper, for instance.

Hand-sewing of any length (hemming, inserting a zipper, working a buttonhole, etc.) should be a pleasant, relaxed activity, done while sitting comfortably and under a good light. While the procedure is simple, you still have to know its basic rules and fine points.

YOU WILL NEED HAND-SEWING FOR:

● Basting, where pin-basting is insufficient and machine-basting impractical—see BASTING, PLEATS, MARKING and TAILORING.

● Hemming most garments—for stitches used see page 122.

● Tacking—see FACINGS, page 96; for making bar tacks, see THREAD LOOPS.

● Sewing on fastenings—see BUTTONS and FASTENERS.

● Finishing zippers in certain fabrics—see ZIPPERS, page 276.

● Overcasting seams in ravelly fabric if your machine is not equipped to do it—see page 224.

● Finishing bound buttonholes—see page 37.

● Hand-worked buttonholes—see page 38.

THREAD and NEEDLE

For any permanent hand-sewing, such as hems, you generally use the same thread as you used in stitching the garment.

For basting, the thread should be regular or lightweight and light-colored.

The size of the needle depends on the fabric and thread (see p. 251).

Snarls can be avoided—or created—by the way you take the thread off the spool. Hold the spool in the palm of your hand and let it roll as you draw off the thread (1).

Beeswax helps to make the thread smooth for hand-sewing and reduces snarling.

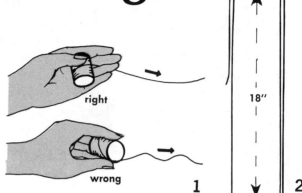

right

wrong

1 | 18" | 2

The **working length** of the thread, single or doubled, should not be more than 18" (2). Cut, never break, the thread. Clip it diagonally and use that end to thread the needle.

STARTING and FINISHING

At the start of any hand-sewing, the thread must be anchored in place. You may do it by taking several small stitches, one on top of the other. Or you can make a knot in the thread-end and tuck the knot under a seam allowance, a hem, etc.

To make this knot, hold the threaded needle in one hand, point up. With the longer thread-end held downward along the needle, wind thread around needle a few times (3); Then, holding wound thread, draw up needle, sliding wound thread over the needle's eye (4) and down to the thread-end.

To finish off hand-sewing, take a few small stitches, one on top of the other, then a few running stitches in an inconspicuous place (a seam allowance, for instance) before clipping off the thread. Or make a knot as in the paragraph above.

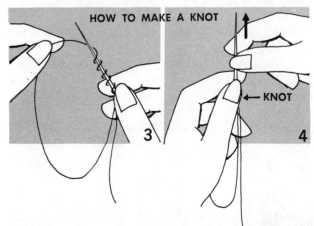

HOW TO MAKE A KNOT

3 | ← KNOT | 4

THE HOW-TO OF HAND-SEWING

• Learn to wear a thimble on the middle finger of your sewing hand. You may have been doing without one, but you will find, after an initial feeling of clumsiness, that with this protection you can push the needle forward faster and with more precision.

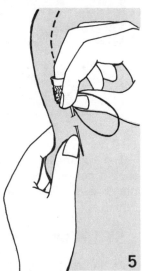

• The needle is held between the thumb and forefinger of your sewing hand as the middle finger pushes it through the fabric.

• The fabric is held over the other hand with thumb on top (5).

• Work with smooth, even motions. Jerking the thread causes it to stretch suddenly and then snarl as it relaxes.

• Stitches are taken from right to left unless otherwise stated (or unless a sewer is left-handed).

• Thread is generally used single. If, for extra strength, you want to use it doubled, make sure that you draw it out smoothly after every stitch, to avoid forming snags and loops.

THE PRINCIPAL STITCHES

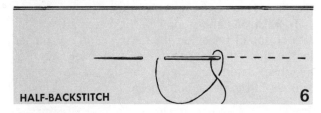

HALF-BACKSTITCH   6

Half-backstitch (6) is good for any seam and for hand-finishing a zipper application (see p. 276). Bring needle and thread out on the stitching line. Take a stitch back about ¹⁄₁₆″; bring the needle out about ⅛″ from where you first came out. Take another ¹⁄₁₆″-stitch back; continue in the same way. In a zipper finish, the backstitches should be tiny and farther apart; the stitch is then called **pick-stitch.**

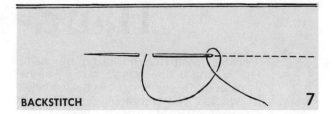

BACKSTITCH   7

Backstitch (7) makes strong seams. On the right side it looks like machine stitching. Bring needle and thread out on the stitching line. Take a stitch back about ¹⁄₁₆″, bringing the needle out ⅛″ forward (that is, ¹⁄₁₆″ from where you first came out). To continue, keep putting your needle in at the end of the last stitch and bringing it out one stitch ahead.

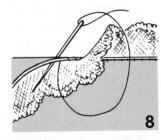

Whipstitch (8) is used to hold two finished or folded edges together in a tight, narrow seam. It is most often used for attaching edgings, lace, etc. as shown. The two edges are placed right-sides-together and the stitches are taken over the two, from back to front, as shown. The stitches should be small and close together, taking in no more fabric than necessary.

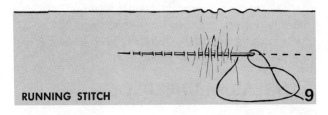

RUNNING STITCH   9

Running stitch (9) is mostly used for gathering and shirring by hand. With the point of the needle, take a number of small forward stitches (¹⁄₁₆″ to ⅛″ long, depending on the fabric) and slide the stitches onto the thread as the needle fills up. If the stitch is used for a seam (not advisable except where there is very little strain), take a small backstitch from time to time.

Other hand-stitches are used for hemming (see p. 122), for finishing seam allowances (see p. 224) for worked buttonholes (see p. 38) and for topstitching (see p. 256).

Hems

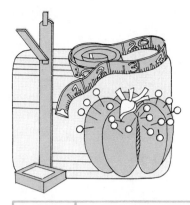

The hem is the last detail, the step that completes a garment. In a ready-made garment, or one that needs bringing up-to-date, the hem is often the only place requiring an alteration.

A good hem is one that is inconspicuous and even, and that, while giving body to the bottom edge, interferes in no way with the hang of a garment.

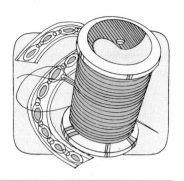

FABRIC	STYLE OF GARMENT	DEPTH OF HEM	CHOICE OF HEM FINISH
All types and weights of fabric except sheers	**Narrow garments** Straight A-line or slightly flared	2″–3″	**For any fabric:** Hem with stretch lace or seam binding Tailor's hem or twice-stitched hem Hong Kong finish or fold-over stretch lace **For lightweight fabrics:** Turned-and-stitched hem
	Full garments Straight (gathered or pleated)	3″	Any of the hems above or machine-stitched hem
	Flared or circular	1″	Hem with stretch lace or seam binding Tailor's hem Hong Kong finish or fold-over stretch lace
	Cuffless pants	1½″–2″	Any of the hems above
Sheer fabrics	**Full garments*** Straight (gathered)	3″–8″ or Very narrow	Turned-and-stitched hem Any of the narrow hems below
	Flared or circular	Very narrow	Rolled hem Edge-stitched hem Tucked hem Horsehair-faced hem French binding (see p. 27)

* A narrow garment in a sheer fabric is usually backed and ceases to be sheer; it is then handled like any other fabric of comparable weight.

Your first consideration should be the proper choice of hem finish for your fabric and garment style. For general guidance on the type of hem you should use, follow the chart above.

NOTE: In a case where there is not enough fabric or the fabric is too bulky for a regular hem, make a FACED HEM (see p. 126).

MARKING THE HEMLINE

The hemline is the line on which a hem is folded up (the finished edge of the garment). It must be at the right level and it must be even—that is, at the same distance from the floor all around.

A pattern usually indicates the depth of a hem. If you know you can use this hemline, for instance, because you have adjusted the pattern to fit, proceed as for "A straight skirt" below.

As a rule, however, you cannot be sure that the length of a garment is right until you have tried it on. And, the human figure seldom being absolutely symmetrical, a skirt with a curved hemline (flared, A-line or circular) may sag at certain points unless the hemline has been measured up from the floor all around. When trying on a garment for marking, wear the proper undergarments; put on the belt, if any; wear shoes with heels of the proper height and stand straight, with arms down and your weight on both feet.

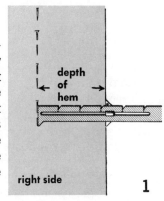

A straight skirt, whether full or narrow, may be marked at one point only, since its hemline is usually on the straight grain. Any unevenness in the hang should have been corrected at the waistline at the time the waistline was finished.

Mark the hemline-level at a seam, on right side. If the fabric has a well-defined crosswise pattern, the hemline will follow that pattern. Otherwise, place the garment right side up on the ironing board. Set the hem gauge or make one for the distance between the mark and the cut edge. Mark the hemline all around with pins or chalk, as shown (1).

An A-line, flared or circular skirt is marked all around, preferably with the help of another person. A circular or bias-cut skirt in a non-treated fabric should be allowed to hang for about 24 hours before

marking the hem, to let it stretch. If you use a yardstick, determine the hemline-level and mark it on the yardstick with a rubber band.

The helper stands the yardstick upright on the floor against the garment and marks the hemline with a horizontal line of pins, about 3" apart (2). With a skirt marker (see p. 65) you may or may not need a helper. If you work alone, keep your body straight as you turn, especially when marking the back.

If you wish, pin up the hem on a trial basis after marking and try on the garment again, to check the length.

For children's clothes of any style, establish the length at one point and proceed as for a straight skirt, in the column to the left.

TURNING UP AND MARKING DEPTH OF HEM

NOTE: For a ROLLED HEM, EDGE-STITCHED HEM or a FACED HEM, skip what follows and turn to pages 125 and 126.

Place the garment on the ironing board, wrong side out. Trim seam allowances in depth of hem to half the original width, as shown (3); trim off corners

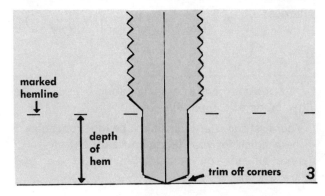

of hem edge. Turn up hem on marked hemline, pinning fold as shown (4) and adjusting fold wherever necessary so line will be even; match at seams. Then baste close to the fold (4), removing pins as you go.

For proper depth of hem, consult the chart on page 119 or your pattern; then set the hem gauge or make one for this depth. Measuring from basted fold (5), mark the hem all around with sharpened tailor's chalk or with pins through **one thickness of fabric only.** Trim off excess fabric all around on marked line.

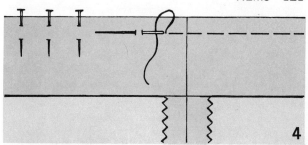

REDUCING FULLNESS IN CURVED HEMS

The excess fullness in curved hems (near seams in A-line skirts, all around in circular ones) is eased as follows:

Make a line of stitching (10–12 stitches to the inch) ¼" from the cut edge through a single thickness, all around. Place the garment on ironing board, wrong side out. Wherever there is a ripple, draw up the bobbin-thread with a pin (6), forming a group of tiny gathers, as shown. Place a piece of heavy paper between hem and garment fabric to avoid a ridge on the outside; press (7), shrinking out the gathers in wool or other shrinkable fabrics. On non-shrinkable fabric, press gathers as flat as possible. Do not put pressure on the basted fold, particularly if you desire a soft hem edge rather than a sharp one.

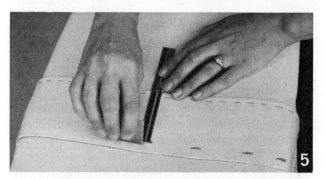

SECURING THE HEM

The last step in making a hem (other than pressing) is securing the upper edge to the garment. This can be done in three different ways: **Hand-sewing** is the traditional way and always suitable. **Machine-sewing,** usually by blind-stitching, is appropriate for certain fabrics and clothing styles. **Fusing** is the quickest way for fabrics that can take it. For all information on fusing a hem, see page 107.

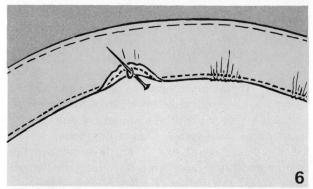

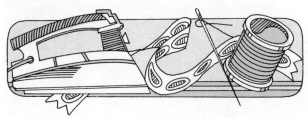

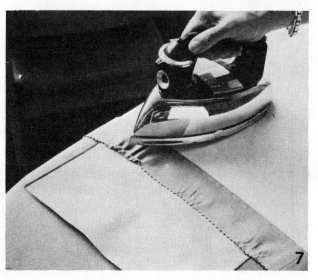

HAND-SEWING

Many stitches are suitable for sewing down a hem. The three most often used are Hemming or Blind-stitch, Catch-stitch and Slipstitch, for which directions follow. These stitches can be used in two different ways, Inside Hemming and Flat Hemming. Except for the Tailor's hem (see p. 123), which is always sewn with inside hemming, the choice is up to you.

Begin your hem at a seam. Take stitches at least ¼″ apart. In the garment fabric, pick up just a thread or two, if possible not going through to the right side. **Do not pull the thread tight,** or the outside fabric will show puckers. To finish a thread-length take a few over-and-over stitches on the hem or in a seam, never in the garment fabric. Cut (do not break) the thread. When sewing is finished, remove the basting and press or steam lightly along the bottom edge, keeping iron clear of upper edge of hem.

In inside hemming, the stitches are taken between the hem and the garment fabric, so that in the finished hem, the thread is protected. To do this, fold the entire hem back against the right side of the garment, with the fold in the garment even with the machine-stitching in the hem-edge (8, 9) or ⅛″ below edge of seam binding (11). On the garment side, take a small stitch through one thread in the fold; on the hem-edge, catch the machine-stitching (9) or the seam binding just below the edge (11).

In flat hemming, the hem-edge is sewn flat to the garment, with stitches taken through the hem-edge (10, 12, 13) and close to this edge in the garment.

HEMMING or BLIND-STITCH is used in both inside hemming (9) and flat hemming (10). Work from right to left. Take a stitch in hem-edge (or line of stitching). Take next stitch in garment, picking up just one thread in fabric and putting needle through the hem-edge (or line of stitching) at least ¼″ ahead before drawing up the thread. Repeat.

CATCH-STITCH is used in both inside hemming (11) and flat hemming (12) and is very good for knit and stretch fabrics because it has "give". Work from left to right, with the needle pointing from right to left. Keep the thread very loose.

SLIPSTITCH (13) is used only in flat hemming where there is a turned edge. It is done like blind-stitching except that the needle is slipped through the folded edge of the hem instead of being put through the edge of the hem.

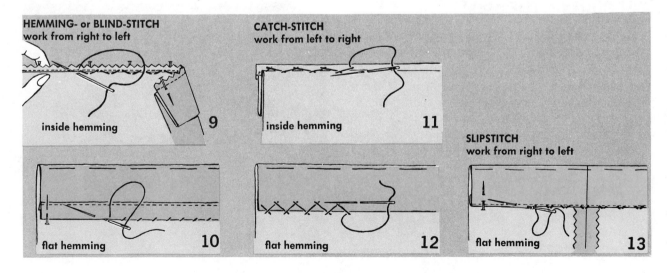

HEMMING- or BLIND-STITCH
work from right to left

inside hemming   9

flat hemming   10

CATCH-STITCH
work from left to right

inside hemming   11

flat hemming   12

SLIPSTITCH
work from right to left

flat hemming   13

MACHINE SEWING

This can be done by blind-stitching, by straight machine-stitching and by shell-stitch.

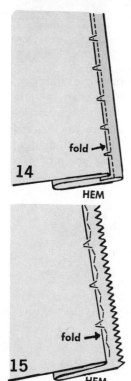

14

HEM

15

HEM

The **blind-stitched hem** is quick and easy, good on straight and A-line skirts and on pants. It eliminates all hand-sewing. The edge is stitched and the hem is caught in place in one operation.

The blind-stitch consists of a few straight stitches in the hem-edge followed by a zig-zag stitch which catches the garment fabric (14). On some machines the straight stitches can be replaced with narrow zigzag stitches, making the hem more elastic (15). For a straight-stitch machine there is a blind-stitch attachment available. See illustrations 14 and 15 for the correct way to fold your hem and consult your manual for the proper machine settings.

The **straight-stitched hem** is turned in the usual way to any depth and stitched by machine instead of by hand. It is generally used for aprons, casual children's clothes, blouses and shirts. (The EDGE-STITCHED HEM, described on page 126, is a more elegant machine hem, suitable for sheer fabrics.)

The **shell-stitched hem** is used mainly on lingerie. See page 139.

PRESSING

Careful pressing can make all the difference between a good hem and a poor one. Remember that pressing is not ironing. In pressing, the iron is moved along the fabric surface with a succession of "pats". "Pats" can be light or heavy as needed, but the iron is never pushed along or rotated. In most cases, pressing is done on the wrong side of the garment, with a steam setting on the steam iron or with a dampened press cloth.

A final pressing is done after the hem is secured and the basting removed. Whether you want a sharp or a soft edge at the fold is a matter of taste; but the top edge of the hem should never show on the right side.

For a **sharp-edged hem** press with a steam iron along the fold. On some wools you may want to use a pounding block.

For a **soft-edged hem** use steam, but do not let the iron rest on the fold. Pat lightly with your hand to shape a curve.

HEM FINISHES

Your garment is ready for one of the following hem finishes after the hem has been folded up, basted along the hemline, and cut to the correct depth.

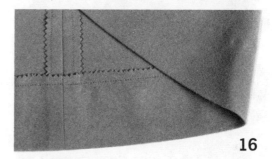

16

TAILOR'S HEM (16)

An excellent hem, flat and inconspicuous, suitable for most heavy and medium-weight fabrics, particularly double-knits. It is sewn with inside hemming or fused.

Make a line of machine-stitching ¼" below the cut edge through a single thickness of fabric (on a curved hem you will already have done it while reducing fullness). On firm fabrics, you may pink the edge; on ravelly fabrics, overcast the edge by hand or machine.

Pin or baste the hem in place about ¼" below the stitching line (17). Sew with inside hemming, using blind-stitch or catch-stitch, or fuse in place.

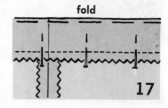

fold

17

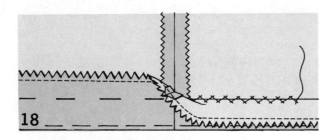

TWICE-STITCHED HEM

For added support, an extra row of hemming stitches may be added on heavy fabrics, especially knits, and on underlined garments.

Make an extra row of hand basting through the center of the hem. Fold the hem back on this basting line. Sew with inside hemming, using blind-stitch or catch-stitch (18). Secure the top of the hem to the garment in the same way.

HEM WITH STRETCH LACE OR SEAM BINDING (19)

Suitable for all fabrics; especially good with fabrics that ravel or roll.

NOTE: For use on a curved hem, prepare the seam binding, which is straight grain, by steam-pressing it into a slight curve (20).

Topstitch lace or seam binding to the right side of the hem about ¼″ from the cut edge, easing it to the fabric (21, 22). Overlap the ends with one end turned under, as shown (23).

Pin or baste the hem to the garment, just below the lace or binding. Sew with either inside hemming or flat hemming, using blind-stitch or catch-stitch; seam binding can be fused in place.

Single fold bias tape can be used on very curved hems. It can be applied either like seam binding (above) or like a packaged hem facing (see BIAS HEM FACING, p. 126).

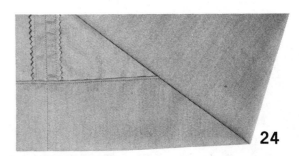

TURNED-AND-STITCHED HEM (24)

For light-weight fabrics in straight or slightly A-line garments. Especially good for washable garments.

Clean-finish the edge as follows: Make a line of machine-stitching ¼″ from cut edge, through a single thickness of the fabric (on a curved hem, you will already have done this while reducing fullness). Turn the edge to the inside on the stitching line and top-stitch through hem edge only, not the garment (25).

Pin or baste the hem in place about ¼″ below the topstitching. Sew with either inside hemming (using blind-stitch or catch-stitch) or flat hemming (using slipstitch).

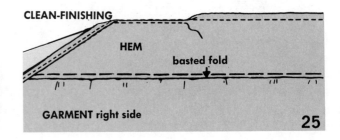

26

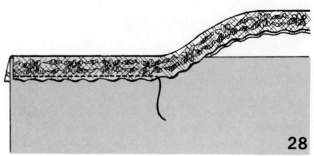

28

HEM WITH HONG KONG FINISH (26)

This is the most elegant hem finish for almost any fabric. The raw edge is encased in a bias strip of lightweight fabric (see p. 24). You may use lining or underlining fabric (cut 1″ wide) or packaged rayon bias tape with the edges pressed open.

Your garment is ready for the following hems immediately after marking the hem-line (see p. 120).

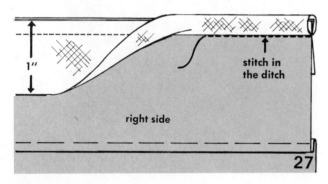

27

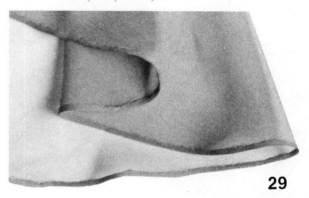

29

With right sides together and raw edges even, stitch the bias to the hem about ¼″ from the raw edge. Trim the seam allowances to ⅛″. Press the strip up; fold to wrong side over raw edges. To secure the bias, "stitch in the ditch" (see p. 152) through hem and bias fabric only—not through the garment (27).

Pin or baste the hem in place, about ¼″ below the stitching. Sew with inside hemming, using blind-stitch or catch-stitch.

HEM WITH FOLD-OVER STRETCH LACE

This is a variation of the Hong Kong finish. Enclose the raw edge of the hem in fold-over stretch lace, inserting the edge in the tape so that the decorative (narrower) part is on top. Edge-stitch with straight or narrow zigzag stitch (28).

ROLLED HEM (29)

This is a very narrow elegant hem finish, used on sheer or lightweight fabrics. There are two ways of doing this hem.

HAND-ROLLED HEM—Make a line of stitching on the marked hemline. Trim hem allowance to ⅛″ outside the stitching. Roll the fabric 3 or 4 times tightly over itself, starting at the line of stitching. Holding the work as shown (30), sew the hem with tiny slipstitches, about ⅛″–¼″ apart.

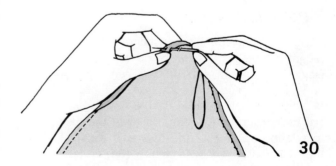

30

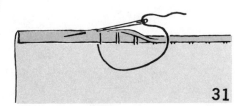

31

HAND-ROLLED HEM, SIMPLIFIED—In this method, the line of stitching is omitted. Trim the hem allowance to ⅛″. Fold in raw edge ⅛″. Slip the needle through the fold. Take a tiny stitch in the garment and again slip needle through the fold; repeat as shown (31), with stitches about ¼″ apart. After every few stitches, draw up the thread, forming a roll.

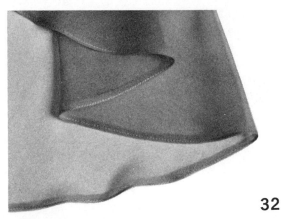

32

EDGE-STITCHED HEM (32)

This is a very narrow hem, used on sheer or lightweight fabrics. It is done entirely by machine and is quick and easy. Make a line of stitching on the marked hemline. Trim the hem allowance to ¼″ outside the stitching. Turn the hem to wrong side, folding on the stitched line (no pinning or basting necessary) and topstitch on **right side,** a scant ⅛″ from fold. If you want a second line of stitching, make the first line a little closer to the fold.

TUCKED HEM

This is a narrow hem, used on sheer or lightweight fabrics. It is easy to do and looks like an elegant bound edge. Trim the hem allowance to ¾″; fold it up to the right side and press. Stitch ⅛″ from the fold (33). Press the raw edge up, over the tuck. Fold the raw edge to meet the tuck, then fold fabric again over the tuck and slipstitch it to the tuck, just above the stitching (34).

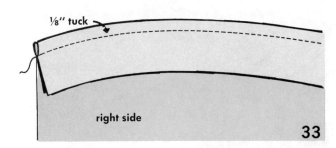

⅛″ tuck

right side

33

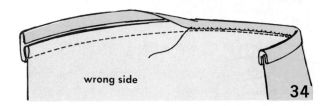

wrong side

34

35

FACED HEM

A hem is faced when there is not enough fabric; when the fabric is too bulky for a regular hem; sometimes for decorative contrast, as in a skating skirt. The facing may be a bias strip or wide stretch lace. If the hem in a sheer fabric needs stiffening, it can be faced with horsehair braid.

BIAS HEM FACING (35) can be bought packaged, as a 2″-wide strip of taffeta or percale with the edges turned under. To make your own, cut 2½″-wide bias strips (see p. 24), join as needed and clean-finish one edge (see p. 124).

Trim away excess fabric ½″ outside the marked hemline. Beginning at a seam, place right side of facing to right side of garment, raw edges even (on packaged hem facing, open out one fold). To join ends neatly, fold back the first end as shown (36). Stitch ¼″ from edge or on the crease. Overlap the

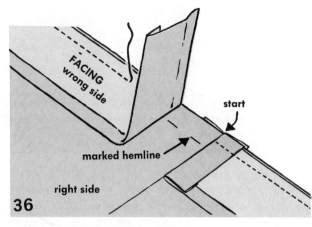

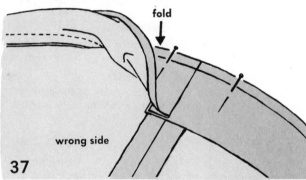

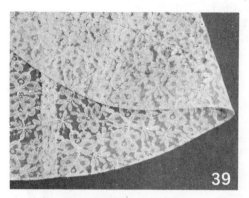

ends. Turn the facing to inside on marked hemline. Pin and baste close to the fold (37); press lightly. Pin the free edge of the facing in place; hem to the garment with slipstitch. Slipstitch the joining together.

HORSEHAIR BRAID is used as a facing to stiffen the hem of a full skirt in sheer fabrics (39). It comes in several widths. Before using it, steam-press out any creases caused by packaging. Trim away excess fabric ¼″ outside the marked hemline.

The cut ends of the braid are sharp and should be encased with a fabric strip. Cut a strip of fabric 2″ wide and about 3″ long; press long edges under ¼″. Place the casing strip over a garment seam, right sides together (40). Starting within the casing, as shown, topstitch one edge of braid to right side of garment edge with edge of braid at marked hemline (40). Overlap ends about ¾″. Wrap the casing around the braid to wrong side; re-stitch the width of the casing, close to the edge, as shown (41). Trim off excess fabric on wrong side.

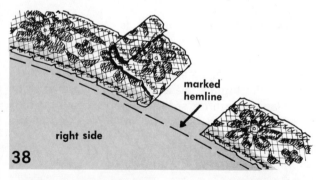

WIDE STRETCH LACE makes a decorative facing. Trim away excess fabric ½″ outside the marked hemline. Topstitch the lace to right side of hem about ¼″ from the cut edge (38). Fold the end under as shown and overlap. Turn to inside on marked hemline. Pin and baste close to the fold; press lightly. Pin free edge of lace in place; hem to garment with blind-stitch. Slipstitch the joining together.

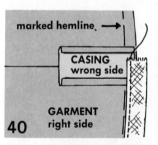

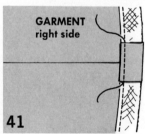

Turn the braid to inside of the garment. On outside, topstitch close to the edge, through braid and fabric, as shown (42). This stitching, so close to edge, is hardly noticeable. Tack the free edge of the braid to the seams of the garment.

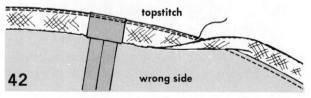

The following hems are for special cases: A hem in a pleat with a seam, a hem in a coat and hems in blouses. For a skirt pleated all around see page 212.

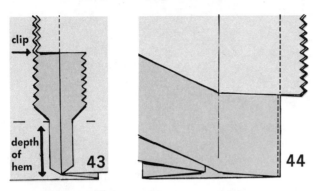

HEM IN A PLEAT WITH A SEAM (43)

How you finish the hem in a pleat with a seam depends on the fabric.

With light to medium weight fabrics, clip both seam allowances above the depth of the hem. Press the seam open below the clip; trim the seam allowances below the marked hemline (43). Turn up and finish the hem as desired. Edge-stitch the inside fold at the pleat through the hem for added sharpness (44).

With bulky or springy fabrics, use the method given in PLEATS (see p. 213, ill. 13).

HEM IN A COAT (45)

A full-length coat is generally 1″ longer than a dress. On any coat, the hem is 2″ to 3″ deep. For interfacing a hem, see TAILORING, page 246. Generally, a hem is put in before the lining. If the lining is put in first, sew it in to within 8″ to 12″ from the bottom edge; at that level, with the coat hanging on a hanger, baste the lining to the coat all around to hold it in place.

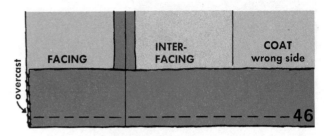

Mark the length of the coat (see MARKING THE HEMLINE, p. 120). At both front edges, trim off the interfacing just above the marked hemline. If an interlining is attached to the body of a coat, trim it at the marked hemline.

Turn up the hem and mark the depth as indicated on page 120, extending the hem through the open facing (46). If the coat has a curved hem, reduce fullness as on page 121. Complete the hem, making either a TAILOR'S HEM or a HEM WITH SEAM BINDING. Overcast the two ends of the hem at the facings (46).

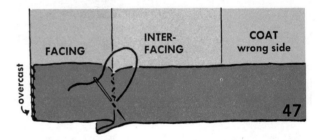

Press the facings to the inside. Any top-stitching should be done at this point. If the front edges of the coat are not topstitched, catch the facing hem to the garment hem ½″ from the facing seam (47).

Catch the facings to the body of the garment with a ½″-long French tack (48) at the hem (see p. 253); or slipstitch the bottom edge of the facings to the coat (49).

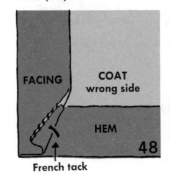

French tack

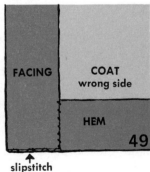

slipstitch

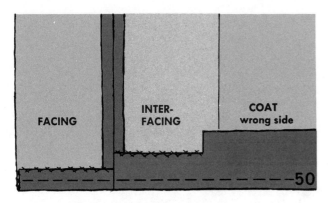

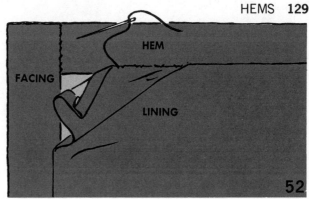

If the fabric is extremely bulky and you are sure the coat will not be lengthened, you will get a flatter corner by cutting out some excess fabric on the hem of the facing and interfacing area (50). Complete the hem and slipstitch the bottom edge of the facings to the coat (49).

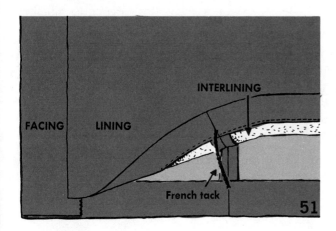

HEMMING THE LINING—a lining may be free-hanging or hemmed to the coat.

Free-hanging lining—Trim the lining to 1″ below the finished coat edge; the interlining, if any, to 2″ shorter than the lining. Finish the lining with a 2″ turned-and-stitched hem (see p. 124), turning it up over any interlining (51).

Slipstitch the front edges of the lining to the facings. At each seam, catch the lining to the coat with a French tack 1″ to 1½″ long (51); see page 253.

Lining, hemmed to the coat—Trim the lining even with the finished coat edge; the interlining, if any, to upper edge of garment hem.

Turn the lining under ½″ and press. Pin the fold of the lining to the upper edge of the garment hem, covering the raw edge; slipstitch (52)—the slight extra length in the lining is for ease. Slipstitch the front edges of the lining to the facings, including the fold made by the extra length.

HEMS IN BLOUSES

In blouses that are worn tucked inside the skirt or pants, the hem should be as flat and narrow as possible.

A machine zigzag finish is good on any fabric.

A stitched-and-pinked finish is good on firmly-woven and knit fabrics: Make a line of stitching ¼″ from raw edge, then pink the edge (53).

For a narrow, flat turned hem, make a line of stitching ½″ from raw edge; turn edge to wrong side on line of stitching; turn raw edge under ¼″ and topstitch (54).

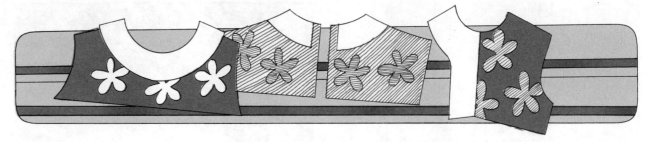

Interfacing

An interfacing is an extra piece of fabric placed between a facing and the outer fabric of a garment. Its purpose is to reinforce, to add body and often crispness, to improve appearance and preserve shape.

Interfacing is usually specified in patterns. If it is not, you should consider adding it, especially if the garment fabric is soft. If you are working with a permanent press fabric that has enough body, however, interfacing may not be necessary.

Interfacing is a must in areas where there are buttons and buttonholes. In tailoring, it is an essential part of the construction and special techniques are used. For specific information, see the chapters on the garment areas to be interfaced, such as the collar and cuffs. For handling darts in interfacing, see TAILORING, page 235.

SELECTING AN INTERFACING

Many different fabrics can be used for interfacing—some are specially made for the purpose and others are ordinary fabrics that happen to be suitable. You may even find what you want among the fabrics you have at home. On page 132, you will find a chart which highlights the most common interfacing fabrics. When selecting an interfacing, keep the following in mind:

- The **purpose**—what you want the interfacing to do. Any interfacing will add a certain amount of body, stability and strength. Often these are all you need. You may, on the other hand, require crispness, shaping, even stiffness. And different parts of a garment—a collar and a waistband, for instance—may need different interfacings.

- The **weight** of the garment fabric. Except for special effects, interfacing should be the same weight or lighter than the garment fabric.
- The **care** demanded by the garment fabric. If it is washable or quick-drying, the interfacing must be that too. If the garment fabric is dry-cleanable only, you are safe with any interfacing, because all fabrics are dry-cleanable.

ORDINARY FABRICS

In order to be suitable for interfacing, a fabric should have a smooth surface—no nap or texture of any kind. Woolen fabrics and knits should not be used.

Lightweight permanent press fabrics—Are washable and pre-shrunk; will add crispness to medium-weight fabrics.

Organdy, voile—Are washable and generally pre-shrunk; are very lightweight; will add crispness to lightweight fabrics. Net may be used on sheers.

Lawn, muslin—Are washable, but may need pre-shrinking; will add body only, to fabrics of related weight.

Self-fabric sometimes works well for interfacing. It can be used with many permanent press fabrics, solid-color organdy, light and medium-weight silks and silk imitations (especially those with a little crispness, such as taffeta).

SPECIAL INTERFACING FABRICS

These specially designed fabrics are made in a great variety. They come **woven** and **non-woven;**

both types may be sew-in or fusible (applied with an iron). In addition, any suitable fabric can become a fusible interfacing if used with a fusible web.

It would be impossible to list here all the interfacing fabrics available. We can just describe the different kinds, and what they will do. After that, keeping your requirements in mind and consulting the labels, you should be able to find what you want.

SEW-IN INTERFACINGS—Available either woven or non-woven and in different types and weights.

Wovens—May be washable or dry-cleanable (check labels); are wrinkle resistant; available in many types and weights; will add body and firmness; help retain shape; have some "give" and can be manipulated. The following are the most common:

> **Permanent press** and other interfacings are sold under various brand names. These are usually washable.
> **Hair canvas** contains goat's hair and can be shaped by steaming, which makes it ideal for tailoring woolen garments; suitable with medium-weight or heavy fabrics.
> **Canvas-like interfacing** (without hair) is often used like hair canvas, although it is less resilient.

Non-wovens—Are washable and non-shrinking; have no grain. There are two types:

> **All-bias** can be stretched in all directions. It comes in several weights: The "featherweight" is soft, excellent with knits; the "lightweight" goes well with any fabric; the thick all-bias "fleece" is used as a cushion for quilted and trapunto effects.
> **Regular** has no stretch at all. It comes in several weights, all providing firmness—from a light crispness to very stiff support. It is used mostly in belts, crafts and home decorating items.

FUSIBLE INTERFACINGS—Consist of fabric with a fusing agent and are applied with heat, steam and pressure. Fusible interfacings are available either woven or non-woven and in different weights: Use a lighter weight than you think the fabric needs because fusing often stiffens a fabric. In addition to their use as interfacing, fusibles are especially good on fabrics that ravel easily, to reinforce points of stress such as

buttonholes (see page 31) or corners of gussets (see page 115).

Always test fusible interfacing on the fabric you are using (see APPLYING FUSIBLE INTERFACING, p. 135). Try to acquire a sample for your test before investing in a large piece. If you follow the manufacturer's instructions, the fusing will survive normal wear, washing and dry-cleaning.

Wovens—Are generally washable; provide considerable firmness. The following are the most common:

> **Fusible hair canvas** contains goat's hair and can be shaped by steaming, which makes it ideal for speed-tailoring; suitable with medium-weight or heavy fabrics.
> **Fusible interfacing** (without hair) often looks like hair canvas but is lighter in weight. It may be used like hair canvas, although it provides less firmness and is less resilient.

Non-wovens—Are washable and non-shrinking; are good with any fabric of suitable weight. The following are the most common:

> **Fusible with one-way stretch** is stable in the lengthwise direction and stretches in the crosswise. It is available in several weights. See page 133 for cutting.
> **Fusible all-bias** can be stretched in all directions; has no grain.

FUSIBLE WEB

Fusible web is a separate, very sheer fusing agent that, when placed between two fabrics, will fuse them together. With it, any suitable fabric can become a fusible interfacing. Where very slight stiffening is needed, just fusing the facing to the outer fabric may be sufficient (see p. 108). Fusible web alone allows the fabric to retain its elasticity, such as in a knit.

PREPARATION

Most interfacing fabrics need no preparation; check the label or the end of the bolt. Never wash or iron any fusible product before application; fusibles need no pre-shrinking or other treatment—use them as they come from the bolt. Washable sew-in interfacing that is not pre-shrunk should be shrunk if it is to be used in a washable garment.

CHART OF INTERFACING FABRICS

INTERFACING TYPES	SPECIFIC INTERFACING FABRICS	PROPERTIES and CARE	USE
SEW-IN WOVENS	Permanent press fabrics Permanent press interfacings	Washable; pre-shrunk; will add crispness	With self-fabric; with other permanent press fabrics
	Organdy, voile		With self-fabric or any lightweight woven
	Lawn, muslin	Washable; may need pre-shrinking; will add body, but not crispness	Lawn with self-fabric or any lightweight woven; muslin for hems and back reinforcement in tailored garments
	Hair canvas, in several weights	Follow manufacturer's recommended care; will provide firmness; hair canvas can be shaped by steaming	With fabrics used for tailoring
	Canvas-like interfacing (without hair)		
SEW-IN NON-WOVENS	All-bias, in featherweight and lightweight	Washable; stretches in all directions	With most knits and wovens
	All-bias fleece		For quilted details and trapunto effects
	Regular, in several weights	Washable; no stretch	For crafts and home decorating items
FUSIBLE WOVENS	Fusible hair canvas	Follow manufacturer's recommended care; do not pre-shrink; will provide firmness; hair canvas can be shaped by steaming	With fabrics used for tailoring and menswear
	Fusible interfacing (without hair)		
FUSIBLE NON-WOVENS	Fusible with one-way stretch	Washable; do not pre-shrink; stretches crosswise, is stable lengthwise	With most knits and wovens
	Fusible all-bias	Washable; do not pre-shrink; stretches in all directions	With light to medium-weight knits and wovens
WEBS	Fusible web	Washable; do not pre-shrink	Alone or with a suitable fabric as interfacing
STIFFENERS	Waistbanding or belting	Washable; non-roll	For waistbands and belts

CUTTING

The following information applies to both sew-in and fusible interfacings.

Woven interfacing—Cut on the same grain as the outer fabric, unless the pattern specifies otherwise.

Non-woven interfacing—Cut in any direction, except for the fusible interfacing with one-way stretch. With this, place the stretch direction crosswise to the body, the stable direction lengthwise.

If your pattern does not have a separate piece for the interfacing, cut the interfacing as follows:

For a shaped facing (1,2,3) cut interfacing from facing pattern.

For an extended facing (4) pin facing part of pattern to interfacing fabric, with edge of fabric along pattern fold line (5). Cut out. A very lightweight interfacing for straight collars and cuffs may be cut from the entire pattern piece, as shown (6).

MARKING

At the neck edge of an interfacing, mark center front and back with a notch, a snip, or other mark.

For perfect curved seams and corners on collars, lapels and cuffs, mark seam lines on the interfacing (7). Use a sharp pencil.

For marking buttonholes, see BUTTONHOLES, p. 32.

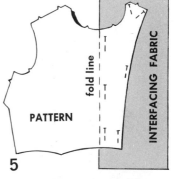

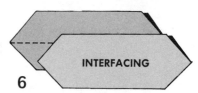

TRIMMING THE INTERFACING

Do the following trimming before applying an interfacing piece: Unless the interfacing is very lightweight, trim away outer corners on collars, lapels, etc. as shown (7). Before applying interfacing that reaches a zipper opening, trim ¾″ from the two edges that adjoin the opening (8).

On sew-in interfacing, prevent free edges from showing below neck or front facing, by trimming ⅜″ from such edges (9); if interfacing tends to ravel, make a line of stitching ¼″ from trimmed edge.

On fusible interfacing, trim ½″ off all edges to reduce bulk; then when the seams are stitched, ⅛″ of interfacing will be caught in the seams (since it is fused in place, it cannot be trimmed after stitching, as a sew-in interfacing would be). In areas where there is no stress, such as pocket flaps, trim ¾″ off the interfacing. See MENSWEAR, page 170.

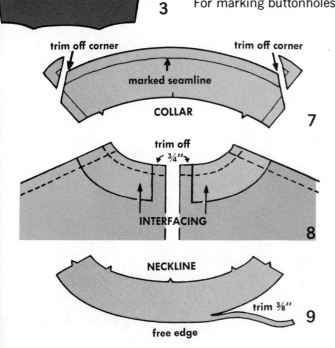

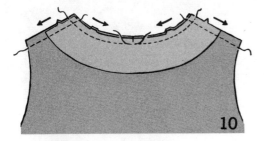

10

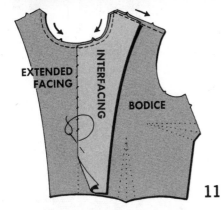

EXTENDED FACING

INTERFACING

BODICE

11

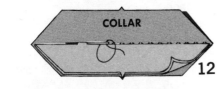

COLLAR

12

UPPER COLLAR PART
fold line

UNDERCOLLAR PART

13

APPLYING SEW-IN INTERFACING

Interfacing is applied to a section before any stay-stitching or construction-stitching is done on the section.

With a shaped facing, pin interfacing to wrong side of outer garment section, carefully matching edges. Stitch directionally (following arrows), ½'' from edges (10). When the edge is curved or slanted, this serves as stay-stitching.

With an extended facing, pin interfacing to wrong side of outer garment section, matching the straight edge of interfacing to garment fold line. Catch interfacing edge to fold line with loose blind-stitch, invisible on right side (11). Stay-stitch neck and shoulders ½'' from edge. The same technique is used if a straight collar or cuff, which will be folded in half lengthwise, is interfaced with a piece reaching just to the fold line.

For a straight collar or cuff where lightweight interfacing has been cut to full outer fabric size, fold the interfacing on the fold line, and slipstitch this fold to the fold line of the outer piece with loose stitches, invisible on right side (12). If you prefer to attach the interfacing by machine, stitch ¼'' away from the fold line, on what will be the undercollar or cuff, where the stitching will not show (13). Open out interfacing and stay-stitch around edges.

On washable garments with worked buttonholes (blouses, children's dresses, etc.), the following finish for an extended facing is very neat and stands up well under washings:

Stitch interfacing to right side of garment facing, edges even (14). Grade seam allowances, clip if necessary. Turn interfacing to wrong side; press. Stay-stitch neck and shoulders ½'' from edge (15-a). Stitch down raw straight edge of interfacing, close to center (15-b); on an open neckline, stop stitching before the point where it would show on outside. Then continue construction (16).

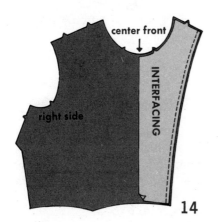

center front

INTERFACING

right side

14

INTERFACING

a

b

wrong side

15

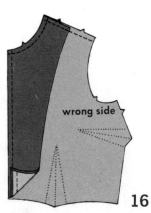

wrong side

16

APPLYING FUSIBLE INTERFACING

Fusibles are easy to apply. First, however, be sure to test any fusible interfacing on your fabric to be certain that your fabric can take the heat, steam and pressure required and that you like the results.

Carefully read the manufacturer's instructions; they are easy, but they vary. For satisfactory results you should have everything right: temperature, amount of steam and pressure, and length of pressing time.

Never slide the iron along—lift it and place it on the next area, over-lapping the former one to make sure of a complete bond (17).

TEST: Use a piece of fabric large enough so you can fuse the interfacing to **half** of it. Then you will be able to compare the fused and the unfused areas. Be sure to follow the manufacturer's instructions.

LOOK AT THE RESULTS: Be sure the fabric has not been adversely affected by the heat, steam and pressure used. Check the right side of the fabric to see if fusing has caused a ridge, an uneven texture, or stiffness. Fold the fabric in half where the inter-facing stops to see if the interfacing looks and feels better on the outer side or the underside.

The fabric, the type of interfacing and the garment style will determine which of the following ways you should use the interfacing.

- If the interfacing edge does not show on the right side, where the interfacing stops in the body of the outer fabric, and you like the look and feel of the interfaced area, you can fuse the interfacing to the **outer fabric,** if desired.
- If the interfacing edge shows on the right side as a line or ridge, but you still like the look and feel of the interfaced area, choose one of the methods that follows, depending on the effect you want.

   Fuse interfacing to the **entire garment section,** such as a jacket front, for a crisp, tailored look (see MENSWEAR, p. 171).

   Fuse interfacing to the **facing sections only** for firm front edges but a softer look to the whole garment.

- If the fusing has adversely affected the outer fabric, you can attach the interfacing to the **facings only,** as above, and/or the undercollar which will not show (normally it is attached to the upper collar and the garment section, so it can lie between the outer fabric and the seam allowance edges).
- If the interfacing is very lightweight, and you find it does not provide enough body and crispness, you may want to fuse interfacing to **both the facing and the entire front.**
- If there is an underlining, fuse the interfacing to the **facing sections only.**

Lingerie

By making your own lingerie, you can duplicate, at a fraction of the store price, elegant slips, gowns and negligees you might not otherwise think of possessing. You can make your favorite styles, which may be difficult to find in stores, and also be assured of the proper fit. Brides, especially, may find it rewarding to make some of their own lingerie.

Nylon tricot, familiar to us through most of the ready-made lingerie we buy, is the most popular fabric for lingerie. It is a knit fabric, with the ribs of the knit running lengthwise on the right side and crosswise on the wrong side. With its stretchability assuring comfort and fit, its easy care and durability, it is hard to beat for lingerie. Tricot is the only fabric we shall cover in this chapter; we shall not deal with spandex power net and the heavy stretch lace used in bras, girdles and swim wear. If you are using a woven fabric, some of these techniques may be used, but also be sure to see the chapter on FABRICS.

PATTERNS

You will find some lingerie patterns at all pattern counters, with the usual size and measurement information on the envelope. There are, however, other lingerie patterns available, offered by fabric shops, shops specializing in knit fabrics, and through direct mail order. These patterns may be sold either by dress size or by ready-to-wear lingerie size; they may include several sizes on one pattern, with special directions for their use.

Do not overlook the possibility of making your own patterns from old garments you have liked for their style and fit (see p. 140).

NOTIONS

Elastic—Use "soft" elastic. This usually has one straight and one fluted or picot edge (1), which may be placed either up or down. Nylon elastic is best, but the most easily found elastics are blends with varying percentages of nylon, rayon and rubber.

Lace edging—Almost any shrink-proof lace can be used, providing it is not too stiff or heavy. Stretch lace, which comes in several widths and usually packaged, is ideal for curved edges because it is easy to manipulate.

Shoulder straps—Ready-made, adjustable straps are available in a limited color range. If you cannot buy straps to match your fabric, you can easily make them of heavy satin ribbon, adding, if you wish, adjustors taken from old or ready-made straps. You can also make straps from self-fabric, either tubing or flat-folded and topstitched.

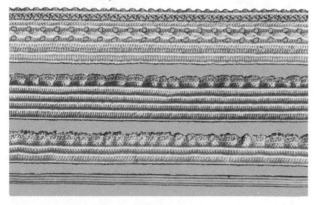

1

THREAD AND NEEDLES

Thread—Use polyester core thread, regular or extra-fine; these threads, while fine, are strong and have the necessary elasticity for tricot.

Needles—For machine stitching, use ballpoint needle #10 with a light ball, or Universal Ballpoint machine needle #11. Both these needles will safely stitch tricot. Change your machine needle often. A new needle assures you of no needle damage to fabric. A blunt or burred needle can damage your fabric and thread and cause skipped stitches (see p. 250).

For hand-sewing, use a #9 or #10 needle.

FABRIC PREPARATION

Tricot can become stretched while on the bolt. To relax the yarns and also to remove any excess finishing solution, thoroughly soak or machine-wash the fabric. Use a fabric softener to reduce static electricity. Gently squeeze out excess water and allow the fabric to dry on a flat surface. When dry, mark wrong side of fabric at the selvage with red or blue pencil or with Magic transparent tape. (If you are in doubt which is the wrong side, stretch the fabric edge on the crosswise grain and it will roll to the right side.)

PINNING, CUTTING AND MARKING

Note the width of your seam allowances; they may be different from those on other patterns and may vary in the same lingerie pattern.

Pinning and cutting—Use the finest, sharpest pins you can find, or ballpoint pins.

Spread the fabric on the cutting table; roll up excess so it won't hang over the edge. When placing pattern pieces on fabric, keep in mind that the direction of greater stretch in tricot is in the crosswise, which should go **around** the body. When an arrow says "stretch", place it on the crosswise grain.

It is a good idea to weight the pattern down to prevent shifting (2). Put pins in seam allowances only, so pin-marks, if any, will not show. Cut notches outward as usual; **do not** make snips into seam allowances. Add notches at center front and center back.

After cutting, indicate the wrong side of each section with a piece of Magic transparent tape which does not damage the fabric and can be easily removed later.

Marking—To transfer pattern markings use pins, basting or a red or blue pencil that you have first tested on a scrap, making sure it will wash out. **Do not** use dressmaker's tracing paper or ordinary pencil, which do not wash out. Mark darts on inside of stitching line, just short of the point.

SEWING

PREPARATION—Before you begin, check your machine cabinet, sewing surfaces and fingernails for rough spots that may cause snags in the tricot. The machine may be either straight stitch or zigzag. **Do not use a zigzag attachment,** because it "grabs" and damages tricot and produces unsatisfactory stitching. See MACHINE-STITCHING, page 148 for adjusting tension, pressure, balance.

Loosen tension but keep a balanced stitch.

Test pressure and adjust your machine, if necessary. An even feed or roller foot may prove helpful and may make handling tricot easier.

Set the machine at 10–12 stitches to the inch for either straight stitch or zigzag. A shorter stitch may damage the fabric. Zigzag stitches that are too close together will make a stiff seam and can cause the fabric to be caught in the needle hole.

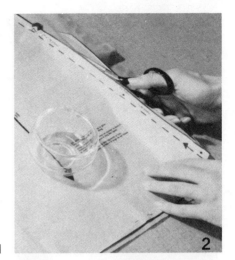

STITCHING—Contrary to usual practice, tricot must be held taut in stitching. This technique puts extra thread in the seams to help reduce puckers. It also holds the fabric down and prevents skipped stitches.

When starting, lower needle by hand and hold both thread-ends back. Otherwise, the static electricity generated by sewing on synthetics may draw the threads to the bobbin area and cause bunching.

Stitch very slowly, holding fabric taut in front and in back of the presser foot as you stitch (3); fast stitching can make the fabric rise and fall with the needle, causing skipped stitches.

Never stitch over pins. This can damage the needle and the fabric. To remove pins, stop before each pin with the needle down.

Don't back-tack. This may cause the fabric to bunch up under the foot. If necessary, pull thread-ends to wrong side; tie and clip threads.

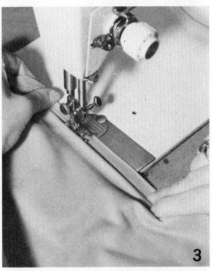

SEAMS—Always make a test seam. Since the seam allowances on lingerie patterns vary, be sure to stitch at the width indicated. Trim off any excess **after** stitching. Make two rows of stitching, as follows:

For the first row, use a straight stitch, which allows better control of the fabric and produces a smoother seam line on the right side. On a zigzag machine, set the needle position to right or left instead of center, to avoid having the fabric pushed down the wide hole.

For the second row, the stitch can be either straight or zigzag. Straight stitch should be ⅛″ from first row (4). With zigzag, stitch close to the straight first row (5). Trim seam, if necessary. In general, tricot seams do not have to be pressed.

If your machine has a stitch that seams and overcasts in one operation, you may want to use it. Test it first, stitching on the ⅝″ seam line and trimming excess fabric after stitching.

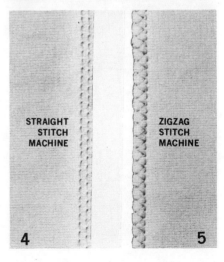

STRAIGHT STITCH MACHINE

ZIGZAG STITCH MACHINE

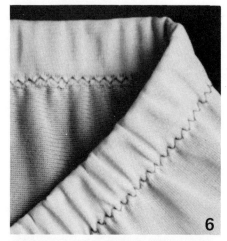

6

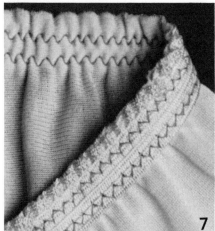

7

8

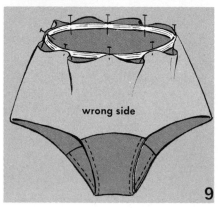

wrong side

9

ELASTIC

RECOMMENDED WIDTHS—¼″ to ½″ for waist of briefs or half-slips; ¼″ for hips of bikinis; ¼″ for all legs.

MEASURING FOR LENGTH—If your measurements are exactly the same as those specified by the pattern, use the ones given on the pattern. Otherwise, figure measurements as follows:

Waist: For elastic in a casing, deduct 2″ from your waist measurement. For topstitched or stitched-and-turned elastic (see below), deduct 3″ (stitched-on elastic doesn't entirely return to its original length).

Hips for bikinis: Try on a pair to see where the top edge comes. Measure around hips at that point. For elastic in a casing, deduct 8″. For stitched-on elastic, deduct 9″.

Legs: For briefs, measure around top of thigh. Cut elastic to this length. For bikinis, which are cut at varying angles, finish waist and try on; hold tape measure around leg along edge of fabric. Cut elastic in a casing to that measurement; for stitched-on elastic deduct 1″.

ATTACHING ELASTIC—Elastic may be inserted in a casing or stitched on. Two methods of stitching on elastic are given below, but the machine stitch will have to be tested first.

Elastic in a casing (6)—Recommended for longer wear, easy replacement, and in cases where the elastic does not match the fabric color. Casing allowance should be the width of elastic plus ¼″. Turn fabric edge to wrong side on fold line; pin. Stitch close to raw edge, with either straight or zigzag stitch, but leave a small opening. Insert the elastic. Overlap ends ½″ and stitch securely; close the opening.

Always test before attaching a stitched-on elastic—the tension used for stitching seams may not be right for elastic. Cut a 4″ length of elastic and a 6″ piece of tricot on the crosswise grain. Pin ends of elastic to ends of tricot. Stitch with elastic side up: For straight stitching, stretch both elastic and tricot; for zigzag or multi-stitch zigzag, stretch elastic just enough to match the tricot, and let it relax gradually as you stitch. **Tie thread-ends securely.** Grasping both ends, stretch elastic and tricot as far as they will go. If either the top or the bottom thread breaks, the tension is off and must be adjusted.

Topstitched elastic (7)—The quickest, easiest application. Cut seam allowance from edge to which elastic is to be attached.

Set the machine for a long stitch. Join elastic ends in a ½″ seam, stitching back and forth several times. Open the seam and stitch the ends down flat, with a rectangle of long stitches (8). On elastic and on garment edge, mark off eight equal sections (you do this by folding and refolding, placing pins at folds). Match elastic to the garment at these points and pin, wrong side of elastic to right side of fabric, top edges even (9). With right side up and elastic on top, make a row of straight or zigzag stitches along both top and bottom edges (7). Or make one row of multi-stitch zigzag through center of elastic (the stitch should be half the width of the elastic).

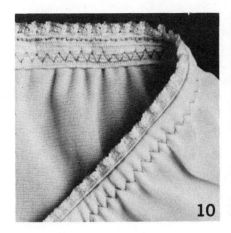
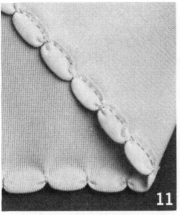
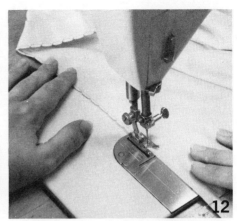

Stitched-and-turned elastic (10)—The elastic may be turned either to the right or the wrong side, enclosing the cut edge of the garment. Seam allowance should equal the width of the elastic.

Follow instructions (joining elastic, pinning to garment) through second paragraph of instructions for **Topstitched elastic,** on the preceding page; but decide first if you want the elastic on the inside or the outside: Pin it to the opposite side, with the **straight edge** of the elastic exactly at the cut edge of the fabric. Stitch along lower edge of elastic, with straight stitch, stretching both elastic and tricot. Trim seam allowance close to stitching. Fold elastic to other side. Using either straight or zigzag stitch, stitch the straight elastic edge to the garment, stretching as before.

EDGE FINISHES

SHELL EDGING—A nice finish that may be done by hand or by machine.

By hand (11)—Trim the hem allowance to ¼″. Fold the hem allowance to wrong side. Working from wrong side, take 2 or 3 small running stitches along the raw edge in **hem allowance only.** Take 2 stitches over edge of hem as shown, pulling the thread taut.

By machine (12)—Use the blind-hemming stitch. Following the instructions below, test the stitch first on a sample of your fabric.

Fold hem under 1″; pin or baste. Place under the presser foot right side up, with hem fold facing left. Stitch slowly with the straight stitches running parallel to the fold and the zigzag stitch going over the fold, not piercing it. Remove pins as you come to them. If the stitch does not pull in the edge enough to form shells, tighten top tension. After stitching, trim away the extra hem fabric on the wrong side.

LACE—Pin the lace to the right side of the fabric. For a **see-through** effect (13), topstitch inner edge with one row of zigzag or two rows of straight stitching; trim away tricot close to stitching (14). For an **opaque** look (15), topstitch both edges with zigzag or straight stitching; if necessary, trim tricot at edge, close to stitching.

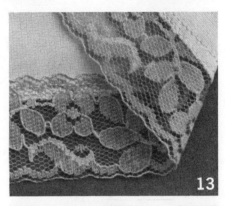
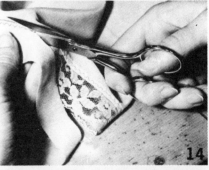
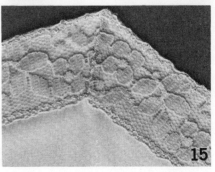

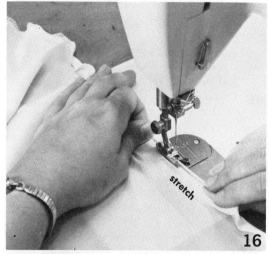

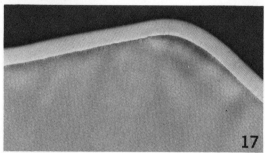

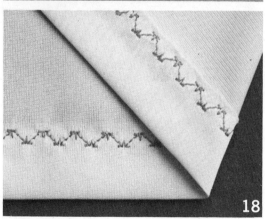

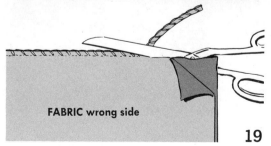

LETTUCE EDGING—This ruffled finish is done with a medium length, narrow zigzag stitch. Since the results vary with the fabric and the machine used, be sure to test it first on a sample of your fabric; if necessary, adjust the length and width of the stitch for the desired effect.

Trim the hem allowance to ¼". With right side up, stretch fabric so edge rolls to the right side. Stitch over rolled edge, **stretching** the fabric as you stitch (16). As the fabric relaxes, lettuce-like ruffles will form.

OTHER NARROW HEMS for lingerie include a simplified hand-rolled hem and an edge-stitched hem (see p. 126).

FRENCH BINDING (17) makes an elegant tailored-looking finish (see p. 27).

STRAIGHT-EDGE TAILORED HEM (18)—Turn fabric under on hemline; baste or pin in place. Stitching with right side up (the cut edge will show through as a guide), secure the cut edge with two rows of straight machine-stitching, or zigzag stitch, or an open decorative machine stitch.

MAKING A PATTERN FROM AN OLD GARMENT

If you have an old garment you have liked for its style and fit, you may want to take the garment apart and make a pattern you can keep. Before taking it apart, make a few pencil marks across each seam and dart to use as matching-points. Mark position of straps, if any, before removing them. Mark garment center front and back. Mark grain line on each section as follows: Lay flat, ribbed side up; holding fabric taut, run a sharp pencil along fabric in the direction of the ribs—the pencil point will automatically rest between two ribs and follow a straight line. Mark a few inches at a time.

Cut the garment apart along stitching lines on wrong side, cutting off the entire seam allowance (19). Do not cut off lace or other trim. Cut off any elastic.

Press each section flat and pin to paper. Carefully trace around the edges and transfer all markings to the paper. Remove the section. Crease the paper through the center back or front. Since the two halves will seldom be exactly symmetrical, straighten and adjust lines. Decide on the edge finish for the top and bottom and add the necessary allowances. Add ¼" seam allowances to the other edges.

FABRIC wrong side

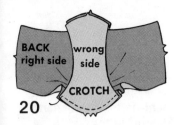

20

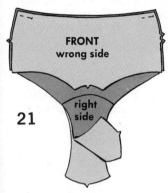

21

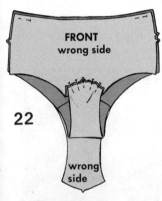

22

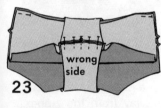

23

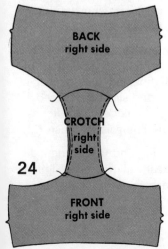

24

CROTCH ON PANTIES

The crotch, cut double, is attached and the seams are enclosed, before any other seams are sewn. Crotch seam allowance is generally ¼''; if not, trim to ¼'', including corresponding seam allowances on pants sections.

a. The wider end of crotch pieces is usually the back. Assemble the two crotch pieces, wrong sides out, with the matching edge of one pants section between them, all edges even. Pin and stitch (20).

b. Pin front to back pants section with right sides together (21). Match the free end of the top crotch section to the corresponding edge of pants. Pin (22).

c. Wrap the remaining crotch section around the pants as shown (23); include the end in the pinned edge, pants edge between crotch edges, as shown. Stitch.

d. Turn the pants out of the crotch sections. Unpin the pants sections. Stitch the open crotch edges together (24). Complete the panties.

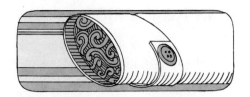

Linings

Since lining, underlining, and interlining all consist of different fabrics added to the inside of a garment, let us begin by explaining them. Each one has a different purpose and is handled in a different way.

A lining is assembled separately, as though it were a second garment. Placed inside a garment wrong side to wrong side and attached along the edges, it provides the garment with a perfectly smooth inside finish. Outer garments that may be worn open or taken off casually, such as jackets, coats, capes, are the ones most often lined.

In other garments, a lining, while not showing, will always add a feeling of luxury. It will also add comfort, if the garment fabric is even slightly rough to the touch. It may make wearing a slip unnecessary. In a straight skirt or pants, a lining will prevent bagginess at the seat and knees. A skirt is sometimes lined to just below the seat to prevent stretching and wrinkling. If made a tiny bit smaller than the garment (see "Assemble the lining" on the next page), a lining will help preserve a garment's shape. However, since it is not caught in the seams, it cannot contribute to the shaping itself. And if the garment fabric needs more body, use an **underlining,** which, as a backing for the garment fabric, is stitched into the garment seams (see UNDERLINING).

Interlining, added to a lining for warmth, is usually handled as a backing for the lining. As such, it is attached to the lining sections before they are assembled and stitched into the lining seams. In tailored clothes, the interlining is a loosely-woven wool. In non-tailored outer wear, a common interlining is non-woven polyester fleece, slightly stiffer than the woven wool. There are also special lining fabrics that are backed with finishes, allowing them to act as both lining and interlining.

LINING FABRICS

Fabrics used for linings may or may not be made specially for the purpose. There is a wide choice of special fabrics in the lining section of fabric stores. On the other hand, many dress fabrics that imitate silk—crepe, taffeta, satin, tricot—also make beautiful linings. To be suitable, a fabric should be smooth to the touch, soft, pliable, and light enough in weight not to interfere in any way with the hang of the garment fabric. Fiber content and construction may vary. China silk to line something soft and dressy, smooth-surfaced cotton blends for casual wear, are excellent.

In an ensemble, the coat or jacket is often lined with the fabric used for the dress or blouse, for a coordinated effect. If this fabric is expensive, or does not slip on and off easily, the sleeves can be lined with a lining fabric.

Fake fur may serve as lining in a winter coat or jacket. In such a case, the coat style should be of loose fit to allow room for the fur. When cutting the lining pieces, eliminate the center back pleat provided in a regular coat lining. For less bulk and ease in slipping the coat on and off, lining fabric can be used in sleeves. See page 76 for handling fake fur.

Yardage needed—When you want to add a lining not given in the pattern, pick out the pattern pieces which will be lined (not facings, collar, cuffs, or waistband); for a jacket or coat with front facings, the front lining will be smaller than the pattern piece (see CUTTING THE LINING on the next page). Use the pattern pieces to figure the yardage, taking into account the width of lining fabric.

LINING A DRESS, SKIRT OR PANTS

The directions that follow are for adding a lining where none is included in the pattern.

CUTTING AND ASSEMBLING

See Yardage needed, above. Cut the lining from the garment pattern, omitting the sections mentioned and a kick pleat, if any. Transfer all markings.

Complete the outer garment except for the upper edge (neck or waist) and the hem on a dress or skirt. On sleeves or pants, turn hems up and catch in place, leaving cut edge raw (not turned under). On a sleeveless dress, leave armhole edges unfinished.

Assemble the lining, leaving all outer edges unfinished, including zipper opening, and any kick pleat or slit in a skirt. To lessen bulk, press darts in the opposite direction from garment darts. Press seams open. Leave lining wrong side out. IMPORTANT NOTE: If you want the lining to serve in preserving garment shape, make it slightly smaller than the garment by taking ¾" seam allowances on the lengthwise seams.

ATTACHING THE LINING

a. Place the lining inside the garment, wrong sides together, lining sleeves inside garment sleeves. Matching seams, darts and markings, pin the raw upper edges together (neck or waist), and the armholes on a sleeveless dress. Baste lining to garment ½" from these edges, turning lining edges under at top of a zipper opening.

b. On a dress, apply any facings or other edge finish. On a skirt or pants, apply waistband or other waist finish.

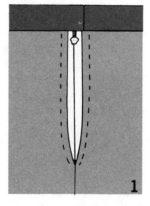 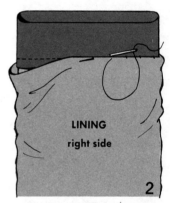

c. At a zipper opening, turn lining edges under and slipstitch to zipper tapes, a scant ¼" from coil or chain. To keep the lining away from the zipper, make a line of running stitches, catching the lining to the garment seam allowance (1).

d. Working with the garment turned so that the lining is entirely on outside, trim lining at bottom of sleeves or pants even with finished outside edge; turn ½" under and press. Pin and slipstitch this edge over the hem, just covering raw edge and stitches. The slight extra length in the lining is for ease (2).

e. Working between the lining and the wrong side of outer fabric, catch one seam allowance of lining to one seam allowance of garment with a long, loose basting stitch at the following locations: On a dress with sleeves, at shoulder seams and side seams from underarm to waist or hips; on a sleeveless dress, at side seams only because the lining is held in place at the armholes; on a skirt or pants, at side seams from waist to hips.

f. On a dress or skirt, complete the garment hem. The lining hem generally hangs free, the lining being made 1″ shorter than the garment. At a slit, turn lining edges under and hem to edges of opening. At a kick pleat, finish lining with a narrow hem and let it hang free.

LINING A JACKET OR COAT

To line a jacket or coat for which your pattern does not provide lining pieces or instructions, follow the directions below.

CUTTING THE LINING

Back—Use the garment back pattern—the necessary changes can be made directly on the fabric. A lining in a tailored jacket or coat requires extra ease in the back. To provide this, place the pattern on the folded fabric, with center back 1″ from fold. Cut out, mark darts if any, and remove the pattern. Pin the neck facing pattern to top of folded lining, shoulder and neck edges even. Mark lower edge of facing with chalk; remove the pattern. Measure and mark another line 1¼″ above chalk line, as shown (3). Cut out the neck on this line.

Front—For this, the lining will need a new pattern piece. Place pattern for facing over pattern for front and mark edge of facing on front pattern. On a sheet of tissue paper, trace the remaining part of the front pattern, adding 1¼″ at marked edge of facing, as shown (4). Cut out. Cut two from lining fabric.

Sleeves—Cut from garment pattern.

ASSEMBLING THE LINING

Baste up a 1″ pleat at center back (5) and press it to one side. Fasten upper end of pleat with a few catch-stitches (6). Catch-stitch pleat at waist level in the same way. Stitch darts halfway, as shown (5). Assemble the lining completely, joining all seams and setting in sleeves.

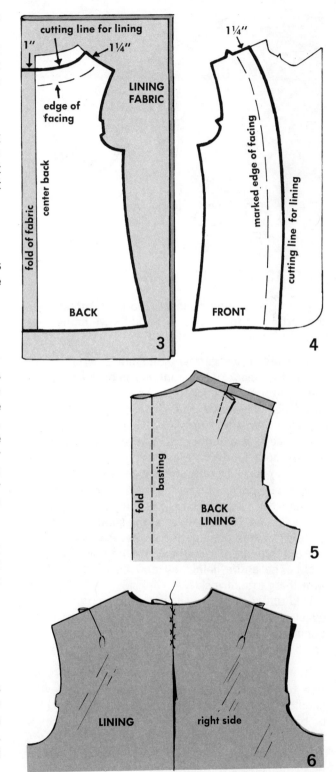

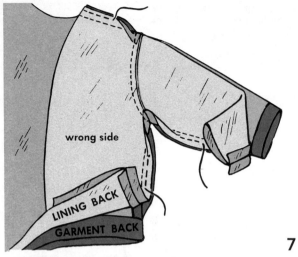

wrong side

LINING BACK

GARMENT BACK

7

ATTACHING THE LINING

This is done after facings have been attached to the garment and the garment and sleeve hems have been completed.

By hand—Have garment and lining wrong sides out. Pin the back of the lining to the back of the garment, wrong sides together, seams matched with open seam allowances on top of each other, as shown (7). With a loose basting stitch, catch one lining seam allowance to one garment seam allowance **exactly** as shown. Join seams in this manner at shoulder, on sleeves to below elbows, and at side seams to hipline.

Now put both your hands inside the lining and through the two armholes, reaching down into the lining sleeves. On both sides at the same time, grasp bottoms of lining and garment sleeves together. Pull sleeves through, turning body of lining over the garment. The entire lining will now be right side out, with the garment inside.

Fold under the seam allowance on front and neck edges of lining and pin to facings ⅝″ from edge. Beginning and ending 3″ from garment hem, slip-stitch lining to facings.

By machine—Place garment and lining right sides together, lining sleeves inside garment sleeves. With shoulder seams matched and raw edges even, pin or baste front and neck edges of lining to facings. Stitch, beginning and ending 3″ from garment hem. Turn to right side. Catch the seam allowances together as for a dress with sleeves; see step **e** on page 142.

HEMS

As a rule, in a jacket the lining hem is attached to the garment hem, while in a coat it hangs free. This, however, is a matter of choice. In sleeves, the lining is always attached.

For a free-hanging lining hem, remove basting at center back pleat, and see HEMMING THE LINING, page 129.

For an attached lining hem, see HEMMING THE LINING, page 129, and then remove basting at center back pleat.

TRIMMING

This is strictly optional, but you may, for a finishing touch, wish to add a line of decoration where the lining joins the facing of a coat or jacket. It can be done in one of two ways: **Rick rack or piping** can be inserted in the seam by machine-stitching it to the lining **before** the lining is attached to the garment (see PIPING, p. 30). **Narrow braid or ribbon** can be blind-stitched over the seam **after** the lining is attached.

LINING REACHING TO GARMENT EDGE

This is for a garment with a front opening, such as a coat, jacket or vest, where the lining reaches to and finishes all edges.

CUTTING AND ASSEMBLING

Cut the lining from the garment pattern, omitting any facings (remember that facings have already been omitted on the garment). Assemble garment and lining completely, joining all seams and setting in sleeves, but leaving all edges unfinished.

ATTACHING THE LINING

a. On both the garment and the lining, mark the hemline and cut away hem allowance ⅝″ from marked line (remember that this makes it impossible to lengthen the garment later).

b. With lining and garment right sides together, and seams and darts matched, pin and stitch around neckline and front opening edges; trim and clip seam allowances; understitch.

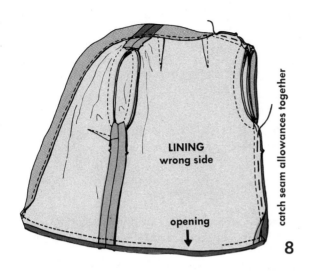

LINING
wrong side

opening
↓

catch seam allowances together

8

e. Push the garment through the opening at bottom and bring it right side out. Reach inside the garment sleeves and through the lining sleeves; grasp the ends and pull the lining through.

Slipstitch the opening together. Press garment edge so that lining will not show on right side. To finish sleeve hems, see step **d** on page 142. On a sleeveless garment, stitch the lining to the armholes and complete with facings.

GARMENT WITH BINDING

Cut the lining from the garment pattern, omitting any facings (remember that facings have already been omitted on the garment). Assemble both garment and lining completely, joining all seams and setting in sleeves, but leaving all edges unfinished. Leave lining wrong side out. On both garment and lining, cut off the entire seam allowance (and hem allowance) on edges to be bound.

Place the lining inside the garment, wrong sides together, the way it will be worn, lining sleeves inside garment sleeves. Matching edges, seams, darts and markings, pin lining in place. Baste together ⅜'' from edges, leaving an opening of about 10'' at bottom edge. Reaching through the opening, catch seam allowances of garment and lining together at shoulder and side seams as directed for a dress with sleeves; see step **e** on page 142. Then baste the opening together and apply the binding.

c. Stitch the bottom edge, leaving an opening as shown (8) through which to turn garment. Press this seam open; trim corners and grade seam allowance.

d. Catch seam allowances of garment and lining together at shoulder and side seams as follows: Reach in between the lining and the garment and bring the front edge of the garment inside the lining until the seam allowances of one side seam on garment and lining can be placed together. Catch one seam allowance to the other with a loose basting stitch (8). Repeat on the other side seam. Catch lining and garment together at shoulder seam allowances (8).

Machine-Stitching

The key to success in stitching any fabric with any thread lies in your sewing machine. Like today's fabrics, today's sewing machines are doing things undreamed-of a generation ago. Naturally, they are a little more complicated than the machines were then; a little study, therefore, is in order, and will repay you a hundred fold. Once you have made yourself truly familiar with your machine, it will adjust to your needs as easily as turning a dial.

Accordingly, before going into the different ways of stitching, let us take a look at the machine that is doing the work.

KNOW YOUR SEWING MACHINE

To begin with, even if you have already been using your machine, take time off to study it with the help of the **sewing machine manual.** Identify its different parts and familiarize yourself with their names. Even if you know how to set in the needle, thread the machine and wind and insert the bobbin, do these things once by following the manual—you may have overlooked some extremely helpful detail.

And read up on the **care** of the machine.

On the pages that follow, there are a few basic things you will want to know about your machine.

ACCESSORIES AND ATTACHMENTS

Many of these come with the machine. Examine the extra ones that are in the box and, with the help of the manual, find out the use of each piece—many are great time-savers. Trying them out is discovery and fun. The manual will also give you a list of other available attachments.

THROAT PLATES—You may not be aware that many machines have more than one throat plate, which can be changed as needed. Most throat plates have guide lines which help you keep an even seam allowance.

General-purpose plate (1)—This is the wide-hole throat plate that comes with the zigzag sewing machine. Together with the general-purpose foot, it allows you to change from straight to zigzag stitch and back without touching anything but a lever or a dial. The only disadvantage of this plate is that, when straight-stitching, the needle may push some light-weight or permanent press fabrics into the wide hole, causing puckering and skipped stitches (see "If the seam is puckered", p. 149).

Straight-stitch plate (2)—This is the throat plate with the small, round hole, that comes with the straight-stitch machine. But even with a zigzag machine, it is a good idea to have one for straight stitching on some fabrics.

GENERAL PURPOSE THROAT PLATE AND FOOT **1**

STRAIGHT STITCH THROAT PLATE AND FOOT **2**

Feed cover plate—This is used to cover the feed dog as needed. When the action of the feed dog is not wanted (as in sewing on buttons, and in free-action work such as darning and some embroidery), the feed dog in certain machines can simply be dropped; for other machines you will need this cover.

PRESSER FEET—Besides the regular presser foot on your machine, you may, as the occasion arises, need some of those listed below. Don't hesitate to buy a special foot—it may be essential to your work, or at least very helpful.

General-purpose foot (1)—For either straight or zig-zag stitching. It comes with the zigzag machine.

Straight-stitch foot (2)—The foot that comes with the straight-stitch machine. Used on a zigzag machine with the straight-stitch plate when the nature of the fabric or the stitching demands close control.

Zipper foot—Essential for inserting zippers (see p. 264 and stitching corded seams.

Special-purpose or pattern-stitching foot—For close decorative zigzag stitching, particularly the raised or satin type. The foot has a wide groove on the underside, behind the needle, to accommodate the embroidery and avoid squashing it.

Even feed or roller foot—These feet may be very helpful for fabrics that need more control (such as some knits), or that are hard to feed, such as piles, leather imitations, plastics.

NEEDLES—To choose the correct type and size of needles for general use, see the THREAD AND NEEDLE CHART on page 251. In addition, a twin needle (3), that makes two rows of stitching at a time, is available for some zigzag machines. There is even a triple needle that makes three rows of stitching. See your manual. **3**

BUTTONHOLE ATTACHMENT—Fitted to the straight-stitch machine, it makes excellent machine-worked buttonholes. (All zigzag machines can make buttonholes and some are automatic.) Do not confuse this with a **zigzag attachment** which has limited use and does not make buttonholes.

NEEDLE POSITIONS

A change in needle position is possible only with zigzag machines. The positions are center (regular), left, and right. These settings can be very useful for stitching at widths different from the usual ones, such as in edge-stitching. Moving the needle to the side may also solve the problem of puckering (see "If the seam is puckered", p. 149).

THE STITCHES AVAILABLE

There are three basic kinds of machine stitching. (For specific details about stitches, see page 150).

Straight or plain stitching, still by far the most commonly used, is made by both the straight-stitch and the zigzag machines. In straight stitch, the needles goes up and down in the same spot while the feed dog (mechanically, "dog" means a gripping device) moves the fabric evenly backward under the presser foot or forward for reverse (back-tacking). Straight stitch can be used anywhere, even for decoration, as in topstitching (see p. 151). It has no variations except in length. (NOTE: Chain stitch, a form of straight stitch, is available on some machines —see your manual.)

Zigzag stitching is made by the needle going from side to side while the feed dog moves the fabric backward (or forward for reverse). The rate at which the fabric moves regulates the separation of the stitches, which is still called the stitch **length,** while the side-to-side motion (or stitch) can be made **narrow** or **wide** (4). Zigzag stitch has a great many variations, designed for different purposes (see p. 150).

Forward-and-reverse stitching is also made by some zigzag machines. In this, the needle may work in one spot and/or from side to side, while the feed dog moves the fabric backward and forward in a programmed motion designed for strength and elasticity. In the straight stretch stitch (p. 150, ill. 19), for instance, the needle takes two stitches forward and one back, putting three stitches in the same spot.

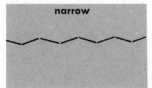
narrow

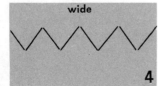
wide

4

FOR BEAUTIFUL STITCHING

Assuming that your machine is in good condition, it should stitch perfectly every time if you make sure that:

> **the machine is clean,**
> **thread and needle are right for the fabric,**
> **needle and bobbin are correctly inserted and the machine is correctly threaded,**
> **pressure, tension and balance are right—see the next page,**
> **you start and end correctly,**
> **you stitch at a steady, even pace (5).**

A CLEAN SEWING MACHINE

● Keep your machine covered when not in use.

● Have a lint brush handy: It is inexpensive and sold in most places that carry sewing machine supplies. Before using the machine, whisk the brush around each side of the feed dog and around the bobbin case.

● How often you clean your machine more thoroughly depends on how much you use it. You must do so in any case after stitching any linty or fuzzy fabrics; also before oiling. Remove the throat plate and bobbin case (if removable) and go over the entire machine with the lint brush.

● Most machines need some lubrication. The manual will tell you how, when, and where to oil. Be careful not to put more than one drop in each place— the oil may spread and get on the fabric later. And be sure to use **sewing-machine oil,** not ordinary machine oil.

● If a scrap of thread is caught in the bobbin case, turn the balance wheel slightly to release it, and draw it out (use tweezers if necessary).

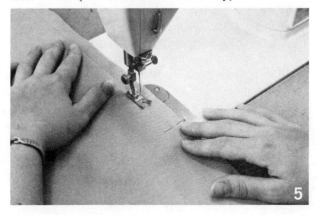
5

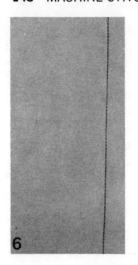
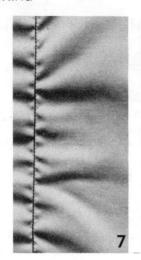
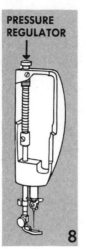
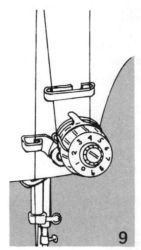

FABRIC, THREAD AND NEEDLE

For coordinating fabric, thread, needle and stitch length, see the THREAD AND NEEDLE CHART on page 251.

NEEDLE AND BOBBIN THREADING

A lot of trouble can be caused by a needle or bobbin not inserted correctly, or by a detail omitted in threading the machine. Check with your sewing machine manual.

PRESSURE, TENSION AND BALANCE

Depending on their weight, finish, fiber and bulk, different fabrics may require more or less pressure on the presser foot, and tighter or looser thread tension. If you have these right, and the top thread and bobbin thread are balanced (at equal tension), you will have smooth seams (6). Having just one of them wrong may cause the fabric to pucker (7); but you can check out and adjust all three by means of a single, very simple test. See TEST SEAM on the next page.

Pressure is what holds the fabric in place between the presser foot and the feed dog. In some machines it is self-adjusting; in this case just check the tension and balance. When the pressure is correct, the two layers of fabric in a seam are held firmly but lightly, and travel under the needle at the same rate. In most machines, there is a pressure regulator usually a thumbscrew (8) connected with the presser foot as shown. The regulator, however, may be a dial on the inside (see your manual).

Tension of thread is regulated by the metal discs on the tension dial (9) for the top thread, and by a screw on the bobbin case for the bobbin thread (10). Today's fabrics require rather loose thread tension.

A balanced stitch means that the stitching looks the same on both sides (top thread and bobbin thread), the two threads having equal tension (11).

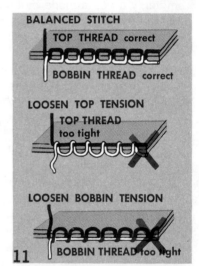

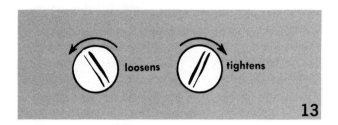

TEST SEAM

This test should be made for each new garment you are about to stitch. Please note that on all screws and dials, a counterclockwise turn loosens, a clockwise turn tightens (13). To adjust a screw, give it only a **small fraction** of a turn (something like 5 minutes on a clock face).

Thread the machine for the garment you are preparing to stitch (thread of different colors on top and in the bobbin, however, will help show up an imbalance). From scraps of your garment fabric, cut two strips, about 3″ by 8″, on the lengthwise grain (with knits, cut crosswise or on the bias, as stitches get lost in the lengthwise ribs). Place the strips together, edges even, and pin together at the bottom with a pin placed crosswise. Seam two edges as shown, from top end to pin (12).

. . . **If a ripple forms** in the top layer, as shown (12), the pressure is too heavy: Loosen the pressure regulator. If the fabric does not feed through properly, the pressure may be too light; tighten the regulator.

. . . **If the stitching is tighter** on one side of the fabric than on the other, the stitch is not balanced (11): Loosen the tension on that side—either the tension dial (9) or the bobbin-case screw (10), using the small screwdriver that comes with the machine.

. . . **If the seam is puckered** while the tension seems loose enough, it may be that your general-purpose throat plate is drawing the fabric into its wide hole. Try moving the needle from center position to left or right position, which gives better support to the fabric. Or try the straight-stitch (small hole) throat plate and presser foot. If the stitching still puckers, the tension must be too tight, even if it is balanced. Loosen both top and bobbin tension.

After making an adjustment on the machine, cut away the test seam on your trial piece, and repeat the test until there is no ripple, and the stitching is smooth and the same on both sides.

STARTING AND ENDING

There are a few motions you should go through as you start and finish a line of stitching. They are essential to good stitching and will quickly become automatic.

Before starting to stitch:

a. Bring the thread take-up lever to its highest point; otherwise the thread will come out of the needle with the first stitch. To raise the lever, turn the hand wheel.

b. Bring the end of the threaded top thread under the presser foot and extend both the top and bobbin thread-ends to the back (diagonally to one side on zigzag machines). Hold the two thread-ends for a stitch or two as you start. This way the thread will not snarl in the bobbin case or get caught in the seam. **Never** let the machine run without any fabric under the presser foot; this snarls and jams up the thread and may even damage the foot.

c. Place the fabric under the presser foot with seam edge to the right and bulk of fabric to the left (always properly supported, never hanging down). Now and then it may be necessary to stitch with bulk to the right, but this is an exception.

d. Before lowering the presser foot, lower the needle into the fabric by turning the hand wheel. This puts the needle exactly where you want it.

e. To secure the row of stitching (optional when it is to be crossed by another row), begin by taking a few stitches in reverse (back-tack).

At end of stitching line:

a. Bring the thread take-up lever to its highest point, turning the hand wheel if necessary. The thread cannot be drawn out otherwise and may break or jam the machine.

b. Raise the presser foot to release the top tension.

c. Remove the fabric by drawing it to the back, then cutting the threads—this prevents strain on the needle.

d. To secure stitching, back-tack before removing the fabric (step **e** above). Or leave thread-ends long enough to tie: Draw one end through to other side and tie the two ends; or tie at fabric edge. Clip thread-ends.

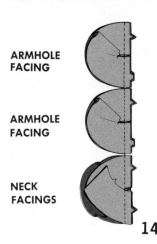

ARMHOLE
FACING

ARMHOLE
FACING

NECK
FACINGS

14

Continuous stitching saves motion. It consists of feeding another seam under the presser foot without clipping thread on the first one. It is especially good for stitching a number of short seams (14). If you wish to secure the stitching on each piece, backtack at beginning and end of each seam.

STITCHING PACE

Stitch at a steady, even pace, even if you have to go slowly. Stitching done in spurts becomes uneven.

SPECIAL STITCHES APPLIED

Do you use your zigzag machine to best advantage? There are some important stitches you may not have tried, and others you may consider just decorative but which have very practical applications. Sewing machine companies may call their stitches by different names and may have slight variations of the stitches we show—check your manual.

FOR SEAMING—Besides the straight stitch you use for most seaming, there are several other stitches

you can use; some will just seam and others will seam and overcast in one operation.

Plain zigzag and **multi-stitch zigzag,** set at the narrowest width (16, 18), can be used in knits when a certain degree of stretch is desired in the seam. Set at regular stitch length or slightly shorter.

Straight stretch stitch (19), which places three stitches in one spot, is highly recommended where strength and elasticity are required (a crotch seam is a good example).

Overlock or **overedge stitches** (20, 21) and **slant overedge stitch** (22) all stitch the seam and overcast the edge in one operation. They are mostly used in knits.

FOR HEMMING—Use the **blindstitch** (23) or the **stretch blindstitch** (24). See your manual; also see BLINDSTITCHED HEMS, page 123.

FOR OVERCASTING—Use the **plain zigzag** (15), **multi-stitch zigzag** (17), or the **universal stitch** (25). These stitches are used for overcasting seams and attaching elastic and stretch lace.

FOR DECORATIVE STITCHES (machine embroidery), consult your manual. In general, when doing embroidery stitches, it is a good idea to change to the pattern-stitching foot mentioned on page 146. Fine or soft fabric can be given stability by a piece of tissue paper, placed between it and the feed dog. In any case, first try out the stitch on a scrap of the fabric.

PLAIN ZIGZAG	SERPENTINE or MULTI-STITCH ZIGZAG	STRAIGHT STRETCH STITCH	OVERLOCK or OVEREDGE STITCHES	SLANT OVEREDGE STITCH	BLIND-STITCH	STRETCH BLIND-STITCH	UNIVERSAL STITCH
15	16 17	18 19	20 21	22	23	24	25

MACHINE STITCHING APPLIED

• **Thread**—For most stitching, top and bobbin thread should be the same, and thread color matched to the fabric (a shade darker makes the best match).

• **Stitch length**—For straight stitching, see the THREAD AND NEEDLE CHART, page 251. In general, remember that well-made, expensive clothes have stitches as short as the fabric requirements allow, while poorly-made ones invariably have long stitches.

• **Pivoting**—When you come to a corner in a stitching line, pivot. In other words, stop with the needle **in** the fabric exactly at the corner (turn wheel by hand if necessary); raise the presser foot, move the fabric around the needle, and lower the presser foot, so stitching can proceed in the next direction.

• **Needle position**—If you change your needle position from center to right or left on a zigzag machine, be sure to maintain the proper seam allowance.

• **Construction-stitching**—Most of the stitching you do will be construction-stitching. This is the stitching that shapes and assembles a garment (as distinct from stay-stitching, gathering, decorative stitching, etc.). It should be done directionally whenever possible (see DIRECTIONAL STITCHING on p. 153). Construction-stitching consists mostly of seams, but also includes darts, and topstitching that attaches clothing details, such as patch pockets. Most construction is done with straight stitch, but the greater elasticity of zigzag and stretch stitches sometimes makes them preferable where stretch is desired.

• **Straight stitching**—The following are common uses of straight stitching. For specific information on SEAMS AND SEAM FINISHES, see that chapter.

TOPSTITCHING is stitching that shows on the outside of a garment. It is sometimes functional, but most often it is purely decorative. Generally, it is done on the right side, not only because there is better control of the stitching from its visible side, but also because on most machines the stitching looks better on top than underneath. Sometimes, however, if you use a heavy thread such as buttonhole twist or pearl cotton for the topstitching, it may not work on top of your machine; in this case, you may put the heavy thread in the bobbin and stitch from the wrong side, checking placement of stitching very carefully.

Stitch length will depend on fabric, thread, and the effect desired. The thread used is very important, but usually it is the same thread as that used in construction. If it is to match the fabric, it should be matched carefully. For decorative effects, there are various possibilities.

Doubled thread makes stitching more prominent. Whether you double the top thread or the bobbin thread, try it out first. Doubling the top thread is relatively easy: If your machine has two spindles, use two spools; if it has only one spindle, fill two bobbins with thread and place them on the spindle, one on top of the other. Then handle the two threads as one. If your machine has a double set of tension discs (for use with the twin needle), bring the threads through the discs separately and then handle them as one. To thread the needle, a needle threader is helpful. Use a #14 needle, or even a #16 needle, if your fabric can take it.

Doubling the bobbin thread is harder for some machines to take. Fill the bobbin with doubled thread, from two spools or two bobbins. If necessary, adjust the bobbin tension.

Buttonhole twist makes very handsome topstitching, with a longer than average stitch. See if your machine will take it as top thread, with a #14 or even a #16 needle, if your fabric allows it. If not, place it in the bobbin (the other thread, top or bobbin, will be regular thread). In this case, however, you must have very exact guidelines to follow on the wrong side, to have it come out as you want it on the right side. CAUTION: Silk twist shrinks and should not be used on garments that will be washed.

A twin needle on a zigzag machine makes a beautiful double row of topstitching. It is used with regular thread. See your manual for directions.

NOTE: Stitching done with buttonhole twist or the twin needle looks quite different on the underside. If used on a front with a lapel, for instance, stop stitching and turn over at the point where the lapel begins.

EDGE-STITCHING is topstitching done close to a finished or folded edge. It is often used for stitching down pleats, or creases in pants. To keep the stitching even, the inside edge of the presser foot usually makes a good guide along which to let the fabric fold travel. A change in needle position may also set the stitching at the right distance from the folded edge.

BASTING STITCH is the longest stitch on the machine (see p. 18). **Speed basting** is a feature found on many machines, making stitches up to 1″ long or more. Check your manual. Speed basting can be used for all basting purposes, but should be tested first on your fabric: Some machines make "empty" stitches between the long ones, and the line of needle holes might show. Hold the fabric taut in front and back, because the basting has a tendency to bunch up the fabric behind the needle.

In **EASE-STITCHING** and **GATHERING,** the line of stitching is drawn up to give either ease or fullness (see p. 64 and p. 109).

UNDERSTITCHING is a line of stitching done on a facing or the underside of a collar. Made close to the edge to prevent seams from rolling to the outside, it does not show (see p. 94).

STITCHING IN THE DITCH means stitching on the right side, in a pressed-open seam, to fasten another piece of fabric underneath. It is here shown on a neck facing (26, 27). Done with matching thread and regular stitch length, it is invisible on the outside because it disappears into the "ditch" of the seam. Draw thread-ends through to wrong side, tie and clip.

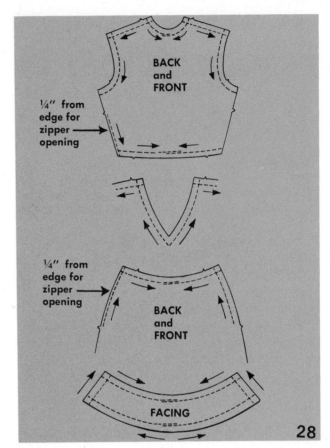

STAY-STITCHING diagrams labeled ¼″ from edge for zipper opening, BACK and FRONT, FACING. **28**

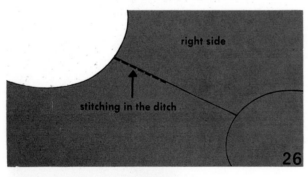

right side — stitching in the ditch **26**

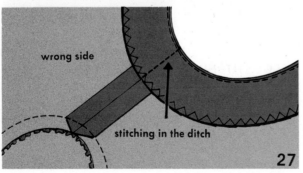

wrong side — stitching in the ditch **27**

STAY-STITCHING is a line of directional stitching, made before construction, to stabilize edges that might be pulled out of shape in handling. It can safely be omitted on fabrics that are firmly woven or tightly knitted. It is a must, however, on off-grain edges in loosely-woven fabrics, also on bias edges and knits where the stretch needs control. On curved edges that will be clipped later, stay-stitching helps prevent the clipping from weakening the seam.

Stay-stitching is done on the separate garment pieces, the first thing after cutting and marking, through a single thickness. When an interfacing or an underlining is added, however, the stitching that attaches it serves as stay-stitching, and is done directionally where required.

The diagrams (28) show where stay-stitching is usually needed, and the arrows show how to do it directionally (see DIRECTIONAL STITCHING). Using regular stitch length, stitch ½″ from the raw edge (to keep clear of the seam line). At a zipper opening, stay-stitch ¼″ from raw edge.

DIRECTIONAL STITCHING

This means, either in knits or in woven fabrics, stitching with the direction of the fabric in mind. It is a very good habit to acquire.

IN WOVEN FABRICS, there is the grain to go by. Most of the seams you stitch are neither straight-grain nor bias, but simply off-grain. Such seams are easily pulled out of shape, particularly if the fabric is loosely woven; stay-stitching, which is done direction-ally (28), is meant to guard against this. But stitching should be direc-tional in any case—that is, it should go **with** the grain and not **against** it.

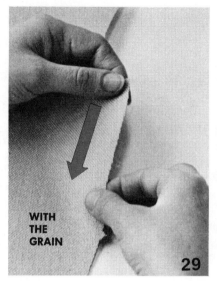
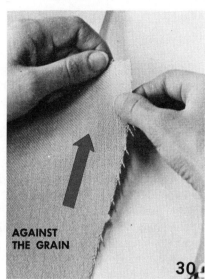

WITH THE GRAIN **29**

AGAINST THE GRAIN **30**

Most patterns have printed arrows at seam lines to show correct stitching direction. In the absence of these, remember that, where the shape allows, you stitch **from wide to narrow.** For instance,
from hem to waist in a skirt,
from underarm to waist in a fitted bodice.

At less clearly-defined cut edges, determine the di-rection by sliding your thumb and forefinger along the edge:
If the edge stays smooth (29), you are going with the grain: stitch in that direction.
If the threads at the edge get ruffled (30), you are going against the grain: stitch in the **other** direction.

IN KNITS, the question is primarily to stitch re-lated seams in the same direction. The seams in a skirt, for instance, should **all** be stitched from bot-tom to top, or **all** from top to bottom. When top-stitching the two edges of an opening, never go down one side and up the other, but interrupt the stitching at one end, and start again in the **same direction.**

ON CURVED EDGES of either woven fabrics or knits, the grain changes direction as the edge turns. When **stay-stitching,** stitch evenly curved edges, such as a neckline, in two separate steps. At an uneven curve, such as an armhole, the stay-stitching is done

in the direction that stays longest with the grain (28). Then, when you do your **construction-stitching,** you may stitch a curve all in one direction because the grain has been stabilized by the stay-stitching.

To sum up, try to make your construction-stitch-ing directional as a matter of habit. In curved seams, however, you may forget about it if it's inconvenient —these edges will have been safely stabilized by stay-stitching if the fabric is loosely woven or stretchy.

TAKING OUT STITCHING

With the rather loose stitch used on today's fab-rics, it has become relatively easy to take seams apart and to remove stitching.

To remove stitching, clip through a stitch of the bobbin thread about every 2″ and draw it out. (Even with a balanced stitch, the bobbin thread is usually looser.) To pick out tiny stitches use a pin or a needle.

A seam ripper is practical and quick to separate seams. It is razor-sharp, however, and must be handled carefully: Hold the two layers of fabric firmly apart and, with the ball underneath to avoid damaging the fabric, touch the blade to the thread only. A seam ripper comes with your sewing machine, or can be bought.

CHECK LIST
IN CASE OF TROUBLE

Common sewing machine failures, such as the ones listed here, usually have a simple explanation. Check the possible causes suggested under each.

THREAD BREAKAGE—TOP THREAD

- Machine improperly threaded.
- Needle improperly set or not all the way up in clamp.
- Bent needle.
- Wrong size or type of needle for fabric and thread.
- Burrs around needle hole or presser foot area, tension discs, or thread guides.
- Spool notch in wrong position so that thread catches in the notch.
- Tension too tight.
- Both threads not extended diagonally to the rear when starting.
- Accumulation of lint.

THREAD BREAKAGE—BOBBIN THREAD

- Bobbin too full or wound unevenly.
- Bobbin case not inserted properly.
- Damaged bobbin and/or bobbin case.

IRREGULAR OR SKIPPED STITCHES

- Stitching done in spurts.
- Pressure too light.
- Needle of wrong size or type for fabric and thread.
- Fabric pulled while stitching.
- Bobbin too full or wound unevenly.
- Dust or lint on feed dog.
- Bent needle.
- Needle improperly set or not all the way up in clamp.
- Accumulation of lint and/or sizing on needle (from fabric finish, especially knits or permanent press).
- Wrong throat plate and/or presser foot—try small-hole throat plate. Or try left or right needle position (while maintaining correct seam allowance).

MACHINE STUCK

- Bits of thread caught in bobbin case holder. Move the hand wheel back and forth to release thread; remove with tweezers.

NEEDLE BROKEN OR DAMAGED

- Wrong type of needle for the machine.
- Very fine needle with heavy fabric.
- Needle improperly set.
- Bent needle.
- Presser foot or attachment improperly set.
- Stitching over pins.
- Pulling fabric while stitching.
- Bobbin inserted incorrectly.
- Machine set for zigzag stitch while presser foot and/or throat plate are for straight stitch.

THREAD LOOPING BETWEEN STITCHES

- Machine improperly threaded.
- Even though threading appears correct, thread may not be properly caught between tension discs, or in bobbin tension; re-thread the machine.
- Upper and lower tension not in balance.

THREAD SNARLING AT START OF SEAM

- Machine improperly threaded.
- Bobbin thread not brought up through hole in throat plate before start of stitching.
- Stitching started without first bringing top thread-end under presser foot and holding both threads to the rear diagonally.
- Stitching started before lowering presser foot.

BOBBIN WINDING UNEVENLY
OR NOT AT ALL

- Thread guide on bobbin winder needs adjusting.
- Machine improperly threaded.
- Bobbin spindle not placed in the winding position.
- Worn rubber friction ring, found on some sewing machines.

Marking

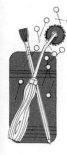

Marking means transferring pattern markings to fabric sections. It is a step professional dressmakers never neglect, but one that a home-sewer often considers unnecessary—which accounts for many a "home-made look."

Marking allows you to sew with precision and assurance, without fumbling. It is by marking that you get the full benefit of the expert guidance a pattern offers. Once you have discovered how quickly marking can be done, and the joy of working with well-marked garment sections, you will never start sewing without first transferring all the necessary markings from pattern to fabric.

WHEN AND WHERE TO MARK

Marking is done the first thing after cutting. Do not separate the pattern pieces from the fabric sections until you have transferred the pattern markings.

After cutting, the sections are almost always wrong side out. In any case, markings are transferred to the wrong side of the fabric (or to the underlining, if there is one).

Construction marks, such as darts, matching-points for assembling, tucks, etc. are needed on the wrong side.

Position marks, for placing buttonholes, pockets, trimmings, etc., are needed on the right side. If you have done them with tailor's tacks, they will show on the right side. Otherwise, bring them from the wrong to the right side with baste- or pin-marking.

WHAT TO MARK

Matching-points on seams are marked with notches, which you include while cutting out the garment.

Center front and center back on all garment sections should be marked as essential matching-points. Often these are not indicated on the pattern as matching-points, because they almost always fall on a fold or a seam. The quickest way to mark these is while cutting out the garment: When the center line

is on a fold, mark both ends of the line (the fold) with a small notch or clip in the seam allowance. If the nature of the fabric makes a clip or notch impractical, mark the center points with tailor's tacks.

Center of sleeve caps, indicated by a dot on the pattern, can be marked with a notch, clip, or tailor's tack as above.

Other matching-points, such as where a collar ends on a lapel, where fabric is joined in a dart, etc., are indicated by matching symbols—small or large dots, two squares, two triangles, etc. The center of the symbol marks the exact point.

Needless to say, you cannot reproduce the matching marks—you just mark their locations carefully. If there is any question about matching them later, you consult the pattern or the pattern guide sheet to check on which ones belong together.

Darts—See HOW TO MARK, on the next page. Or, better still, consult the chapter on DARTS.

Positions—The location of buttonholes, pockets, pleats, and trimming should be marked on the right side. See MARKING ON THE RIGHT SIDE, page 159. Also see BUTTONHOLES, page 32, and PLEATS, page 212, for additional information.

Certain special seam lines—Mark the corners on a square neckline, so you will know when to pivot.

You may want to mark the seam line on two edge-seams that face each other, such as lapels or the two ends of a collar, and must match perfectly; this is most necessary where the outline is curved. In such a case, mark the section that will be on top while stitching; in other words, the smaller section, such as the facing of a lapel. When the outer section, the facing, and the interfacing are all the same size, as in a collar or cuffs, mark the interfacing (interfacing may be marked with an ordinary pencil, but other fabrics may **not**).

Such a seam line can be stitched without marking if a **special paper guide** is used (see SEAMS, p. 221).

Do not mark the arrow showing grain direction. This arrow serves only for placing the pattern correctly on the fabric.

HOW TO MARK

There are many methods of marking. Some work better than others on certain fabrics and for certain details. You would do well to try them all, so you can be sure to select the method that works best for you in each case.

DRESSMAKER'S TRACING PAPER AND TRACING WHEEL

Works well on most firmly-woven fabrics. It should not, however, be used on leather or vinyl, where the impression might show through on the right side. On loosely-woven fabrics and on sheers and laces, the color from the paper might show through. On tweeds, spongy fabrics, or fake fur, the marks are unreliable and sometimes don't show.

In any case, always begin by **making a test** with a scrap of fabric, doubled as shown (2).

Dressmaker's tracing paper is a specially-prepared waxed paper that comes in many colors. Select one of not too great a contrast with the fabric, as it will not come out in washing or dry-cleaning. White is safest, and visible even on white fabrics. Such paper can also be used for marking with a hard pencil.

Tracing wheels are available with or without teeth. Wheels with teeth can be used on most fabrics. The smooth wheel makes a firm, continuous line and is recommended for hard-to-mark fabrics and for tricots, which may be damaged by the teeth.

Mark two layers of fabric (with pattern on top) at the same time. Fold a sheet of tracing paper in half across its width, with the marking surface **inside.** For most marking, cut a strip about 3″ wide (1); a strip can be used many times. For marking larger areas, such as pocket positions, use a doubled piece of suitable size.

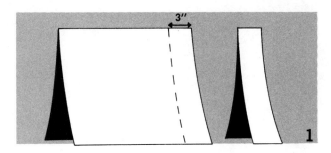

Place a piece of cardboard or a magazine under the fabric to protect the table surface. Slip the bottom half of the folded tracing paper under the two layers of fabric and insert the upper half between pattern and fabric (remove pins only as needed). In this way, the two marking surfaces are against the wrong side of the two garment sections. Follow the pattern markings with the wheel (2): On straight lines, use a ruler; on curved lines, go very slowly or use a French curve as a guide.

If the fabric has been cut right side out, fold the tracing paper with the marking surface **outside** and slip it between the two layers of fabric.

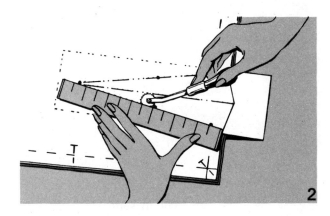

When marking darts, make a short crossline (3) at the point of the dart and at matching-points (dots). Be careful, however, not to make marks that may show through on the right side. If the pattern does not give the center line of darts, measure center of dart at its wide end and draw a line to the point. You will fold the dart on this line.

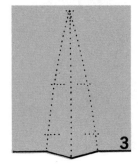

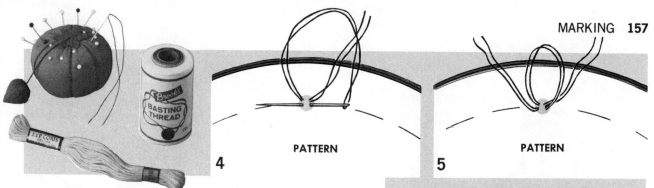

PATTERN

4

PATTERN

5

TAILOR'S TACKS

Marking with tailor's tacks has all kinds of advantages. It is suitable for most fabrics. It does not leave permanent marks on the fabric. It marks both sides and both layers of fabric at the same time. If made with the right kind of thread, it does not fall out, but can easily be removed. While the method may appear slow, it is rather quick once you get used to it.

Tailor's tacks are made with needle and thread. Soft threads such as embroidery floss, darning cotton or cotton basting thread are best, because they stay in the fabric better than other threads. Use white or pastel colors and a long thread, doubled, without a knot.

To mark a point, take a small stitch through pattern and both layers of fabric. Draw the thread up, leaving a 1½″ end. Take another stitch at the same point (4), leaving a loop of about 1″ (5). Cut the thread, leaving another 1½″ end, as shown. When all points are marked, remove the pattern (if you stitched through it, gently tear it off). Carefully separate the layers of fabric to the extent of the thread loops, and cut through the threads, as shown (6). Little tufts of thread will remain as markings in each fabric layer.

To mark a line, make a loop at the beginning of the line; take a 2″ to 3″ long stitch along line of marking and make another loop. On darts, for instance, make loops at matching dots (7). Continue along line in same manner. Clip the long stitches between loops (7), then remove pattern. Separate the two thicknesses of fabric and cut through threads (6).

On long lines, the loops can be omitted. Make the stitches 3″ to 5″ long. Clip thread and remove the pattern. When separating the two thicknesses of fabric, be very careful not to pull the fabric off the thread-ends.

Sometimes the two methods above can be used together. For instance, on a front section that ends in a curve, omit loops on straight edge, but make loops around the curve, fairly close together (8).

Some machines have a stitch which can be used for tailor-tacking. Consult your manual.

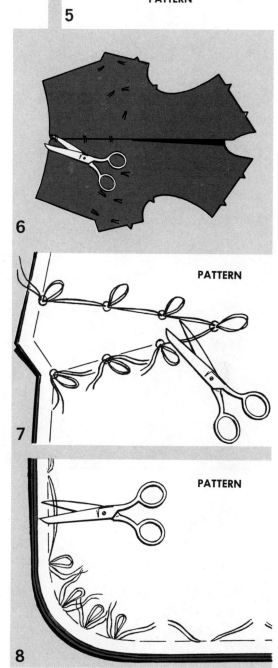

6

PATTERN

7

PATTERN

8

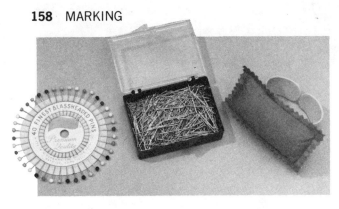

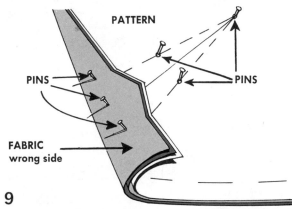

PATTERN

PINS

PINS

FABRIC
wrong side

9

PINS

Quick, and usable on most fabrics. On certain fabrics, however, they may leave permanent holes or snags—if in doubt, you will have tried them out before pinning down the pattern. On loosely-woven fabrics, pins may slip out easily. Pins can be very useful for bringing markings from the wrong side to the right side.

To mark with pins, put a pin straight through the pattern and fabric at each point to be marked so it sticks out on the other side (9). Remove the pattern, easing the tissue over the pinheads and being careful not to pull out the pins. Then turn the sections over and, as close as possible to each pin, insert a pin in the other direction. Separate the two layers of fabric, each one bristling with pins on the right side, as shown (10).

On the wrong side, without ever entirely removing a pin from the fabric, draw out each pin and pick up a few threads of fabric at the same point (11). Push pins in far enough so they won't slip out.

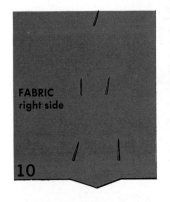

FABRIC
right side

FABRIC
right side

10

TAILOR'S CHALK

Chalk comes in flat squares and in marking pencils. It is quick and easy to use, but does not show on all fabrics and does not make reliable marks on nubby weaves. It can be very useful for quick marking and for drawing long lines with the yardstick. For exact marking, sharpen the chalk well.

Do not mark with chalk until you are ready to sew, because it tends to rub off. At each point to be marked, put a pin straight through pattern and fabric, to stick out on the other side. Remove pattern carefully. On wrong side of both layers of fabric, use marking pencil or sharpened chalk to mark an X where pins are. Remove pins. If desired (in darts, for instance), connect marks with chalk lines.

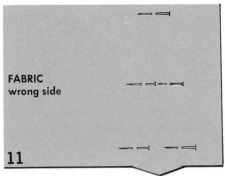

FABRIC
wrong side

11

BASTE-MARKING

This is often used to bring position marks from the wrong side to the right side. It can be done either by hand, with uneven basting stitches, or by machine, set for the longest stitch. For uneven basting make long stitches on top and short stitches through the fabric (12).

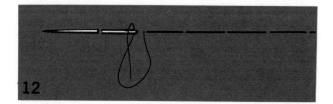

12

MARKING ON THE RIGHT SIDE

The position of details such as pockets or trimmings must be marked on the right side of the fabric. There are two ways of doing this.

If you are using thread, transfer pattern markings directly to right side of fabric by making tailor's tacks or by baste-marking through the pattern.

If you are using dressmaker's tracing paper, transfer pattern markings first to the wrong side of the fabric, as usual; then transfer these marks to the right side with baste-marking or pin-marking. Use this also when transferring markings to the right side from the underlining or the interfacing.

Mending

We all need to do a bit of mending now and then to keep our clothing neat; a timely stitch may even prolong the life of a garment. General family mending has been made quicker and easier by iron-on fabrics and fusible webs which, if your fabric can take them, will make almost invisible repairs in a jiffy.

Meanwhile, there are still the tried and true methods of mending, by hand and machine. Some are very simple, others require skill and even imagination, but they are all very useful to know.

Self-fabric, it must be remembered, is a great help in mending. You will have some on hand if a garment is home-sewn. In the case of ready-to-wear, you may have saved some when a garment was shortened.

TO MEND OR NOT TO MEND

There can be no question about repairing things that have come undone, such as buttons, snaps, hooks and eyes, thread loops, hems, linings and seams.

Whether or not to undertake more extensive mending depends on a number of factors: How valuable the garment is and how much wear is left in it; the value of your time and how much you can spare; your ability to do the job to your satisfaction; and the state of your budget. There is no point in laboriously repairing an article that can be replaced cheaply, or that will not last much longer in any case. On the other hand, if you can save a good garment, it may be well worth your time.

PREVENTIVE MENDING

Preventive mending is the true "stitch in time", but is not real repair work, because it is done **before** damage occurs. Ready-to-wear garments should be gone over for this kind of mending even before they are worn.

Dangling threads—Thread the ends into a needle, bring to inside of garment and tie.

Hem—If stitches are loose or if the fabric is pulled off grain, remove stitches and resew (see page 122). Resew any section that may be loose.

Buttons, snaps, hooks, eyes that are not properly attached should be resewn. If the existing thread has not begun to come loose, it need not be removed—just sew over it. In the case of **buttons with a shank,** however, it is better to remove buttons and scraps of thread entirely and start again as described on page 43.

Buttonholes—You can double the life and improve the looks of machine-made buttonholes by going over them with a hand-buttonhole stitch, or a zigzag machine stitch (see p. 38).

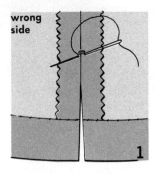

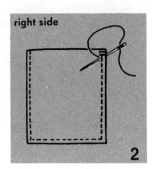

Zippers—Overcast any loose or fraying fabric edges that might catch in zipper.

Slits and patch pockets—Strengthen with a few firm overhand stitches at top of slit (1) or pocket (2).

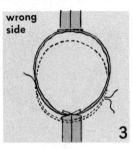

Seams — Strengthen all sleeve and crotch seams with a second line of machine-stitching on top of the existing stitching (3). This is especially recommended when seams are narrow or crooked, or the stitches are long.

Underarm seams of raglan and kimono sleeves, which are put to extra strain, should be reinforced with seam binding: Place the binding over the seam line and stitch through it (4); if there is a sharp curve, fold the tape as shown (5).

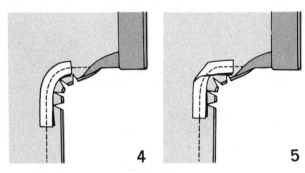

Areas of hard wear can be reinforced either when the garment is new or when such an area begins to show signs of wear.

Elbows, knees and the seat of pants (especially on children's clothes) can be doubled on the inside with iron-on patches. Patches of leather or suede add quite a smart note when stitched to the outside.

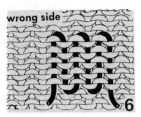

Thinning elbows on sweaters can be strengthened by running yarn invisibly through the back of the knitting, as shown (6).

Set-in pockets may be reinforced at the bottom with iron-on patches.

IMAGINATIVE MENDING

This means turning repair work into decoration or some other plus. It can be done in various ways. For instance: Use contrasting rather than matching fabric for a patch, and repeat the patch on the undamaged elbow, knee or other corresponding area to make a planned design. Place a decoration, such as an appliqué (see p. 16) over the damage (7); or place a pocket over the damage, if the location allows it. Embroidery, in bold, simple designs, is often good—it should extend beyond the damaged area, with a light fabric reinforcement on the wrong side. Braid, lace, ribbon may provide effective camouflage, but if you add braid or a frill to frayed sleeve edges, for example, be sure to add it also at the neck, even if that edge is unfrayed!

Patches or appliqués that are applied with a hot iron (see below) make wonderful cover-ups for spots and tears on casual clothes and children's wear. Cut them out in gay colors and attractive shapes (coloring books may provide you with outlines).

Needless to say, whether or not such mending is suitable will depend, not only on the garment, but also on the location and nature of the damage.

MENDING WITH FUSIBLES

This is quick and easy, whether you use fusible fabric which is applied with an iron, or fusible web with a patch of fabric. Both, if they are suitable for the fabric you are mending, are excellent for tears and threadbare areas.

Iron-on patches come in plain or twill weave, denim, jersey and corduroy in many colors and prints; they are particularly useful for imaginative mending (see preceding page). There are ready-cut patches in different shapes and sizes, also strips that can be used for pressing on the wrong side of a tear. Large white pieces are excellent for mending sheets.

Fusible web, if your fabric can take the heat and steam (see FUSIBLES, p. 107), will firmly attach a patch to the wrong side of a garment. For tears and general reinforcement, use lining or other lightweight fabric of matching color; cut this and the web slightly larger than the area to be covered. To mend a hole, a patch of self-fabric can be inserted almost invisibly with fusible web—see FUSED PATCH on page 166.

In every case, round off corners of patches or designs because sharp corners tend to lift off, and follow package instructions exactly. Be sure to apply enough pressure and heat.

FASTENINGS

Loose buttons, snaps, hooks and eyes, thread loops, must be removed entirely before resewing, including all bits of broken thread. For resewing, see the chapters on BUTTONS, FASTENERS, and THREAD LOOPS.

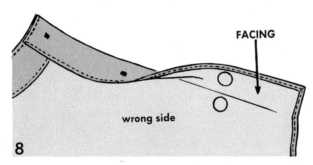

FACING

wrong side

8

If the fabric under a button is torn or worn, mend or reinforce it with iron-on fabric in matching color: Remove the button. Snip frayed threads around the damaged spot. Cut two identical circles of iron-on fabric or fabric and fusible web, slightly larger than the hole. Spread the facing open, wrong side up, and attach the circles over the button location on both outer fabric and facing (8). Close the facing and sew on the button.

Worked buttonholes that show signs of wear should immediately be gone over with buttonhole stitch by hand or by machine (see p. 38). Badly raveled but-

tonholes can be renewed from scratch, if the garment is worth it, as follows:

Carefully remove all stitches with sharp, pointed scissors or a seam ripper. Steam-press the buttonhole.

If you are refinishing the buttonhole by machine, back the slit on both outer fabric and facing with a lightweight patch, either iron-on or with fusible web; or, if backing is not convenient, hold the buttonhole edges a hair's breadth apart as you work the buttonhole.

If you are refinishing the buttonhole by hand, first make a line of very small machine-stitching on each side of the slit, as close to the edge as possible.

Zipper—If the zipper stitching is ripped, baste zipper back in place and machine-stitch with matching thread. To replace a zipper, see page 278.

HEMS AND SEAMS

Ripped hem—If this is simply a matter of broken thread, remove the loose thread and sew the hem back (for hemming stitches, see p. 122). If, however, the seam binding is worn through, the worn length must be replaced. Remove it neatly, then edge-stitch the new binding over the raw hem-edge, either by machine, or by hand with a running stitch and an occasional backstitch for reinforcement (9). Turn ends under and sew hem back in place.

Ripped lining—Lining often rips at the armhole and center back seams. Sew them up as described in the next paragraph. If the lining comes loose at the hem, fold it under as it was and slipstitch it invisibly in place.

Split or ripped seams should be sewn up from the inside if possible, beginning and ending at least ½″ beyond the split. Machine-stitching is preferable, because it is stronger; otherwise, do it with a hand-backstitch (10).

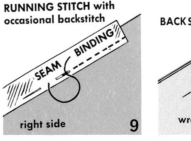

RUNNING STITCH with occasional backstitch

SEAM BINDING

right side **9**

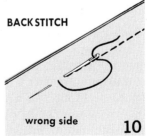

BACK STITCH

wrong side **10**

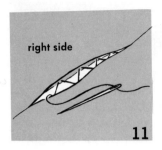
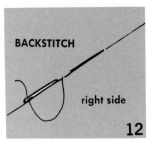
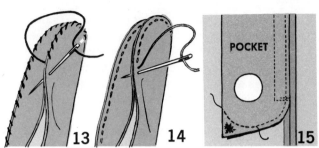

When you cannot work from the inside, the work must be done by hand, invisibly. Use a single thread with a knot at the end (the knot will be trimmed off when the mending is completed). Start well beyond the split, running the thread along the seam. At the split, work the needle back and forth between the two edges of the split, catching two or three fabric threads at a time (11). After a few stitches, draw up the thread, take a backstitch through the seam line (12), and repeat. To finish off, run thread along seam well beyond end of split; clip the thread.

Split underarm seams in raglan and kimono sleeves should be sewn up and reinforced with tape on wrong side, as shown on page 160. If such a tear extends into the bodice, it may be necessary to insert a gusset (see GUSSETS).

In gloves, open seams should be mended in the manner of the original stitching—whipstitch (13) or running stitch (14). Even if you cannot duplicate the stitch exactly, a mended seam is not nearly as conspicuous as an open one. Match the thread as closely as possible to the thread used in the glove. Thread and needle should be of a fineness or coarseness suited to the glove material. A glover's needle, though not absolutely necessary, may be helpful for leather. Start without a knot; secure the stitching carefully, and conceal thread-ends inside the glove.

POCKETS

To repair a hole in a set-in pocket, use a small iron-on patch, or a fabric patch attached with fusible web. If the hole is in the very corner, however, as often in men's trouser pockets, you can eliminate it by rounding off the corner with hand- or machine-stitching (15). Men's trouser pockets damaged beyond this easy repair can be replaced with pocket-replacement kits sold at most notion counters.

DARNING

Darning to strengthen worn spots or repair tears and small holes can be done by machine or by hand. It should extend well beyond a torn area, to avoid having edges pull out and to include all weakened spots. Thread should always be color-matched.

Machine-darning is faster and stronger than hand-darning, but can be done only where appearance does not matter, as on sheets and work clothes. Stitching is done on the right side, with or without a backing. If you can find a fine thread, such as Dual Duty Plus® Extra-Fine, you will have a softer darn.

Hand-darning is done on the wrong side, unless the darn is reinforced with a backing, in which case it is done on the right side. Use matching thread. The best, if it can be managed, is a thread drawn out of the fabric, either from a left-over piece or from a straight-cut seam allowance. If drawn from wool, such threads should be shrunk before use. The needle should be as fine as possible; the thread should be used single and be no longer than average (drawing out a long thread pulls fabric out of shape). Make no knot, but let the thread-end extend on wrong side. Never pull thread tight.

SMALL HOLES

In general, this means holes small enough to be filled in with thread. Trim ragged edges without changing the shape of the hole. If you should want to back the hole for reinforcement (though this makes a stiffer darn), use a very lightweight fabric, let it be caught in the darn (either hand or machine), and trim away excess backing fabric afterward (16).

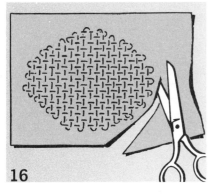

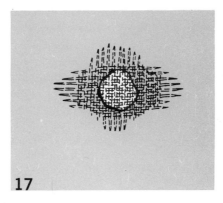

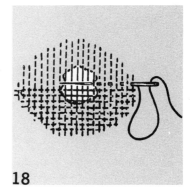

For machine-darning, use a **long** straight stitch, going back and forth across the hole (guide the fabric by hand, holding it taut over any empty space). Then switch to a **short** straight stitch and work back and forth in the other direction. Keep the outer edges of darn irregular (17).

For hand-darning, fill in the lengthwise threads as close together as the original weave or knit, if possible. Weave crosswise threads over and under (18).

Chain-stitch darning is used for sweaters and other knitted garments, as it reproduces the knit stockinette stitch. Steam-press the damaged area lightly. Pick away worn stitches around holes, so you have straight edges. Use matching yarn and a darning needle. Run yarn invisibly through surrounding area, then work it crosswise across hole, one line to a row, as shown (19).

Working from the right side and starting at the top, chain-stitch down the crosswise threads, as shown (20). Run the thread back invisibly, over and under, to the top, and start the second row. Repeat until the hole is filled. Steam-press.

TEARS

Machine-darning of tears should be done with many small stitches in order to bring the fabric edges together and keep them flat: Use either a multi-stitch zigzag, which is found on some machines, or a straight stitch; do not use a plain zigzag.

With multi-stitch zigzag, use a wide, fairly short stitch. For stability, place a piece of organdy or thin lining fabric of matching color under the tear. Make a row of zigzag stitching down the middle of the tear, drawing the edges as close together as possible (21). If the tear is badly frayed, or if the fabric ravels easily, make another row of stitching on either side of the middle row. Cut away excess backing.

For straight-stitching, first draw the edges together with hand fishbone stitch as shown (22). Stitch back and forth across the tear, keeping outer edges of darn irregular (23). Reinforce any corner by stitching across the stitching just completed, as shown for hand-darning (24).

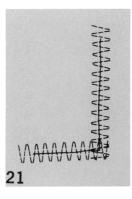

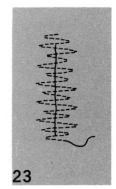

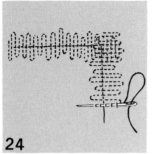

24

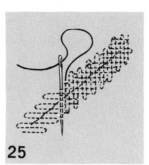

25

Hand-darning, done from the wrong side unless the darn is backed, can be almost invisible in certain fabrics. (Backing is seldom necessary, but if it is done, use lightweight fabric of matching color). With wool fabric, a human hair makes a strong and inconspicuous sewing thread. First draw the torn edges together with fishbone stitch (22). If these stitches do not disappear in the darning, snip them later and draw them out gently. Starting ¼″ from the end of the tear, make rows of tiny running stitches back and forth across the tear (24). Keep in line with the fabric grain and keep the outside edges of the darn irregular. **Be sure** to slip your needle **under** the fabric edge as you cross the tear. Reinforce the corner of L-shaped tears by darning in both directions (24). Do the same with diagonal tears (25).

PATCHES

A patch is generally used to mend a hole or a badly-worn spot. There are various methods of attaching patches—by machine, by hand, and by fusing. To make a patch as inconspicuous as possible, you need matching fabric. However, if it is not important for the patch to be inconspicuous or if the patch is meant to be decorative, it is treated as an appliqué. See IMAGINATIVE MENDING on page 160.

The ideal patch is made of self-fabric—which, however, may have to be pre-shrunk and faded to match the present state of the garment. (To fade, wash in suds and baking soda and dry in the sun). In every case, the patch should be of the same weight as the garment fabric. It should be cut on exactly the same grain, and placed so that the lengthwise and crosswise threads match the surrounding area. When there is a design, match it before cutting out the patch. Be sure to make the patch large enough to include all of the damaged area. Use regular thread, color-matched.

PATCHING BY MACHINE

Overlapped patch with zigzag stitch—This is done on the right side, with either plain or multi-stitch zigzag. With woven fabrics, cut the patch square; with knits, round off the corners.

  a. Cut a patch at least ½″ larger than the damaged area on all sides.

  b. Center the patch over the damage, both fabrics right sides up, matching the grain or design. Pin in place.

  c. Stitch around, just covering the edges of the patch. On a square patch, reinforce corners by going over the end of a completed side as you start the next one (26).

    With multi-stitch zigzag, use a wide, fairly short stitch. Go around once (27).

    With plain zigzag, use a medium wide, fairly short stitch. Go around once, then make a second row of stitching ⅛″ to ¼″ inside the first row of stitching (28).

  d. On the wrong side, cut away the damaged fabric close to the stitching.

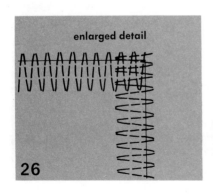

enlarged detail

26

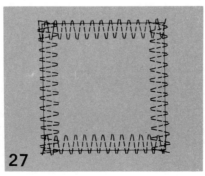

27

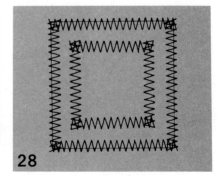

28

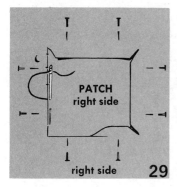

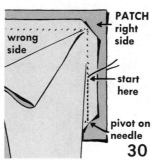

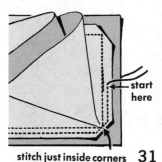

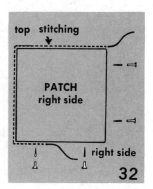

Set-in patch—Trim the damaged area all around to make a square or rectangular hole, carefully following the lines of grain or design.

a. Cut a patch 1″ larger than the hole on all sides. Place it under the hole with right side showing through. Pin in place, matching grain or design. Make a ¼″ diagonal clip into each corner of hole. Turn all edges of the hole under ¼″ and press carefully.

b. Slip-baste edges in place as shown (29): Take ¼″ stitches alternately in fold and in patch, always putting needle into the patch at the exact point where it came out of the fold.

c. Fold the garment fabric back as shown (30) and stitch on the wrong side along the line of basting, pivoting at corners.

If it is particularly important for the patch to be inconspicuous, trim patch seam allowances to ¼″ and trim off corners. Press the seams open and overcast the raw edges (35).

If strength is more important, make a second line of stitching ⅛″ from the first, through the two seam allowances, stitching across corners (31). Trim patch seam allowances to ¼″.

This patch can also be topstitched in place (32) after following steps **a** and **b**.

PATCHING BY HAND

Set-in patch—Follow the instructions above for doing this by machine, substituting hand-backstitch for machine stitching.

Hemmed patch—Insert the patch in exactly the same way as the set-in patch, through step **a**. Then, instead of slip-basting the edges, hem them down with fine, invisible stitches (33), taking several stitches at the corners.

On washable articles, trim the patch edges on the wrong side to ½″; turn edges under and hem them down (34).

On others, trim edges to ¼″ and hem lightly to the garment fabric.

For a flat, almost invisible patch, trim patch edges to ¼″ and trim off corners. Press seams open and overcast raw edges (35).

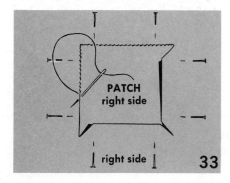

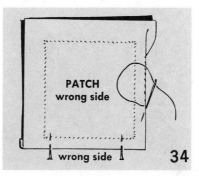

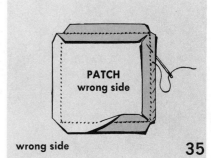

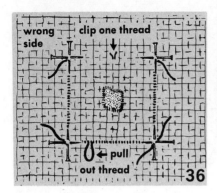

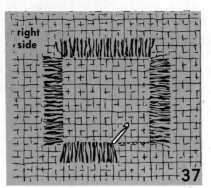

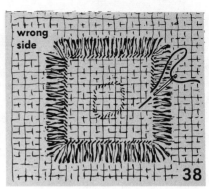

Woven-in patch—For loosely-woven wool and similar fabrics, this is neat and surprisingly quick. It is particularly good for small holes, such as the ones made by moths and cigarette burns.

a. Work on wrong side. Around the hole, mark out a straight-grain square with pins at each corner. This will be the size of the patch. With pointed scissors, clip through **one** thread at center of each side of the square, as shown. Draw out these threads as far as the corner pins (36). This is the outline for the patch.

b. Out of matching pre-shrunk fabric, cut a square 1″ larger on all sides than the marked-out square. Draw threads out on all four edges until you have the center exactly matching the outline (be accurate!), surrounded by an inch of fringe.

c. Pin the patch to right side of garment, matching the outline. Using a fine metal crochet hook, draw a raveled thread-end to wrong side through each corner of outline. Then draw the rest of the ravelings through to wrong side along outline, taking one thread at a time and advancing one thread at a time (37).

d. Fasten fringe in place on wrong side with fine hemming stitches along outline (38). Steam-press. Trim fringe to ¼″.

Darned-in patch—This is a flat, inconspicuous and fairly sturdy patch, good in wool and similar fabrics. After trimming the damaged area to a square or rectangular hole along lines of grain or design, cut the patch to fit the hole exactly and baste it to a piece of net, extending 1″ on all sides. Place patch in hole from wrong side, face down, and pin net to surrounding fabric (39). On right side, darn the raw edges together all around (40)—see HAND DARNING, page 162.

FUSED PATCH

Cut edges of damaged area to form a square or rectangular hole, with edges following grain or design. Cut a patch of fabric and web ¾″ larger than the hole all around. Center web under hole, trace outline of hole on it and cut out. With web between patch and garment fabric (41), fuse as directed in FUSIBLES, page 107.

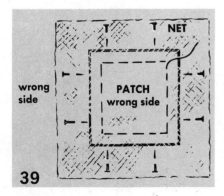

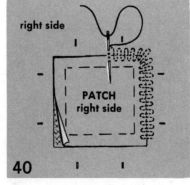

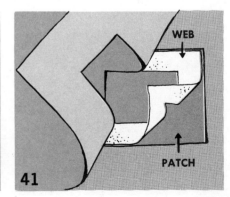

TURNING COLLAR AND CUFFS

Turning a collar and French cuffs, which fray or pill long before the rest of the shirt or blouse shows wear, is as good as getting a new shirt or blouse. If there are stays in the collar, just make sure they are not the kind that show on the reverse side.

a. Fold collar (or cuff) carefully in half and place pins as shown (42, 43), in collar and neckband, and in cuff and sleeve, all placed close to the seam line. On neckband, mark positions of front collar edges with pins.

b. Carefully take out stitching, attaching collar to neckband or cuff to sleeve. Remove all threads.

c. Reverse the collar and reinsert into the neckband, matching center pins. Baste through all thicknesses along original seam line, matching ends to front pins (42). Machine-stitch on inside of band over old stitching line.

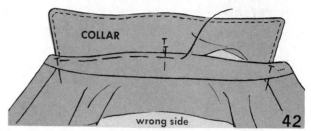

Reverse the cuff and insert the sleeve-edge into it as before, matching pins (43). Baste and stitch as for collar, on outside of sleeve.

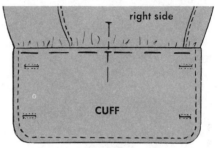

Menswear

The field of home sewing has expanded to take in men's clothes—sometimes made by the men themselves. Patterns, fabrics and notions specially designed for the purpose are now generally available and allow a careful "home tailor", female or male, to turn out menswear with a professional finish.

As usual, the pattern guide sheets take you through all the necessary steps. There are, however, a number of techniques that may be different and give beautiful results. We suggest that, before starting work on a man's jacket or pants, you look over this chapter. If you decide to use any of these methods, mark your pattern guide sheet at the point(s) where you plan a change. It may involve a different sequence in the construction steps.

FABRICS AND NOTIONS

If you want a washable garment, make sure that everything you put into it, including notions, is washable. The best policy is to launder all your ma-

terials before using them, in the same way that you intend to launder the garment, except fusibles, which are ruined if washed before application, but are safely washable after they are in place.

MENSWEAR FABRICS are of tight, firm construction, generally of finer yarns. This is particularly true of knits. Any fabric used for men's clothes must have definite body and firmness.
Other JACKET materials needed:

LINING FABRIC should be a medium-weight synthetic or blend. For inside pockets, use a firmly-woven polyester/cotton blend.

UNDERCOLLAR FABRIC should have the same care requirements as the jacket fabric.
With a knit or a lightweight washable woven fabric, use self-fabric.
With medium-heavy washable woven fabric, use polyester double-knit.
With dry-cleanable woven fabric, use tightly-woven wool flannel or special undercollar fabric.

INTERFACING is generally called for in patterns. We have found that fusible interfacings, which do away with pad-stitching, also make the work more stable and easier to handle, and provide beautifully smooth end-results. With few exceptions they are perfect companions for today's fabrics (see APPLYING FUSIBLE INTERFACING, p. 135, for preliminary testing).

The fusible interfacings used in menswear tailoring may be woven or non-woven. There are two woven types: **fusible hair canvas,** very resilient and good for shaping, and **fusible interfacing (without hair),** softer but providing body and stability. Of the nonwoven types, the only one we recommend for menswear is the **fusible interfacing with one-way stretch;** it compares to fusible interfacing (without hair).

• **For jacket front, undercollar,** and **chest pieces,** use **fusible hair canvas.**

If this is unavailable, or if the jacket will be made in a lightweight washable, woven fabric, use the same **fusible interfacing** (without hair, or non-woven with one-way stretch) that you will be using in the details mentioned below. In such a case, however, you will also have to fuse interfacing to the **jacket facing** and to the **upper collar,** which will double the interfacing in those areas.

• **At details and edges,** such as lapels, hems, vents, pocket flaps, use **fusible interfacing** (without hair, or non-woven with one-way stretch) because they are lighter in weight.

• **In pocket welts and underlays,** use Magic Polyweb® (see FUSIBLES, p. 107).

ADDITIONAL SHAPING AIDS can be bought ready-made, as notions, or be made to fit the individual.

Chest pieces fill and smooth out the chest area and provide a roll line for the lapels.

Shoulder pads fill out and square the shoulder line.

Sleeve heads round out the sleeve cap and make the sleeve hang smoothly. The ready-made ones are sold in a kit with chest pieces.

TWILL TAPE, ¼" and ½" wide, is needed to stabilize edges and roll lines. Whether it is polyester or cotton, always shrink tape before use.

Other PANTS materials needed:

LINING FABRIC for waistband and fly facing and for inside pockets should be a firmly-woven polyester/cotton blend, in a color suited to the outer fabric.

WAISTBAND STIFFENER is a very firm backing strip that keeps the waistband from rolling during wear. Buy it in the width planned for the finished waistband. There are two types:

Plain, to be faced with a bias strip of your lining fabric; it is similar to belting in stiffness, and is sometimes elastic. Widths are from 1½" to 2", and it comes packaged or by the yard.

Ready-faced with lining color-matched to your lining. Measure the width from raw edge of stiffener to line of stitching that attaches the facing (width does not need to be too exact as the lower edge extends below waistline seam).

TROUSER ZIPPERS come in a single length (11"). Any conventional zipper, however, is suitable, since it will be cut to fit during application (see p. 177).

PATTERNS

Jacket and suit patterns are bought by chest measurement, taken on the man himself. Pants patterns are bought by waist measurement, unless hips are out of proportion to the waist, in which case you buy by hip measurement (for measuring, see p. 182).

After buying the pattern, make sure the pattern will fit by checking the measurements. One very good way is to first measure a well-fitting, similar garment at the points given below. As you go along, jot down each measurement.

MEASURING A JACKET

1. **Back width**—At widest part of back, just below armhole from underarm to center back.
2. **Back Length**—Center back seam from base of collar to bottom of jacket.
3. **Shoulder**—Across shoulder from neckline seam to armhole seam.
4. **Underarm sleeve length**—At underarm seam from armhole to bottom of sleeve.
5. **Sleeve length**—From center top of armhole seam to bottom of sleeve.
6,7. **Sleeve circumference**—At fullest part of sleeve, 1" below armhole at underarm (6) and at wrist (7).
8. **Front width**—At widest part of chest, from just below armhole to center front (buttons).
9. **Hips**—At greatest width in lower part of jacket from center front to center back.
10. **Pocket height**—From pocket top to jacket bottom.

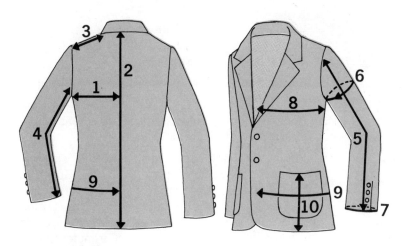

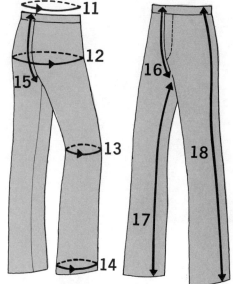

MEASURING PANTS

11. **Waistband**—Measure it closed.

12. **Hips**—At fullest part of pants. Note how far down this is from waist.

13. **Width at knees**—Circumference of pants legs at a point about halfway down the inner leg seam.

14. **Width of leg bottom**—Circumference of leg at hem.

15. **Length of center back seam**—From top of waistband to inner leg seam.

16. **Length of center front seam**—From top of waistband to inner leg seam.

17. **Inner leg seam**—From the juncture of inner leg seam and crotch seams to bottom of pants leg.

18. **Side length**—From top of waistband to bottom of pants leg.

19. **Length of crotch**—Subtract the inner leg seam measurement from the side length measurement.

CHECKING THE PATTERN FOR FIT

To check the above measurements against those of the pattern, follow the procedure below. Then adjust the pattern as necessary (see PATTERN ADJUSTMENTS, p. 193). If you don't want to leave anything to chance, make a trial garment of muslin from the adjusted pattern.

• Iron out the creases in pattern with a warm, dry iron.

• Have pattern pieces flat on table.

• With pencil and yardstick, extend the grain line on each piece the entire length of the piece.

• Measure the pattern pieces at exactly the points at which you have taken the corresponding measurements on the garment.

• Take all measurements from seam line to seam line. Do not include seam allowances or the width of any darts.

THE JACKET—
SPECIAL METHODS

USING FUSIBLE INTERFACING

Read about FUSIBLE INTERFACING on pages 131 and 135. Don't neglect to make a test as instructed, to be sure the edges of the interfacing that are not stitched into a seam will not cause a ridge on the right side.

SPOT STABILIZATION

Begin by fusing the **lighter weight fusible interfacing** (without hair, or non-woven with one-way stretch) to various points that require stabilization: Use the garment pattern pieces for cutting and follow the instructions on the next page; at places where there is no stress, ¾″ is trimmed from seam allowance edges to avoid bulk; otherwise, ½″ is trimmed off so that ⅛″ is left to be stitched into seams. Cut two of each piece, one for each jacket side.

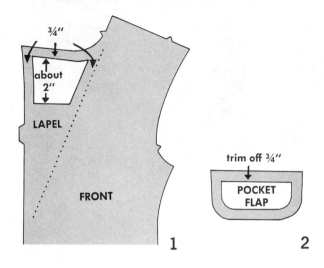

Lapel—Cut a piece as shown (1), about 2″ deep and ¾″ in from lapel edges and roll line (this will keep the lapel tips from curling).

Pocket flap (2)—Cut as shown, with ¾″ trimmed off all around.

Underarm on side section—Cut a piece as shown (3a); trim ½″ off seam allowances.

Pocket locations that extend into side section—For a welt pocket, cut a piece as shown (3b), trimming ½″ off the seam allowance. For a patch pocket, cut a piece as shown (4b), adding ½″ at top, bottom and side of pocket location and trimming ½″ off the seam allowance. After fusing, transfer pocket markings to interfacing, as shown.

Hems at side (3c), back (5a) and sleeves (6)—Cut interfacing as shown, the width of the space from fold line to raw edges. Trim off ¼″ at hem edges, ½″ at seam allowances.

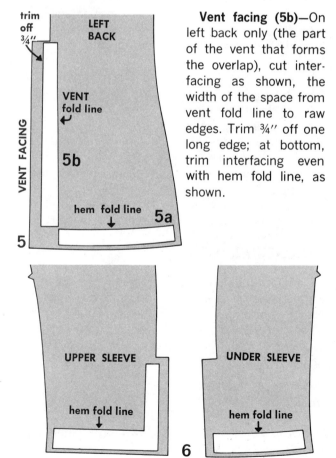

Vent facing (5b)—On left back only (the part of the vent that forms the overlap), cut interfacing as shown, the width of the space from vent fold line to raw edges. Trim ¾″ off one long edge; at bottom, trim interfacing even with hem fold line, as shown.

OVER-ALL INTERFACING

The jacket front and the collar are interfaced in their entirety (although the interfacing on a jacket stops at the underarm mark if there is no side front seam). For the correct interfacing, be sure to see INTERFACING, FOR JACKET FRONT on page 168.

As for the collar, do not cut out **any part** of it before looking over the method for the COLLAR, found on page 173.

For jacket front, cut interfacing from jacket pattern. If there is no side front seam, end interfacing at underarm marking. Trim ½″ from seam allowances all around; at hem, end interfacing at hem fold line; trim ¼″ off corner of lapel. Fuse to wrong side of garment section, covering the interfacing already on the lapel (7).

Transfer all markings—roll line, dart, buttonholes, pocket placement—to interfacing. For placement of chest piece, mark an additional line just inside the roll line, as shown: ¼″ from the line at top and ⅝″ at the bottom (7).

For the front facing (only if you are using the lighter weight interfacing), cut interfacing from facing pattern. Trim ½″ from seam allowances; if facing reaches to hem, end the interfacing at hem fold line; trim ¼″ off corner of lapel (8).

CHEST PIECES

For fused chest pieces use the same type of interfacing you used for the jacket front. You may also buy ready-made chest pieces (non-fusible).

When cutting a chest piece (9), have the grain line parallel with shoulder line of jacket front pattern. Cut out chest piece ¾″ from shoulder and armhole edges and even with the line just marked on jacket interfacing (see above); end the piece 1½″ above bottom of roll line. Draw in the bottom line of the chest piece as shown, curving above front dart and ending just short of side seam line. Mark position of chest welt pocket, if any; to reduce bulk, mark and cut out a rectangle ¼″ outside the pocket marking all around. Fuse the chest piece in place over the previously fused front interfacing (9).

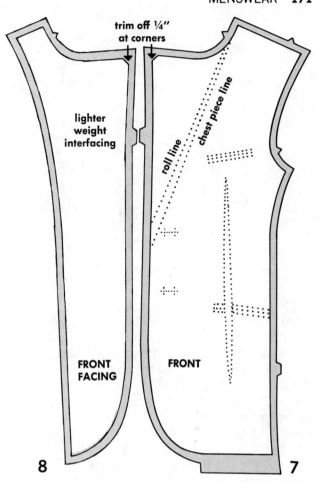

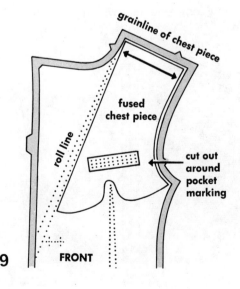

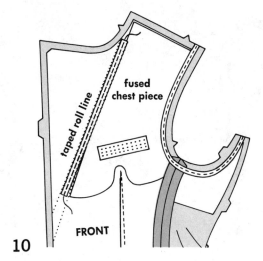

10

TAPING THE JACKET

The roll lines and edges subject to strain must be stabilized with pre-shrunk twill tape. This is done after jacket front and side section (if any) are joined.

Roll line—Use ½" wide tape; cut ¾" shorter than the measurement from neck seam line to bottom of chest piece. Pin as shown (10) with one edge along the roll line; ease jacket to tape (this helps the lapel to roll over smoothly). Machine-baste the tape in place through center. Whipstitch edges of tape to interfacing and chest piece, being careful not to catch the jacket fabric. Remove machine-basting.

Front armholes—Use ¼" wide tape. Cut to the measurement of armhole on the pattern. After side front seam (if any) is stitched, stitch the tape to the armhole, on wrong side, just within the seam allowance (10).

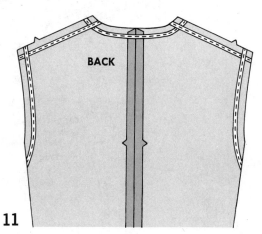

11

Back armholes, shoulders, neck (11)—Use ¼" wide tape. Cut to the measurements of armhole and neck on the back pattern, but use the **front** pattern for the shoulders. After stitching center back seam, stitch the tape lengths in place, on wrong side, just within seam allowances. At shoulders, ease garment to tape.

POCKETS

For patch pockets, follow the directions for DE-SIGNER PATCH POCKET on page 218.

For welt pockets, follow your pattern guide sheet. These pockets are made on the same principle as a bound buttonhole. Since the welt and the pocket opening on a jacket are made much the same as they are for pants, you might want to look over the WELTED HIP POCKET on page 178.

ADAPTING SHAPING AIDS FOR YOUR USE

Shoulder pads come in different sizes, with different amounts of padding. They can be trimmed if too large; if they are too thick, part of the padding can be removed. Be sure to preserve location of clip at edge, marking shoulder line.

After setting in the sleeves, trim armhole and sleeve seam allowances to ⅜". Make a second line of stitching ¼" from seam line. Match edge of shoulder pad to trimmed armhole edge, with clip at shoulder seam (12). If you have a fused chest piece (to which the pad cannot be tacked), tack it securely by hand to armhole and shoulder seam allowances.

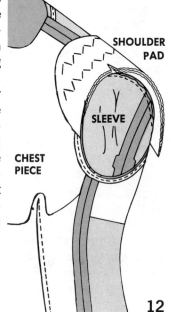

12

RIGHT-HAND SLEEVE   RIGHT-HAND SLEEVE

SLEEVE HEAD   SHOULDER PAD   SLEEVE HEAD

clip

SLEEVE   SLEEVE

JACKET FRONT   JACKET FRONT

SIDE   SIDE

13   BACK   **14**   BACK

Sleeve heads can be made from non-woven poly-ester fleece. For each sleeve, cut a strip 18″ long and 3″ wide. Fold one long edge over 1″, and ma-chine-stitch ⅜″ from fold.

After shoulder pads are in place, attach sleeve heads inside the armhole: Starting at back side seam of **jacket,** place the prepared strip on sleeve seam allowance, with wide side next to sleeve and fold even with raw armhole edge. Hand-stitch to seam al-lowance as far as 1½″ above back seam of **sleeve.** At this point, make a ¼″ clip through fold of sleeve head. At the clip, flip the sleeve head up so fold now lies along armhole seam line; whipstitch fold to seam line (13) around top of armhole. About 5″ down from shoulder seam at front of jacket, clip again through sleeve head fold, flip strip so fold is again even with raw armhole edge. Hand-stitch as before to seam allowance as far as front seam of **sleeve.** Cut off end of sleeve head even with seam. Finish off; turn sleeve head into sleeve (14).

LINING

If you have decided to make your collar according to the method that follows (in which the collar is at-tached last), complete the lining and stitch the jacket facings to it. Then stitch the facings to the jacket, handling lining and facings as a unit. Baste the raw neck edges of jacket, facings and lining together.

COLLAR

The collar achieved by this easy method is one any tailor would be proud of. Fit is perfect and corners are sharp and flat. The secret lies in the construction of the two collar ends.

UNDERCOLLAR

For suitable fabrics, see page 167. Note that, with the exception of the lightweight woven fabric (self-fabric), they are non-raveling.

Match undercollar pattern against pattern for upper collar: For the finished collar to fold down properly, the undercollar should be slightly smaller. If it is not, trim as directed below.

If jacket and undercollar are made of a lightweight washable, woven fabric, trim the seam allowance off the end(s) of undercollar pattern—not at center back seam. If undercollar pattern is not smaller than the upper collar, trim ⅛″ off its two long edges (15).

Cut undercollar and lighter weight interfacing from the adjusted pattern. On interfacing, trim ¾″ off long edges.

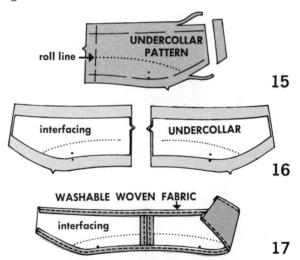

roll line → UNDERCOLLAR PATTERN   **15**

interfacing   UNDERCOLLAR   **16**

WASHABLE WOVEN FABRIC

interfacing   **17**

Fuse the interfacing to wrong side of undercollar section(s). Transfer roll line to interfacing (16). On a two-piece undercollar, join the center seam, press open, topstitch ⅛″ on each side of seam, trim seam allowances. Fold the long seam allowances to wrong side and edge-stitch close to fold; trim close to stitch-ing (17). Then fold the undercollar and steam-press as directed on the following page.

For all other fabrics, trim all outer seam allowances off the undercollar pattern (**not** at center back seam, if any). If pattern is not smaller than upper collar, trim an additional ⅛″ off the two long edges.

Cut undercollar and interfacing from the adjusted pattern; use the same type of interfacing you used for the jacket front.

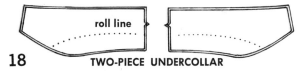

18 TWO-PIECE UNDERCOLLAR

Fuse interfacing to wrong side of undercollar sections. Transfer roll line to interfacing (18). On a two-piece undercollar, join the center seam, press open, topstitch ⅛″ on each side of seam, trim seam allowances (19).

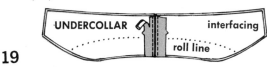

19

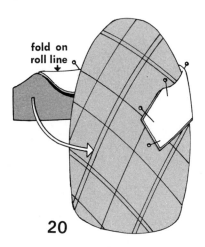

Fold undercollar on roll line, interfacing side out, as it will be worn. Pin to a pressing ham or tightly rolled towels and press with lots of steam to set the shape (20). Allow to dry thoroughly before handling further.

20

UPPER COLLAR

Lengthen the collar pattern by adding 1″ to each end (21). Cut upper collar from adjusted pattern.

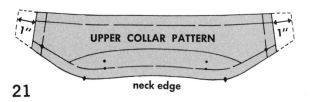

21

Interfacing is not needed if hair canvas was fused to the undercollar. If the lighter weight interfacing was used, however, cut another interfacing piece from the adjusted upper collar pattern. Then trim ½″ off the seam allowance on notched (neck) edge—⅛″ will be caught in seam. Trim ¾″ off the unnotched (outer) edge. Trim 1⅝″ off each end (on seam line). Fuse to wrong side of collar section (22).

Transfer all marks except roll line to wrong side of collar, whether interfaced or not. On outer edge, turn the ⅝″ seam allowance to wrong side; press. Baste close to fold.

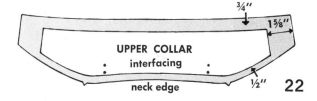

22

ATTACHING AND FINISHING THE COLLAR

a. Pin right side of upper collar to wrong side of jacket neck edge (including lining); match markings; clip neck edge as necessary and baste. Stitch a ⅝″ seam between end-marks (23). Trim jacket seam allowance to ¼″ and collar seam allowance to ⅜″. Press all seam allowances and collar up, away from garment.

For lightweight washable woven fabrics only, finish raw ends by folding ends ⅜″ to wrong side and edge-stitching.

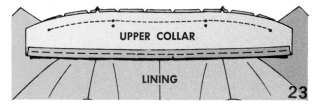

23

b. Pin undercollar to upper collar (24), wrong sides together, with outer edge of undercollar (raw or stitched, depending on fabric) 1/16″ from folded outer edge of upper collar, and neck edge of undercollar on jacket seam line. Sew down these two long edges with catch-stitch or blanket-stitch, taking small stitches, close together (24).

c. Fold ends to underside of collar and catch-stitch or blanket-stitch them down all around (25). Fold collar down so that bottom edge covers neck seam.

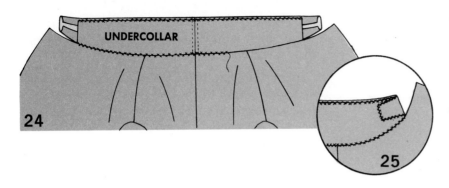

UNDERCOLLAR

24

25

MACHINE-WORKED KEYHOLE

26

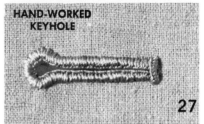

HAND-WORKED KEYHOLE

27

KEYHOLE BUTTONHOLE

The keyhole buttonhole is generally found on menswear, but also on tailored women's garments. This buttonhole is always horizontal, with the keyhole near the garment edge, where the button rests. It is usually corded for body and strength. Some machines are equipped to make keyhole buttonholes (26)—follow your sewing machine manual for instructions. Below you will find instructions for corded keyhole buttonholes made by hand (27).

For thread, use buttonhole twist, waxed, as this type of buttonhole is always used in heavier fabrics. To wax thread, draw it over a piece of beeswax; use wax sparingly.

For cording, use Button & Carpet thread, doubled, twisted and waxed; or a single strand of pearl cotton.

For measuring and marking the buttonholes, read pages 31 and 32.

a. Overcast the buttonhole by hand or machine before hand-working, holding the cord in place at the same time:

   By hand—Cut the buttonhole slit between end-lines, making small slashes at keyhole end as shown (28). With the cording held close to edges, overcast edges (29).

   By machine—Starting at bar tack end and working over a cord, make a buttonhole, leaving the keyhole end open; use a narrow, open zigzag stitch and be careful not to stitch into the cord (30). Cut the buttonhole slit between end-lines, making small slashes at keyhole end as shown (28). Draw up the cord-ends gently to bring the loop close to keyhole slashes.

b. Starting as for the REGULAR HAND-WORKED BUTTONHOLE (step **b**, p. 39), work over the edges with buttonhole stitch. At slashes, make a round keyhole; continue to bar-end (31).

c. Before making the bar tack, gently draw up both cord-ends to firm up the buttonhole. Thread cord-ends into a tapestry needle and bring them through to the inside, between facing and interfacing. Cut off, leaving short ends. Make the bar tack (see p. 39).

Steam-press, shaping the keyhole with an awl.

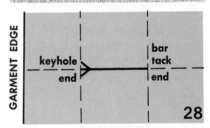

GARMENT EDGE
keyhole end
bar tack end

28

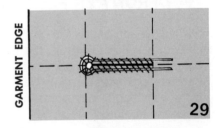

GARMENT EDGE

29

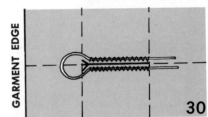

GARMENT EDGE

30

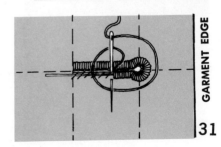

GARMENT EDGE

31

THE PANTS—
METHODS RECOMMENDED

CROTCH LINER

Before stitching any seams, add crotch reinforcement to the front sections. Cut from lining fabric, using the front pattern from notch in crotch to notch on inner leg seam (32); cut the inside edge on a curve, as shown. Pink the curved edge if lining fabric does not ravel; if it does, overcast the edge. Stitch liner to front sections ½″ from raw edges.

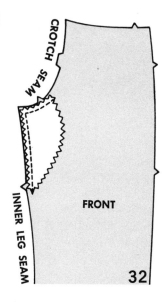

FLY-FRONT ZIPPER APPLICATION

While the application (33) is standard for an opening with a separate facing, the fly shield extension (optional) is a detail special to custom tailoring and the more expensive ready-to-wear clothes. Buttoned to the waistband, it provides extra security and reduces the strain on the zipper.

The zipper can be any conventional zipper of sufficient length or over. Any excess length will be cut off at completion of application (see illustrations).

a. On left front, mark curve of topstitching with basting.

b. Match crotch edges of front sections, right sides together. At bottom of fly, stitch the short curve from pattern marking to within 1″ or 1½″ from inner leg seam (34).

c. Pin left fly facing to left front edge, right sides together, matching markings. Stitch seam from marking at bottom of fly facing to waist (34). From waist to marking, trim facing seam allowance to ¼″ and pants seam allowance to ⅜″. Open out facing; press seam allowances toward facing; understitch (p. 94).

d. Pin closed zipper face-down on right side of open facing (if zipper is too long, let it extend beyond waist edge as shown): Right edge of zipper tape should lie along facing seam, and the **bottom stop** of the zipper should be ¾″ from lower raw edge of facing. Fold up bottom end of right-hand tape as shown, to keep it away from stitching in the next step (you release it later); baste right edge of tape to facing, through fold at end. Using a zipper foot and regular stitch, stitch left tape from bottom to top close to coil or chain; stitch again along edge of tape (35). Turn facing to inside on seam line. Press.

e. On outside, pin front to facing and topstitch from bottom to top along baste-marked line (at bottom, avoid folded-up zipper tape). Pull thread-ends to wrong side and tie. Remove all basting (36,37).

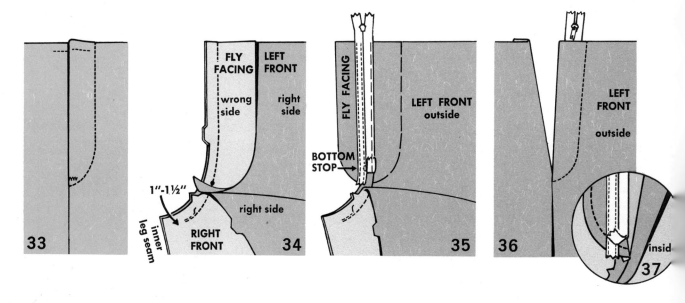

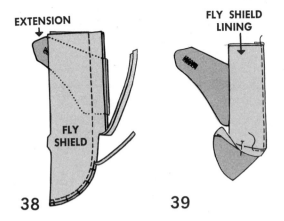

38   **39**

f. **Make the fly shield extension** (optional)—If your pattern does not have it, use the pattern below. Cut two from pants fabric or one from pants and one from lining fabric. Right sides together, stitch a ¼″ seam around, except at straight-grain edge. Trim seam and corners, turn, press. Make a machine-worked buttonhole as marked.

g. **Place extension as shown** (38) between right sides of sections for fly shield and fly shield lining: Straight raw edges even with edges of shield, finished top edge of extension even with raw top edges of shield. Stitch seam, through all thicknesses, on un-notched edge of shield. Grade and clip seam allowances. Turn shield and press.

h. **On raw (notched) edge of shield,** trim ⅜″ from pants fabric only. Fold lining over this edge and stitch close to fold (39).

i. **On inside of pants pin shield over zipper,** with curve of shield matched to line of topstitching (40). On right front make a ¼″ clip in the seam allowance at end of zipper. Press raw opening edge ¼″ to wrong side (40). Working from the outside, place this fold over the free zipper tape, with fold very close to coil or chain; pin through tape and fly shield.

Remove other pins holding the shield in place; open the zipper. Using a zipper foot and working from top to bottom, close to coil or chain, stitch on right side, through all thicknesses (edge of right front, zipper tape, fly shield). Pull thread-ends to wrong side and tie.

j. **If the zipper extends beyond raw waist edge,** trim it as follows: While it is still **open,** stitch across top end of each zipper tape, about ¼″ from raw edge, carefully guiding needle between coils or teeth. Cut off excess zipper at edge (41).

At bottom of fly, make a bar tack by hand or by machine, catching in the shield underneath (41).

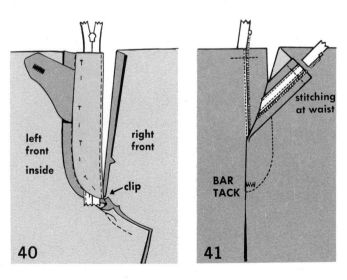

40   **41**

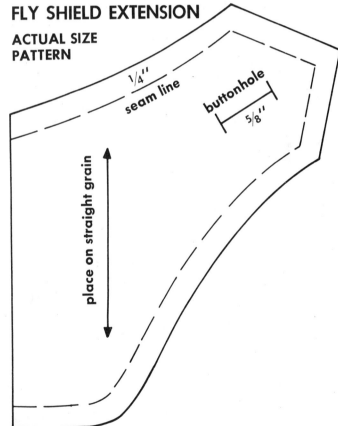

FLY SHIELD EXTENSION
ACTUAL SIZE PATTERN

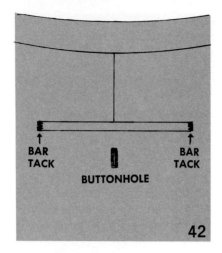

BAR
TACK

BAR
TACK

BUTTONHOLE

42

WELTED HIP POCKET

In this pocket (made on the same principle as the patch buttonhole), the inside fabric extends upward and is caught in the waistband seam, a feature that allows the pocket opening to keep its shape. Whether or not your pattern has a welted hip pocket, you may want to follow these directions. The pocket position is just below the hip dart, either centered across it, or with the outside end 2″—3″ from the side seam.

The single welt in this pocket (42) is ¼″ wide. For a wider welt, cut a wider welt strip and draw a wider opening on the pocket fabric.

Make the pocket in the back pants section(s) before stitching any seams, immediately after making darts.

a. **For each pocket, cut the following sections.**
From lining fabric: **pocket,** 21″ × 7″.
From pants fabric: **welt,** 6″ × 1½″ (lengthwise, crosswise, or bias); **underlay,** 6″ × 3″ (same grain as welt).
From Magic Polyweb: a strip 5″ × ¼″ for **welt;** a piece 6″ × 3″ for **underlay.**

b. **On wrong side of pocket piece,** draw the pocket opening, 5″ × ¼″, in the position shown (43). At the other end of the piece, fuse the underlay with Magic Polyweb to right side of fabric in the position shown. Finish underlay edges with plain or multi-stitch zigzag.

c. **To make the pocket opening,** pin pocket piece to pants section, right sides together, making sure the marked pocket position is just below the hip dart. Place pins about 1″ away from pocket markings (44). Set machine stitch at 12–15 per inch. Beginning at center of one long side, stitch carefully around marked opening. Pivot at corners; at end, stitch over beginning stitches. Starting at center of opening, cut carefully toward each end, stopping ½″ short of ends. Clip diagonally into corners (forming triangles, as shown), being careful not to cut through stitching.

Put the entire pocket piece through the opening to wrong side of pants section. Before pressing, place strips of brown paper between seam allowance and pants fabric, to prevent ridges on the outside. Press, using more steam than pressure, and making sure the opening is an exact rectangle.

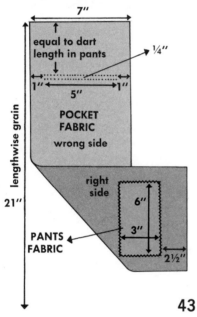

7″

equal to dart
length in pants

¼″

1″   5″   1″

POCKET
FABRIC

wrong side

lengthwise grain

21″

right
side

6″

3″

PANTS
FABRIC

2½″

43

WAIST EDGE

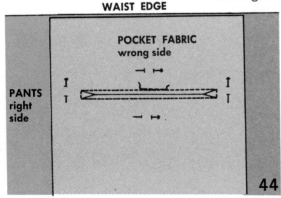

POCKET FABRIC
wrong side

PANTS
right
side

44

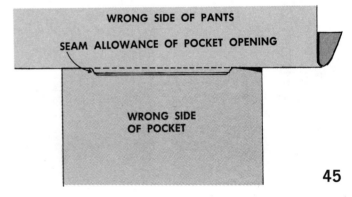

WRONG SIDE OF PANTS

SEAM ALLOWANCE OF POCKET OPENING

WRONG SIDE
OF POCKET

45

d. Fold the welt strip in half lengthwise, wrong sides together. Place the Magic Polyweb strip inside, along fold; fuse. With pants section right side up, place the welt under the pocket opening: fold of welt must touch upper edge of opening and the two ends underneath must extend evenly at both ends of opening. From right side, pin ends in place. To secure welt for permanent stitching, either slip-baste edge of welt to edge of pocket, or baste with a long, narrow zigzag stitch, barely catching the two edges.

e. To stitch bottom of welt in place, fold pants fabric out of the way, so the seam allowances of pocket opening are exposed (45). Baste through all thicknesses on pressed crease line of opening. Check on right side to make sure welt is straight and even; then stitch exactly over basting, with regular machine-stitch; back-tack at both ends (45).

At each end of opening, stitch end of welt in the same manner, basting over base of triangle and checking to make sure line is straight. To secure the triangles, carefully stitch back and forth two or three times.

On welt, trim the underneath seam allowance (46). Zigzag over raw edges of welt, attaching them to **pocket fabric only** (47).

A buttonhole, if any, should be put in now. Make a vertical worked (hand or machine) buttonhole ⅜″ below welt seam through all thicknesses (42).

f. To sew up the pocket, first remove basting from pocket opening. In order to make French seams, put pocket piece through to right side. Fold in half crosswise, wrong sides together, top and side edges even. Stitch ¼″ seams on sides (48). Trim seam allowances to ⅛″. Put pocket back through opening to wrong side, pulling out corners; press. Seam allowances are now on inside of pocket. Fold pants fabric out of the way. Make ¼″ seams at sides and bottom—at corners, instead of pivoting, shorten stitch length and round corners off (49).

g. To secure top edge of opening to pocket, fold pants fabric down over welt, exposing top seam allowances of pocket opening (49). Baste along crease line through all thicknesses and check; stitch, back-tack and press, as you did before.

h. Machine-baste raw top edges of pocket to pants section, ½″ from waist edge. On right side of pocket opening, make a machine bar tack at each end, the width of the welt (42).

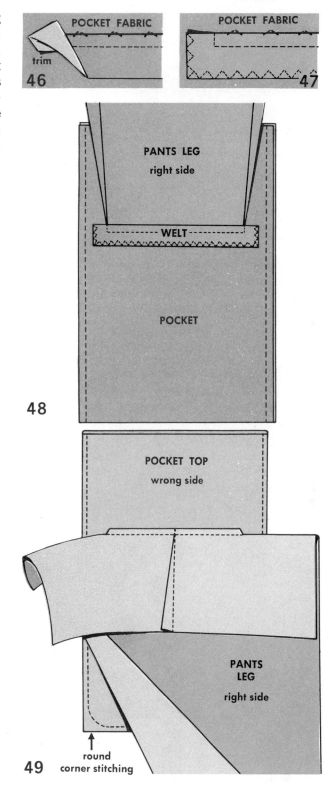

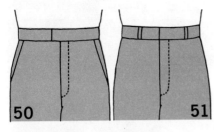

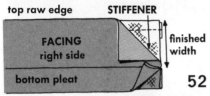

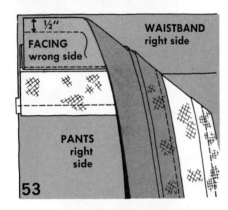

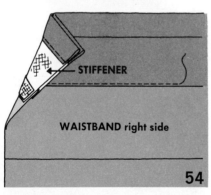

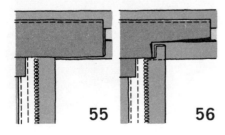

WAISTBAND

In many patterns, the waistband is a doubled strip of pants fabric, with stiffener in between. In custom-made and ready-to-wear trousers, however, the waistband is faced with lining fabric. The directions that follow will enable you to make such a waistband. On page 168 the two kinds of stiffeners available are listed and described. Both kinds, applied according to the two methods that follow, give excellent professional-looking results.

On pants worn without a belt, there may be an extension of the waistband front overlap (50). On dressier pants, worn with a belt, one front edge is generally flush with the fly edge (51), while the other is flush with the fly shield underneath. Decide **before** you cut the waistband if you want an extension.

The waistband in men's pants is made in two sections, with a seam at center back to allow for alterations. It is attached before center back seam is stitched.

WAISTBAND WITH READY-FACED STIFFENER

a. Cut the waistband from pants fabric, 1¼″ wider than desired finished width. Use the pattern for length and for marking the notches.

- If the pattern gives an extension, add about 4″ to the left-hand waistband section, to allow folding back (see ill. 57).
- If you want to add an extension not given in the pattern, add 6¼″ to the cut length of waistband section (this allows for a 2″ extension).

b. Cut the stiffener to the same length as the two waistband sections. Examine ill. 52, showing the construction of ready-faced stiffener.

- When there is no extension, trim the ⅝″ seam allowance at front edges off the **stiffener only,** not the facing.
- If the pattern gives an extension, cut stiffener and facing to the pattern seam line at front.
- If you are adding an extension, cut stiffener and facing 2″ beyond center front.

c. Match fabric waistband to pants, right sides together, notches matched. Stitch seam exactly ⅝″ from edges. Press waistband up.

d. Place right side of facing on stiffener to right side of waistband, raw edges even. Stitch at exactly ½″ from edge (53). Fold facing up on stitching, and fold stiffener in place, enclosing seam allowance of waistband between facing and stiffener. Topstitch as shown, through all thicknesses (54).

e. Finish front edges as follows:

- On a section without extension, turn stiffener and facing to right side, making a fold in waistband even with edge of stiffener; stitch a seam flush with fly edge. Grade seam, trim corner, turn waistband right side out and press.

• On an extension, press the long seam allowances to wrong side; stitch across end to secure them, as shown (57a). Trim off bottom of stiffener and facing to the width of waistband as far back as center of zipper tape (55). Clip fabric seam allowance ½″ in from edge of fly, and slip stiffener under seam allowance of extension (56).

To finish the raw edges along zipper, trim ¼″ from stiffener only; clip facing, fold it over stiffener and slipstitch down (57b).

Fold waistband end back over stiffener. Slipstitch top and bottom edges together (57c). The end may be stitched down from right side as a continuation of the zipper fly topstitching; or it can be hand-sewn in place (end turned under ¼″ if fabric is ravelly).

f. To stitch center back seam, extend stiffener up, out of the way. Pin seam, matching waistline seams. Starting ½″ below stiffener (which is not seamed in this stitching), back-tack 2 or 3 stitches, then stitch across the waistband and down the back, tapering to meet the front crotch seam. Do not trim seam allowances.

g. Press center back seam open, including the seam allowances of the unstitched stiffener. Fold stiffener to wrong side of waistband, as shown, and slipstitch to center back seam allowances (58). Press.

h. Hand-tack underpleat of stiffener to pockets and seam allowances at sides and center back. The button for the fly shield extension goes on the waistband seam. Sew on waistband fasteners.

WAISTBAND WITH PLAIN STIFFENER

a. Cut the waistband from pants fabric 1⅝″ wider than stiffener. Use the pattern for length and marking notches. If there is an extension, see step **a** on the opposite page.

b. Cut two bias strips for facings from lining fabric, 2¼″ wider than stiffener and the length of each waistband section. On one long edge of each bias strip, press 1″ to wrong side. **Cut stiffener** the length of each waistband section minus ⅝″ (stiffener should not extend into front seam allowance of facing). If there is an extension, see step **b** on the opposite page.

c. Match fabric waistband to pants, right sides together, notches matched. Stitch seam exactly ⅝″ from edges. With end of stiffener matched to raw center back edge, pin stiffener over seam allowance of waistband and pants, one edge along stitched seam line (59). Stitch as shown. Press waistband up.

d. To attach facing, pin raw (not pressed) edge of facing to raw (top) edge of waistband, right sides together. Stitch exactly ⅝″ from edges. Press facing up. Turn facing to inside over stiffener; pants fabric will also fold ¼″ to inside. Press (60).

e. To finish front edges and back seam, see steps **e,f,** and **g,** beginning on the opposite page.

f. Attach bottom edge of waistband, by stitching in the ditch of the waistband seam, on right side. The button for the fly shield extension goes on the waistband seam.

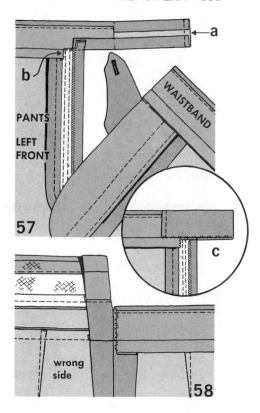

57

a

b

PANTS LEFT FRONT

WAISTBAND

c

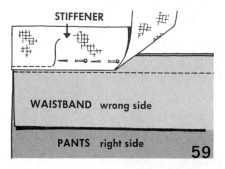

wrong side

58

STIFFENER

WAISTBAND wrong side

PANTS right side

59

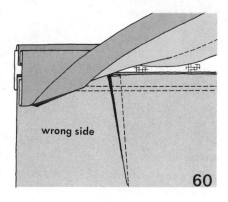

wrong side

60

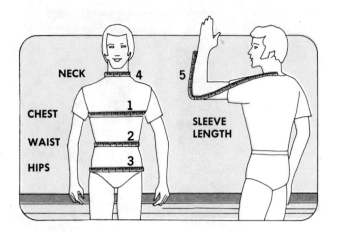

TAKING BODY MEASUREMENTS

Patterns are bought according to body measurements. Jacket and suit patterns are bought by chest measurement. Pants patterns are bought by waist measurement, unless hips are either unusually large or narrow in proportion to the waist, in which case you buy by hip measurement. For shirts, neck measurement can be omitted and pattern can be bought by ready-to-wear shirt size. Take the measurements as shown. From the charts at right, determine the correct size pattern.

1. **Chest**—Measure around fullest part of chest.
2. **Waist**—Measure at natural waistline over shirt.
3. **Hips**—Measure at seat or fullest part of hips.
4. **Neck**—Measure loosely.
5. **Sleeve Length**—Measure from base of neck in back across shoulder and around bent elbow to wrist.

BOYS and TEEN-BOYS

These size ranges are for growing boys and young men who have not yet reached full adult stature.

Chest	26″	27″	28″	30″	32″	33½″	35″	36½″
Waist	23″	24″	25″	26″	27″	28″	29″	30″
Hip (seat) . .	27″	28″	29½″	31″	32½″	34″	35½″	37″
Neckband . .	11¾″	12″	12½″	13″	13½″	14″	14½″	15″
Height	48″	50″	54″	58″	61″	64″	66″	68″
Boys' and Teen-boys' size	**7**	**8**	**10**	**12**	**14**	**16**	**18**	**20**

MEN

Men's patterns are sized for men of average build about 5′10″ without shoes.

Chest . .	34″	36″	38″	40″	42″	44″	46″	48″
Waist	28″	30″	32″	34″	36″	39″	42″	44″
Hip (seat) .	35″	37″	39″	41″	43″	45″	47″	49″
Neckband . .	14″	14½″	15″	15½″	16″	16½″	17″	17½″
Shirt sleeve	32″	32″	33″	33″	34″	34″	35″	35″
Men's size	**34**	**36**	**38**	**40**	**42**	**44**	**46**	**48**

The Metric System

One of these days the metric system will be our system of measurement, and we should be prepared to welcome it. Once the change-over is in effect, it will definitely make life easier for us. The reason why most of the rest of the world, as well as our own scientific community, uses the metric system is that its divisions are all by 10, 100, 1000. Obviously, this greatly simplifies figuring.

The basic unit of length in the metric system is the **meter (m),** an internationally established measure, a little longer than our yard. The meter is divided into 100 **centimeters (cm).** Each centimeter is divided into 10 **millimeters (mm).** All that is needed for these divisions is a decimal point, the way it is done now with dollars and cents. For instance: 2.35 means 2 meters plus 35 centimeters.

In sewing, once the metric system has been accepted, all the basic measurements we work with will be in m, cm and mm. We ourselves will not have to do any converting from yards and inches—although no doubt, until the new measurements mean something to us, we will for a while think in terms of their old equivalents. But you will take your measurements with a tape measure marked in centimeters (with results that may seem funny at first— 91.5 cm for a 36″ bust!). Your pattern size will be the same as before, but the body measurements on the back of the pattern envelope will correspond with yours in centimeters, too; and the amount of fabric you need will be given in meters. At the fabric counter, the fabric will be sold to you by the meter, which is about 40 inches. Notions, such as zippers etc., will be identified and sold by centimeters (2.5 cm equal 1 inch).

Our pattern companies are already geared to the metric system for the simple reason that American patterns are sold all over the world. You may have noticed that many pattern companies, besides the notations in inches on the pattern, also give their equivalent in "cm" (for example, the ⅝" seam allowance is also marked 1.5 cm or 15 mm).

One thing you can do now is to buy a tape measure that has inches on one side, centimeters on the other —a good way to get a feeling for the relationship between inches and centimeters.

As mentioned before, you will not be called upon to do any converting to speak of; it will all be done for you. The only time you may have to convert is if you want to use an old pattern—one of the old favorites you have kept. There, the amount, given in yards, will have to be changed into meters, for buying fabric.

In case you like to follow what is going on, one of the charts below will allow you to compare yards and meters in either direction (for convenience's sake, the figures have been slightly rounded off). There is also a chart to convert inches to centimeters and millimeters.

meters into yards read this way ←		yards into meters → read this way	
1⅛ yds ← = meter	1	yard = →	0.915 m
2¼ yds ← = meters	2	yards = →	1.83 m
3⁵⁄₁₆ yds ← = meters	3	yards = →	2.74 m
4⁷⁄₁₆ yds ← = meters	4	yards = →	3.66 m
5½ yds ← = meters	5	yards = →	4.57 m
6⅝ yds ← = meters	6	yards = →	5.49 m
7¾ yds ← = meters	7	yards = →	6.40 m
8¹³⁄₁₆ yds ← = meters	8	yards = →	7.32 m
9⅞ yds ← = meters	9	yards = →	8.23 m
11 yds ← = meters	10	yards = →	9.15 m

inches	millimeters mm	centimeters cm
⅛"	3 mm	0.3 cm
¼"	6 mm	0.6 cm
⅜"	10 mm	1.0 cm
½"	13 mm	1.3 cm
⅝"	16 mm	1.6 cm
¾"	19 mm	1.9 cm
⅞"	22 mm	2.2 cm
1"	25 mm	2.5 cm
2"	51 mm	5.1 cm
3"	76 mm	7.6 cm

inches	centimeters cm
4"	10.2 cm
5"	12.7 cm
6"	15.2 cm
7"	17.8 cm
8"	20.3 cm
9"	22.9 cm
10"	25.4 cm
11"	27.9 cm
12"	30.5 cm

Notions

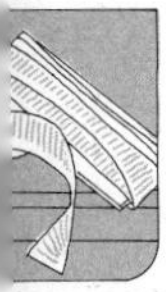

The notions which follow consist of all the small articles that go into the making of a garment and become part of it. They are listed alphabetically with a brief description of each product and its uses. If you want more information, refer to relevant chapters in this book.

Notions which are used as **tools** in the construction of a garment are listed under EQUIPMENT. For interfacing, see that chapter.

Be sure to select notions that have the same care requirements as the garment (washable or dry-cleanable) and pre-shrink notions wherever possible.

BELT BUCKLES are available in many materials— for instance in metal, plastic, bone, mother-of-pearl or wood. Fabric-covered buckles can be ordered in notions or sewing stores and departments, or made with the help of a kit (see BELT BUCKLES, p. 23).

BELTING comes in three types, each with its own purpose:

Washable belting is used for backing fabric belts. It is available by the yard in widths from ½″ to 3″, in black or white; also in belt-and-buckle kits (see BELTS).

Grosgrain belting is stiff grosgrain ribbon used for waistbands of skirts and pants; it may be used inside the waistband or as a waistband backing. It is sold by the yard, in widths from ½″ to 2″, in black or white. Soft **grosgrain ribbon** may be used as a facing in skirts and pants. It is sold by the yard or in packages, in widths from ¼″ to 2″, in colors.

Waistband stiffener is a non-roll backing strip used in waistbands of skirts, pants and men's trousers. It is always used inside the waistband. It is available by the yard or in packages, in widths from ½″ to 2″. It is sold plain or with a facing of lining fabric attached (see MENSWEAR, pp. 168 and 180).

BIAS TAPES are pre-folded bias strips, packaged in various widths and lengths and most commonly used for binding and facing edges. See the chart below.

BONING and **STAYS,** the modern, lighter substitutes for whalebone, are used where vertical support is needed, as in strapless tops and cummerbunds. They are available by the yard or in packages, in black or white. Packaged stays come in 4″, 6″ and 8″ lengths.

BUTTONS, for fastening or decoration, come in a great variety of materials, shapes and sizes. You can arrange to have buttons covered with your own fabric by notions stores or departments; or you can make them yourself, with or without the help of a kit (see BUTTONS).

CABLE CORD is soft cotton cord, used as a filler for corded tubing or corded piping (see BIAS, pp. 29, 30) and for corded buttonholes (see BUTTONHOLES, p. 33). It comes in many sizes, in black or white.

DECORATIVE TRIMS are available in so many varieties and sizes that we cannot cover them all here. They include: braids (knit, fold-over knit, middy, soutache), rick rack (baby, medium, jumbo), laces (plain or ruffled), embroidered ribbons, appliqués, iron-on patches, and many others. They are sold at notions or sewing stores and departments, by the yard or in packages (see TRIMMING).

BIAS FOLD TAPES

WIDTH	NAME	FIBER CONTENT AND COLORS	DESCRIPTION	USES
½″	**SINGLE FOLD BIAS TAPE**	Rayon, cotton, and polyester/cotton; black, white and colors	Bias strip, raw edges folded to wrong side, meeting at center	Binding (¼″ wide), facing, casing, accent trim; can be used with binder attachment; see BIAS
¼″	**DOUBLE FOLD BIAS TAPE**	Cotton, polyester/cotton; black, white and colors	Bias strip, same as single fold plus extra fold just off center	Extra-quick binding (¼″ wide), accent trim; see BIAS
1″	**WIDE BIAS TAPE**	Same as above	Bias strip, raw edges folded ¼″ to wrong side	Facing, binding (½″ wide), accent trim; see BIAS
2″	**HEM FACING**	Rayon taffeta, cotton, polyester/cotton; black, white and colors		Hem facing, binding (1″ wide), craft items; see BIAS
⅛″	**PIPING (corded)**	Cotton, polyester/cotton; black, white and colors	Bias strip (corded), ¼″ seam allowance	Piping; see BIAS

ELASTIC comes in many varieties with different fiber contents, weights (firm or soft) and constructions. It may be made in polyester, nylon, cotton, rayon, or blends and can be woven, knitted or braided. Be sure to consider its use and the garment care when selecting elastic. It is sold by the yard or in packages, from ⅛″ to several inches in width, in black or white. Lingerie elastic, which is soft and lightweight, is also available in pastel colors (see LINGERIE).

FUSIBLE WEB is a fusing agent used between layers of fabric. It comes packaged in strips ¾″ to 2″ wide or in pieces up to 9″ × 36″, or is available by the yard (see FUSIBLES).

HOOKS AND EYES are the reliable fasteners used at points of strain (see FASTENERS). Regular hooks and eyes come in several styles and sizes, in black or nickel. Large hooks and eyes, such as coat hooks for outer wear and flat hooks for waistbands, are available in black or nickel. Coat hooks also come silk-covered; flat hooks are available in sew-on and hammer-on varieties.

HORSEHAIR BRAID is used to stiffen hems of flared or full skirts (see HEMS). It is available by the yard or in packages, in ½″ and 1″ widths, in black or white.

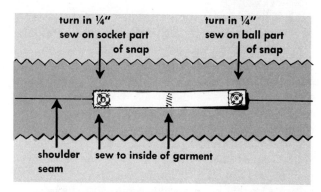

turn in ¼″ sew on socket part of snap

turn in ¼″ sew on ball part of snap

shoulder seam

sew to inside of garment

LINGERIE STRAPHOLDERS are attached on the inside of a garment shoulder seam to hold lingerie straps in place. They are available in black, white and limited colors, or can be made as shown, using 3″ of narrow tape or ribbon for each.

NYLON TAPE FASTENERS consist of two pieces, one with tiny hooks and one with tiny loops, which interlock (see FASTENERS). They are good for closures where there is an underlay. Sew-on and iron-on types are available by the yard or in packages, in black, white and limited colors.

POCKET REPLACEMENT KITS include a pair of constructed cotton pockets in white or black that can be sewn on or ironed on.

SEAM BINDING is used for finishing hems and for staying seams such as at a waistline or shoulder. See the chart below.

SEAM BINDING				
WIDTH	**NAME**	**FIBER CONTENT AND COLORS**	**DESCRIPTION**	**USES**
½″ 1″	**SEAM BINDING**	Rayon; black, white and colors	Ribbon-type, straight grain, woven edges	Edge of hem, see HEMS; waistline stay, see p. 277
½″	**IRON-ON SEAM BINDING**	Same as above	Same as above, with heat sensitive adhesive	Edge of hem
¾″	**STRETCH LACE SEAM BINDING**	Nylon; black, white and colors	Decorative lace	Edge of hem, sleeves, see HEMS; facings, binding (⅜″ wide)
1¾″	**STRETCH LACE HEM FACING**			Hem facing, binding (⅞″ wide), craft items
½″	**FOLD-OVER STRETCH LACE**		Decorative lace, folded just off center	Extra-quick binding (½″ wide), accent trim

SHAPING AIDS for both men and women are available ready-made or can be made to fit the individual. Shoulder pads are sold covered or uncovered in many styles and sizes; menswear shaping aids—chest pieces, shoulder pads and sleeve heads—are available in kits; sleeve heads can also be bought separately. Use washable items in washable garments (see MENSWEAR and TAILORING).

SNAPS, HAMMER-ON, are used on children's clothes, work clothes, pajamas and sportswear. They are sold packaged in various types and colors, with instructions on the package. Some are very decorative.

SNAPS, SEW-ON, are good for closings that have little strain (see FASTENERS). They are available in many sizes from 4/0 (smallest) to 4 (largest); in metal (black or nickel) and nylon (clear and limited colors). Silk-covered snaps are also available in two sizes and many colors. Instructions for covering snaps are on page 100.

THREAD—See the chapter on THREAD AND NEEDLES.

TWILL TAPE is strong cotton or polyester tape, ¼″ to 1″ wide, used as a waistline stay, in tailoring, menswear, and for drawstrings. It is sold in packages, in black or white only.

WEIGHTS are used to give body to the hang or drape of a garment. They may be placed at hems, or, for example, in a cowl neckline. They come in various types:

Round lead weights resemble coins and are of different sizes (weights). Inquire as to reaction to washing or dry cleaning. They may be sewn permanently within the layers of a garment or, covered with lining fabric, attached in place with a small safety pin.

Lead weight by the yard consists of small flat slugs (in two weights) encased in ½″ tape, or small pellets covered with a knitted sleeve. Attach along the top edge of a hem before sewing down the lining.

Gold chain weight is pretty enough to be tacked along the lining, not covered by it. It comes in various weights, by the yard or packaged.

ZIPPERS are usually constructed of synthetic coils or metal teeth attached to knit or woven tapes (see ZIPPERS). A small number of novelty zippers with nylon or plastic teeth are also available.

Conventional zippers (skirt, dress or neck) are made in lengths from 4″ to 24″, in fashion colors. They are used in garments and home decorating items.

Invisible zippers (7″–9″, 12″–14″, 16″–18″, 20″–22″) are coil zippers which are entirely concealed in a seam. They are used in garments and home decorating items. Available in fashion colors.

Separating zippers are usually made of metal, in two weights: lightweight (12″ to 22″) for jackets and dresses, in limited colors; heavy (14″ to 22″) for outer wear, in neutral colors only. Other types include: reversible jacket (16″ to 22″) in limited colors; parka, which includes a dual slider (20″ to 60″), in limited colors; a nylon teeth zipper in limited colors and one size (20″) which must be shortened at the top to fit the garment; a coil separating zipper is also available.

Zippers for special applications:

Trouser zippers (9″ to 11″) are made of metal or coil. Shorten at the top to fit the garment (see MENSWEAR, p. 176).

Blue jean zippers (6″) are made of metal.

Ring pull zippers (7″, 18″, 22″) are large coil zippers with a decorative pull-tab, in limited colors. They are used for sportswear and children's clothes. Some zippers of this type are also available with nylon teeth in limited colors and sizes (7″ and 20″).

Snowmobile zippers (20″ to 40″) are large coil zippers with dual sliders, in black only.

Slipcover zippers (24″ to 36″) are heavy zippers made of metal, in beige only.

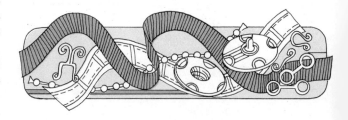

Patterns

Patterns are offered in countless styles, for all kinds of figure-types, and in just about as many sizes as people come in.

Style, important as it is, has nothing to do with fit and so is of little concern to us here. Besides, like fabric, it can change with each new garment you make.

Figure-type and size in the right combination are what make for good fit. Moreover, they can and should be established once and for all (unless you gain or lose noticeable weight). We would like to show you how to make the correct choice; and, if the fit is not perfect, how to adjust the pattern to your figure. **Any major adjustment for fit must be made on the pattern.**

American patterns are very accurately drafted. They are based on figures supplied by the U.S. Bureau of Standards from surveys made of the body measurements of a representative segment of our population. The basic body measurements, therefore, are standard and mean the same thing in all pattern brands—the measurement of bust, waist, etc. as it is on your body.

Garments, however, must have an ease allowance in order to be wearable. It is this ease allowance, and the way it is distributed, that varies with the different pattern companies.

The information in this chapter is for women's and teenage girls' clothes only. See the chapter CHILDREN'S CLOTHES for measuring and buying a pattern for a child; the chapter MENSWEAR for doing the same for a man or teen-age boy.

As general information about patterns, you will also want to know that most pattern brands have certain designs planned for quick, easy sewing, which are marked accordingly. Also, certain patterns are good only for given fabrics, and are so marked (for example: "For stretch knits only").
Please note that patterns are never returnable.

THE RIGHT PATTERN FOR YOU

You may prefer the styles of one pattern brand to those of another. Which one gives you the best fit, however, can be discovered only by actual trial, because no measurements will furnish a clue to their subtle differences in line and cut. For a first garment, choose something simple (or a Basic Pattern) in any brand. Unless the fit gives you entire satisfaction, try another pattern-brand for your next garment. In time you will know which brand is best for you.

Style—Styles are related to figure-type only to the extent that they are designed with certain body proportions in mind. Otherwise, style is a separate consideration about which we have only one recommendation at this point: Steer clear of anything complicated until you are an expert.

On the other hand, correct choice of figure-type and size means not only good fit, but few, if any, adjustments.

Figure-type is what is meant by "Misses", "Half-sizes", "Juniors", and the other categories listed in the charts on the next page. These categories, based on the variations in our shapes, are very important —even the pattern books are divided and indexed according to figure-types. The measurements for the different figure-types are based on the body build or proportions generally belonging to certain age groups. This classification is quite loose, and a person in one age group may very well have the proportions of another. The styles designed for one figure-type, however, may not be suitable for another.

Size is established by the four measurements—bust, waist, hips, back waist length—that are usually listed under Standard Body Measurements on pattern envelopes. If only the bust measurement is shown, you will find the other measurements for the same figure-type and size on the charts on the next page. Correct bust measurement is, however, the most important in any garment that takes in the bust.

The back—neck to waist measurement (back waist length) is determined by a person's height. A very rounded back, of course, may throw the measurement off.

For how to take your measurements, see page 192.

CHARTS of FIGURE-TYPES and SIZES

These charts cover all the figure-types and sizes as they are used by all the pattern companies. The classifications and measurements are standard, and are meant to take in all the variations of the feminine form.

MISSES'

Misses' patterns are designed for a well-proportioned and developed figure; about 5'5" to 5'6" without shoes.

Bust	30½	31½	32½	34	36	38	40	42	ins.
Waist	23	24	25	26½	28	30	32	34	ins.
Hips (9" below waist)	32½	33½	34½	36	38	40	42	44	ins.
Back waist length	15½	15¾	16	16¼	16½	16¾	17	17¼	ins.
MISSES' SIZE	**6**	**8**	**10**	**12**	**14**	**16**	**18**	**20**	

WOMEN'S

Women's patterns are designed for the larger, more mature figure; about 5'5" to 5'6" without shoes.

Bust	42	44	46	48	50	52	54	ins.
Waist	35	37	39	41½	44	46½	49	ins.
Hips (9" below waist)	44	46	48	50	52	54	56	ins.
Back waist length	17¼	17⅜	17½	17⅝	17¾	17⅞	18	ins.
WOMEN'S SIZE	**38**	**40**	**42**	**44**	**46**	**48**	**50**	

HALF-SIZE

Half-size patterns are for a fully developed figure with a short back waist length. Waist and hips are larger in proportion to bust than other figure types; about 5'2" to 5'3" without shoes.

Bust	33	35	37	39	41	43	45	47	ins.
Waist	27	29	31	33	35	37½	40	42½	ins.
Hips (7" below waist)	35	37	39	41	43	45½	48	50½	ins.
Back waist length	15	15¼	15½	15¾	15⅞	16	16⅛	16¼	ins.
HALF-SIZE	**10½**	**12½**	**14½**	**16½**	**18½**	**20½**	**22½**	**24½**	

JUNIOR

Junior patterns are designed for a well-proportioned, shorter-waisted figure; about 5'4" to 5'5" without shoes.

Bust	30	31	32	33½	35	37	ins.
Waist	22½	23½	24½	25½	27	29	ins.
Hips (9" below waist)	32	33	34	35½	37	39	ins.
Back waist length	15	15¼	15½	15¾	16	16	ins.
JUNIOR SIZE	**5**	**7**	**9**	**11**	**13**	**15**	

JUNIOR PETITE

Junior Petite patterns are designed for a well-proportioned petite figure; about 5' to 5'1" without shoes.

Bust	30½	31	32	33	34	35	ins.
Waist	22½	23	24	25	26	27	ins.
Hips (7" below waist)	31½	32	33	34	35	36	ins.
Back waist length	14	14¼	14½	14¾	15	15¼	ins.
JUNIOR PETITE SIZE	**3jp**	**5jp**	**7jp**	**9jp**	**11jp**	**13jp**	

MISS PETITE

This size range is designed for the shorter Miss figure; about 5'2" to 5'4" without shoes.

Bust	30½	31½	32½	34	36	38	ins.
Waist	23½	24½	25½	27	28½	30½	ins.
Hips (7" below waist)	32½	33½	34½	36	38	40	ins.
Back waist length	14½	14¾	15	15¼	15½	15¾	ins.
MISS PETITE SIZE	**6mp**	**8mp**	**10mp**	**12mp**	**14mp**	**16mp**	

YOUNG JUNIOR/TEEN

This size range is designed for the developing pre-teen and teen figures; about 5'1" to 5'3" without shoes.

Bust	28	29	30½	32	33½	35	ins.
Waist	22	23	24	25	26	27	ins.
Hips (7" below waist)	31	32	33½	35	36½	38	ins.
Back waist length	13½	14	14½	15	15⅜	15¾	ins.
YOUNG JUNIOR/TEEN SIZE	**5/6**	**7/8**	**9/10**	**11/12**	**13/14**	**15/16**	

DETERMINING YOUR FIGURE-TYPE AND SIZE

Take your four basic measurements. You can do it alone if you have no one to help you, but it must be done right—see page 192.

Then check the measurements with the chart for the figure-type in which you buy your ready-to-wear clothes. The chances are that this is the category in which you belong, especially if your ready-to-wear fits you well.

Otherwise, read the description of each figure-type on the charts to the left and decide which ones seem best suited to you. If your measurements should place you in a category whose styles you find quite inappropriate for you, you may want to look under another figure-type, where the combination of measurements may not come as close to yours (and may necessitate an adjustment in the pattern), but where your taste is satisfied.

On each chart which you consider a possibility, circle the measurements that match yours. If any one of your measurements falls between two on a chart, place the circle between the two; if it is closer to one than the other, circle the closer one (see the EXAMPLE to the right).

Then, compare the charts marked and see which one does best in combining your measurements **within one size.** You may end up choosing a type and size in which no measurement is exactly yours, but all come reasonably close.

PATTERN SIZE AND TYPE OF GARMENT

In cases where your measurements do not clearly fit one pattern size, a deciding factor can be the kind of garment you are planning, and whether an adjustment will be easy or difficult. For instance:

• In a dress, blouse or jacket, the **bust** measurement should be correct, because adjustment of the armhole-and-neck area is difficult. Pattern ease, however, will take care of a bust up to 1″ larger than the body measurement given on the pattern envelope.

• A straight skirt or pants should have correct fit at the **hips**—the waist is easy to adjust.

• A full skirt goes by **waist** measurement.

• A loose-hanging or semi-fitted garment needs correct **bust** size and nothing else.

HOW TO USE THE CHARTS ON PAGE 188—AN EXAMPLE

Suppose we imagine a girl with the following measurements, using these charts to establish her figure-type and size:

Bust	33½″
Waist	25″
Hips	37″
Back waist length	15⅝″

Since she knows that she does not have a child's figure, she can eliminate the category Young Junior/Teen. Nor are her measurements anywhere near Women's. Her back waist measurement is too long to fit her into Junior Petite or Miss Petite. As for Half-size, she does not have the bust-waist-hip fullness and comparatively narrow shoulders that are characteristic of this figure-type, generally representative of the older, more mature woman. This leaves the Misses and Junior categories, whose styles are also the most suitable for her age anyway and offer the most variety. On the two charts she now checks, her measurements fall like this:

Bust	30½	31½	32½	(34)	36	38	40	42	ins.
Waist ...	23	24	(25)	26½	28	30	32	34	ins.
Hips (9″ below waist)	32½	33½	34½	36	38	40	42	44	ins.
Back waist length ...	15½	15¾	16	16¼	16½	16¾	17	17¼	ins.

MISSES' SIZE	6	8	10	12	14	16	18	20

Bust	30	31	32	(33½)	35	37	ins.
Waist........	22½	23½	24½	25½	27	29	ins.
Hips (9″ below waist)	32	33	34	35½	(37)	39	ins.
Back waist length	15	15¼	15½	15¾	16	16	ins.

JUNIOR SIZE	5	7	9	11	13	15

On the Misses chart, the back waist length is entirely out of line, which means that the up-and-down points (points of bust, elbow, etc.) will fall in the wrong places. On the Junior chart this measurement is almost perfect, while the important bust measurement is right, too. It is no trick to take off a half-inch at the waist and add 1½″ to the hips.

Her pattern will be a Junior 11.

YOUR PERSONAL MEASUREMENT CHART

When you take your measurements (see p. 192), it is a good idea to record them on a personal measurement chart, as an easy reference for checking pattern measurements, as long as your weight stays the same. Date the chart and check your measurements against it from time to time.

PERSONAL MEASUREMENT CHART

To make a chart, mark off four columns on a sheet of ruled paper. In the first column, list the points to measure, numbered as on page 192. Mark the three remaining columns **Body measurements, Ease,** and **Total.** See the sample chart below. There are three more columns for **Pattern measurements, Difference,** and **Adjustments,** which you can add to your chart in pencil since the figures will change with each pattern, or you can put these on a separate piece of paper.

In the second column of the chart, enter your **body measurement** for each point measured.

ADDING EASE

A garment made to exact body measurements would be unwearable. For comfort and freedom of movement, ease allowances are therefore added to patterns, particularly in the width. These allowances are not standard, but vary with each pattern company.

Ease is entered on your personal measurement chart in order to check the pattern measurements against your body measurements. However, if you have a well-fitting garment of a similar design, you can check the pattern measurements against the measurements taken from this garment, which already includes ease.

Below are the average amounts of ease added to patterns. Note that there is a range, so you can add the larger or smaller amount, depending on whether you like your clothes loosely or closely fitted. Remember too, that large sizes require more ease than small ones. However, if your fabric is a very stretchy knit and you want the garment close fitting, you will need little or no ease.

Enter these allowances in the third, or **Ease,** column of your chart, after each body measurement. Where no ease is listed, it means that none is needed—just make a dash in the column.

1. Bust—2½″ to 3½″ for a fitted bodice.
2. Waist—½″ to 1″.
3. Hips—2½″ to 3″.
4. Back waist length—⅛″ to ½″.
5. Front—shoulder to waist—¼″.
8. Bust front—half the ease allowed for Bust.
9. Back width—¼″ to ½″.
13. Upper arm—1″ to 2″ for a fitted sleeve.
14. Crotch depth—½″ to 1″.
15. Thigh—1½″ to 2½″, depending on fabric.

Jackets and coats, of course, require considerably more ease:
1. Bust—4½″ to 6″.
2. Waist—3½″ to 5″.
3. Hips—3½″ to 6″.
13. Upper arm—1¾″ to 3½″.

YOUR WORKING MEASUREMENTS

On each line across your chart, add up body measurement and ease allowance and enter the total in the **Total** column. Where there is no ease, enter the body measurement. **Compare these figures with the actual pattern measurements.**

PERSONAL MEASUREMENT CHART

	Body meas.	Ease	Total	Pattern meas.	Diff.	Adjustments
1. Bust	33½″	2½″-3½″	36″-37″	37⅛″	⅛″	none diff. negligible
2. Waist	25″	½″-1″	25½″-26″	25″	½″ needed	add to seams
3. Hips	37″	2½″-3″	39½″-40″	37½″	2″ needed	add to side seams
4. Back Waist Length	15⅝″	⅛″-½″	15¾″-16⅛″	15¾″	none	none
5. front						

CHECKING THE PATTERN FOR FIT

Checking the pattern for fit is something that a great many home-sewers neglect to do. If you are lucky, both in your figure and in your choice of pattern-brand (and/or if your garment is of a loosely-fitted design) you may achieve acceptable fit without it; or fitting may be sufficient for the adjustments needed (see that chapter). If, however, you do not have such luck, you may have an unsuccessful garment—very discouraging for any dressmaker. Your only option in such a case will be to make the adjustments on your **next** pattern.

Checking the pattern measurements may prevent a lot of trouble. As mentioned before, there are two ways of doing this:

You can compare the pattern measurements against your body measurements plus ease (the figure in the **Total** column on your personal measurement chart).

OR

If you have a well-fitting garment of a similar design, it already includes the right amount of ease. Check the pattern measurements against the measurements taken from this garment at exactly the same points.

THE PATTERN MEASUREMENTS

First of all, let us make clear the difference between the ease we have just been talking about, whose purpose is to make a garment wearable, and **design ease,** such as in a free-hanging garment, a gathered top or skirt, etc. Where there is such design ease (fullness), it is not necessary to measure the pattern, as the ease must always be left in. When the fullness consists of pressed or stitched pleats, the pleats should be folded in the pattern before the pattern is measured.

Otherwise, measuring a pattern is not difficult, although it must be done with care. Even if your four basic measurements are exactly those of your pattern figure-type and size, you cannot be sure the pattern will fit at all points. Ease allowances not only vary, but may be changed without notice.

To measure a pattern:
- Iron out the creases in pattern with a warm, dry iron.

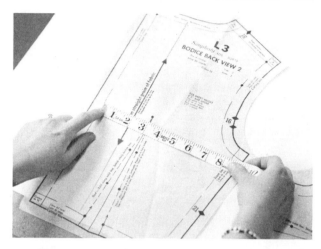

- Have pattern pieces flat on table.
- With pencil and yardstick, extend the grain line on each piece the entire length of the piece.
- Mark the point of bust, as follows:

If a bodice front has only one dart, point of bust will be ½″ to 1″ beyond point of dart.

If a bodice front has both waist and side darts, draw a line through the center of each dart to beyond the point; where the two lines meet is the point of bust.

- Measure the pattern pieces at exactly the points at which you have taken the corresponding measurements on your body.
- Take all measurements from seam line to seam line. Do not include seam allowances, or the width of any darts.
- When only half a pattern is given, be sure to double the measurement before writing it down.
- As you go along, jot down each measurement. The easiest way to compare these figures with the ones on your chart is to note them as shown in the sample chart under **Pattern measurements** (use a pencil, as suggested earlier). If you wish to use a separate piece of paper, be sure to identify each measurement properly, either by number or by name.

WHAT ADJUSTMENTS ARE NEEDED?

Now compare the pattern measurements with those in the **Total** column on your chart. Note the difference, if any, in the **Difference** column. Then write down, as shown, what adjustment is needed.

How to make adjustments is described in the following pages.

TAKING YOUR MEASUREMENTS

Measurements should be taken over well-fitting undergarments, with a narrow ribbon, seam tape or string tied snugly around the waist to mark the exact waistline location.

The first four measurements (the ones you need to establish your figure-type and size and buy your pattern) can, if necessary, be taken by yourself without help. For some others you will need someone to help you.

1. **Bust**—measure around fullest part.

2. **Waist**—at ribbon around waist.

3. **Hips**—around fullest part: usually 9″ below waist for Misses', Women's, and Junior sizes; 7″ below waist for Half-sizes, Junior Petite, Miss Petite and Young Junior/Teen.

4. **Back waist length** (back—neck to waist)—from prominent vertebra at back of neck to waistline ribbon. If you are taking this without help, use one

hand to hold end of measuring tape on vertebra, which can be felt even better than seen. With the other hand, hold tape at waist, marking location of ribbon with thumbnail. Release upper end of tape and note measurement.

5. **Front—shoulder to waist**—from middle of shoulder over point of bust to waistline ribbon.

6. **Point of bust**—from middle of shoulder to point of bust—note when taking preceding measurement.

7. **Point of bust** (distance from center)—measure from one bust-point to the other: divide measurement in half.

8. **Bust front**—from side seam to side seam over fullest part of bust.

9. **Back width**—across back, 4″ down from prominent vertebra, between body folds formed by arms hanging straight.

10. **High hip**—around hips (hip bones) 2″ to 4″ below waist.

11. **Sleeve length**—from edge of shoulder, where sleeve would be set in, over bent elbow to wrist bone or desired length.

12. **Point of elbow**—preceding measurement to point of elbow only.

13. **Upper arm**—around arm 1″ below armpit; if one arm is larger, use larger measurement.

14. **Crotch depth**—sit on a flat chair with your feet flat on floor; measure from waist to chair at side seam, following curve of body.

15. **Thigh**—around fullest part; note distance from waist.

16. **Skirt length**—favorite skirt length from waist to hem; measurement can be used for a dress, from marked waistline to hem.

17. **Pants length**—along the side seam; measure your favorite pants from waist to hem.

Needless to say, you will not need all these measurements at any one time. You might just take the ones that apply to the garment you are about to make. If, however, you plan to take your sewing seriously, it is an excellent idea to take all the measurements now and make up **a personal measurement chart,** as shown on page 190.

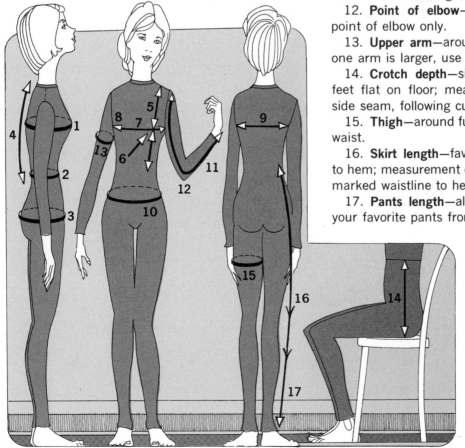

PATTERN ADJUSTMENTS

Adjusting a pattern means adding to it where it is too small for fit, and reducing it where it is too large. When this is done right, the basic outline of the pattern is maintained, the sections still fit together, and the garment keeps its intended shape and style.

If you have followed the first part of this chapter by taking your measurements and comparing them with those of the pattern you have noted a difference where the pattern needs an adjustment. The AD-JUSTMENTS FROM MEASUREMENTS, starting on page 195, will show you how to do it.

There are, however, a number of problems of fit that do not show up in the comparison of measurements, but only as a garment is tried on. The more common of these problems are taken care of under OTHER ADJUSTMENTS, page 202. If you have already encountered such faults of fit in your ready-to-wear clothes, you would do well to make a BASIC MUSLIN (see p. 205) on which you can make all the necessary corrections, to be used in adjusting **all future** patterns.

BASIC PRINCIPLES

Adjustments in **width** and **length** can be made either along the edges or through the body of a pattern piece.

Adjustments along edges are simply drawn on the pattern either inside the existing cutting line to reduce size or outside in the paper margin to increase size (you may have to add some paper). In adjusting **width,** you cannot add or take off more than ½″ at edges without spoiling the shape of a pattern. A garment, however, has a number of lengthwise seams, and a very small change in each one, plus in the darts, can add up to a sizable amount. Even with just two seams, you can make an adjustment of 2″ by adding or taking off ½″ at each edge involved. In adjusting **length** you have more freedom, especially at straight edges, such as hems, where quite large adjustments can be made. **Never attempt** to make an adjustment at the edge of an armhole, a sleeve cap, or any other carefully drafted outline.

Adjustments through the body of the pattern are made where larger amounts must be added or taken in, as they preserve the pattern outline, the place of darts, etc. They are made by folding a pattern section to reduce size, or cutting and spreading it to increase size (in which case you will need extra tissue paper). Such changes are almost always made along an **adjustment line,** which may be printed on the pattern or drawn in by yourself with pencil and ruler. Printed adjustment lines are only for changes in length. If a pattern does not carry such lines, it may mean that the pattern company considered the pattern design too difficult for adjustments. In the case of a simple design, however, it is easy to add an adjustment line where needed—where to place it is shown in individual adjustments that follow. How to fold or spread a pattern is described on the next page.

With most adjustments, an adjustment in one pattern section must be carried over to the adjoining section in order to keep the sections matching at the edges.

WHEN MAKING ADJUSTMENTS
- Have your pattern piece spread flat on the table.
- Secure adjustments with pins or transparent tape.
- If there is more than one adjustment on one pattern piece, you can often combine the two—for instance, changing the place of darts as you lengthen or shorten a bodice or a sleeve (see p. 197, ill. 16).

AFTER ADJUSTMENTS HAVE BEEN MADE
- The pattern must still lie flat.
- Matching seam lines must still match.
- Printed lines (seams, grain line, etc.) broken by an adjustment must be redrawn—straight lines with a ruler, curved lines by hand or with a French curve.

HOW TO FOLD A PATTERN TO REDUCE SIZE

a. Measuring from the adjustment line, mark the amount to be taken out. Draw a second line as shown, either parallel with the first (1) or on a slant (2), as necessary.

b. Fold the pattern on the first line, and bring the fold to the second line. Smooth out pattern carefully (3). Secure the fold.

c. With a ruler, redraw all lines crossing the fold to connect smoothly and maintain the pattern shape. With a slanted fold (p. 196, ill. 10), this means that, beyond the fold, lines must be redrawn as a continuation of the original line, and that side edges will be trimmed on one side and added to on the other.

HOW TO SPREAD A PATTERN TO INCREASE SIZE

a. Cut pattern piece along adjustment line.

b. Secure cut edge of main section to a piece of tissue paper (4). With pencil and ruler, extend all straight lines across tissue (grain line, center line, center of dart).

c. Measure on tissue the amount to be added. To mark the amount, draw a line either parallel with the cut edge or on a slant, as necessary (see page 196, ill. 12, 13).

d. Secure remaining pattern section to tissue, with cut edge on marked line (5), matching at vertical lines drawn in.

e. Redraw all lines to connect smoothly and maintain the pattern shape. If the inset tapers, this means that, on the smaller pattern section, lines must be redrawn as a continuation of the original line, before the section was cut off, and that side edges will be trimmed on one side and added to on the other (p. 196, ill. 12).

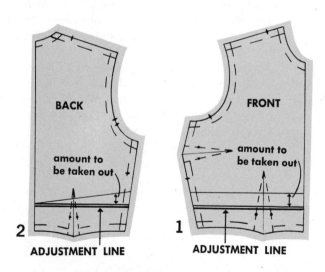

BACK — amount to be taken out — ADJUSTMENT LINE

FRONT — amount to be taken out — ADJUSTMENT LINE

2   1

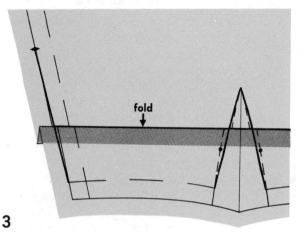

fold

3

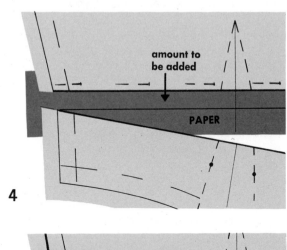

amount to be added — PAPER

4

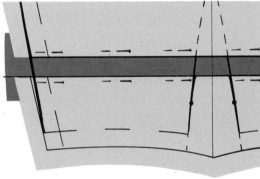

5

HOW TO RESTORE A CUTTING LINE

After an adjustment has been made, it is often necessary to redraw the cutting line. This is especially true for a dart which has been altered in size or direction. Pin the altered dart together (6) and fold (down at side, toward center at waist). Redraw cutting line across fold (6), with ruler for a straight seam, freehand or with a French curve for a curved seam (waistline) and cut. Remove pins (7).

Of course, if you change only the length of a dart, the seam line will not be affected.

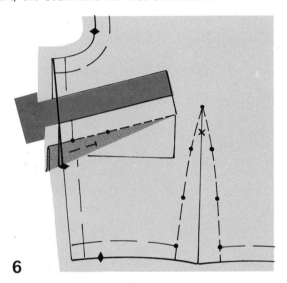

6

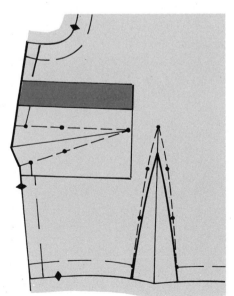

7

ADJUSTMENTS FROM MEASUREMENTS

These include any adjustments you may have decided upon after checking the pattern against the measurements on your personal measurement chart (the Total column).

For HOW TO FOLD A PATTERN to reduce size, or spreading it to increase size, see the preceding page.

BODICE

The garment used for demonstration here is a fitted bodice, which requires the most exact fit. Most of the adjustments, however, can be used for any more-or-less fitted garment for the upper part of the body (such as a blouse, jumper, jacket or dress). The measurements on your personal chart that may be involved are meas. 1, 2, 4, 5, 6, 7, 8 and 9, with ease added as in the Total column.

Shortening or lengthening (meas. 4, 5, 6, plus ease).

If the pattern has no printed adjustment line, draw one with a ruler 2″ to 3″ above the waistline, at right angles to center front and/or center back, as shown (8, 9).

On the **bodice front,** an adjustment in length will often involve the placement of bust dart (meas. 6), in which case the two adjustments can be combined; an adjustment line placed above the bust dart (METHOD II under LOWERING OR RAISING BUST DARTS on the next page) will take care of part or all of the adjustment in overall length.

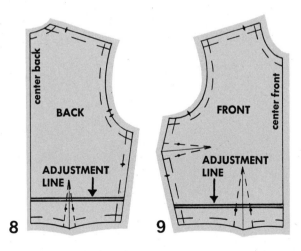

8   **9**

If the **bodice back** has the same adjustment as the front, the seam lines will continue to match. If, however, the adjustment is made on only one of the two sections (10, 11), or on both but in different amounts (12, 13), taper the fold (10) or tissue inset (12), as the case may be, to keep the side seams matching. Then slightly trim one edge and add to the other (10, 12), as required to restore their original cutting line.

NOTE: If the bodice has buttons and buttonholes, check their spacing after an adjustment in length; they may need re-spacing (see p. 31).

Lowering or raising bust darts (meas. 6)

Darts **must** be correctly placed for good fit. An underarm dart should point directly toward point of bust and stop ½″ to 1″ short of it. Moving an under-arm dart is a simple operation that can be done by either of the two methods below: Use Method I if the length of the front bodice (meas. 5) needs no change; use Method II if the length needs adjustment also.

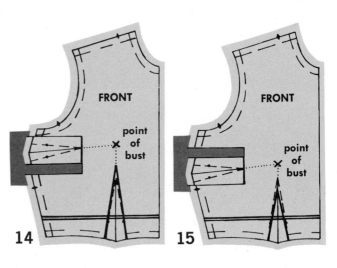

14   15

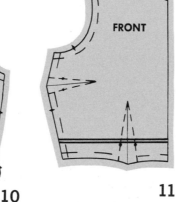

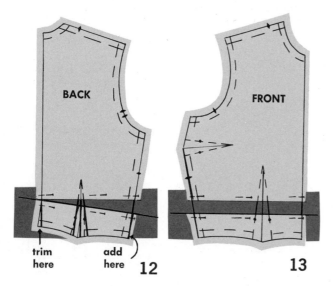

Method I—when no adjustment is needed in bodice length. Mark the desired location of the dart point. With a ruler, draw a rectangle around the underarm dart at right angles to the center front line: 1″ be-low the armhole seam line and ½″ below the dart. Cut out the rectangle and place tissue paper under the open area. Move the dart up or down, as desired (14, 15), matching vertical lines. Tape in place. Raise or lower the point of waist dart (if any) the same amount.

Method II—when an adjustment is needed in bodice length also. Draw an adjustment line above the bust dart.

> **To lower the dart,** cut the pattern on the ad-justment line and spread to the amount needed as shown (16).

> **To raise the dart,** fold the pattern on the adjustment line to the amount needed (17).

You may find that this change in the dart position has taken care of the necessary adjustment in bodice length. If not, draw a second adjustment line 2″ to 3″ above the waistline; spread or fold the pattern on that line as needed. On the waist dart, if any, draw new lines from the point to the two base points.

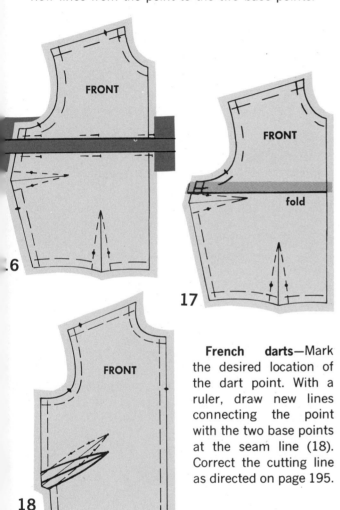

French darts—Mark the desired location of the dart point. With a ruler, draw new lines connecting the point with the two base points at the seam line (18). Correct the cutting line as directed on page 195.

Adjusting bust measurement (measurements 1, 8, 9, plus ease)

A bust adjustment is generally divided equally between the front and back of the bodice. If you are either full-busted or flat-chested (meas. 8), the adjustment may need to be made entirely on the front. If your back is very broad or very narrow, the adjustment may need to be made entirely on the back. Or it may be divided unequally between the front and the back.

NOTE FOR BOTH FRONT AND BACK—After completing any of the adjustments below:

• Restore the original waist measurement; measure the amount that the pattern has been overlapped or spread at the waistline, then add or trim away an equal amount at side seam and draw a new cutting line with a ruler.

• Redraw the waistline to conform with the original line, trimming the pattern where there was a decrease in width (20), adding to the pattern for an increase (21).

Front adjustment—Using a ruler, draw lines as shown (19):

a to c—from the point of waistline dart (a) to ⅛″ from the point of underarm dart (b), to the armhole seam line at the notch (c);

d to e—through the center of the underarm dart (unless it is already printed on the pattern).

Starting at waistline, cut along the outer line of the waistline dart (the side nearer the seam) and along the line drawn from points a-b-c. Do **not** cut through the armhole seam line.

To reduce size, mark one half of the total front adjustment needed just above point b. Lap the edge containing the waistline dart over the other as far as the mark; smooth out the pattern carefully and secure the overlap at point b. Cut through center of underarm dart (d-e). Shift the bottom section of pattern so that the bust dart and the waist overlap about the same amount. Secure overlaps (20). Restore the original waist measurement and waistline. The waistline dart retains its original size while the bust dart is made smaller.

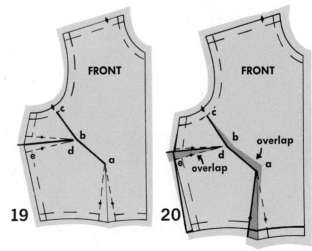

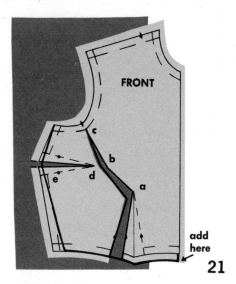

FRONT

c
b
e d
a

add here

21

To increase size, slip tissue paper under the pattern. Spread out the cut, measuring on the tissue, just above point b, one half the total front adjustment needed. Secure cut edges to the tissue at point b. Cut through the center of underarm dart (d-e). Shift the bottom section of the pattern so that the bust dart and the waist are spread about the same amount (21). Secure all cut edges to the tissue. Restore the original waist measurement and waistline. The waistline dart retains its original size while the bust dart is made larger.

Back adjustment—Using a ruler, draw a line from the point of the waistline dart to center of shoulder line (22). Starting at waist, cut along the outer line of dart (the side nearer seam) and along the line drawn. Do **not** cut through the shoulder seam line.

The amount of adjustment is measured at a level 1″ below the bottom of the armhole seam line.

To reduce size, measure one half of the total back adjustment from the cut toward side seam; mark. Lap the edge containing the waistline dart over the other to the mark and secure the overlap (23). Restore the original waist measurement and waistline. The waistline dart retains its original size.

To increase size, slip tissue paper under the pattern. Spread the pattern to one half the total back adjustment and secure the cut edges to the tissue (24). Restore the original waist measurement and waistline. The waistline dart retains its original size.

Adjusting the waist (meas. 2, plus ease)

For a garment with a waist seam, a waist adjustment must be made on both bodice and skirt.

For an adjustment of 2″ or less add or take off at the side seams; **one-fourth** the amount (½″ for a 2″ adjustment) added or taken off each edge will add up to the total needed. Then draw new cutting lines: On a bodice, pin up the bust darts, if any, and draw the new cutting line from underarm to waist. On a skirt or pants, taper to join the existing cutting line at the hip (25, 26).

For an adjustment of more than 2″ adjust the side seams as above to take out or add 2″. Divide the **remaining** amount by the number of waist darts. Then draw new stitching lines for the darts: **inside** the existing dart for an increase in size (25), **outside** the existing dart (26) for a decrease (a change of ⅛″ at each stitching line will make a change of 1″ on a garment with 4 darts).

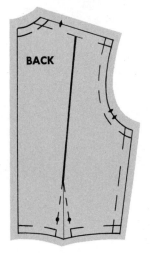

BACK

22

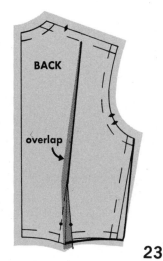

BACK

overlap

23

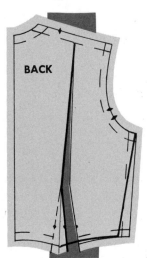

BACK

24

SKIRT

Adjusting the waist (meas. 2, plus ease)
Follow the directions on the preceding page.

Adjusting the hips (meas. 3, plus ease)
An adjustment in the hipline width must be carried all the way to the hem, both in a skirt and in pants.

For an adjustment of 2″ or less add or take off at the side seams. **One-fourth** the amount (½″ for a 2″ adjustment) added or taken off at each edge will add up to the total needed. Measure down from the waistline to the level of the hip measurement. Mark the adjustment at that point; then, using a yardstick, draw a new line down to the hem, parallel to the old one. Above the point marked, draw a line tapering to the waistline, as shown (27, 28).

For an increase of more than 2″ add 2″ at side seams, as above. Then, with a yardstick draw an adjustment line through the dart to the hem, on back and front sections (if there are two darts, use the dart nearest the side seam). Spread each piece one-fourth the total amount needed. Adjust the waistline by taking deeper darts.

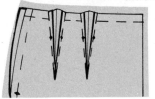

FRONT

increasing width

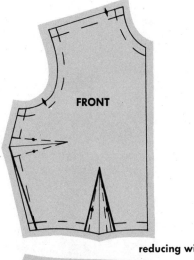

25

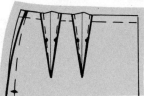

FRONT

reducing width

26

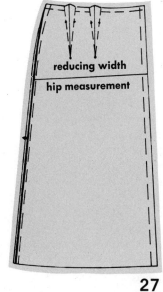

reducing width

hip measurement

27

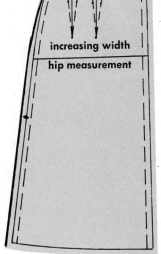

increasing width

hip measurement

28

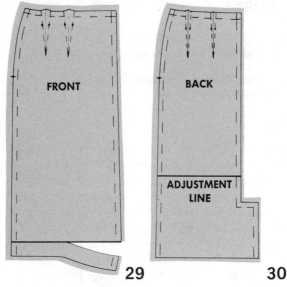

FRONT

BACK

ADJUSTMENT LINE

29   **30**

Adjusting length (meas. 16 or 17)

A skirt is usually shortened or lengthened at the hemline (29). If there is a kick pleat, however, the adjustment line should come above the pleat (30).

PANTS

Adjusting the waist (meas. 2, plus ease)

Follow the directions under that heading on page 198.

Adjusting the hips (meas. 3, plus ease)

Follow the directions under that heading on the preceding page.

Crotch depth (meas. 14, plus ease)

On front and back pattern pieces, you will need two lines at right angles to the grain line: a crotch line, from point of crotch to side seam, and an adjustment line 2″ to 3″ above it (31). Measure crotch depth near side seam, from waist seam line to crotch line. Make the necessary adjustment at the adjustment line, folding or spreading the pattern to shorten or lengthen it (see p. 194).

ADJUSTMENT LINE
CROTCH LINE
GRAIN LINE
SIDE SEAM
INNER LEG SEAM
ADJUSTMENT LINE
31

Leg length (meas. 17)

Measure at side seam. Straight-leg pants can be shortened or lengthened at the hem, like a skirt (29). For other styles, make the adjustment at an adjustment line place half-way between crotch and hem. In either case, deduct or add just the necessary amount for the adjustment, leaving the hem allowance untouched.

Thigh (meas. 15, plus ease)

This adjustment is done at the edge of the inner leg seam allowance. You were asked, when taking the measurement, to note the distance from the waist seam line at which you were taking it. On front and back pattern pieces, measure down this same distance, and draw a line (thigh line) at right angles to the grain line (32, 33). Make the adjustments at that level.

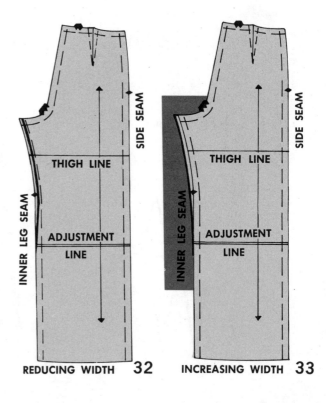

SIDE SEAM
THIGH LINE
INNER LEG SEAM
ADJUSTMENT LINE
REDUCING WIDTH **32**

SIDE SEAM
THIGH LINE
INNER LEG SEAM
ADJUSTMENT LINE
INCREASING WIDTH **33**

To reduce size, measure in from inner leg edge, one-half of the adjustment needed.

To increase size, add tissue paper along the crotch and inner leg, and measure out from inner leg edge, one-half of the adjustment needed.

In both cases, draw a new cutting line where it is needed. Depending on the amount taken out or added, take more or less distance (but a minimum of 2″) to taper to the original cutting line above and below the adjustment. The curve of the crotch should remain untouched.

SLEEVE

Length (meas. 11)
A fitted or semi-fitted long sleeve should have adjustment lines above and below the elbow. If there are none on the pattern, draw them in, 5″ below the underarm and 5″ above the bottom edge (34). Fold or spread at one or both adjustment lines as necessary.

On a straight, short sleeve, shorten or lengthen at the bottom edge.

Sleeve darts (meas. 12)
The correct adjustment in length, above, will automatically move the darts to the right place. The middle dart, or mid-point between notches, should be directly at the bend of the elbow.

Width (meas. 13, plus ease)
A sleeve sometimes needs widening, practically never narrowing. Narrowing the lower part can be done by taking in the seam after trying on the garment. A short sleeve can usually be widened or narrowed at the underarm seam, as shown (35).

The upper part of a long or three-quarter sleeve can be widened by the method that follows, which leaves the armhole untouched. Not more than 1″ should be added in this manner, however.

Using a yardstick, draw a line parallel with the grain line from center of sleeve cap to center of wrist; then a second line across the first, 1″ below the upper end of underarm seam as shown (36). Starting and stopping inside seam lines, cut through both lines—**do not cut into any seam allowance.**

Slip tissue paper under the pattern. Spread the lengthwise cut the necessary amount, letting crosswise edges overlap to keep the pattern flat. Secure all cut edges with transparent tape. Draw a new grain line through the center of the tissue insert. Redraw the wrist cutting line (37).

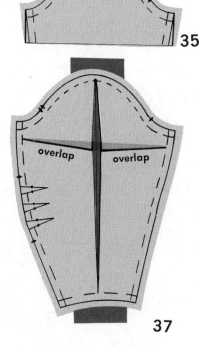

35

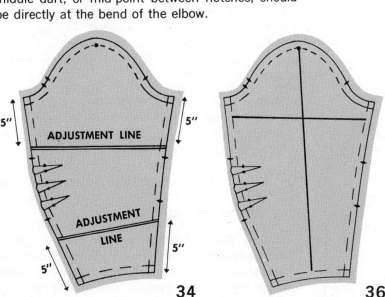

34

36

37

OTHER ADJUSTMENTS

These are the problems of fit, already mentioned on page 193, that do not become apparent from the measurements on your chart, and generally cannot be corrected by measurements alone. The necessary adjustments can and should, however, be made on the pattern, once you know what is called for. This can best be established by MAKING A MUSLIN (see p. 205). Since the need for these adjustments is established as a garment is tried on, we strongly urge you to look through the chapter on FITTING, much of which is applicable here.

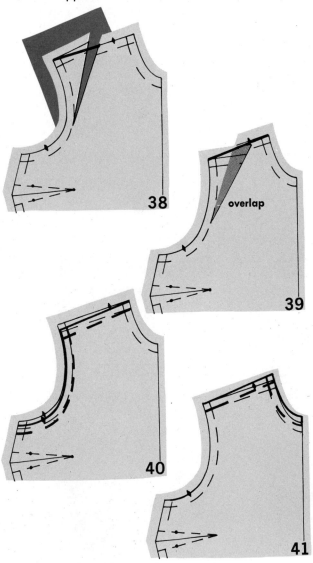

Tightness across shoulders and top of sleeves (shoulders broader than average).

To establish the amount of the adjustment needed, measure a well-fitting garment (or basic muslin) across the back from one armhole seam to the other where it meets the shoulder seam. Divide this measurement in half and compare it with your pattern.

On the patterns for both front and back, draw a line with a ruler from the middle of the shoulder seam line to about halfway down the armhole seam line (38). Cut through shoulder seam allowance and along the line to—but **not through**—the armhole seam line. Place tissue paper under the cut edges and spread them apart to the adjustment needed. Tape in place. Redraw shoulder cutting lines (38).

Armhole seams falling off the shoulders (shoulders narrower than average).

Measure and cut the pattern as directed for broad shoulders, above. Then lap the cut edges the desired amount and tape in place. Redraw the shoulder cutting lines (39).

Folds from bottom of armholes, pointing toward the neck (sloping shoulders).

Begin by pinning up the shoulder seam to fit, taking it up at the armhole and tapering to the normal seam line at the neck. The difference between the old and new seam lines at the armhole will be the amount of adjustment needed. The correction can be made by one of the two methods below. If you are combining it with an adjustment in bodice length, use Method II.

Method I—On front and back pattern pieces, lower the shoulder seam line at the armhole. Redraw the shoulder seam line and cutting line, tapering to the original lines at the neck. Make tracings of the entire original armhole (one tracing for the back, one for the front, each from shoulder to underarm), and use them to redraw the armhole from the new, lowered shoulder line (40).

Method II—On front and back pattern pieces, raise the shoulder seam line at the neck. Redraw the shoulder seam line and cutting line, tapering to the original lines at the armhole. Redraw the neckline, bringing it to its original size and curve (41).

Wrinkles from top of armholes across front and back (shoulders squarer than average).

Open the shoulder seam. If the shoulders are extremely square, place a piece of fabric under the open seam and pin it in place, tapering to the original seam line at the neck. One half the amount added at the armhole will be the amount of the adjustment needed. The correction can be made by one of the two methods below. If you are combining it with an adjustment in bodice length, use Method II.

Method I—On front and back pattern pieces, raise the shoulder seam line at the armhole. Redraw the shoulder lines and the armhole (42) as for sloping shoulders, Method I, on the preceding page.

Method II—On front and back patterns, lower the shoulder seam line at the neck. Redraw the shoulder lines and the neckline (43) as for sloping shoulders, Method II, on the preceding page.

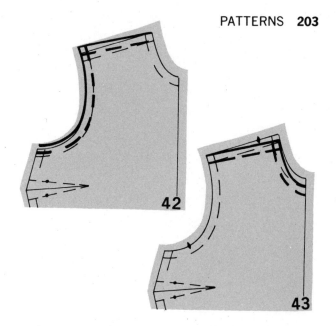

Wrinkles in back, above or below waistline (sway-back).

On a dress with a waistline seam, open the seam across the back and determine the amount of adjustment needed by taking up the excess fabric at center back. Measure the excess on bodice edge and skirt edge. On the pattern, redraw the waistline on bodice and skirt, taking out the amount of adjustment at center and tapering toward the side seams (44). Darts will become shorter.

On a skirt or pants, make the same adjustment as above.

On a fitted one-piece dress, determine the amount of adjustment needed by pinning out the excess fabric, tapering the fold to the side seams. On the pattern, shorten the center back by folding and tapering the same amount. Redraw the grain line, lower part of darts, and cutting lines. Darts will become shorter (45).

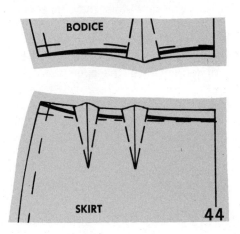

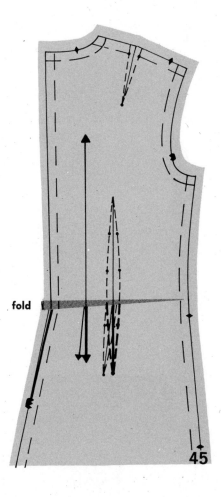

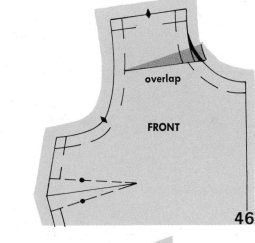

overlap

FRONT

46

Neckline gaping in front (most common in a scoop neck or V-neck).

To determine the amount of adjustment needed, pin out the excess fabric where it occurs, starting at the neckline and tapering to the armhole seam. Measure the excess amount at the neck.

On the front pattern, draw a line from the neckline to the armhole, the same distance from the shoulder (46). Cutting through the neckline seam allowance, cut along this line, but **not through** the armhole seam allowance. Lap the cut edges at the neckline the amount of the adjustment needed. Tape edges in place. Redraw the neckline (46). Trace the new neckline to adjust the facing and the collar, if there is one.

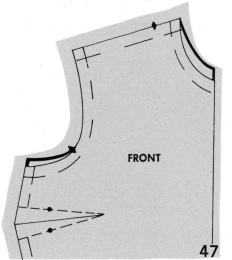

FRONT

47

High neckline or sleeveless armhole too tight or too wide.

In either one of these cases, the pattern can be adjusted by redrawing the cutting line, placing it higher (47), or lower (48), as the case may be. Trace the new neckline or armhole to adjust the facing and the collar, if there is one.

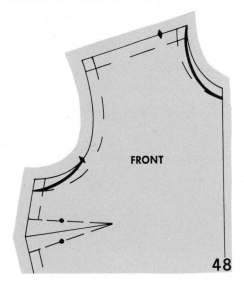

FRONT

48

Tightness in the crotch area, indicated by horizontal wrinkles (large buttocks).

Be sure you have adjusted CROTCH DEPTH (see p. 200), if necessary—this may take care of the problem. If the crotch area is still tight, determine the amount of adjustment needed by opening the inner leg seam and waist seam. If necessary, place a piece of fabric under the open seam and pin in place.

On the back pattern, place tissue paper in the crotch and inner leg area, and at the waist (49). At the back crotch line, add the adjustment needed, tapering to the original cutting line at the crotch seam and inner leg seam. Raise the waistline at the center back for the adjustment needed and redraw, tapering to the original cutting line at side seam. Adjust darts, if necessary (49).

Bagginess at crotch in back (flat buttocks).

Be sure you have adjusted CROTCH DEPTH (see p. 200), if necessary—this may take care of the problem. If the crotch area is still baggy, determine the amount of adjustment needed by pinning out the excess fabric along the high hip line (meas: 10) and down the back of the leg. Measure the excess amount.

On the back pattern, draw a line along the side seam from the waist to the knee (50). Starting at the waist, cut along this line, but **not through** the side seam allowance. Lap the cut edges the amount needed. Lower the waist at the center back and redraw the waistline, tapering to the original cutting line at side seam. Adjust darts, if necessary (50).

MAKING A MUSLIN

A "muslin" is a garment model on which you can work out problems of fit and adjustment, especially those that cannot be corrected by measurements alone, in fact, those that don't show up until a garment is tried on (like a gaping neckline or armhole). In this case, "muslin" refers to the garment and not necessarily to the type of fabric used. A muslin is finished only to the point where fit is established. The corrections are then transferred to the pattern, allowing the garment fabric to be cut correctly.

There are two kinds of muslins:

A basic muslin is made from a perfectly simple, basic or classic pattern, if possible out of pre-shrunk, firmly-woven cotton—unbleached muslin or an old sheet. Most pattern companies have such a basic pattern for a fitted dress, sometimes in more than one style (with or without a waistline seam); pick the one you use most often. For pants, just buy a well-cut, classic pattern. Once you have fitted a basic muslin to your satisfaction, you can use it as a permanent guide in correcting patterns, for as long as your shape stays the same. A basic muslin is of great use in the following instances:

when you are first learning to sew and fit clothes,
if you know you have a fitting problem,
the first time you make a different kind of garment—pants, for instance,
sometimes just for the part of a garment where you know you have a fitting problem.

A trial muslin is made for an individual garment, from its own pattern, if possible out of a fabric that will drape and behave the way the garment fabric does. A trial muslin is recommended in the following instances:

if a garment style is difficult or unusual,
if your fabric is very expensive,
for the part of a garment about which you are not sure, such as the depth of a neckline.

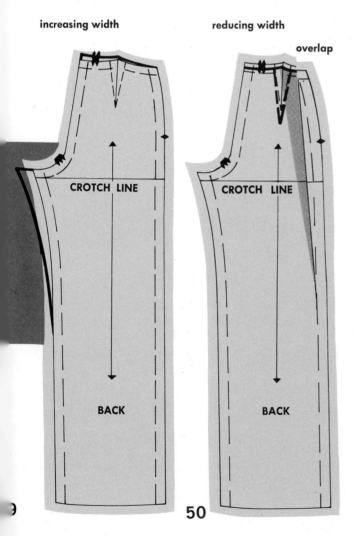

increasing width   **reducing width**

overlap

CROTCH LINE   CROTCH LINE

BACK   BACK

50

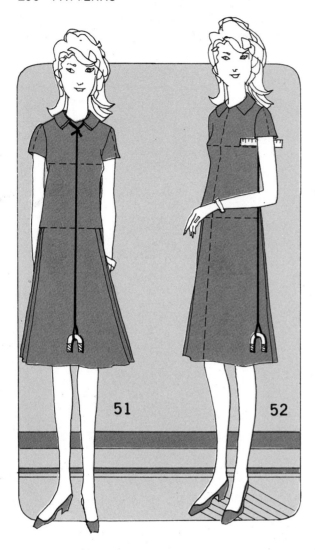

51   52

With any muslin, you have the great advantage of being able to mark, slash, add fabric where needed, pin up folds to remove fullness, etc., as you could never do on the garment itself.

Do not, however, omit any of the pattern preparations just because this is a muslin—this, in fact, is where you will try them out: Select your pattern as directed in the preceding pages, check it against your own measurements, carefully make all the adjustments from measurements that may be needed.

• When cutting out a muslin, allow for possible alterations by making the seam allowances 1″ instead of the usual ⅝″.

• After cutting out, transfer the usual markings from pattern to muslin with dressmaker's tracing paper and tracing wheel (see p. 156). In addition, mark all seam lines, so that any alterations made on the muslin will be easier to transfer to the pattern. On right side of muslin, mark vertical lines at center front, center back and sleeves; horizontal lines at bust, back, sleeve cap and hips. These will be grain lines on straight-cut garments, but direction lines on bias-cut garments. You may use an ordinary pencil and a yardstick for this.

• For construction, use machine basting (it may be necessary to open seams) and follow the pattern guide sheet.

• Leave all edges (neck, hem) and zipper opening unfinished. To check the fit of a neckline or a sleeveless armhole later, make a line of stitching directly on the seam line, and clip all around, through the seam allowance to the stitching.

• Try on the muslin, following the procedure in FITTING, page 102. Check the fit against STANDARDS OF GOOD FIT, page 102. For minor fitting adjustments, see the list of problems and solutions beginning on page 103.

Since you are working on a muslin, however, you can make much greater adjustments than if you were working on a regular garment with regular seam allowances: You can mark, slash and spread and add another piece of muslin if necessary; you can also pin folds to remove excess fullness. See PATTERN ADJUSTMENTS, starting on page 193.

• To check seams and center lines, you may want to make a plumb line: Attach a string to a metal weight (a magnet, for instance) and attach the other end to a piece of seam binding placed around your neck (51). Vertical seams and lines should be parallel to the plumb line. To check side seams, attach the plumb line to a ruler and place it under your arm (52). Alter the muslin as necessary.

• When you are satisfied with the fit of the muslin, mark any new grain or directional lines, seam lines and darts etc. on the muslin with pencil or pen. Take the muslin apart and transfer any adjustments to the paper pattern.

• Note the adjustments on your personal measurement chart. Unless your figure changes, you will know exactly what adjustments to make on your patterns in the future.

Plackets

A placket is a slit opening, with finished edges, that allows a garment to be put on and taken off. It is most often in a seam, but may be a slash cut in the fabric. Plackets may be closed with zippers, buttons, snaps, hooks and eyes, etc. For standard zipper plackets, see ZIPPERS.

A regular placket may be finished with a strip of fabric (continuous lap) or with a facing. The FACED PLACKET at a cuff seam line on page 209 is really not a placket at all but a very easy and practical way to avoid a placket. Another version of this is given on page 55 under QUICK METHODS FOR ATTACHING CUFFS.

PLACKET WITH A CONTINUOUS LAP

A continuous lap means a single strip of fabric, finishing both edges of the slit. It may finish a placket in a seam or in a slash, and is seen most often in long, cuffed sleeves. The "raw edge" in the illustrations that follow would in this case be the edge gathered into the cuff.

LAPPED PLACKET IN A SEAM

a. At end of stitched seam, clip through seam allowance to seam line (1).

b. For lap, cut a strip of garment fabric, either straight-grain or bias, 1¾'' wide and twice as long as the opening.

c. Spread out the opening and pin it to the strip (2), right sides together, edges even. Stitch as shown, taking the regular ⅝'' seam allowance. At center, where the seam allowances are clipped, make a second reinforcing line of stitching for about 2''; trim placket seam allowances to ¼''.

d. Press strip and seam away from garment. If fabric is ravely, turn free edge of strip ¼'' under and press; otherwise this is unnecessary. Fold the strip in half lengthwise. On right side, topstitch along seam as shown (3), or "stitch in the ditch."

e. On inside, fold lap as shown (4), and stitch diagonally across the fold.

f. On outside, turn lap to left or right, as it should go, and press (5).

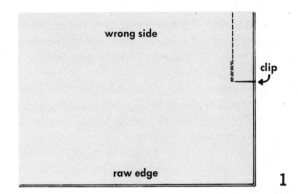

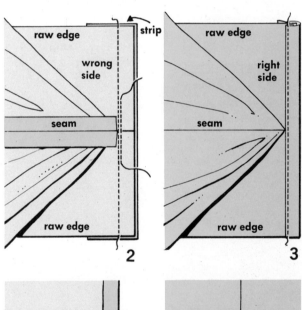

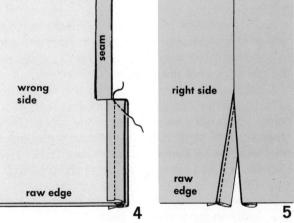

LAPPED PLACKET IN A SLASH

DO NOT CUT THE SLASH until after you have reinforced its edges with stitching as directed below.

a. If a stitching line for the slash is not indicated on the pattern, draw a line on each side of the slash-line with a ruler as shown (6): from end of line to ¼″ from it at fabric edge.

b. Set the machine for 20 stitches per inch. Stitch on the line you marked, taking two stitches across the point. Cut on slash-line, being careful not to clip through the stitching at point.

c. For lap, cut a strip of garment fabric, either straight-grain or bias, twice as long as the slash and 1¼″ to 1½″ wide (the heavier the fabric, the wider the strip).

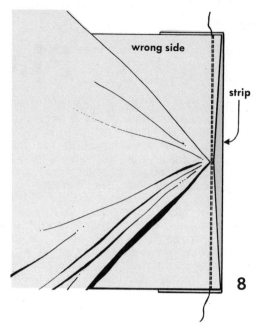

8

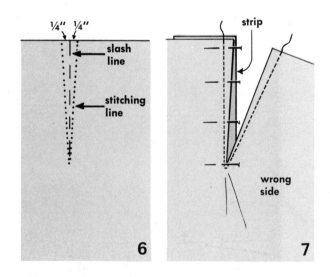

6   7

d. Pin right side of one edge of slash over right side of strip, keeping the stitched line (not the edge of the slash) ¼″ from edge of strip (7). **Note that the raw edges will not be even.**

e. Stitch (still with short stitch) just outside the existing stitched line, going toward the point. At the point, **leave the needle down** in the fabric. Bring other edge of slash forward and match the end to end of strip, so that the stitched line is ¼″ from edge of strip as before. Continue stitching to end of slash (8).

f. To finish, follow steps **d, e, f,** for the PLACKET IN A SEAM, on the preceding page.

FACED PLACKETS

FACED PLACKET IN A SLASH

This is usually used at a neckline, but is also suitable for a sleeve. We show two variations: One may be used for a zipper in a centered application or for a button or hook at the top; the other is used for a zipper in an exposed application. Generally the facing is made of garment fabric. If the garment is underlined, you may use the underlining to face the slash: mark and stitch as directed for the facing; then turn it to the inside, press and stay-stitch in place at raw edges as usual.

DO NOT CUT THE SLASH until after you have stitched it.

a. If a stitching line for the slash is not indicated on the pattern for facing or underlining, draw a line on each side of slash-line with a ruler as follows:

from end of line to ¼″ from it at fabric edge (9) for a centered zipper application or for a button or hook;

parallel to slash-line, ⅛″ from it all the way (10) for an exposed zipper application.

Transfer lines to facing or underlining.

b. Pin the facing (with free edges finished if necessary) or the underlining to the garment, right sides together. Set the machine for 20 stitches per inch. Stitch along marked line, going toward bottom of slash; at bottom, **leave needle down** in fabric, pivot, and stitch across bottom:

make two stitches at slash point for ill. 9; stitch to the next line for ill. 10;

pivot again and stitch along other side.

c. Cut on slash-line through both thicknesses. For ill. 10, stop ½″ before bottom of slash and clip into corners (10a). For **either version,** be very careful not to clip through the stitching at bottom of slash. At top, trim away corners of seam allowances, grade, clip, and understitch the neck seam. Turn facing to inside; press (11, 12).

d. Add whatever closure you have decided upon. To insert a zipper, center it under the slit (edges of slit meeting for a centered application), and topstitch by hand or machine, folding tape-ends under at top. If some other closure is used, reinforce bottom of opening with a bar tack on wrong side (11).

NOTE: For facing a **slash in a sleeve,** follow the instructions for ill. 9. A placket facing should extend about 1¼″ beyond sides and end of slash; cut a strip to fit. To hold free edges of facing in place, sew down invisibly, or attach with fusible web.

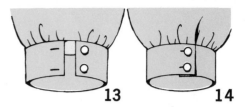

FACED PLACKET AT A CUFF SEAM LINE

This method is suitable for the sleeve closure shown (13, 14).

a. On sleeve pattern, find center of placket opening and mark a dot ½″ on each side of center. Transfer dots to sleeve.

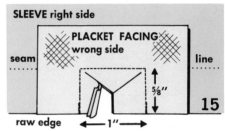

b. For each sleeve, cut a rectangle of fabric on the bias, 1¼″ × 2¼″. Center patch over marked dots, right sides together, one longer edge even with raw edge of sleeve. Pin. Set the machine for a short stitch. At edge, stitch as shown (just the depth of the seam allowance and 1″ wide from dot to dot). Clip through center and diagonally into corners (15), being careful not to cut through stitching. Trim seam allowances within stitching.

c. Turn patch to wrong side; press (16). Tack in place as necessary. Attach cuff.

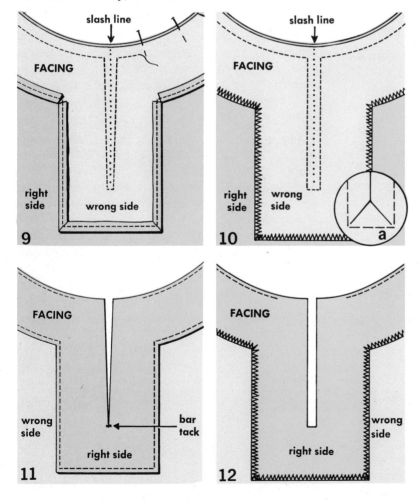

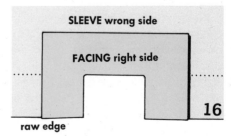

Pleats

Pleats are folds that add controlled fullness to a garment as a definite part of the design. They may be placed singly or in a series, appearing most often in skirts or the skirt of a dress. Pleats may be pressed sharply, or even edge-stitched to keep a sharp crease. Sometimes, however, they are left unpressed to roll softly. They may start at the waist or at a dropped waistline.

For pleats placed singly, you only need to follow the directions of your pattern guide sheet. This includes the kick pleat sometimes added for walking ease in a straight skirt. You will, however, find on page 215 directions for a simulated kick pleat that has certain advantages over a regular one.

In serial pleating you will also follow pattern directions. What follows are general principles and information you will find useful.

FABRIC IN PLEATS

The "hand" of a fabric determines how well an unpressed pleat will hang and hold its place. When it comes to pressed pleats, however, what matters is fiber content, fabric construction and finish. These will determine whether the fabric will take a sharp crease (its pleatability), and whether the crease will stay in (pleat retention).

Pleatability—Some fabrics, such as nubby weaves and knits, resist pleating. Most fabrics, however, if pressed with enough steam, will take a crease; how well they will retain it, especially through washings, is the question. To keep a sharp crease in a knit, or a weave that is either very resilient or very limp, it may be necessary to edge-stitch it in (see p. 214).

Pleat retention—With a garment that is to be dry-cleaned, there is no problem—the pleats will be re-pressed with each cleaning.

In washable fabrics, pleats will always withstand washing if they have been heat-set by a manufacturer either in a ready-to-wear garment or in pre-pleated fabric (see p. 215). Pleats set by a commercial pleating process (see p. 215) also stand a better chance of surviving washings than home-pressed ones.

In general, polyester, acrylic, nylon, and triacetate fibers have good pleat retention, but cotton and rayon only if they are blended with synthetics or treated with a resin finish. As for fabric construction, a smooth, closely-woven fabric will hold a crease better than a loosely-woven one, and especially better than a knit. A permanent press fabric, however, cannot be permanently pleated at home. Although creases may be present after washing, they may need re-pressing to look right.

Size of pleats (width and depth) should be consistent with weight of fabric. In general, lighter weight fabrics take narrower pleats, heavier fabrics wider pleats. Sometimes, in order to reduce bulk or save fabric, or both, wide pleats are not folded in all the way—in other words, they are not as deep as they are wide (1).

Amount of fabric—While your pattern will give you the yardage necessary for a particular garment, there is an easy way of figuring the yardage for a fully-pleated skirt. For one length: skirt length plus 4". For width: three times your hip measurement plus ease, plus about 5"–8" for seams and adjustments. This allows for a full pleat which has three layers. For pleats folded in only partway (1), you will of course need proportionately less fabric.

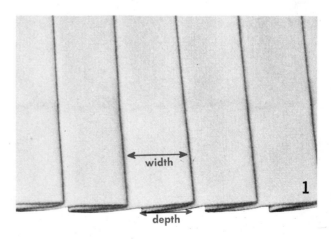

width

depth

1

Plaid fabric in pleats—Here, the grain is of the greatest importance. With wool, which can be straightened, you have no problem. In the case of fabric in which the grain cannot be straightened (synthetics, blends, treated cottons), make very sure before buying that the horizontal stripe is at true right angles to the selvage (SEE CHECK A DESIGN, p. 74), because you cut along a horizontal stripe at the hem, and fold along vertical stripes for the pleats.

With a plaid, you do not transfer pattern markings for pleats. You just select one vertical stripe on which to fold, and keep folding on the same stripe in the design so as to achieve a uniform effect.

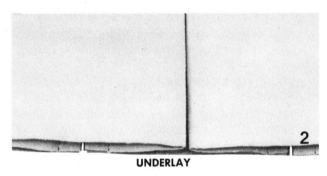

UNDERLAY 2

KINDS OF PLEATS

SHAPED PLEATS WITH SEPARATE UNDERLAYS are most often inverted box pleats in which the underfold is a separate piece of fabric (underlay) so that the two side folds actually are two seams (2). These pleats usually have a separate pattern piece —follow your pattern guide sheet.

PLEATS MADE FROM A SINGLE PIECE OF FABRIC folded to fit (1) fall into certain basic styles:

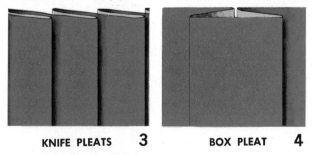

KNIFE PLEATS **3** BOX PLEAT **4**

Knife or side pleats (3) have folds all turned in one direction. The folds go around the body with the last pleat covering the zipper placket.

Box pleats (4) consist of two equal folds turned away from each other, with underfolds toward center underneath. The underfolds may or may not meet. Generally, box pleats are not made singly.

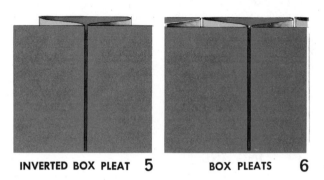

INVERTED BOX PLEAT **5** BOX PLEATS **6**

Inverted box pleats (5) are described by their name, the two equal folds meeting on the outside. This pleat is the one most often made singly. A series of box pleats and inverted box pleats looks the same on both sides (6).

The three kinds of pleats above may be pressed in at home or made commercially, or be left unpressed. They may be stitched down as far as the hips (15, 16 on p. 214). They may also, especially if the fabric resists pleating, be edge-stitched along the outer fold, the inner fold, or both (see page 214, illustration 17).

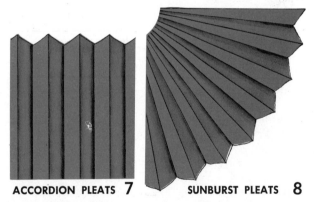

ACCORDION PLEATS **7** SUNBURST PLEATS **8**

Accordion pleats (7) and **sunburst pleats** (8) can only be made commercially. The first are narrow pleats that open out accordion-like. Sunburst pleats, made in a piece of fabric cut on the principle of a circular skirt, start at nothing at waist to widen and fan out at hem.

PLEATED SKIRT MADE FROM A PATTERN

When buying a pattern, note that the line drawings on the back of the envelope often show the pleats more clearly than the picture on the front.

Buy a skirt pattern by your hip measurement, so that the pleats will hang straight. The waist can easily be adjusted, if necessary. In the case of a dress with a pleated skirt, buy the pattern by the bust measurement, as usual. If the hip measurement is not right, the adjustment can be made while forming the pleats.

CUTTING AND MARKING

Cutting and marking are both done through a single thickness of fabric, with the pattern placed on right side of fabric. Taking the time to transfer all markings will save a great deal of time and trouble later when forming the pleats. Pleats may be formed on either the right or the wrong side and should be marked accordingly.

For each pleat, the pattern gives two lines—one on which the fold is made, the other to which the fold is brought. They are marked differently: one may be solid, the other broken. When transferring them, keep them differentiated as indicated below. Do the marking before unpinning the pattern to cut the next section.

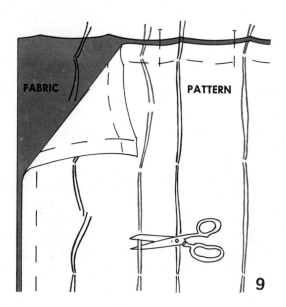

For pleats formed on the right side, marking is done on the right side as follows: Indicate the two different lines by using two pastel colors of thread, one for each. Use a double thread, slightly longer than the skirt. Take a small stitch through pattern and fabric at beginning of fold-line, leaving 1″ thread-ends. Leaving thread slightly loose, take a small stitch about every 3″ all the way down the line. When all lines have been basted, snip thread between stitches (9) and remove pattern carefully to avoid losing thread markings.

For pleats formed on the wrong side, use dressmaker's tracing paper and a tracing wheel, if the fabric can be so marked. Place the paper underneath and mark the wrong side. If the fabric is not suitable, mark on right side as described above, as the thread marking will show on both sides.

SEAMING AND HEMMING

Follow instructions on your pattern guide sheet for seaming. Note that seams should always fall on the inner fold of a pleat. The last seam (to contain the zipper) is left completely unstitched until all pleats except the last one are basted.

If pleats are to be pressed, the skirt is hemmed before pleats are put in. Determine the skirt length, carefully, but play safe by figuring a little long; you can always shorten at the top later, but you cannot lengthen. Press each seam open only where it will be enclosed in the hem.

Clip both seam allowances above the hem so the seam will lie flat; trim seam allowances within hem (10). Choose a hemming method with minimum bulk. Finish the hem and press it well. For completing the hem through the last seam, see FITTING AND COMPLETING on the next page.

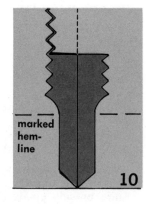

marked hem-line

If pleats are to be unpressed, hemming is the last step and presents no special problem.

FORMING PLEATS

This is done on your cutting surface or ironing board, right or wrong side of fabric up, depending on which side the pleats are to be formed. Start at the open seam and work around. Whether pleats are to be pressed or not, each pleat should be basted in place for the full length in order to hang well.

If an alteration in width is needed, distribute it evenly through all the pleats so that their width remains uniform. A **very small** adjustment in each pleat will take care of the 2″ (the difference between pattern sizes) which would be the maximum alteration. For larger hips or waist, make pleats slightly narrower; for smaller hips or waist, make pleats slightly wider.

To form pleats on right side, anchor fabric to working surface with a pin at the hem and one at the top. Fold along fold line, bring fold to next line, and pin in place from top to hem. Secure pleat with diagonal basting, as shown, through all thicknesses (11).

To form pleats on wrong side, carefully match and pin together the two pleating lines from top to hem. Then baste exactly on marked line (12) by hand or with machine-speedbasting (if using speedbasting, see p. 152).

DO NOT REMOVE BASTING IN PLEATS until the garment is entirely finished, even if the pleats are unpressed.

The tapering toward the waist is done by gradually taking more fabric into the pleats, as the pattern markings show. If you are doing the pleating without a pattern (with plaids or stripes, for instance) do the tapering as follows:

In knife pleats, deepen the inner fold, keeping the outer fold straight.

In box or inverted pleats, the outer folds will have to be tapered, each one going off grain.

In either case, more tapering is usually needed at the sides than at front or back. Later, if pleats have been stitched between waist and hips, bulk around hips can be reduced by cutting away fold of fabric on inside.

FITTING AND COMPLETING

To fit, pin the open seam together, except for the zipper opening; pin the last pleat in place; pin the top edge to waistband, yoke or bodice and try on the garment. Check the length all around and be sure hem is even; adjust at top edge, if necessary. Check the fit at waist and hips; adjust if necessary. Check the pleats to be sure they hang straight—a plumb line is helpful for this (see p. 206). Even with the pleats basted closed, they should hang straight with no pulling and the hem should be even.

Stitch the open seam. How you finish the hem in the last seam depends on the fabric:

With any fabric, but especially if it is heavy or springy, stitch the seam through the finished hem. Turn in corners of seam at hem edge and whipstitch edges together (13).

With lightweight fabrics, you may use the method on page 128.

Insert the zipper. Baste in the last pleat.

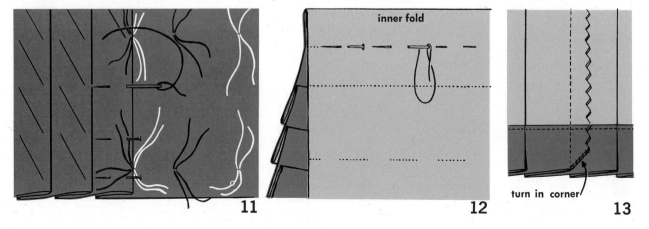

inner fold

turn in corner

11 12 13

PRESSING

Be sure your garment fits, hangs straight and looks right before you press in any pleats. See page 219 for the general principles of pressing. Work slowly, so that steam and heat can penetrate. Use plenty of steam. Do not let the full weight of iron rest on the fabric, as it might leave an impression. Remember to raise the iron and lower it again—not to push it along. When working on right side of garment, always use a press cloth. Let pressed area cool before moving garment to next pleat.

Pleat folds are pressed, first on one garment side, then on the other.

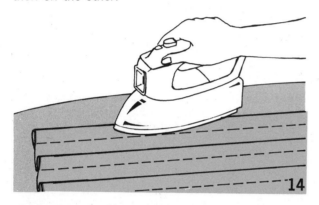

For pleats basted on wrong side, begin by pressing a sharp crease on each inner fold (14), then turn skirt to right side. Along skirt top, make a line of basting to secure the pleats turned in the proper direction. Press on right side.

STITCHING PLEATS

If stitching is desired, it is done after pressing, unless pleats are to be left unpressed. Pleats can be stitched down between the waist and the hips (topstitching or inside stitching); or the folds can be edge-stitched for a sharply creased effect; or these can be combined.

Stitched-down pleats—Measure and pin mark, on each pleat, the exact point on the hipline at which the stitching is to start.

To topstitch (15, 16), slide skirt under presser foot with hem away from you. Topstitch through all thicknesses along folds, using inside or outside edge of presser foot as a stitching guide. On inverted pleats (16), start the second row by stitching across the two folds at the hipline and pivoting.

For inside stitching, back-tack at the hip and stitch over the basting on the wrong side.

Edge-stitched pleats are especially good in fabrics that do not hold creases well. When done on the inner fold only, the stitching is invisible. For a really sharp look, however, the stitching must be done on the outer fold as well. To edge-stitch, place the folded edge alone under the presser foot and stitch very close to the edge (17).

To combine edge-stitching and topstitching, first edge-stitch the top fold of a pleat between hipline and hem; then start again at the hipline and topstitch through all thicknesses to the waist, as described above.

Attach waistband, yoke or bodice.

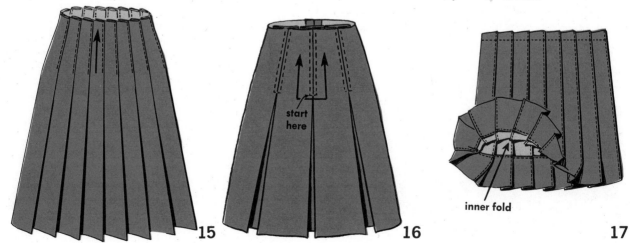

start here

inner fold

SKIRT PLEATED COMMERCIALLY

To locate a commercial pleater, consult the Yellow Pages, and look for ads in women's magazines; inquire at your dry-cleaner's and at fabric or notions stores. The services offered vary; find out what your pleater can do. Send or take to him a swatch of your fabric; ask him how much you will need and how he wants it prepared for the kind of pleating you want.

Pre-pleated skirt lengths, with some kind of hem finish, can be purchased by the yard. Buy enough so pleats will lie flat over the hips (hip measurement plus about 8″ for ease and seam allowances).

To finish a commercially-pleated skirt, baste pleats in place across the hipline to make sure this measurement is right. Then proceed as described under FITTING AND COMPLETING on page 213.

Accordion pleats are attached almost open to waistband or yoke, and hang better from a yoke. With lightweight fabric, make a row of gathering stitches along the raw top edge and draw it up slightly to ease pleats to whatever they hang from. In any case, it is a good idea to have an overblouse covering the upper end of accordion pleats.

SIMULATED KICK PLEAT

If a skirt fabric is heavy, or if you wish to avoid the way a kick pleat sometimes sticks out, substitute for it a slit with an underlay, the two giving the effect of a short inverted box pleat. The underlay is attached to a partial lining or underlining.

a. Begin by adjusting the skirt back pattern as shown: trim away pleat allowance, leaving only a ⅝″ seam allowance (18).

b. From skirt fabric, cut the two back sections, plus a rectangle 18″ wide and 13″ long for underlay. From lining (or underlining) fabric, cut two skirt back sections 12½″ shorter than outer sections.

c. On skirt sections, stitch darts. Stitch center back seam, starting 10″ from bottom (back-tack for ½″ at start). Hand- or machine-baste edges of the slit together on seam line. Press seam open from top to bottom. Press darts. At basted slit, stitch an 11″ length of seam tape or lace over each seam allowance edge; blind-stitch free edge loosely to garment. On underlay, make a 1″ hem along each 13″ edge. Press.

d. On lining sections, stitch darts and center back seam; press. Pin underlay to lining as shown (19), wrong side of underlay to right side of lining, centers and raw edges matched. Stitch ½″ seam, extending stitching across lining edge as shown. Fold seam up on stitched line and topstitch (20).

e. Match lining and outer sections, wrong sides together; pin. Stay-stitch waist and side edges. From here on, handle this as a single piece.

f. After completing the skirt except for the hem, remove basting in slit. When putting in hem, make underlay ½″ shorter than skirt (21).

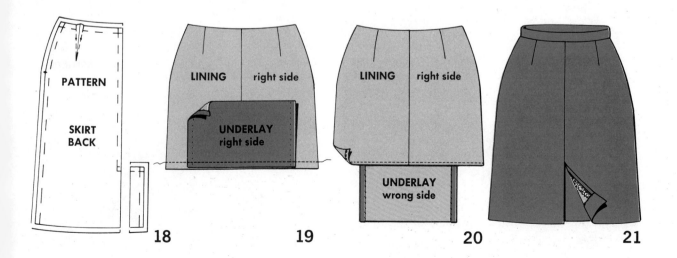

18   19   20   21

Pockets

A pocket hidden in a seam (1) is merely functional. All other pockets are part of the outer design of a garment and in most cases are functional as well.

Hip pockets (2), single welt (3) and double welt (4), and flap pockets (5) are inside pockets with an outside finish or detail. Patch pockets (6), made from the garment fabric, are entirely on the outside.

Even a hidden pocket is in a very visible seam, and all pockets, which are important details in a garment design, need to be made with precision.

The pattern guide sheet will tell you how to make your pocket, but a few additional pointers may help you achieve the precision you want. The DESIGNER PATCH POCKET on page 218, is an elegant extra, a special technique you can use on a man's jacket as well as on women's garments.

GENERAL POINTERS

Position markings for all pockets except 1 and 2 should be transferred to the right side of the fabric with hand- or machine-basting.

Welt pockets (3, 4) and flap pockets (5) are slashed, with openings constructed on the same principle as a patch buttonhole. Like the buttonhole (see p. 36), they need interfacing to reinforce their edges.

Pockets at seams (1, 2) need interfacing if your fabric lacks firmness and/or stability. They require a sharp, firm seam-edge; grade, clip and understitch seam allowances (7) as directed for facing seams (see BEFORE TURNING THE FACING, p. 93).

Patch pockets are unlined on a shirt or blouse, usually lined on a jacket or coat. Neat corners are assured with the procedures that follow.

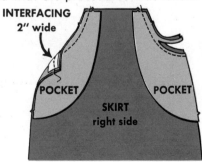

INTERFACING 2" wide

POCKET   POCKET

SKIRT right side

7

UNLINED PATCH POCKET

a. Turn raw top edge of pocket section ¼″ to wrong side and stitch. Fold hem to right side, on fold line indicated on pattern. Stitch through single thickness along seam line around remaining edges, as shown. Trim seam to ⅜″, and trim corners at top fold (8). Turn hem to wrong side.

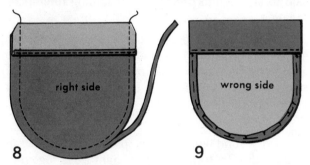

b. On a rounded pocket, clip through seam allowance at curves. Turn to wrong side on stitched line, baste and press (9).

On a square pocket, fold corners to wrong side (10); press. Then turn seam allowance on stitched line; mitering corners as shown (11); baste and press the pocket.

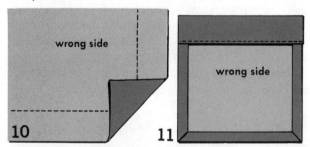

c. Baste pocket to garment; topstitch. To reinforce top corners, you can either:
  • Stitch a triangle (12).
  • Make close zigzag stitch, about ⅛″ wide, for ½″ (13).
  • Reverse stitching for about ½″ (14).

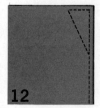

LINED PATCH POCKET

Follow this procedure if you wish to add a lining not given in pattern.

WITH A HEM AT THE TOP

a. Cut out pocket. Cut lining from pocket pattern with top edge of pattern folded on fold line; trim off 1/16″ on all edges (seam will then roll to wrong side). Press top edge of lining ¾″ to wrong side. Pin to pocket, right sides together, side and bottom edges even (15).

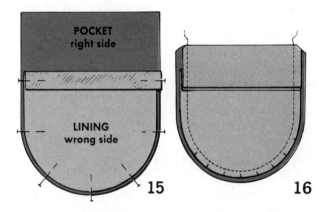

b. Fold top edge of pocket over lining on fold line indicated on pattern; pin. Stitch on seam line around raw edges, as shown. Grade seam allowances; trim corners at top (16). If pocket is rounded, clip through seam allowance at curves; on a square pocket, trim off corners.

c. Turn pocket right side out, carefully pushing out corners and seams. Press carefully. Slipstitch the lining to the hem (17).

d. Baste pocket to garment. Either slipstitch in place, or topstitch. Reinforce top corners, if desired, following directions for UNLINED PATCH POCKET.

WITH LINING EXTENDING TO ALL EDGES

a. Cut out pocket. Cut lining 1/16″ smaller on all edges (seam will then roll to wrong side).

b. Pin lining to pocket, right sides together. Stitch all around. Trim corners, grade and clip the seam allowance.

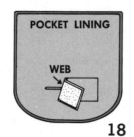

POCKET LINING

WEB

18

c. Near bottom of pocket, cut a slit in the lining (18). Through this slit, turn pocket to right side. Press.

d. If pocket is purely decorative and lining fabric does not ravel, the slit can be left as is. Otherwise, cut a patch of lining fabric and fusible web slightly longer than the slit and fuse the patch over the slit as shown.

DESIGNER PATCH POCKET

This method is fine for pockets with rounded corners. Instead of being topstitched to the garment in the usual way, this patch pocket is machine-stitched from the inside (odd as it sounds, this is perfectly feasible). There is no visible stitching and the pocket is very securely attached.

While the pocket can be made with or without lining, the lining given here is particularly neat: It is made slightly smaller than the outside, and prevents the outer pocket from being pulled out of shape by its contents.

a. Mark fold line at top of pocket. If pocket is unlined, finish this edge (see SEAM FINISHES, p. 224), skip to step **e** and proceed, disregarding references to lining.

b. Cut two lining sections the same size as pocket, minus seam allowances and top fold. Center one lining section at top edge of pocket section, right sides together (19). Stitch a ⅝″ seam, starting and stopping ½″ short of lining side edges, as shown. Press lining up.

c. On second lining section, press top edge ¼″ to wrong side. Pin to first section, right sides together, cut edges even. Stitch these edges together in a ⅝″ seam (20). Trim seam to ¼″, as shown.

d. Fold top edge of pocket section to wrong side along marked fold line. Press.

e. Make a line of stitching on pocket, ½″ from edge (do not catch lining). At the two rounded corners, make a line of ease-stitching ¼″ from edge. Fold entire seam allowance to wrong side so stitched line is rolled ⅛″ in from edge. Hand-baste close to folded edge (21), drawing up ease-stitching at curves, as shown. With edge of lining under seam allowance of pocket, press folded edge lightly.

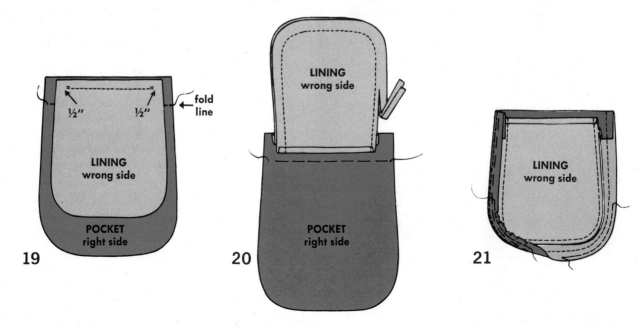

19 — ½″ ½″ fold line — LINING wrong side — POCKET right side

20 — LINING wrong side — POCKET right side

21 — LINING wrong side

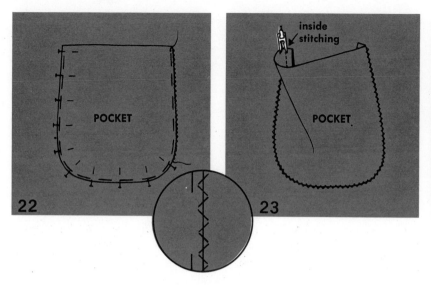

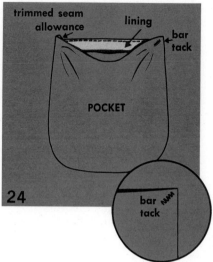

f. Pin pocket to garment, placing sides just inside position marking to allow a little ease at the top for the curve of the body. Set the machine for longest, narrowest zigzag stitch and use it to machine-baste pocket edges to garment, the stitch just catching the edge (22). If your machine does not do zigzag, slip-baste the pocket edges in place by hand (see p. 19).

g. Place work on machine with top inside corner of pocket under presser foot, as shown (23). Stitch,

just inside the row of machine stitching, around the entire pocket on the **inside.** Remove zigzag or hand-basting. If curves of pocket are bulky, clip seam allowance.

h. At top of pocket, trim off corners of seam allowance. Pin folded top edge of lining to garment and topstitch in place. Fasten the two top pocket corners with diagonal bar tacks long enough to catch in the lining (24).

Pressing

Pressing is part of sewing—if there is a golden rule of good dressmaking, this is it. "Stitch-and-press" makes for professional-looking work all the way through. It also reduces the final pressing to almost nothing, which is a great help.

On page 68 you will find all the information you need on pressing equipment—not only the iron and ironing board, but such helpful articles as a pressing ham, point presser, needleboard and others.

When and where pressing is done is indicated throughout the chapters of this book. When a fabric or a detail requires special pressing directions, you

will find them under their subject—FABRICS, SEAMS, BUTTONHOLES, etc.

What follows are the general rules of good pressing and their use with standard fabrics.

PRESSING PRACTICE

● Iron and ironing board should be kept set up and ready at all times while you are making a garment. They are, in fact, the first things you need—to smooth out the creases in your pattern, and perhaps in the fabric before you cut it (see PATTERNS, CUTTING, FABRICS).

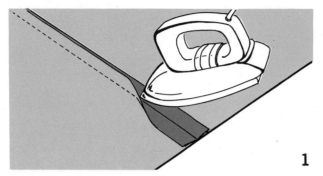

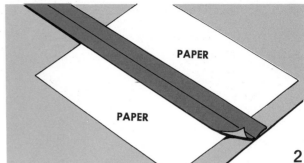

- Do not confuse **pressing** with **ironing.** Ironing, usually done after laundering, is a bearing-down and stroking operation. In pressing, you lower the iron, in most cases lightly, then lift and lower it again a little farther on; now and then you use a light, sliding motion without ever letting the full weight of the iron rest on the fabric—which might leave an impression, or, if done on the right side, cause a shine. On most fabrics, pressing action comes from a combination of heat, steam and partial weight of iron.

- In pressing seams open (1), you work with the tip of the iron only.

- Most construction pressing (pressing as you go) is done on the wrong side. Pressing in general should be done on the wrong side whenever possible. Where it is necessary to press on the right side, certain precautions are needed with most fabrics (see the next column).

- Do not overpress. It may flatten and deaden a fabric.

- Stitch-and-press—the basic principle of construction pressing—does not mean that you have to press each seam and dart, immediately after it is stitched. You can usually press several of them at one time. Just make sure that each one is pressed **before it is crossed** by another seam.

- Never press over pins—they will leave an impression on your fabric. They may also scratch the iron, causing it to snag fabrics later.

- Remove basting whenever possible before pressing. Always remove it before a final pressing, as even a thread may leave a mark.

- If your fabric is of a kind that will cause an edge to leave an impression on the outside, place a strip of brown paper between such edges (seam allowances, darts, hem) and the garment fabric before pressing (2). Pressing seams open over a seam roll with a point presser will also prevent such impressions.

- Before pressing a sharp crease anywhere, make sure that the line will not be altered; in other words, that the seam, pleat, etc. is in the right place.

- Pressing done on the right side requires certain precautions. On any fabric, a shine will tend to occur at bulky places such as pockets, facing edges, zipper openings, etc. To prevent this, use a dry press cloth with a steam iron. With a dry iron, dampen one half of a press cloth, fold the damp half over the dry half and use the cloth dry-side-down. A very satisfactory solution to the problem is a slipcover over your iron which you can either buy or make yourself. There is also a very good attachment which fits over the sole plate of the iron.

- Keep your iron clean—there are several products on the market which will safely remove any starch, fusible, etc., which may have built up on the bottom of your iron.

- If you have been careful to press details as you went along, the final pressing of a garment should be just a matter of touching up here and there.

PRESSING STANDARD FABRICS

Most irons show clearly what heat setting to use for various fibers—linen taking the highest, synthetics the lowest. With all the new blends and finishes, however, you will do well to try the iron on a scrap of fabric before touching it to the garment itself.

Steam may and should be used on most fabrics. Again, however, play safe by testing the steam first on a sample to see how much your fabric can take. Use a piece large enough so you can compare the pressed and unpressed parts; steam may dull the surface of some fabrics (such as satin), and flatten others (crepe, for instance).

Cotton presents no problem. Except when it is of dark color (when it may tend to shine) it can be pressed on either side, either with a steam iron, or with a dry iron after having been directly dampened with a sponge.

Linen is as easy to press as cotton, but is more apt to shine if pressed on the right side. With dark colors, use a press cloth.

Wool requires considerable steam in pressing. It responds excellently to the steam iron, or to a dry iron with a press cloth, used half-damp, half-dry as described on the preceding page. If wool is pressed on the right side, the press cloth should preferably be a piece of the same wool, especially if the fabric is dark. Wool lends itself well to shrinking and shaping by means of steam.

NOTE: Wool crepe needs special care. Never let the iron rest on it, as it will leave an imprint. Use very little steam, as it will shrink even if it is pre-shrunk.

Silk is handled according to its weight. Heavy and medium-weight silk is handled like wool. Sheer silk, such as chiffon, is pressed with a dry iron only. As for silk crepe, see the note above for wool crepe.

Rayon requires a moderately warm iron, and should not be exposed to direct steam.

Acetate should not be exposed to direct steam. Use a dry press cloth with a steam iron; with a dry iron, use the half-damp, half-dry press cloth as described on the preceding page. For the degree of heat, make a test with a scrap or scraps of fabric; discoloration caused by heat is usually temporary. Fabric edges will mark through to the right side, so put paper between them and outer fabric as described on the preceding page.

Blends must be handled according to their fiber content—set the iron by the fiber requiring the lowest heat setting. In any case, test first on a fabric scrap.

PRESSING SPECIAL FABRICS

For pressing fabrics that need special handling (bonded fabrics, fake fur, knits, lace, leather and suede, leather look, permanent press, pile fabric, sheers, and suede look) see those headings, beginning on page 75.

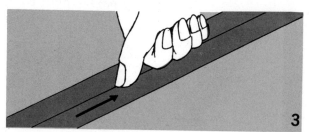

Finger-pressing, mentioned in connection with a couple of these fabrics, means opening a seam or forming a crease by running your thumbnail firmly along the crease (3). It is used mainly with fabrics that cannot take pressing.

FABRICS WITH A SURFACE TEXTURE must be pressed with care to retain the beautiful texture. For pile fabrics, one of the most common textured fabrics, see page 89. For other textured fabrics, follow the guidelines given below:

Napped fabrics should be pressed on the wrong side on a softly padded board, or on the right side under a press cloth of self-fabric. Press in the direction of the nap. After pressing, brush the nap lightly with a soft brush.

Fabrics with a raised surface, such as woven, embossed or embroidered designs, should be pressed on the wrong side on a softly padded board or over terry cloth. Use plenty of steam. On woven or embossed fabrics, use light pressure; on embroidered designs, use heavier pressure.

Crepe fabrics must be pressed with great care to avoid shrinking or stretching the fabric. Press with the grain, using as little steam as possible.

Glossy fabrics, such as glazed chintz or polished cotton, should be pressed on the right side without a press cloth and with little or no steam to retain the luster.

Non-shiny fabrics should be pressed on the wrong side to maintain the dull finish on the right side.

Seams and Seam Finishes

A seam is the line of stitching, usually done by machine, that holds two fabric edges together. Seams are the most basic and indispensable construction stitching, and are most often plain. They can, however, be double-stitched in various ways for strength or neatness. They can also be made decorative with added topstitching, or cording or piping inserted between the two fabric edges. The way seams are made, pressed and finished depends on the design and purpose of a garment and on the fabric.

Read the chapter on MACHINE-STITCHING for the things you **must** know before making a seam.

SEAM ALLOWANCE AND STITCH LENGTH

The seam allowance is the fabric between the seam line and the raw edge. After a seam is stitched, the seam allowances are on the wrong side of a garment. The standard seam allowance in patterns is ⅝″, sometimes trimmed afterward to a narrower width. Lingerie patterns may have a narrower seam allowance; in any case, the allowance is always clearly marked on the pattern or indicated in the instructions.

To maintain the size and lines of a garment, it is essential to keep the seam allowances even and at the given width. For this you need a guideline, running parallel to the presser foot. The distance between the needle and the guideline is the width of the seam allowance, and you keep the fabric edge moving smoothly along the line as you stitch. (Be sure to keep your eye on the **fabric edge** as you guide it along, not on the needle or the presser foot). There are several kinds of seam guides:

• Some machines have guidelines etched on the throat plate, ⅛″ apart for seam allowances of different widths.

• Seam-guide attachments of different kinds can be bought. One that is very easy to use consists of

a magnetized guard that is set on the throat plate at the desired distance from the needle—either to the right or to the left of it.

• You can also make your own. There is an adhesive **sewing tape,** pre-marked with lines ⅛″ apart, that you can buy and fasten to the throat plate. Just be careful to have the lines the right distance from the needle and parallel to the presser foot. Or use a **3″ strip** of ordinary **adhesive tape** (1) and mark it yourself. For turning corners, measure and mark a line (or lines) across the width of the tape, the same distance from the needle as the seam allowance. This guide can be placed either at the right or the left of the needle.

• In places where two finished edges face each other and must match perfectly (lapels, the two ends of a collar, etc.) you may need a special seam guide. This is particularly true with curves. In such cases, you can mark the seam line (see MARKING, p. 155); but the easiest procedure is to draw the outline you want on brown paper, cut it out, pin it even with the desired seam line, and stitch along it. By using the same guide for both edges, you are assured of a perfect match.

The stitch length in seams will depend on the fabric, the type of garment, etc. (see THREAD AND NEEDLES chart on p. 251). The average stitch length is 10 to 12 per inch. A seam on the bias, however, requires the added strength of a shorter stitch.

For starting and ending and **for directional stitching,** see MACHINE-STITCHING, pages 149 and 153.

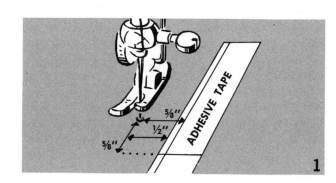

THE PLAIN SEAM

This is the basic seam, used everywhere; most other seams begin with a plain seam.

a. Place the two sections right sides together, edges even, notches and other construction marks matched (2). The edges to be stitched may be pinned or basted as necessary.

b. Stitch on the seam line. Either set the machine for a straight stitch or for the narrowest zigzag if you are working on a knit (the slight zigzag will give elasticity to a seam by adding more thread). If your machine has a straight stretch stitch, you may want to use it for extra strength.

c. Press in three steps: First press the line of stitching as is, without opening the seam (3); then open the seam with the point of the iron, applying light pressure (4); then lightly press the open seam. Even if the seam allowances are finally to be pressed to one side (as in a facing), press them open first—you will have a much smoother seam line.

Plain seams are often made with two fairly different edges. In such cases, proceed as follows:
● When stitching a curved or a bias edge to a straight edge, do so with the curved or bias side on top.
● When stitching a fuller (eased) edge, or a gathered or pleated edge to a plain edge, do so with the fullness on top, so you can control it.

Princess seam—This is a curved seam and takes special handling. Stay-stitch both edges ⅛″ from the seam line. Clip the inward curve and notch the outward curve, both to the stay-stitching (see p. 94). Then stitch the two edges together on the seam line (you would probably do well to baste first) and press the seam open (5).

Corner in a seam—When you come to a corner in a stitching line, **pivot:** Stop with the needle **in the fabric,** exactly at the corner (move wheel by hand if necessary), raise the presser foot, shift fabric around the needle, and lower presser foot so stitching can proceed in the next direction.

Crossing a seam—This means stitching over a seam-end with another seam. Never neglect pressing (and if possible finishing) a seam before crossing it. When two seam-ends come together to be crossed, carefully match the seam lines with a pin as you place them right sides together. Then put pins through the seam allowances, as shown, to keep those on the underside from folding under as the cross seam is stitched (6). After stitching, trim the seam allowance ends, as shown, to reduce bulk (7).

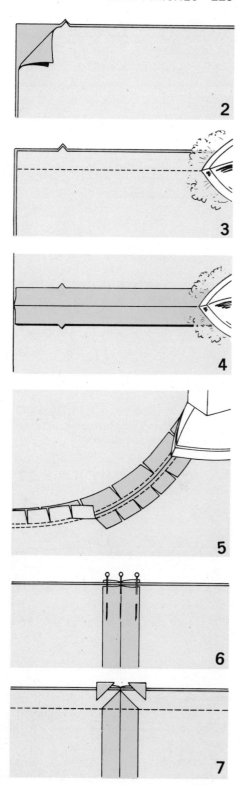

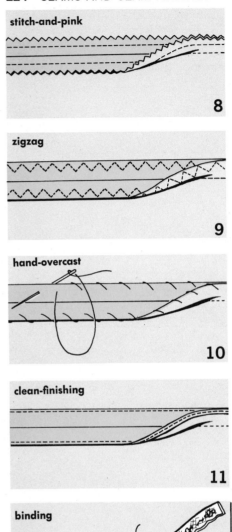

stitch-and-pink

8

zigzag

9

hand-overcast

10

clean-finishing

11

binding

12

SEAM FINISHES

With knit fabrics and very firmly-woven fabrics, the edges of plain seams may be left as is. Otherwise, the seam allowances must be finished to prevent raveling, and for neatness, unless a garment is lined. For handling the allowances of enclosed seams, see BEFORE TURNING THE FACING, page 93. In other seams, different fabrics call for different finishes.

Most fabrics—Trim seam allowances with pinking shears, or stitch-and-pink (8).

Ravelly fabrics—Finish seams by machine with multi-stitch zigzag (9), plain zigzag, or blind stitch; for any one of these, stitch ¼″ to ½″ from the raw edge and trim away excess fabric.

Seam allowances can also be overcast by hand. Hold your work with the edge to be overcast up; you can go either from right to left or from left to right. Take stitches ⅛″ to ¼″ deep and ¼″ apart, over the edge as shown (10).

Lightweight fabrics—Turn edges of seam allowances under about ⅛″ and stitch (11). This is called clean-finishing and is excellent anywhere, but is especially good in unlined jackets.

Heavier fabrics in an unlined jacket or coat—Enclose the edge of each seam allowance in double-fold bias tape or fold-over lace, inserting the edge in the tape so that the narrower half of the tape is on top. Edge-stitch (12). If you want to apply the elegant Hong Kong finish to your edges, see page 125.

NARROW SEAMS

For fabrics that can take a narrow seam, such as knits, lace and sheers, you may use one of the following seams:

Double-stitched seams—Make a plain seam; do not press the seam open. With seam allowances together, make a second line of stitching, straight or zigzag, in the seam allowance, ⅛″ from the first stitching. Trim close to second line (13, 14). Press to one side.

Overedge seam—If your machine has a convenient overedge stitch, it does the stitching and overcasting in one operation. You stitch on the regular seam line, and trim the seam allowance to the narrower width either before or after stitching (15).

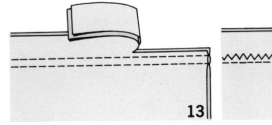

13

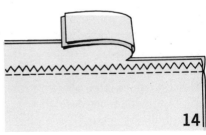

14

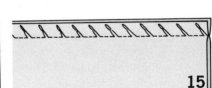

15

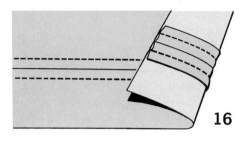

16

TOPSTITCHED SEAM

This is a decorative seam. After pressing a plain seam open, place the work on the machine right side up and topstitch on each side of the seam line, being very careful to make both sides equal (16). The distance from the seam line will vary according to thickness of fabric and your preference. Stitch with the grain, and always start **both** sides at the **same end** of the seam. See page 151 for more on topstitching. NOTE: Be careful about topstitching permanent press fabrics, as they tend to pucker; make a test first.

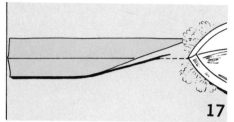

17

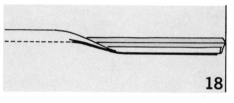

18

FLAT FELL SEAM

This seam, also called felled seam or fell seam, is strong and neat, good on garments that are laundered often. The fell (stitched-down overlap) may be made on the inside or the outside of a garment, the outside fell usually being a feature of sports clothes, men's shirts, pajamas, etc. An armhole seam can be felled only if the top of the sleeve is almost straight, as in a man's shirt sleeve, with no cap to speak of and no ease.

a. Make a plain seam, as on page 223 (wrong sides together if you want an outside fell).

b. After pressing the seam open, press it again with both seam allowances turned to one side (17).

c. Trim the bottom seam allowance to about ⅛″ (18). Fold the top seam allowance under to half its width (with some fabrics, you may wish to hand-baste or press this before stitching). Edge-stitch the fold (fell) to the garment (19).

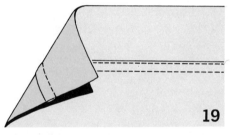

19

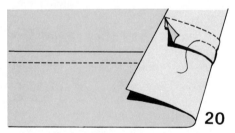

20

WELT SEAM

An easy variation of the fell seam, mostly used on knits and heavier fabrics, because it is flatter. The second line of stitching is done from the outside.

a. Make a plain seam. After pressing it open, press it again with both seam allowances turned to one side.

b. Trim the bottom seam allowance to about ¼″. Then topstitch from the outside, enclosing the narrower seam allowance in the wider one, without turning the raw edge under (20).

For a double welt seam, which looks like a seam with an outside fell, make a second line of stitching, close to the seam, on the outside (21).

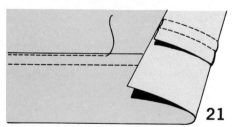

21

FRENCH SEAM

A very neat seam, used on sheer fabrics, where a raw edge would show through, and on carefully-made blouses. The first line of stitching is done on the right side; the second stitching, done on the wrong side, falls on the regular seam line.

a. With fabric **wrong sides together,** stitch a plain seam a **scant** ½″ from raw edges. Trim seam allowances to ⅛″ (22).

b. Press seam allowances to one side. Fold the work on the stitched line, right sides together. Stitch again (23), ⅛″ from fold, encasing the raw edges (this stitching will be on the regular seam line).

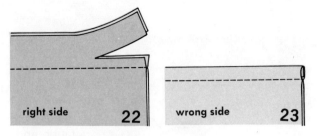

right side 22 wrong side 23

MOCK FRENCH SEAM

A French seam cannot be made on a curve—in an armhole, for instance. You can, however, simulate one by making a plain seam in the usual way, then turning the edges in on both seam allowances and edge-stitching them together. For a narrow seam, trim the seam allowances before turning them in.

Sewing Area

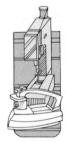

Many an efficient home-sewer gets by with a portable sewing machine, an ironing board, and perhaps a cutting board, taken out when needed and set up any place. Others may keep their sewing equipment ready in a convenient closet that opens into a sewing nook. Some may have the corner of a room, screened off or not, reserved for the purpose. The lucky few with plenty of space may have a sewing room. How much space you have is on the whole not nearly as important as how well you organize and use it.

A proper sewing set-up, however, whether permanent or temporary, has certain basic requirements. These, plus proper planning, can save you any amount of time and effort.

WHEREVER YOU DO YOUR SEWING:

• Have proper lighting, not just at the sewing machine (which has its own light), but anywhere that you work with patterns or fabric. Lamps should be adjustable with a strong enough light.

• Make sure of sufficient electrical outlets, and try not to plug the sewing machine, the iron and the light into the same outlet.

• Have a good working surface for cutting out fabric, for transferring markings and for adjusting patterns. If you do not have a cutting table (33″ to 36″ high and accessible from all sides), place a cut-ting board (see EQUIPMENT, p. 67) on a dining-room or ping-pong table or even on a bed.

• If your sewing machine does not have its own cabinet, set the machine on a table or desk at a comfortable height from the floor. There should be enough surface extending to the left for your work to lie on and spread out.

• Your chair should have no arms preferably, but should have a good, supporting back. A swivel chair is ideal because of its mobility.

• An ironing board of adjustable height, set up at right angles to the sewing machine, allows you to turn around and press a seam or dart without getting up from your chair.

• A full-length mirror is a necessity for checking fit, length, etc.

• A hardwood or vinyl floor will be more practical than carpeting—it is harder to pick up pins, threads etc. from rugs.

• Have a wastebasket within reach wherever you happen to be working; or tape a paper bag to the machine, the ironing board and the cutting table.

AS FOR ORGANIZATION

Not only sewing, cutting and pressing surfaces, but everything pertaining to your sewing activity should be kept together, within easy reach.

Boxes and containers should be either of clear plastic or clearly labelled. Look around for other storage ideas. There are containers which are specially made for sewing notions and equipment, such as portable sewing baskets in a variety of sizes, chairs with a storage area under the seat, and even hassocks on rollers with storage room under the top.

Equipment may be kept in a handy drawer or storage container mentioned above. It will help, however, if you sort it so that the articles you need most often are the most accessible.

Machine attachments: Separate the frequently-used ones and keep them with the machine.

Bobbins: Have plenty of spares. Keep some always filled with the thread colors most often used—white, black, etc. When you know you will need more than one bobbin of one color, fill several bobbins beforehand to avoid interrupting your work.

Scissors, tape measure, yardstick, ruler, French curve can be kept available by being hung. A pegboard is excellent for this—place it on a wall if it can be kept visible, or hide it on the inside of a closet door.

A pincushion attached to the right side of the sewing machine, near the hand wheel, is a great help. Use nylon tape fastener or double-face tape, not glue.

Notions—Buttons (sorted if possible), other fastenings, trims, etc. are most readily available when kept in transparent containers—not only plastic boxes, but apothecary or food jars.

Spools of thread are best placed, arranged by color, in shallow boxes or box lids. Attach ribbon or bias tape handles to the boxes and stack them in a drawer. To prevent the thread from unwinding, be sure to catch the thread-end in the slit or notch on the spool. Or tape the thread-end to the spool.

Patterns which you want to use again should be folded into their envelopes, together with the guide sheet; since most patterns have several views, even if you do not want to make the same garment later, you may want to save the pattern for a different view the next time. File them in a shoe box or other boxes according to type of garment, but keep your favorites together.

Fabrics can be stored in drawers or boxes, sorted by kinds. Interfacings, linings, underlinings should be kept together; leftovers from existing garments likewise. Be sure to label fabrics as to yardage and width, fiber content, care requirements, and whether or not they have been pre-shrunk.

Sewing books, leaflets, product instructions, should be kept together. For loose leaflets, use a file folder or a box.

The work on hand—This is important. Avoid mislaying any part of it by keeping all of it—pattern, garment sections, notions—together in a large box.

In general, avail yourself of whatever you have in the way of shelves, drawers, etc. to store your material, but keep it all together as much as possible, sorted and properly labelled. Filing cabinets or file boxes make great storage places for fabrics. Wicker baskets, carboard boxes, even coffee cans will hold notions and small equipment.

A SAMPLE SEWING AREA

The most convenient set-up for sewing has proved to be the U-shaped one, with the sewing machine at center and the ironing board and the working surface forming the sides. If you have a permanent sewing room, you may be able to place low cabinets (two-drawer filing cabinets, for instance) under the cutting table, in addition to the drawers connected with the sewing machine cabinet. Any shelves you can install to hold boxes and containers will be a plus. A pegboard can be attached, not only to a wall, but to the back of a cabinet or door. If your sewing area contains a closet, it might hold a dress form.

Whether it is permanent or temporary, make sure your sewing set-up is convenient so you will be inspired to sew!

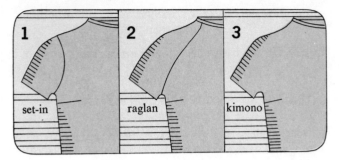

1 set-in   2 raglan   3 kimono

Sleeves

Sleeves, and the way they are set in, are one of the focal points in the changes of fashion. They not only widen or narrow the shoulders, but can affect the entire silhouette by the shape they take around elbows and wrists. A dropped or raised armhole means a major variation in style; so does a smooth or a gathered sleeve cap.

With all their variations, however, sleeves fall into just three basic categories:

The set-in sleeve (1) is cut separately from the body of the garment and seamed into an armhole. This sleeve may have a smooth cap, a darted cap, or a full, gathered cap.

The raglan sleeve (2) is cut separately from the body of the garment, but continues over the shoulder to the neckline. The seam attaching it to the body of the garment forms a sort of modified armhole.

The kimono sleeve (3) is cut in one with the body of the garment. If it is cut narrow, it usually has an underarm gusset.

The lower edge of any sleeve is finished by a cuff, a hem, a facing, etc., as indicated in the pattern. For additional help, see those chapter headings. Remember that on wide sleeves the hem can be seen; make the hem or facing deep or add a decorative finish.

THE SET-IN SLEEVE

The directions that follow are the standard method for setting in sleeves. There is also a flat construction method, used mainly for sportswear and children's clothes (see p. 48), for stretchy knits (see p. 81), and for leather (see p. 85).

For perfectly set-in sleeves, you must do three simple things:

- Line-up matching points exactly—underarm seams, notches, shoulder seam to sleeve center mark. Don't forget the center marking, preferably a notch, as shown here (4).
- Distribute ease in sleeve cap evenly—see directions below.
- Keep stitching around armhole even and seam allowance the correct width.

Setting in a smooth-cap sleeve

a. Before stitching the underarm seam in the sleeve, make a row of ease-stitching (8–10 stitches per inch) on the seam line of the sleeve cap, between dots. To help control the fullness, stitch a second line within the seam allowance, ⅛″ from first one (4).

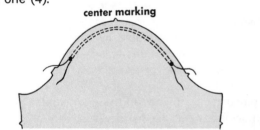

center marking

4

b. Stitch underarm seam; press open. Finish sleeve bottom if it consists of a cuff or a facing. A hem may be done later—follow your pattern instructions.

c. With garment wrong side out, place the sleeve in the armhole, right sides together. Pin edges together at underarm seams, notches, shoulder seam; add a pin ½″ to each side of the shoulder seam (5) —this inch of fabric at the top of the sleeve cap is straight grain and needs no easing. Draw up the threads gently between the dots and these two pins until the cap fits the armhole loosely—do not pull up tightly. Distribute ease evenly and pin remaining edges together with pins ½″ apart; or baste, if you prefer.

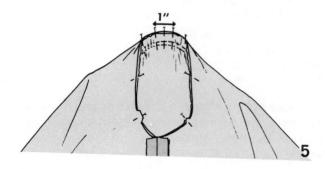

1″

5

Optional: If your fabric can be shaped by steaming, tie the easing threads after drawing them up, and distribute the ease. Then carefully unpin the sleeve, remove it from the armhole, and place the cap over a tailor's ham or the end of a sleeve board (6). Shrink out the ease with the point of the steam iron. Pin or baste the sleeve back into the armhole as described in step **c**.

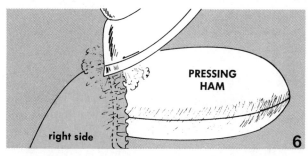

d. Starting at underarm seam, with sleeve side up, stitch around carefully, removing pins as you come to them. Make a second row of stitching within seam allowance, ⅛″ from first (7).

e. At underarm, between front and back notches, trim the seam allowance close to the stitching (8). Trim the remainder of the seam to ⅜″. Press seam as sewn, without turning it to one side; then, without pressing, turn it toward the sleeve.

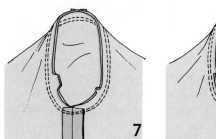
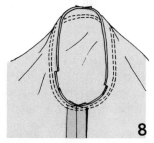

THE RAGLAN SLEEVE

Raglan sleeves are cut into two sections shaped by a shoulder seam, or in one section shaped by a large curved dart that tapers from neck over the top of the arm. Mark, stitch and press this dart carefully (see DARTS) because it outlines the curve of your shoulder. When seaming the sleeve to the garment body, be careful not to stretch the seam.

THE KIMONO SLEEVE

Kimono sleeves are usually shaped by a shoulder seam, and may or may not have a gusset at the underarm. If the pattern does not call for a gusset, you may wish to add one for comfort, especially if the sleeve is narrow (see GUSSETS). Otherwise, reinforce the underarm seam by one of the two following methods:

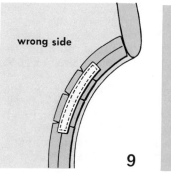
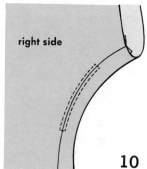

Method I—Shorten stitch at curve of underarm. Then clip seam allowance and press seam open. Baste a piece of seam tape 3″ to 4″ long over opened seam (or pin, putting pins through **from right side**); stitch on right side of garment, ⅛″ to each side of seam line (9, 10).

Method II—Pin a piece of seam tape 3″ to 4″ long over the seam line before stitching underarm seam (11). If there is a sharp curve, fold the tape as shown (12). Stitch seam with shortened stitch. Clip seam allowances **without clipping through the tape.** Press the seam open.

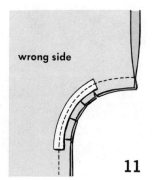
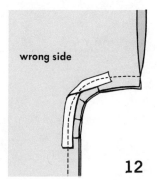

Tailoring

Tailoring is a set of sewing techniques involving extra materials and extra work on the inside of a garment. Men's jackets and coats are always tailored. A woman's jacket or coat may be of a tailored style without being tailored—it all depends on the way it is made. It is perfectly possible to turn out a dressmaker suit or a tailored suit from the same pattern. The tailored suit will have a firmer, smoother look and a more precise outline. It should also keep its shape a good deal longer.

In tailoring, the interfacing is firmer and extends over a wider area; twill tape stabilizes edges; there is often underlining; pad-stitching holds layers together; continuous steam-pressing insures shape. Everything, including fitting, is done with extra precision.

Tailoring may be done in three different ways:

Hand- or custom-tailoring is the traditional tailoring that truly shapes. A collar or a lapel made to roll by hand pad-stitching cannot be flattened out. Throughout the garment, careful hand-stitching stabilizes and shapes.

Machine-tailoring often gives good results. Since machine-stitching is conspicuous, however, the pad-stitching must be limited to the undercollar, the one place that does not show.

Tailoring with fusibles, or speed-tailoring, can be very satisfactory (see MENSWEAR), but is limited to certain fabrics.

In view of the amount of work and precision called for in tailoring, we do not suggest that you tackle it until after you have successfully made garments merely in a tailored style. Furthermore, the amount of wear you plan to get out of the garment, and the quality of the fabric used, should justify the time and care you put into it.

EQUIPMENT

The only extra equipment you will need is pressing equipment. Important as pressing is in dressmaking, it is twice as important in tailoring. You probably already have most of the pressing equipment mentioned on page 68—for tailoring, you will find that a **sleeve board, dressmaker's ham,** and a **point presser** all become necessities. A **pressing mitt** can be used instead of a dressmaker's ham; it goes over your hand for steaming curves or over the end of the sleeve board for pressing sleeve caps (1). A **pounding block** (4) is a wooden block about 9" long; when clapped down and left for a few seconds over a just-steamed edge or seam, it will make a knife-sharp crease without causing a shine. Some point pressers have a bottom designed as a pounding block (2).

A tailor board, an additional pressing aid not mentioned on page 68, is a board with various different-shaped surfaces for pressing points, curves and small flat parts. It allows any stitched area to be shaped and molded. For pressing, it has a padded cover (3); uncovered it is used with a pounding block (4).

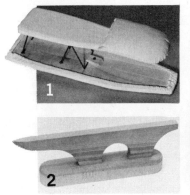

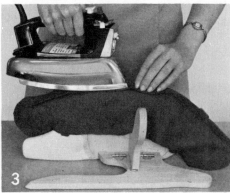

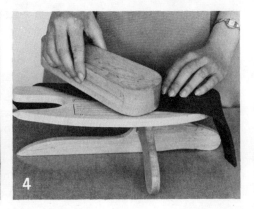

PATTERN

Most pattern companies have designs meant for tailoring, with tailoring instructions. What follows is meant to supplement such instructions, giving you in detail what the pattern guide sheet may take for granted.

Check and adjust your pattern (p. 191) even more carefully than usual, including garment length. If the style is one you have not worn before, you would be well advised to make a trial muslin, especially if your fabric is expensive. See MAKING A MUSLIN on page 205. Remember the extra thickness of underlining, interfacing, lining, perhaps interlining, and be careful not to fit too tightly. Making such a trial muslin before buying your fabric may also save you some expensive yardage.

FABRICS AND NOTIONS

GARMENT FABRIC

Buy quality fabric—you are about to put a lot of work into it. If the pattern envelope says that this design is not suitable for diagonal fabrics, avoid twills such as gabardine—a diagonal, often used in tailoring. Menswear fabrics, now generally available, are excellent. As a rule, firm fabrics are best, but tweeds, among other good fabrics, may be loosely-woven—they will just have to be made firm with underlining.

Be very sure to read and note all the information on the label of any fabric you are considering. See PREPARING FABRIC FOR USE, on page 74. Make sure that the fabric grain is straight, the fabric pre-shrunk. If you have the slightest doubt on that score, shrink the fabric as instructed.

UNDERLINING FABRIC

Underlining is generally a lightweight fabric that may or may not be specially made for the purpose. It is a necessity with soft or loosely-woven outer fabrics. The chapter on UNDERLINING will give you useful information on the subject, although in tailoring it is handled somewhat differently. Underlining is sometimes added even when the garment fabric does not absolutely demand it, as a matter of style, the need for more body, and personal preference.

When deciding on an underlining, **consider the weight and thickness of outer fabric, underlining and interfacing as a whole.**

Lightweight muslin, cheaper than specially-made fabric, makes excellent underlining. Muslin, however, is heavily sized and should be washed a few times before use, to get rid of all the sizing. Muslin used in a trial garment that did not need many alterations can be used for underlining if it was properly prepared first.

For loosely-woven outer fabric that might let color show through, buy one of the special underlining fabrics in a matching color. Be sure to shrink it unless it is marked pre-shrunk.

If underlining is not specified on the pattern, buy the same yardage as for the outer fabric, taking fabric widths into account (see the FABRIC CONVERSION CHART, p. 73). If you underline only part of the garment, figure accordingly.

INTERFACING FABRIC

In tailoring, the garment is literally constructed on the interfacing, which sometimes extends to take in the armholes, and gives the garment its shape. It cannot be chosen with too much care. Be sure to look up the chapter on INTERFACINGS. If you are interested in fusibles, also see pages 168–171 in MENSWEAR.

Interfacing should have ''give'', allowing it to be shaped and manipulated; therefore it should be woven or, if non-woven, either all-bias or with one-way stretch. The most suitable is hair canvas. It comes in a variety of weights and properties, depending on fiber content—the higher the content of goat's hair, the better the quality. Standard sew-in hair canvas is used in hand- or machine-tailoring. There is also fusible hair canvas, which does away with pad-stitching, and lighter weight fusible interfacing for lightweight fabrics (interfacing must never be heavier than outer fabric).

LINING FABRIC

A tailored coat or jacket is always lined. Select a smooth fabric, light enough in weight not to interfere with the hang of the garment, but opaque enough not to let the complex inner construction of the garment show through. Crepe, taffeta, satin, china silk, synthetics and blends all make good linings. An attractive print can give special character to the inside of a garment. If you decide to line a winter garment with pile fabric, you may still want a smooth fabric in the sleeves for ease in slipping on and off. A smooth finish plus warmth are combined in quilted fabrics, and in certain others that look like satin on one side and are finished for insulation on the other. Whatever you buy, let it be of good quality—a lining wears out all too soon. Read the chapter on LINING.

INTERLINING FABRIC

Interlining, usually made of loosely-woven wool, is an extra layer of fabric added inside a lining for warmth. It is sometimes omitted in sleeves. Fabrics such as quilting, that combine lining and interlining, are handled like lining.

NOTIONS

Twill tape, specially designed for tailoring, is used to stabilize seams, roll lines and edges. It may be cotton or polyester. For front edges, where it is used to reduce bulk, buy the ½″ width. With fusibles, use the ¼″ width for reinforcing seams (see MENSWEAR, p. 172). Shrink any tape before use, even if it is labelled pre-shrunk. To do this, remove wrapping, but leave the tape on the card. Immerse the whole thing in water. Take out; bend the card slightly as shown (5), and allow to dry.

For the **hand-sewing** to be done in tailoring, use a short needle (No. 7 or 8 Betweens). A short needle gives better control in picking up the tiny amounts of fabric called for in pad-stitching and blind-stitching. If you do not wear a thimble, this is the time to acquire the habit: with the rather resistant materials used, your fingers will suffer otherwise.

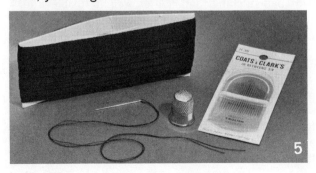

CUTTING

Press out center crease in fabric; re-fold the fabric on grain for cutting. If the crease has become soiled or discolored, avoid the line when laying out the pattern.

Cutting must be done with special accuracy.

THICK OR SPONGY FABRIC

Trim off excess pattern tissue (not seam allowances) before laying out the pieces.

Make sure that pins go through both layers of fabric—you may have to use longer (glass head) pins.

Extremely bulky fabric should be cut out through a single thickness. Have the fabric folded, as usual, but cut just one layer first, then the second layer, following the cut edge (6).

Use lighter weight fabric in a matching color for undercollar, and lining fabric for cuff and pocket-flap facings, if outer fabric is very bulky or loosely woven.

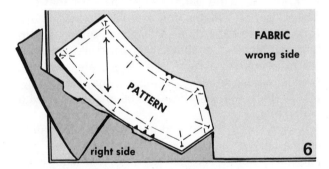

FABRIC
wrong side

PATTERN

right side   6

CUTTING FRONT INTERFACING

The front interfacing may be cut in two ways:

Extending half way into the armhole if there is no great need for support (if there is underlining, for example); this will reduce bulk at the underarm (p. 238, ill. 25).

Extending over the entire front of armhole and below it, if outer fabric needs support (p. 238, ill. 27).

In either case, cut the inner edge of interfacing ½″ wider than facing, to avoid having the two edges at the same place which might cause a ridge on the outside.

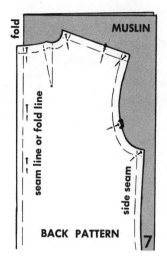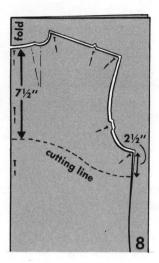

BACK PATTERN 7

fold MUSLIN

seam line or fold line

side seam

fold

7½"

2½"

cutting line

8

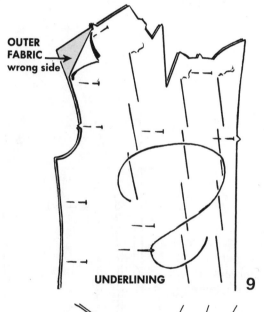

OUTER FABRIC wrong side

UNDERLINING 9

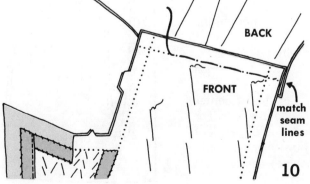

BACK

FRONT

match seam lines

10

MUSLIN REINFORCEMENT FOR BACK

Use back pattern piece. If garment has a center back seam, place the **seam line** on a straight-grain fold in the muslin (7). Cut around neck, shoulder and armhole edges, and about 2½" down the side. Remove pattern. On the muslin, measure and mark 7½" down from neck edge; measure and mark 2½" down from bottom of armhole. Draw a curved line (8) and cut out. This reinforcement is used even if there is an underlining.

To preserve the stretch in a knit garment, you may wish to omit the reinforcement described above. In such a case, reinforce the seams with twill tape (see MENSWEAR, p. 172).

CUTTING UNDERLINING

Use the garment pattern. Underline the collar, facing and undercollar only if the fabric weave is so loose that interfacing would show through.

BASTING

Two kinds of basting are special to tailoring. Use light-colored thread, as usual.

Tailor-basting (9) is diagonal basting used in both hand- and machine-tailoring for attaching entire areas of fabric together. It is worked in up-and-down rows, with the fabric flat on a table. Start with a short backstitch rather than a knot. Make the diagonal stitches about 2" long and the right-to-left stitches short; place the rows 3" to 4" apart. Avoid putting a row directly over darts or buttonholes. Tailor-basting is left in until the garment is ready for the final pressing.

Overlap-basting (10) means lapping one edge over the other, bringing the two seam lines exactly one on top of the other, and basting firmly through the seam line. It is necessary for fitting, because seams basted in the usual way would be too bulky, since they cannot be pressed open at this stage.

UNDERLINING

What follows is for underlining used together with **sew-in** interfacing. If you wish to use fusible interfacing in a garment that requires underlining, proceed as directed in the chapter on UNDERLINING, and fuse the interfacing to the facing section only—it should not be fused to the underlining.

• Underlining is marked only **after** it has been attached to the outer fabric section—this insures that markings will fall in the right places.

• It is attached to the garment, not by stitching around, but by overall tailor-basting (see the preceding page).

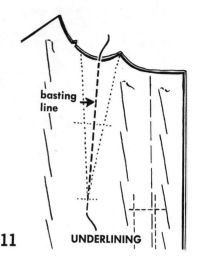

To apply underlining, spread out the garment section wrong side up:

On front sections, match underlining to garment at front edges (along fold line if there is an extended facing); pin edges together. Smooth out the two layers; if necessary, trim underlining to match garment section. Pin together at notches, corners, and various points over the entire area. Begin tailor-basting down the front edge and work across the section, but avoid the buttonhole and lapel areas and, if possible, the places where you will mark darts.

On back and sleeve sections, match the curved edges and pin the two layers together through the center line (straight grain). Smooth out toward the sides. Tailor-baste from center out. If there is a center back seam, match side edges and work toward center back. If necessary, trim underlining to match the garment section.

After you have marked the underlining (see below), hand- or machine-baste the darts to outer fabric as shown: straight darts through the center (11); curved darts just inside the marked line (12).

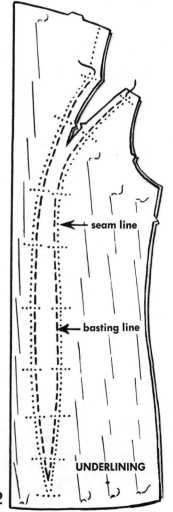

MARKING

Underlining and lining can be marked with dressmaker's tracing paper (see p. 156); muslin and interfacing with tracing paper or blue pencil. An outer fabric used in a tailored garment, however, is almost always of a texture that requires thread-marking, which is usually done with tailor's tacks (see p. 157).

If there is no underlining, mark garment sections as follows after cutting them out:

Darts, pockets and construction-markings are marked with tailor's tacks.

Front and neck seam lines are marked with tailor's tacks at one-inch intervals.

Center front line and buttonholes are marked with basting: at center front put pins through both layers (see PINS, p. 158) at wide intervals. For buttonholes put the pins through each end in right-hand side of garment only. With ruler, check straightness of center front line and straightness and intervals of buttonholes. Baste-mark (by hand or machine) center front lines and buttonholes on right side (see p. 159).

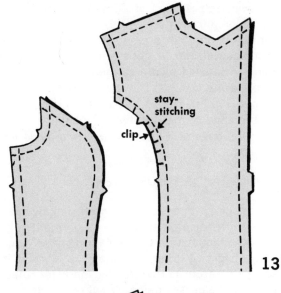

13

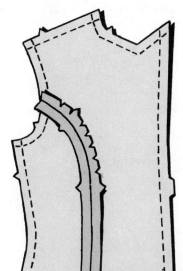

14

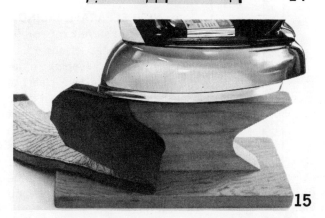

15

If there is an underlining, after tailor-basting underlining sections to garment sections, replace pattern over underlining and mark all details, including front and neck seam lines. Baste-mark center front lines and buttonhole markings through to right side (see p. 159).

If fusible interfacing is used, mark all details, including darts, after fusing the interfacing to the flat garment sections.

CURVED SEAMS

Before basting curved seams together, clip the **concave edge** to the stay-stitching (13). This will allow the seam allowance to spread as needed (14).

PRESSING

Press each part of the garment as it is stitched, using the proper piece of equipment to give it the right curve and shape. Do not press too heavily. After steam-pressing, allow fabric to cool (dry) before handling. Handle fabric as little as possible.

All seams, even the edge seams such as collar and front facing seams, should be pressed open over a point presser (15) to have a really sharp edge when they are pressed together afterwards.

When pressing on the right side of the fabric, always use a press cloth, even with a steam iron. When doing final outside pressing on wool, use a piece of garment fabric as a press cloth. If more steam is needed than the iron produces, put a damp press cloth over the woolen one.

THE FRONT INTERFACING

The handling of the interfacing is the very essence of tailoring. What follows applies to hand- and machine-tailoring. For tailoring with fusibles, see MARKING on the preceding page and MENSWEAR, pages 168–171.

In order to avoid bulk, some patterns have the interfacing cut without seam allowances along front, neck and shoulder edges. Where there is a seam allowance, mark the seam line. Mark darts, if any, and construction markings.

DARTS

To avoid a bulky seam, cut along one side of dart to point (16). Lap cut edge over other edge to other line. Secure with two lines of stitching ⅛″ from edge. Trim close to stitching (17). If interfacing ravels, reinforce point with a piece of fabric stitched over it as shown, or zigzag over the point.

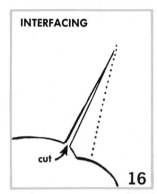

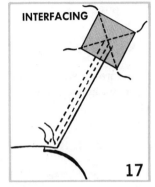

Another way of handling darts in interfacing, that completely eliminates any bulk, is to cut out the dart entirely (18). Slip it over the stitched dart in the garment; catch-stitch its edges to the fabric dart as shown (19).

If fusible interfacing is used, see MARKING on the preceding pages. Stitch darts through fabric and interfacing; slash and press open if necessary.

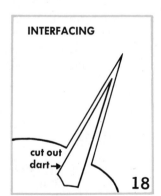

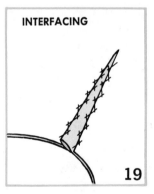

FRONT EDGE

Twill tape or a strip of lightweight fabric (organdy or underlining) is added for reinforcement. If there is a seam allowance at the front edge, it should be cut away either before or after to insure a crisp, sharp edge.

If twill tape is used, it does not extend into the seam allowance; interfacing is attached to the garment by hand. With a fabric strip, which extends to form a new, lighter weight seam allowance, the interfacing is stitched to the garment at the same time as the facing.

When you are ready to stitch the facing in place, use the edge of the twill tape or (if fabric strip was used) the edge of the interfacing as a guide for the stitching.

TWILL TAPE REINFORCEMENT

The tape is attached to the interfacing by machine and the interfacing is applied to the garment by hand. Whether you have a **separate facing** or an **extended facing,** begin by trimming away top edge of interfacing (20) from corner to the mark for attaching collar, ¼″ below seam line (or cut edge if there is no seam allowance).

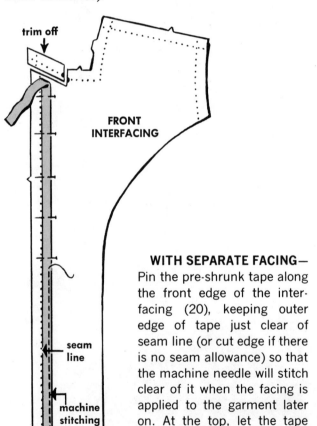

WITH SEPARATE FACING— Pin the pre-shrunk tape along the front edge of the interfacing (20), keeping outer edge of tape just clear of seam line (or cut edge if there is no seam allowance) so that the machine needle will stitch clear of it when the facing is applied to the garment later on. At the top, let the tape extend an inch or so beyond trimmed edge.

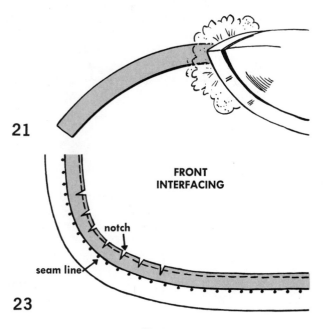

21

**FRONT
INTERFACING**

notch

seam line

23

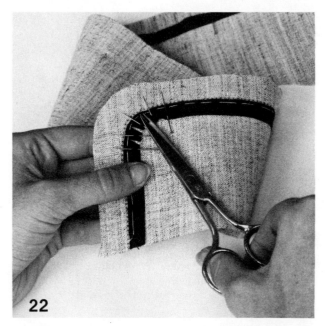

22

**FRONT
INTERFACING**

24

If garment front ends in a curve, the tape can be attached in two ways, depending on the degree of the curve:

Slight curve—"Swirl", that is, steam-press part of tape into a curve before applying (21).

Sharp curve—Carefully baste outer edge of tape along line of application, then notch inner edge of tape around curve (22), that is, remove excess fullness at the edge by cutting out little notches. Steam-press flat before machine-stitching (23).

Machine-stitch inner edge of tape to interfacing (24). Under tape, trim away interfacing edge ¼" from seam line (or cut edge) as shown (24).

Place interfacing to wrong side of front garment section, over underlining if there is one. Pin, matching all notches, marks and edges at neck, shoulder and armhole; along the front edge, keep tape just clear of seam line on outer fabric or underlining. Starting along the front edge, tailor-baste interfacing in place.

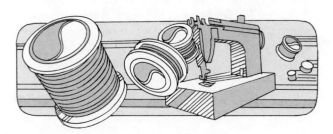

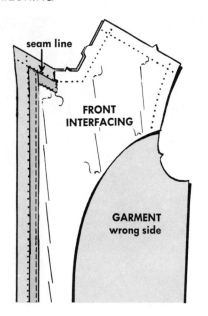

25

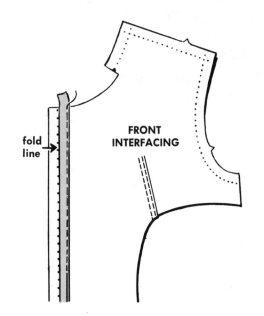

26

At top, trim end of tape to just clear of seam line on outer section. Add a short piece of tape as shown (25) from edge of long tape to the mark for attaching collar. Pin, keeping top edge of tape just clear of seam line. Blind-stitch lower edge to interfacing, being careful to pick up only the interfacing, not the outer fabric, with your needle.

If there is no lapel (meaning that the garment is to be worn closed at the top, or either open or closed): Blind-stitch all free tape edges to outer fabric or underlining, using thread to match outer fabric. Always keep clear of seam lines. Pick up no more than one thread in outer fabric with each stitch.

If there is a folded-back lapel, leave the tape edges unattached until after the **roll line** on collar and lapels has been established and taped, and the lapels pad-stitched (see p. 241).

WITH EXTENDED FACING—The interfacing may have an extra ⅝″ or so along front edge, meant to be folded to give body to the edge in the absence of seam allowances. Pin the pre-shrunk tape along this fold line, outer edge of tape even with the fold, or even with the cut edge if there is no such extension. At the neck, let the tape extend an inch or so beyond trimmed edge. Machine-stitch inner edge of tape to interfacing (26).

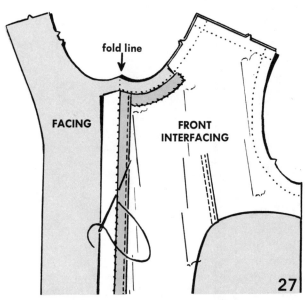

27

Pin and tailor-baste interfacing to front garment section as for separate facing (see p. 236), matching tape edge exactly to fold line on outer fabric or underlining. At the top, trim end of tape just clear of seam line on outer fabric or underlining. Blind-stitch free edge of tape to fold line, picking up no more than one thread in outer fabric with each stitch. Add a short piece of tape to neck edge as for separate facing (27).

FABRIC STRIP REINFORCEMENT

The fabric strip is machine-stitched to the interfacing and the interfacing is applied to the garment also by machine. Use underlining, or any other firm, lightweight fabric.

If the interfacing has a seam allowance, pin the front interfacing pattern to the fabric, on the grain indicated. Cut along front and neck edge, and for about 3″ along bottom and shoulder edges. Remove the pattern. Measure and mark a line 3″ back from cut edges; cut along this line. Pin the strip to the interfacing, matching notches and outer edges (be sure to make a right and a left side). Attach with two lines of stitching, one ¾″ from cut edge, the second ¼″ in from first (28), or with a row of multi-stitch zigzag. Trim away the entire seam allowance of the interfacing, exactly on the seam line, as shown. On reverse side, trim the inside edge of the fabric strip ¼″ from stitching (29).

If the interfacing has no seam allowance, pin the interfacing pattern to the fabric and mark the seam line along front, lapel and neck edges (30). Remove the pattern. Draw a line ⅝″ **outside** the seam line, and another line about 2″ **inside** the seam line (31). Cut out the strip. Pin the interfacing to the fabric strip, matching front and neck edges of the interfacing to seam line on strip (be sure to make a right and a left side). Attach with two lines of stitching, one ⅛″ from interfacing edge, the second ¼″ in from first. On the reverse side, trim the fabric to about ¼″ from second line of stitching.

Pin interfacing to wrong side of garment section, outer edges even. Starting along the front edge, tailor-baste the interfacing in place, keeping clear of buttonhole and lapel areas. When the facing is stitched on later, the lightweight seam allowance will be caught in the seam.

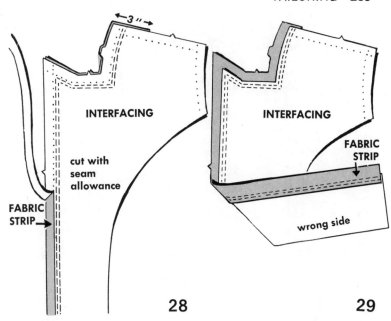

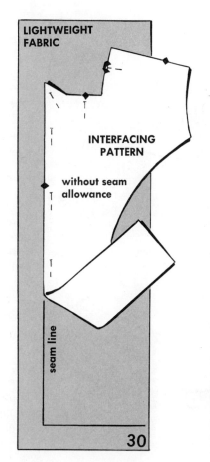

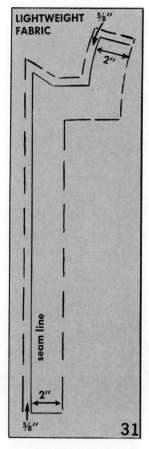

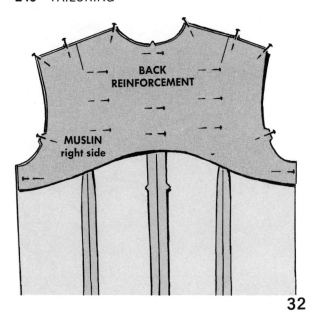

32

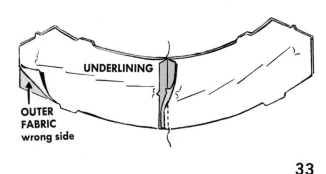

UNDERLINING

OUTER
FABRIC
wrong side

33

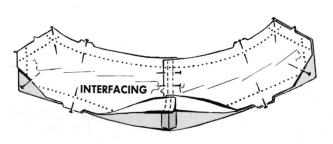

INTERFACING

34

BACK REINFORCEMENT

The back reinforcement described under CUTTING (see p. 233) is applied after seams and darts in the garment back section have been completed and pressed. Stitch darts in the reinforcement piece and press in the opposite direction from those in the garment. Pin the piece to wrong side of outer section, center back lines matched. Pin to entire area from center out (32). Tailor-baste. The bottom edge is left unfinished.

FITTING

Read the chapter on FITTING carefully—the information there is applicable to tailored garments. In tailoring, you need at least three fittings:

First fitting—This is mainly to check position of darts before any stitching is done; darts, shoulder and side seams are basted.

Second fitting—This is done after darts and back seam have been stitched and pressed, and interfacing is in place on front sections; shoulder and side seams are basted.

Third fitting—This is done after shoulder and side seams have been stitched and pressed, sleeves have been stitched and sleeve-caps shrunk (see pp. 228, 229). Sleeves are basted in (determine the sleeve length). Undercollar is overlap-basted in place to determine the roll line (see the next page).

UNDERCOLLAR AND LAPEL

If underlining is used on undercollar, tailor-baste underlining to wrong side of outer section. If undercollar is in two sections, join the center seam and press it open; trim the underlining seam allowance close to the stitching; trim fabric seam allowance to about ¼'' (33).

On interfacing mark seam lines. To join the two sections, avoid bulk by lapping one side over the other, matching seam lines. Make two lines of stitching ⅛'' apart. Trim close to stitching. Trim off outer corners ⅛'' inside seam line. Place interfacing over wrong side of undercollar, marked side out, matching notches, etc. Pin. Working from one end to the other, tailor-baste the layers together through the center with one row of 1''-long stitches (34).

If fusible interfacing is used, see COLLARS, page 50.

THE ROLL LINE

Establishing the roll line is of the utmost importance. The undercollar must be temporarily attached to the garment: Starting at center back, lap right side of undercollar over wrong side of garment at neck edge, matching seam lines; pin with a vertical pin on inside; do the same at front points and shoulder seams. Overlap-baste on seam line, easing as necessary (35).

The roll is best established **on your person** with someone helping you. The next best thing is a **dress form** in your size. In the absence of both helper and dress form, place garment on a **man's suit hanger** with fully-shaped shoulder and neck (36) and make very sure that the shoulder seams are in correct position.

Pin the garment front sections together at the top buttonhole and let lapels (if any) and collar roll back. Now make sure that outer edge of the collar will cover the neck seam by at least ½″: This means that the finished edge of the collar—deduct the seam allowances—must cover the neck seam which is now the basted seam line. (Make doubly sure of this if you are working on a clothes hanger). Depending on the style, the collar may spread well beyond ½″, but the **edge must not fall short of that.**

Once the roll is established, place a row of pins exactly along the roll line (soft fold) of the undercollar and the lapel (if any) as shown (37). If you are working alone, try on the garment and make sure that the roll is to your liking and the neck seam at back is well covered.

Remove the undercollar from the garment. Since pins tend to fall out during work, replace them with a line of basting along the roll line, making sure that the two halves of the collar are symmetrical. Do the same on the lapels.

Pad-stitching is the next step. It is done on the collar (or, more precisely, the undercollar) and the facings (the garment side that is folded back) in order that interfacing and garment fabric may be attached together throughout these sections, and the finished collar (and lapel) will keep its shape and fit when worn. In the collar, pad-stitching can be done by hand or machine. In facings it is done by hand or not at all.

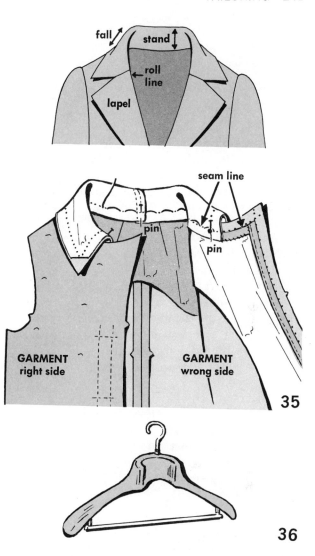

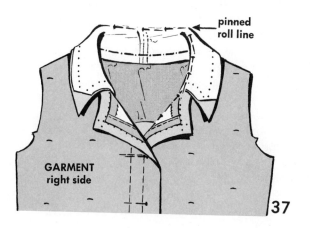

HAND PAD-STITCHING

Hand pad-stitching does by far the better job than machine pad-stitching because it allows the section actually to be shaped, so that it does not flatten out when laid down. While working, hold the section over your hand in the shape it will have when worn (38). The stitch, motion and direction are the same as in tailor-basting, but the padding stitch (39) is much smaller and closer and stays in the finished garment.

Ideally these stitches will be invisible on the outer fabric. In lightweight fabrics, however, the stitch may be slightly perceptible and the padding as a whole will produce a surface impression on the outer fabric.

Work on the interfacing side. Use thread to match the outer fabric and a short needle (No. 7 or 8 Betweens). Start with a small backstitch, not a knot. In general, make the diagonal stitches about ⅜'' long and the right-to-left straight stitches very small, just catching a thread of the outer fabric through the interfacing. Make the next row ⅜'' away. **Do not pad-stitch seam allowance**—stop stitches just short of seam line.

Pad-stitches can be as short as ¼'' or as long as ½'', depending on where they occur. In general, they are shorter and closer together (¼'') on the collar "stand" (the part that stands against the neck). In the back-and-forth lines on the collar "fall", they are longer and farther apart (½''). In a lapel they are in between.

PAD-STITCHING
THE UNDERCOLLAR

a. Collar stand (inner part of collar)—Make a row of pad-stitching along the roll line. Always holding the collar in the shape it will have when worn, make the next rows parallel to first until you reach neck seam line (40).

b. Collar fall (outer part of collar)—Start at center back seam at roll line. Making the stitches slightly larger and farther apart than on the stand, work toward outer seam line of collar, following the grain of the interfacing, as shown (41), and still keeping the collar shaped over your hand. Cover the entire area in this manner.

NOTE: For the sake of clarity, the two drawings show the undercollar flat. Once pad-stitched, how-

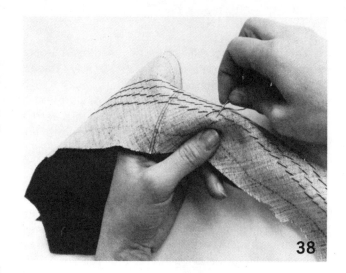

38

HAND PAD-STITCHING

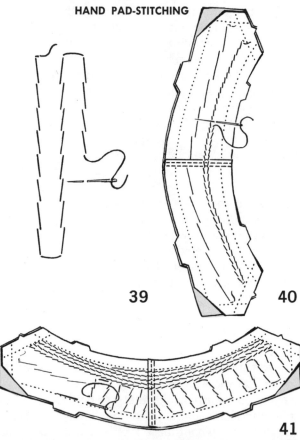

39 **40**

41

ever, it will tend to stand up as shown in the photograph (44). Before the raw edges of interfacing are trimmed, they will have drawn back slightly from the fabric edges.

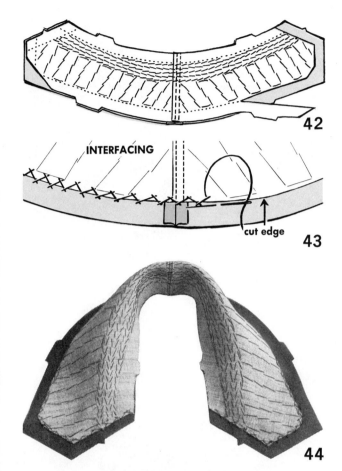

42

INTERFACING

cut edge 43

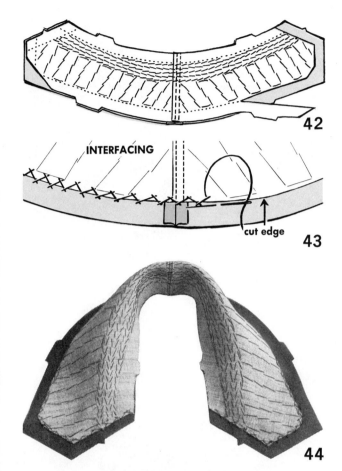

44

45

MACHINE PAD-STITCHING

46

c. Trim away interfacing seam allowance close to seam line at ends and outer edges of collar (42). Catch-stitch the cut edge to the outer fabric (or underlining, if any). If there is no underlining, be careful to pick up no more than a thread in outer fabric. Place stitches about ½″ apart and do not pull them up tight (43).

d. Press the undercollar with plenty of steam and use a ham for shaping, or a tightly-rolled towel. The photograph (44) shows the undercollar completely finished and ready for the next stage in construction. Pin front edges together and keep the section pinned and upside down as shown (45) until you are ready to use it. Once pad-stitched, the section should never lie flat—if you are interrupted while pad-stitching, fold and pin together in front in the same way.

MACHINE PAD-STITCHING, or machine-tailoring, merely reinforces the undercollar without shaping it.

a. Collar stand (inner part of collar)—Make first row of stitching along the roll line, and succeeding rows about ¼″ apart, working toward neck seam line (46).

b. Collar fall (outer part of collar)—Start at center back seam at the roll line. Following the grain of the interfacing, stitch to outer seam line, then along seam line for ½″ to ¾″; pivot and repeat in the other direction. Continue as shown to front of collar, always following the grain. Then repeat on other half of collar, starting again at the center (46).

c. Press the undercollar over a ham for shaping.

WITH FUSIBLE INTERFACING, cut a curved strip to fit between the roll line and the seam line at neck edge; cut woven interfacing on the bias, non-woven interfacing in the direction of the stretch. Fuse the strip over the undercollar interfacing (47). Press undercollar, using a ham for shaping.

FUSED INTERFACING

47

TAPING AND PAD-STITCHING THE LAPEL

Taping and pad-stitching the lapel were mentioned under IF THERE IS A FOLDED-BACK LAPEL on page 238. You were instructed to leave the twill tape unattached along front and top edges.

a. Taping the roll line (fold) of a lapel is done to prevent stretching and give more body. Place tape over baste-marked roll line (48). Blindstitch the edges to the interfacing only, being careful not to stitch through garment fabric. Cut tape-ends diagonally, as shown, just short of neck seam line (48) and even with edge of front tape.

49

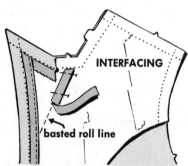

48

b. Pad-stitching the lapel area can be done by hand only; if you are machine-tailoring, omit it. Start at the roll line and fill in the lapel with parallel lines of pad-stitches, holding the work over your hand, rolled in the direction it will roll when worn (49). Press carefully, using the ham to maintain shape. Note that after the padding has been completed, the tape at front edge no longer quite reaches the garment seam line.

c. Blind-stitch free edges of twill tape to outer fabric or underlining along front and top, being careful not to pick up more than one thread of garment fabric with each stitch.

d. Catch-stitch free edge of interfacing loosely to outer fabric or underlining, leaving the curved part at the bust area unattached, as shown (50). This catch-stitching should be done only if it will not show on the outside.

BUTTONHOLES

Tailored women's garments almost always have bound buttonholes. Make them after the interfacing is attached, but before the free edge is catch-stitched

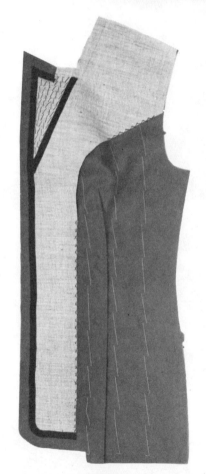

50

down. See BUTTONHOLES for heavy fabrics. The patch method (see p. 36) is best, because of its wider seam allowance. For reducing bulk in heavy interfacing, see page 37. For keyhole buttonholes, see page 175.

POCKETS

The pattern guide sheet always gives instructions for making the pockets in your garment. Like button-holes, they have to be made with great care. **Always interface the opening edge** of a pocket in a tailored garment. Once a slashed pocket has been made, close it with diagonal basting until the garment is finished. See the chapter on POCKETS.

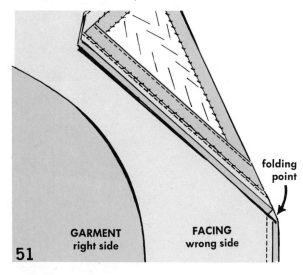

GARMENT
right side

FACING
wrong side

folding
point

51

REDUCING BULK

In tailoring, where so much of the final effect depends on general smoothness and sharply-defined edges, and where fabrics tend to be heavier, it is particularly necessary to reduce bulk wherever it is possible.

Edge-seams along facings and collar are the most important. Before trimming their seam allowances (except for interfacing), press them open over a point presser (p. 235, ill. 15) in order that they may have a really sharp edge when they are pressed together afterward. Then grade and clip as directed under BEFORE TURNING THE FACING on page 93. (Do not, however, understitch as directed on page 94). Where there is a lapel, reverse the order of widths at the point where lapel is folded back (51)—that is, if along the front edge you have trimmed the outer fabric to ¼″ (slightly more if fabric is heavy) and the facing to ⅛″, along the lapel, trim the outer fabric to ⅛″ and the facing to ¼″.

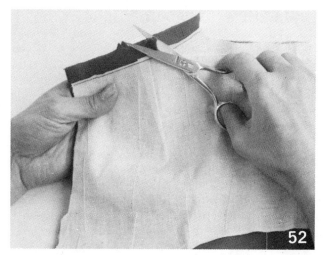

52

Interfacing, when it is caught in a seam, is always trimmed as close to stitching as possible.

Ends of darts caught in seams are trimmed diagonally with the scissors held at an angle, as shown, to grade the layers of fabric (52).

Ends of seams crossed by another seam are trimmed diagonally like darts (53).

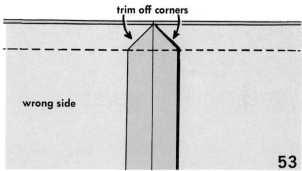

trim off corners

wrong side

53

In hems, at bottom of garment or sleeves, trim seam allowances from raw edge to marked hemline, as shown (54).

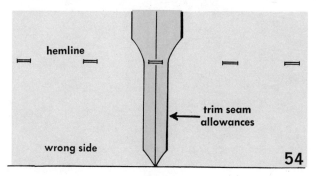

hemline

trim seam
allowances

wrong side

54

SLEEVES

To set in sleeves, follow the instructions on pages 228 and 229, being sure to include the part marked OPTIONAL which tells you how to shape a sleeve cap —in tailoring, this is a necessary step. Even if your fabric is not of a shrinkable kind, this step will help control and smooth the ease in the cap.

Sleeve heads—After attaching shoulder pads, make sleeve heads to round out the sleeve caps. For each sleeve, cut a strip of lambs wool or polyester fleece, 2½″ × 6½″. Fold one long edge 1″ under. Place the strip inside the sleeve, with wider side against sleeve and folded edge even with armhole seam line. Slipstitch fold to seam line. Round off corners (55).

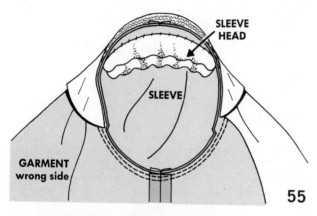

INTERFACING IN HEMS

On jackets, coats, and cuffless sleeves, the hem is given body by means of a bias strip of muslin or lightweight interfacing. Front interfacing should be cut even with marked hemline.

Upper edge of interfacing should never stop at the top edge of the hem—in order to avoid a ridge, the interfacing either goes above as shown (56) to be used with an attached lining hem, or stops below as shown (57).

Hem with a soft edge—Cut bias strips 1″ wider than hem allowance. Place the strips on the wrong side of the garment, with bottom edge ⅝″ below marked hemline. To join strips, cut ends straight and just let them overlap. Catch-stitch both edges of strip to garment (56). Ease-stitch hem allowance if necessary; catch-stitch hem to strip.

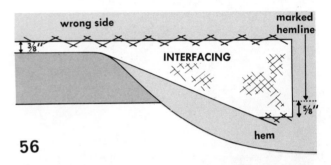

Hem with a sharp edge—Cut bias strips 2″ wide. Fold one long edge ¼″ over and press. Pin strip along marked hemline with fold up (not against the garment) and folded edge exactly even with marked hemline (57). Slipstitch the folded edge to hemline, picking up no more than a thread in outer fabric with each stitch. To join strips, cut ends straight and just let them overlap (fold within fold at bottom edge). Catch front ends loosely to interfacing and upper edge to vertical seam allowances, as shown (57).

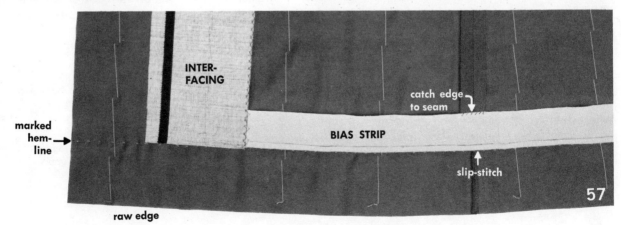

For sleeves, interface and finish the hem in the same way as the garment hem.

If using fusible interfacing, the interfacing is fused to the hem allowance: Cut interfacing the width of the space from marked hemline to ¼'' from raw edge. If hem edge is shaped, use the garment as a pattern.

For putting up the hem, see the directions under HEM IN A COAT on page 128.

FINAL PRESSING

When the garment is finished except for the lining, tack front facing loosely to interfacing and the back facing to back reinforcement, underlining or outer fabric. Take long running stitches. (If you plan to put in your lining by machine, this basting will have to be removed after pressing). Remove all tailor-basting and thread markings. Carefully press the garment or, better, have it pressed by a tailor, by hand(!) with attention paid to each detail. This will give your garment a professional finish that will be out of your reach once the lining is in.

LINING

If the pattern does not provide pieces for the lining, see LINING A JACKET OR COAT on page 143.

FINISHING DETAILS

Seam allowances in areas that are to be covered with a lining need not be finished unless fabric is extremely ravelly—in that case make a line of ma-chine-stitching along edges, straight or zigzag.

Covered snaps (58) are sometimes used to fasten the upper edge of front facing under the collar (see FASTEN-ERS, page 100).

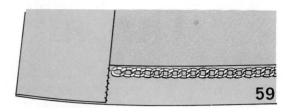

A gold chain weight (59) may be added at the hem of a jacket to give the garment a better hang. Chains designed for this purpose are available packaged or by the yard and in different weights. If it is necessary to change the length, you can remove some links or join two chains.

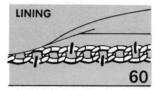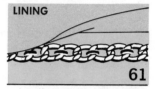

Place the chain along the hem on the inside of the jacket. It may extend from facing to facing or just across the back between side seams. Sew the chain in place along top and bottom edges, using an overcast stitch in alternate links (60). Catch the hem only, not the outer fabric. If the chain is light-weight, you may sew it in place with running stitches through the center (61).

It is a good idea to remove the chain before the garment is dry-cleaned to avoid press marks which might show on the outside.

French tacks are used to hold facings to the body of the garment at the hem. They are also used to hold a free-hanging lining loosely in place along the hem at side seams (see HEM IN A COAT, pp. 128, 129 and THREAD LOOPS, p. 253).

Arrowhead tacks (62) are sometimes used as a "stop" and a decoration at the top of single pleats or at pocket-corners (see page 253).

Thread and Needles

Thread and needle are practically a unit in sewing—one is useless without the other. For best results, however, they must be suited to each other and especially to the fabric you want to stitch.

Many threads are available in different spool sizes—the largest spools, of course, are the most economical.

THREAD

Thread may be made of synthetics, cotton, silk, or a combination of these fibers. Like fabrics, threads are often treated with finishes to impart special qualities and improve performance.

Mercerization, applied to cotton thread and cotton-covered polyester thread, adds smoothness, luster and better dye affinity.

Glacé finish, used on quilting thread and button and carpet thread, produces a hard, smooth surface, as waxing does.

SYNTHETIC THREAD

Synthetic threads today may be cotton-covered polyester, spun polyester, or nylon. These threads provide the strength and elasticity necessary for today's knits, permanent press, and stretch fabrics.

Dual Duty Plus ®—The cotton-covered polyester thread on the golden spool: The polyester core is wrapped in cotton to make a single strand; two (or more) strands are twisted together to create the thread (1). The one thread for every purpose—for hand and machine sewing, for every fabric from chiffon to sailcloth, for natural fibers and synthetics. It sews and irons like a cotton thread, yet the polyester core gives the flexible, more durable seams of a synthetic thread.

It is mercerized and comes in fashion colors. Regular spool and large spool. Extra large dressmaker spool in white and in black only.

Dual Duty Plus ® Extra Fine for Lightweight Fabrics —Cotton-covered polyester thread for tricots and other very lightweight fabrics. In limited colors.

Dual Duty Plus ® Extra Strong, Button & Carpet— Cotton-covered polyester thread for buttons and hand sewing on heavy fabrics. In basic colors.

Spun polyester thread—A 100% polyester thread (2) which can be used on natural fibers and synthetics. In fashion colors. Regular spool and large spool.

Nylon sewing thread—A 100% nylon thread which can be used for hand or machine sewing on synthetics. In fashion colors. Regular spool and large spool.

Clear nylon thread—A continuous filament nylon thread used mostly on sturdy fabrics where strength is essential. Transparent for easy color blending. Adjust your machine for a very loose tension when you start using it.

Polyester buttonhole twist—A strong thread specially designed for hand-worked buttonholes and decorative stitching by hand or machine. In fashion colors.

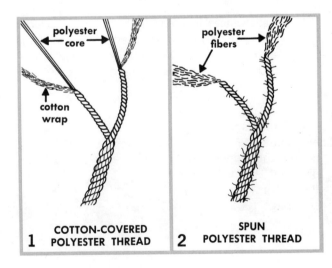

1 COTTON-COVERED POLYESTER THREAD

2 SPUN POLYESTER THREAD

COTTON THREAD

Cotton thread, which has less strength and less stretch than a synthetic thread, may be used on natural-fiber fabrics that have no stretch. It comes in a variety of sizes (thicknesses), usually indicated by a size number on the spool—the higher the number, the finer the thread, with 50 as a general-purpose medium size.

Mercerized sewing thread—For light and medium-weight fabrics of every kind. Size 50 only. In fashion colors. Regular spool and large spool. Extra large dressmaker's spool in white, sizes 40, 50, 60 and in black, size 50.

Mercerized Best Cord ® thread—White and black only, in 6 sizes, from coarsest, size 8, to finest, size 60. For white and black cottons and linens. Also used on fabrics too heavy for other thread, even though thread color may not match. Small spool, regular spool and large spool.

Button and carpet thread—Extra-heavy, extra-strong, glacé-finished cotton thread. For hand-sewing only. In basic colors. Large spool.

Quilting thread—Fine, strong glacé-finished cotton thread for hand- and machine-quilting. In limited colors. Large spool.

Basting thread—Soft, fine cotton thread for hand-basting; breaks easily and is therefore easy to remove. Large spool in white only.

SILK THREAD

Because silk is a natural fiber, its availability becomes more limited every day.

Silk sewing thread—For use with silk and lighter-weight wool fabrics. It handles differently from other threads—test the tension on your machine when you start using it. Comes in one size (A), in fashion colors.

Silk buttonhole twist—A strong thread specially designed for hand-worked buttonholes and decorative stitching by hand or machine. In fashion colors. Not recommended for topstitching washable garments, as it may shrink.

NEEDLES

Needles are made in different types to suit the kind of work for which they are used. They are available in many sizes, in order to draw threads of different sizes easily through fabrics of various weights.

Buy good quality needles—inferior needles may have a blunt point or a rough eye which can cause the thread to fray or break.

MACHINE NEEDLES

Check your sewing machine manual for the type of needle you should buy. Some needles, such as those by Coats & Clark, will fit most popular makes of sewing machines—see the needle package. The following needles are **standard needles** (3), which vary mainly in the type of point.

Universal ballpoint needles have a special taper, designed for knits and wovens alike.

Sharp-pointed needles are designed to pierce woven fabrics.

Ballpoint needles have a rounded point, designed for use on knit fabrics; the ballpoint pushes the yarns aside, instead of piercing them.

Wedge needles have a wedge-shaped point, designed for use on leather and leather-look fabrics.

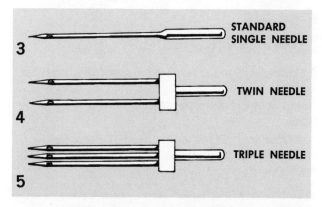

STANDARD SINGLE NEEDLE

3

TWIN NEEDLE

4

TRIPLE NEEDLE

5

Twin needles (4) and **triple needles** (5) have two or three needles joined together with a common body or shank. They can be used on some machines for straight or decorative stitching (see your sewing machine manual).

The correct machine-needle size is determined by the weight of the fabric to be sewn (see the chart on the next page). The numbering system for needle sizes varies depending on the brand—some are numbered according to the U.S. system of sizes, while others are numbered according to the European system. The following are commonly used sizes in both numbering systems for fine, medium and coarse needles:

U.S. SIZES		EUROPEAN SIZES	MACHINES NEEDLES (actual size)
10	fine	70	
11	fine	75	
14	medium	90	
16	coarse	100	

Change your machine needle often especially when sewing on synthetics. A new needle assures you of no needle damage to fabric. A blunt or burred needle (6) can damage your fabric and thread.

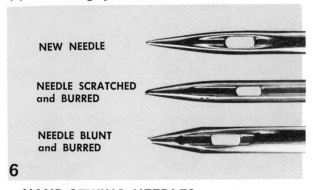

NEW NEEDLE

NEEDLE SCRATCHED and BURRED

NEEDLE BLUNT and BURRED

6

HAND-SEWING NEEDLES

Hand-sewing needles come in ten sizes, from No. 1, very coarse, to No. 10, very fine (see actual size illustrations). The following are the most common types:

Sharps are medium length needles, most commonly used for general sewing. Most other hand-sewing needles differ from them mainly in length.

Embroidery (also called crewel) needles are exactly like Sharps but have a longer eye for easier threading. They are excellent for sewing.

Betweens are shorter needles, good for detailed handwork, such as fine stitching on heavy fabric, as in tailoring. **Quilting needles** are size 7 Betweens.

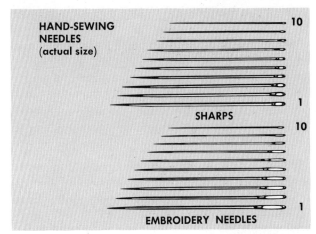

HAND-SEWING NEEDLES (actual size)

10

1

SHARPS

10

1

EMBROIDERY NEEDLES

Milliners are longer needles, best for basting and millinery.

Calyx-eyed Sharps are open at the top for easy threading. Very helpful for people who have difficulty threading ordinary needles.

CALYX-EYED NEEDLE

Ballpoint needles, with a rounded point, are made specially for knits.

SPECIAL NEEDLES

The following needles are made for various purposes; the numbering for sizes may vary somewhat from the hand-sewing needles above.

Beading needles are very fine, long needles, used for bead work and sewing sequins on fine fabrics.

Tapestry needles are heavy needles with a blunt point for work on canvas, such as needlepoint.

Chenille needles are similar to tapestry needles but have a sharp point for heavy embroidery on closely-woven fabric.

Glovers needles have a tapered point with three sharp edges to pierce leather without tearing it; used for hand-sewing on leather.

Darners are long needles, used for basting and darning with cotton.

Yarn darners are the heaviest needles with large eyes, used for stitchery and darning with yarn.

Special assortments are available with various straight and curved needles for crafts, upholstery, rugs, etc.

HOW TO CHOOSE THE CORRECT THREAD AND NEEDLE

Choose your thread and needle according to your fabric—the chart below will show you how to coordinate the essentials in your sewing—fabric, thread, needle, and the machine stitch-size best suited to them.

For knits and permanent press fabrics, use the finest needle the fabric will take and the longest stitch which will still look good (this is to avoid puckering or splitting the fabric yarns).

For sewing buttons on light and medium-weight fabrics, use Dual Duty Plus ®. For buttons and for hand sewing on heavy fabrics, use Dual Duty Plus ® Extra Strong, Button & Carpet thread.

FABRICS		J. & P. COATS THREAD			J. & P. COATS NEEDLES	
The fabrics listed below may be made of any fiber or combination of fibers; they are listed only as an example of weight.		For all fabrics including knits	For all fabrics except knits	Cottons and linens in white and black	Hand-sewing	Machine-sewing UNIVERSAL BALLPOINT
LIGHT WEIGHT	nylon tricot for lingerie batiste, chiffon, dress-weight tricot, dotted Swiss, net, organdy, sheer crepe, voile	DUAL DUTY PLUS® EXTRA FINE FOR LIGHTWEIGHT FABRICS	SUPER SHEEN® MERCERIZED SEWING thread use thread one shade darker than fabric	MERCER-IZED BEST CORD® thread size 60	sizes 9, 10	size 11 10-12 sts per inch for tricots 12-14 sts per inch for wovens
MEDIUM LIGHT WEIGHT	challis, crepe, gingham, jersey, percale, taffeta, wool crepe	DUAL DUTY PLUS® POLYESTER thread with cotton covering; mercerized			sizes 8, 9	size 11 12-14 sts per inch
MEDIUM WEIGHT	broadcloth, corduroy, double knit, flannel, linen, piqué, polished cotton, poplin, satin, shantung, suiting, velvet, velveteen			sizes 50, 60	sizes 7, 8	size 11 or 14 12-14 sts per inch
MEDIUM HEAVY WEIGHT	bonded fabrics, coating, denim, double knit, drapery fabric, felt, fleece, gabardine, leather, leather-look, quilted fabric, sweater knits, terry cloth	use thread one shade darker than fabric		size 40	size 6	size 14 or finest needle fabric will take 10-12 sts per inch
HEAVY WEIGHT	awning cloth, canvas, duck, fake fur, sail-cloth, ticking, upholstery fabric		MERCERIZED BEST CORD® thread sizes 8, 20, 30	sizes 8, 20, 30	sizes 1-5	size 14 or 16 6-8 sts per inch

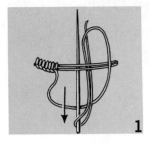 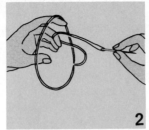 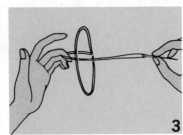 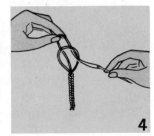

Thread Loops

"Thread loops" include all reinforced threads, even if, like the bar tack and the French tack, they are not really loops. They may consist of a core of several threads covered with blanket stitch, or of a finger-crocheted chain. The blanket-stitched loop is stronger, since it is attached by several threads instead of one or two.

Use single or double thread. Where possible, put the needle through from the wrong side, with a knot in the thread-end; otherwise start with a couple of tiny stitches.

The blanket-stitched loop can be used for any purpose: button loop, belt carrier, thread eye for hook, bar tack, French tack or hanging snap (see p. 99). Blanket stitch on a loop differs from blanket stitch in embroidery in that the needle never goes through the fabric and is used eye-first (1). After taking three or four stitches for the core, cover them entirely with blanket stitch, worked close together but not too tight. Fasten thread securely (on wrong side when possible), and cut off.

The finger-crocheted loop is generally used only for a button loop, belt carrier or French tack. After bring-

ing the thread to the right side, take a tiny stitch in the fabric at the same place. Draw thread up to form a loop. Put a finger through the loop (2, 3) and using it as a hook, make a chain of the required length (4). Put needle through last loop and pull up tight. Attach loop-end firmly but invisibly where it belongs, finishing off on wrong side when possible.

BUTTON LOOP (5)—An inconspicuous loop for a small button, usually placed at the neck of a front opening. Attach loop securely, keeping beginning and finishing stitches invisible. Use single thread. For a blanket-stitched loop, take stitches as shown (6), with enough slack for the button. Complete as directed.

BELT CARRIER (7)—Used on side seams of dresses to keep a belt in place. Mark placement (width of belt, one-half above and one-half below center of belt line). Use double thread, long enough to complete one loop (a long loop, blanket-stitched, may need a 48″ long thread before doubling).

For a crocheted loop, proceed in the usual way, leaving a comfortable slack in the loop.

For a blanket-stitched loop, take small horizontal stitches at top and bottom marks (8) and draw thread

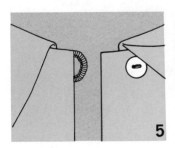 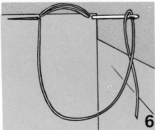 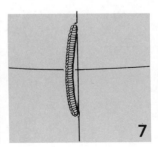 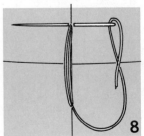

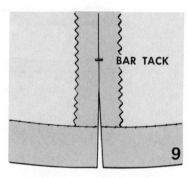

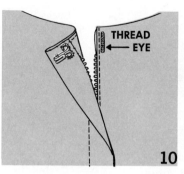

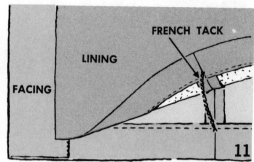

up, leaving the necessary slack in the loop. Repeat three or four times, as shown; take an extra stitch to fasten thread. Complete in the usual way.

BAR TACK (9)—An inconspicuous reinforcement, placed on wrong or right side of a garment at points of strain, such as the top of a slit, the bottom of a fly front, or the top corners of patch pockets. It is

hardly more than ⅛″ long. Draw up thread completely, leaving no slack.

THREAD EYE FOR HOOK (10)—Used in place of a metal eye. Make "eye" about ¼″ long, and draw up thread so "eye" is straight with practically no slack.

FRENCH TACK (11)—Used to hold two parts of a garment, such as lining and coat, loosely together at the hem. It may be blanket-stitched or crocheted.

Trimming

Trimming may be added to a garment just for decoration, or it may be a necessary detail (most often an edge finish) applied so as to serve as decoration as well. Bias binding and piping (see pp. 26 and 30) are good examples of this. So is self-fringe. The decorative details that follow are the ones you are most likely to use. They are given in alphabetical order. For APPLIQUÉ, see that chapter.

ARROWHEAD TACK

The arrowhead tack is a decorative stop, placed at the upper end of single pleats and slits, and at the

corners of slit pockets. It consists of a triangle of embroidery, done with buttonhole twist or embroidery floss. The three sides of the tack are equal in size, seldom more than ¾″ and sometimes as small as ⅜″. At a pleat or slit, the tack is centered at the top (1), so that the stitches can go through both seam allowances or pleat fabric. At pocket-opening ends (2), the tack should span the two lips of the opening.

Mark out the triangle with basting thread. Bring out the thread at left-hand corner (3a) and fill in the area, proceeding as shown (3b, c). Keep threads very close together.

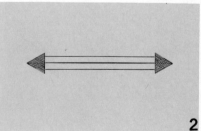

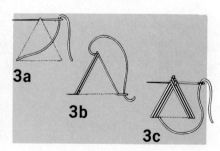

BEADS

Beads are usually attached along an outline lightly marked on the outside of the fabric. Sometimes they are used to enhance a printed or woven design in the fabric. They can be sewed on singly or in groups.

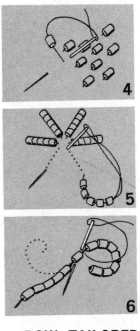

For attaching beads as shown in illustrations 4 and 5, use a very fine needle or a beading needle, and wax the thread with beeswax to prevent twisting. Sew on single beads with a backstitch, working from right to left, as shown (4). For short straight lines, use double thread; take 5 or 6 beads on the needle and sew on as shown (5). For a long continuous line, string beads on a heavy thread and attach them by taking stitches over the thread between beads (6). When attaching beads, it is particularly important to fasten thread-ends securely.

BOW, TAILORED

A tailored bow (7) is made from ribbon or flat tubing (see BIAS, p. 29). Cut a length three times the desired size of bow, plus 1″. Trim ends diagonal-ly; in the case of tubing, turn in raw edges, slip-stitch and press. Fold and tack through center, either flat (7a) or with a pleat (7b). Fold another piece of ribbon or tubing across the center, as shown (7). Sew ends together underneath.

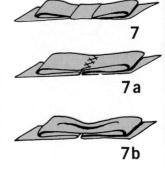

EMBROIDERY

Embroidery can be mentioned here only briefly. For machine embroidery see your sewing machine manual.

Hand embroidery includes fagoting, openwork, appliqué, and every kind of decorative stitch made on fabric. Illustrated below (8) are some stitches most commonly used. The thread is generally six-strand embroidery floss, in which the strands can be divided for finer work.

FAGOTING

Fagoting is decorative openwork, used to join two finished edges, with either a natural finish (like ribbons) or folds. The most commonly used fagoting stitches are the bar or ladder stitch and the criss-cross stitch.

The bar or ladder stitch is quite time-consuming, so we will not go into it here. A trim, imitating ladder fagoting, is sold by the yard. It is attached by machine like insertion lace (see the next page).

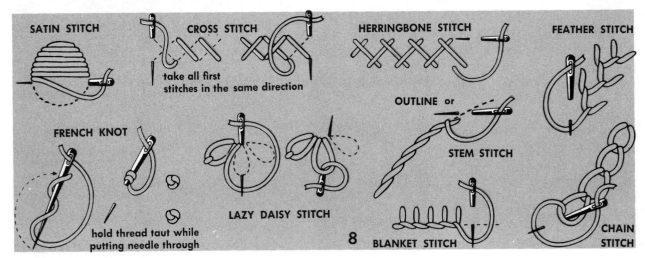

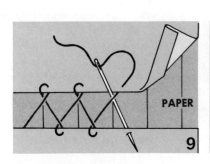

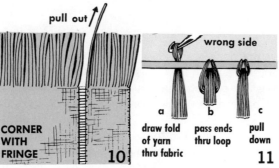

CORNER WITH FRINGE

pull out

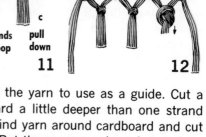

wrong side

a
draw fold
of yarn
thru fabric

b
pass ends
thru loop

c
pull
down

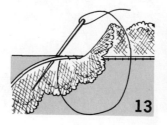

PAPER

9

10

11

12

Crisscross fagoting is an easy stitch, done with buttonhole twist or embroidery floss. It can be done at a seam or by cutting the pattern apart at the desired place. **For fagoting at a seam,** fold back the seam allowances plus one-half the width of the fagoting; press and trim to ¼″. **If pattern has been cut to add fagoting,** one-half the width of the fagoting will be folded back; add to the cut edge if necessary, so there will be ¼″.

To do the fagoting, draw two parallel lines down a sheet of ruled paper, the width of the fagoting apart. Baste the two edges to be joined along the two drawn lines. The printed lines will help you make stitches of even distance. Starting at left, bring the needle up through the lower edge. Slant the needle to the right and take a stitch through the upper edge. Work back and forth as shown (9), passing the needle each time **under** *the thread of the preceding stitch.*

FRINGE

Fringe comes and goes as a fashion finish. The three main kinds are described below.

Ready-made fringe comes in various widths. Sold by the yard, it is simply stitched on through the heading, which as a rule is decorative and placed on the outside.

Self-fringe (10) can be very chic, especially in woolens. The fabric edge must be absolutely straight-grain—trim the edge evenly along a drawn thread. With a pin, draw out a thread at the desired fringe-depth. Unless the fabric weave is very firm, make a line of machine-stitching along that line. Beginning at the stitched line, draw out threads.

Knotted fringe (11, 12) is made with yarn and a crochet hook. It requires a finished edge. To determine the length of the yarns, cut a few strands, fold and draw them through the fabric edge with the hook, looping as shown (11 a,b,c). Trim ends as

desired. Remove the yarn to use as a guide. Cut a piece of cardboard a little deeper than one strand folded in half. Wind yarn around cardboard and cut along one edge. Put the same number of strands in each tassel, place each at the same depth, and space evenly. If you wish, you can make a much deeper fringe and shorten it by knotting together the halves of two adjacent tassels (12).

LACE

Lace for trimming comes in many types, weights, and widths. **Edgings** have one straight and one shaped edge. **Beading** has a row of openings to thread a ribbon through. **Insertion** has two straight edges. **Galoon** has two shaped edges. It is used in the same way as insertion.

To attach an edging, the fabric edge should be finished. If the lace is to be gathered, use one and one-half to two times the length of the edge to which it is to be applied.

- To attach by hand, place the lace along the fabric edge, right sides together, straight edges matching. Sew together with whipstitch (13).
- To attach by machine, lap the straight edge of lace very slightly over the fabric edge, right sides up (14). Attach with narrow zigzag or straight stitch.

For an insertion, place the lace right side up on the right side of the fabric. Attach both edges by hand or machine. For a see-through effect for lace inserted by machine, cut away the fabric underneath the lace (see p. 139, ill. 14).

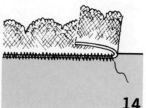

13

14

MACHINE QUILTING

Machine quilting is frequently done for a decorative effect. You can quilt an entire garment or just an area, such as a yoke, collar or pocket. Quilt the fabric before cutting out the pattern as quilting reduces the size of the fabric.

For quilting, use an outer fabric, a filler (cotton or polyester batting or polyester fleece) and a backing of lining fabric (may be omitted with fleece). Baste the layers together every 4″ to avoid slippage. Use polyester core thread or quilting thread. Make a test sample and adjust pressure, tension and stitch length, if necessary (see p. 148).

To quilt a design in the fabric (or one you have marked yourself), stitch from the center of the design out. Avoid stitching over a line twice. Bring thread-ends to the wrong side and tie.

To quilt parallel lines, use a quilting bar. Mark only one line in each direction near the edges. Stitch the marked line, and then, using the quilting bar as a guide, proceed across the fabric, always in the same direction to prevent shifting.

POMPONS AND TASSELS

Pompons (15) are made from yarn. Cut a rectangle of cardboard, a little wider than the desired diameter of the pompon. Along one long edge, hold a 6″ piece of yarn (doubled, unless yarn is very strong). Then wind a considerable amount of yarn around the cardboard, as shown. Tie very tightly with the short piece; cut through yarn at the other edge of cardboard. Fluff out the yarn and trim around the pompon with scissors until you have an even ball. **Tassels** (16) are started like pompons, but much less yarn is wound on the cardboard. After cutting the yarn off the cardboard, wind another short piece just below the fold, as shown, and tie. Trim ends.

RICK RACK

Rick rack (17), which comes in several widths, makes a charming trimming for children's and casual clothes. It can be sewn on by hand as shown; it can also be attached by machine with straight or zigzag stitch through the center, as shown. For a special effect, two strips of rick rack can be interlocked and applied as a single strip. Rick rack can also be inserted in a seam, like piping (see p. 30).

SEQUINS

Sequins, a dressy decoration, can be bought in strips or loose. For a continuous line of sequins, mark the design lightly on the right side of fabric. To attach a strip, cut it a little longer than needed. Remove a few sequins at ends and tie thread-ends. Attach with invisible stitches under the sequins. To make a line of single sequins, work from right to left with a backstitch (18). To attach single scattered sequins, sew them on with a bead on top (19).

TOPSTITCHING

Topstitching is used as decoration at a finished edge or along a seam. It can be done by machine or by hand. **For topstitching by machine,** see page 151. **For topstitching by hand,** use buttonhole twist or separate out 2 or more strands of embroidery floss. **Saddle stitching** consists of even running stitches at least ¼″ long. Take one stitch at a time, making all stitches the same length and the same distance apart. If you have difficulty with this, mark off the length of stitches and spaces on a strip of paper and pin it alongside your work. Keep thread loose enough to lie on top of the fabric. **A smaller hand-topstitch** is made with half-backstitch. It is done like the pickstitch for a hand zipper application (see p. 276), except that you do not go through all layers with every stitch.

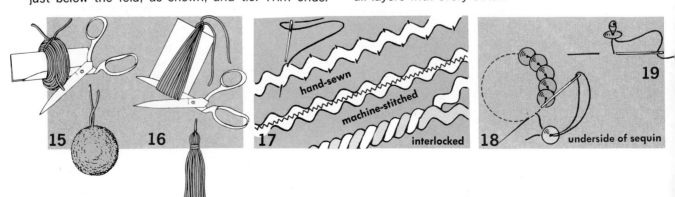

15 16 17 hand-sewn machine-stitched interlocked 18 underside of sequin 19

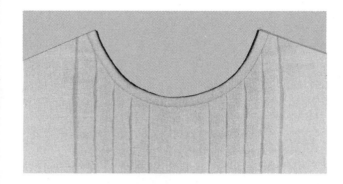

Tucks

A tuck is a fold of fabric, usually not very deep, that is stitched along all or part of its length. A tuck stitched in its entire length serves as decoration only. A tuck stitched only to a certain point furnishes fullness and may contribute to fit; it may be decorative as well.

Marking tucks—Most pattern markings for tucks consist of two lines, indicating where the fabric is brought together and stitched. It is much easier, however, to mark the **fold** line, and then stitch at the given distance from the fold. To do this, draw a pencil line on your pattern exactly between the two stitching lines, and transfer only this line to your fabric. The method of marking will depend on the fabric; in any case, it will be preliminary for press- or crease-marking the length of the tuck. With stable fabric and straight-grain tucks, a pin at each end will be sufficient; otherwise, baste-mark before you press. In most cases, the fold will have to be on the right side, where most tucks are stitched.

To stitch, carefully measure depth of tuck from the needle and locate a point on the sewing machine to keep the distance even. The outer edge of the presser foot may be right; or put down a strip of adhesive tape as a seam guide (see p. 222). On zig-zag machines, a change in needle position may also set the stitching at the right distance from the folded edge. For hand-sewing or basting, use a gauge (1), self-made or other.

As a general rule, stitching on decorative tucks is done on the outside and is a visible part of the design. Thread is carefully matched. While stitching is generally done by machine, it can be done by hand with a tiny running stitch.

Press tucks first as stitched, then to the side you want them to lie, then the entire area on the wrong side of the garment.

DECORATIVE TUCKS

These may be plain as just described, or scalloped (2)—follow instructions for SHELL EDGING, page 139. Some may be made with a twin needle. In all three cases, if you desire tucks where the pattern does not call for them, stitch them in **before** cutting out the garment.

Twin-needle tucks are not really tucks, because they only consist of narrow raised rows of fabric drawn up between the twin lines of stitching. They are done on the right side, through a single thickness of fabric. Consult your sewing machine manual. Tightening the tension will give more of a raised effect.

TUCKS USED FOR SHAPING

Pin tucks are very narrow, stitched close to the fold. They are often stitched on the wrong side of a garment (3).

Dart-tucks serve the purpose of darts, but do not come to a point in the body of a garment section. They release fullness at one or both ends (4, 5).

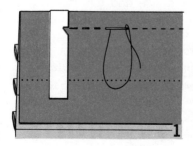

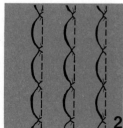

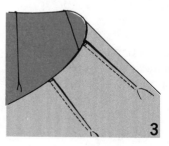

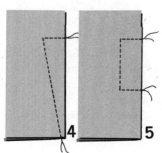

Underlining

Underlining is a backing for the garment fabric. Each section is cut from the same pattern pieces as the garment and stitched to the corresponding garment section; the two layers are then handled as one.

The purpose of underlining is to add body to a garment fabric (also making the garment more durable). While underlining helps preserve shape, it does not, like interfacing, add stiffness or crispness. Neither can it serve as an inside finish, since its edges are part of the raw seams. Coats and jackets are often both underlined and lined (see the chapter on LINING).

Pattern directions seldom specify underlining. Whether to add it is generally up to you, depending on whether your garment fabric is firm enough to take on and maintain a certain garment shape, such as an A-line. However, where part of a garment generally loses its shape through use, underlining should be added without question. The back section of a straight skirt should be underlined at least from the waist to 8″ to 10″ below the hips to prevent "sitting out". In pants, even if added only at the knee area, underlining will prevent bagginess at the knees.

With some soft fabrics, underlining will prevent pulling out at the seams. With lace and sheers, it will provide opacity. While knits are not usually underlined, where there is too much stretch you may want to add a lightweight knit underlining, such as nylon tricot.

UNDERLINING FABRICS

There are a number of fabrics in a variety of weights, that are made specially for use as underlinings. Many ordinary fabrics, such as organza, batiste, muslin, organdy, China silk and taffeta, can be used as well.

The important thing about an underlining fabric is that it should be entirely suited to the garment fabric in weight, drapability, and in care requirements. Generally, the underlining should be of a lighter weight than the garment fabric—often much lighter. A formal garment of satin or similar fabric can, how-ever, be given a special richness with an underlining of lambs wool or baby flannel which is much less expensive.

As for care, be sure to pre-shrink your underlining. An underlining that shrinks in washing or dry-cleaning can ruin a garment.

A word of caution: The whole performance of an underlined garment rests on the fact that the two fabrics must react as one. The underlining must enhance, not overpower or interfere with, the garment fabric. Be sure that if your pattern calls for gathers or draping, the underlining fabric is soft.

UNDERLINING A GARMENT

• Use the garment pattern pieces to cut the underlining on the same grain as the garment.
• Never cut out the garment fabric and the underlining together—it would make both inaccurate.
• Underlining can be omitted in sleeves, avoiding bulk at armholes and elbows.

a. Pattern markings are transferred to the underlining, except position markings, such as buttonholes, which are transferred to the right side of the garment fabric before the pattern is removed (see the chapter on MARKING).

b. Place the unmarked side of underlining to the wrong side of the matching garment section. Match centers and pin down the entire center length; smooth out and pin edges together. If the underlining is slippery, hand-baste the two layers together through the center and along edges.

Partial underlinings: In a skirt, finish the bottom edge before attaching the side and top edges. On underlining at pants knees, stitch and pink top and bottom edges; attach side edges. After the garment seams are stitched, sew the free edges to the pants fabric with loose stitches, invisible on the outside.

c. Place the two layers on the machine with underlining side up. Stitch ½″ from all edges, except the hem edges which you leave free. Stitch with the grain, which means that you will have to start from the same edge to stitch two opposite sides, even if the bulk of the work is on the right when you do the second edge (see DIRECTIONAL STITCHING, p. 153).

d. Darts—To prevent the underlining from slipping when darts or dart-tucks are folded and stitched, first baste the two layers together along the center to ½″ to 1″ beyond the point (unless needle-marks would show).

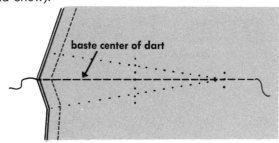

baste center of dart

In bulky fabrics, stitch darts separately in the garment fabric and in the underlining. You can then handle them in one of two ways:

- In the garment fabric, slash darts and press open; in the underlining, slash or trim.
- Do not slash darts. In the garment fabric, press darts toward the center or down; in the underlining, press darts toward the seam or up.

e. Interfacing—Sew-in interfacing is applied to the underlined garment section. Fusible interfacing is applied to the facing.

f. Construct the garment as usual, handling the underlining and garment fabric as one.

g. Hem—After marking the hemline, hand-baste the two layers together all around, ¼″ above the hemline; leave this basting in until the hem is finished. To reduce bulk, you may cut off the underlining at the hemline. Use stretch lace, seam binding or the Hong Kong finish. Sew the hem to the underlining only, every few inches catching the garment fabric with a stitch invisible on the outside. An alternative is the TWICE-STITCHED HEM—see page 124.

Waistbands

A waistband is a straight-grain strip of garment fabric stitched to the top edge of a skirt or pants for the purpose of holding the garment in place. A waistband is always reinforced, usually by being doubled and interfaced. As a rule, it is closely fitted. The garment waist edge, however, is always slightly fuller to fit the body curves and is eased to the waistband.

A waistband, like a belt, may be wide or narrow. On women's clothes, the ends of the band lap right over left on a front or a side closure, and left over right on a back closure. Often the overlapping end,

which has the buttonhole or the hooks, is even with the opening edge, while the other end extends as an underlay of about 1½″ (1). Some styles, however, have the overlapping end extended (2).

Occasionally a waistband is omitted. See FACED WAISTLINE FINISH on page 261.

Although the pattern will include instructions for applying your waistband, you may wish to substitute one of the following methods. A contoured waistband, however, should be made strictly according to pattern directions.

STANDARD WAISTBANDS

A standard waistband is doubled lengthwise and usually reinforced with interfacing or some other stiffener, or with elastic. If it is no more than ¾″ wide, its own seam allowances serve as interfacing. The standard methods are suitable for all fabrics except where bulk makes a facing of grosgrain ribbon or belting preferable (see FACED WAISTBAND, p. 261).

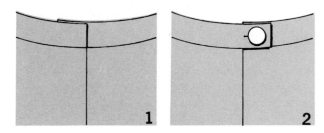

WAISTBAND WITH INTERFACING

a. Cut the waistband on the lengthwise grain, if possible, and preferably on a selvage:

Length—Waist measurement plus 2¾".

Width—On a selvage, twice the desired finished width plus 1" (3). If no selvage is available, either finish the cut edge with zigzag stitch, or add ¼" to the width, turn under and edge-stitch; this will be your "selvage edge".

b. The interfacing, whether sew-in or fusible, should be firm (not lightweight). Cut it to match the waistband.

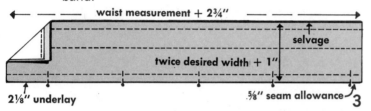

Sew-in interfacing—Stitch interfacing to wrong side of waistband with a line of stitching ½" from each long edge. Trim interfacing seam allowance close to stitching. To keep interfacing from buckling when folded, make a third line of stitching to fall just inside the top fold: to do this, measure from the selvage edge the width of finished waistband plus ⅛" (3).

Fusible interfacing—Trim away ½" on all edges, which will leave ⅛" to be caught in the seams. Center the interfacing carefully on wrong side of waistband and fuse, following manufacturer's instructions.

c. Measure and pin-mark raw edge of waistband as shown (3): 2⅛" at underlay end, ⅝" at overlap end; divide the length between into four equal parts. Divide and pin-mark garment edge into four equal parts, starting and ending at the zipper opening (4).

d. With right sides together and raw edges even, pin garment to waistband, matching pins. Hand-baste, easing the garment edge. Stitch. Trim seam allowance of garment to ¼". Press band up (5).

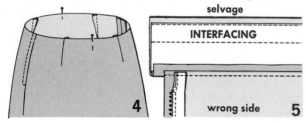

e. Fold waistband in half, wrong side out. Selvage edge will extend ¼" below waistline seam. Pin ends. Stitch across overlap end (6). Stitch edges of underlay, pivoting at corner (7). Trim all corners, grade end-seams. Turn waistband right side out and press.

f. Attach selvage edge by machine or by hand:

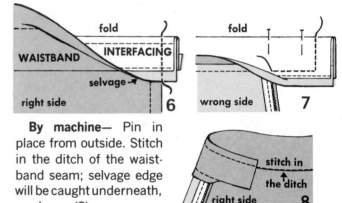

By machine— Pin in place from outside. Stitch in the ditch of the waistband seam; selvage edge will be caught underneath, as shown (8).

By hand—Pin in place on wrong side and blind-stitch edge to the seam allowance with inside hemming (see p. 122, ill. 9).

g. Press. Sew on hooks and eyes, or make a worked buttonhole and sew on a button.

SELF-INTERFACED WAISTBAND

Good for light- and medium-weight, firmly-woven, washable fabrics, this eliminates the need for a separate interfacing. It is especially nice for children's clothes.

a. Cut the waistband on the lengthwise grain, if possible, to the following size:

Length: Waist measurement plus 2¾".

Width: Four times the desired finished width plus 1¾" for seam allowances.

b. Fold waistband in half lengthwise, right side out, and stitch raw edges together about ½" from edge. Press. From the pressed fold, measure the width of finished waistband plus ⅛". At that point, make a line of stitching the length of the band: this will keep the inside layer from rumpling, while not showing on the outside.

c. Complete by following directions for WAISTBAND WITH INTERFACING, beginning with step **c,** and using the pressed fold as "selvage edge".

WAISTBAND WITH NON-ROLL STIFFENER

This stiffener is designed to keep a waistband from rolling. It is available in various widths. Buy it in the width you want the finished waistband to be and have it on hand **before cutting the waistband.**

a. See WAISTBAND WITH INTERFACING on the preceding page. Skip step **b**, which refers to interfacing. Follow steps **a, c,** and **d,** but **do not press waistband up.** Then proceed as follows:

b. Cut stiffener 1½″ shorter than waistband so it stays clear of end seams.

c. Place stiffener over seam allowance of waistband (9), one edge even with waistline seam and each end ¾″ from ends of waistband. Machine-baste edge of stiffener to seam allowances of waistband and garment as shown.

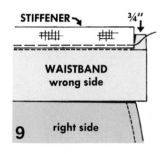

d. To complete the waistband, follow steps **e** through **g** of WAISTBAND WITH INTERFACING on the preceding page.

FACED WAISTBAND

To reduce bulk on certain fabrics (leather, suede, fake fur, heavy woolens, etc.) instead of being doubled, a waistband can be faced with grosgrain ribbon or belting. Both come in various widths, and some belting has rubber strips to keep blouses and shirts in. Both should be pre-shrunk if garment is washable.

Buy the grosgrain or belting ¼″ wider than the width you want the finished waistband to be; have it on hand **before cutting the waistband.**

a. Cut the waistband on the lengthwise grain, if possible, to the following size:
Length: Waist measurement plus 2¾″.
Width: Width of grosgrain or belting plus 1″.
Cut grosgrain or belting the same length as the waistband.

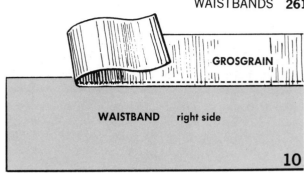

b. Lap grosgrain or belting ¼″ over one long edge of waistband and edge-stitch (10).

c. To complete waistband, follow directions for WAISTBAND WITH INTERFACING on the preceding page, from step **c** to the end. When folding the waistband in step **e**, be sure the grosgrain or belting falls ⅛″ to the inside of the band.

FACED WAISTLINE FINISH

This eliminates the waistband entirely and is often part of the design. It may also be done to reduce bulk in heavy or stiff fabrics (leather, fake fur, deep pile, etc.). The garment top must be well fitted. The facing can be grosgrain ribbon ½″ to ¾″ wide, or belting ⅞″ wide. Pre-shrink if garment is washable.

a. Cut grosgrain or belting to 2″ longer than waist measurement or the measurement where top edge of garment will be when worn. Shape the strip to a curve by "swirling" it—see page 26.

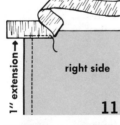

b. Lap grosgrain or belting ½″ over waist edge of garment, with 1″ extending at each end. Edge-stitch (11). Trim the seam allowance of the garment to ¼″.

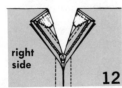

c. Fold grosgrain or belting to inside of garment, with top edge ⅛″ below fold. Turn ends under and slipstitch over zipper tape as shown (12).

d. Fasten facing in place either by tacking it to seams and darts, or by stitching in the ditch of seams and darts. Sew on a hook and eye, if desired.

1

2

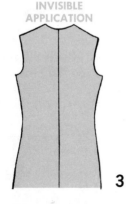

3

Zippers

The zipper in a garment is part of the garment's style. There is variety, not only in zippers, but even more in the ways in which they are inserted. Needless to say, a zipper application that is suitable and well made contributes to a garment's quality.

Contrary to what many people believe, putting in a zipper is not hard at all. You need two things, however: a zipper foot for your sewing machine (see p. 264), and a willingness to follow instructions one step at a time, omitting nothing.

Begin by reading this page and the next to familiarize yourself with the various zippers and the basic applications. Be sure to check over THINGS YOU NEED TO KNOW on page 264 for whatever applies to your work.

THE BASIC APPLICATIONS

While different situations may call for a variety of ways of inserting a zipper, three basic applications account for most of the zippers in garments. They are the lapped application and the centered application for conventional zippers, and the invisible zipper application. For all three, the opening is in a seam.

In the **lapped application** (1), one side of the zipper opening forms a lap over the zipper and is the only visible edge. One line of topstitching holds the lap in place. This application has the advantage of covering the zipper entirely because the fabric edges overlap, while keeping the fabric away from the slider. It is suitable for all light- and medium-weight fabrics and is good almost anywhere.

In the **centered application** (2), the zipper is centered under the opening and attached by a line of topstitching along each side. The two edges of the opening meet over the zipper. This application is suitable for all fabrics, but in medium-weight to heavy ones, it is better than a lapped application, because there is no bulk from the overlap.

In the **invisible zipper application** (3), the stitching is done entirely on the inside, and when the opening is closed, it looks exactly like a seam except for the pull-tab at the top. Since it interferes in no way with fabric design or line of the garment, this application is good anywhere. It is suitable for all weights of fabric. It requires the use of a special foot (see page 264) but the application is very easy.

EXPOSED—SLASH
page 272   EXPOSED—TRIM
page 273   FLY-FRONT
page 274   FLAT-FELL SEAM
page 275   KNITTED JACKET
page 275

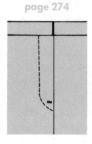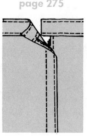

Besides the three basic applications above, you will find in the pages that follow directions for the applications shown at the left. Also, how to replace a zipper in various garments on pages 278, 279. For applications in special fabrics, such as leather, etc., see the chapter on FABRICS.

THE BASIC ZIPPERS

A zipper consists of two rows of either synthetic coils or metal teeth fastened to two fabric tapes. A slider, as it moves, meshes and locks the coils or teeth together. In quality zippers, the slider can be locked in place. Zippers come in many weights and lengths to suit their different uses—for a listing, see page 186 in NOTIONS.

Basically, however, there are just three types of zippers. Two of them are of the same conventional construction—one with synthetic coils, the other with metal teeth. The third type is the invisible zipper—with synthetic coils only.

CONVENTIONAL ZIPPER—COIL

Polyester or nylon coils are stitched to knit or woven tapes of polyester or a blend. When closed, the two coils mesh into a single coil that is as strong as metal, though much lighter; it is also flexible and drapable. A polyester coil is stronger than one of nylon, and a 100% polyester tape is treated to eliminate shrinkage (check the labels). The coil is sometimes covered for protection. This zipper is "self-healing"—see ZIPPER CARE on page 277.

CONVENTIONAL ZIPPER—METAL

This zipper has metal teeth that are referred to as a chain when closed. The teeth may be die-cast directly on to the tape or stamped out and clamped to the tape. The enamel finish on a colored zipper should be bonded to insure against color chipping (see the label). Heavier than the coil zipper, this zipper is used mostly with medium-weight to heavy fabrics. For use in washable garments, pre-shrink the zipper.

INVISIBLE ZIPPER

This zipper is constructed so that, when closed, it disappears in the seam and only the pull-tab shows. The coil is of polyester or nylon (polyester is stronger), stitched to knit or woven tapes of polyester or a blend. The 100% polyester tape is non-shrinking—check the label. The size of the coil varies, the narrower ones being very light and flexible.

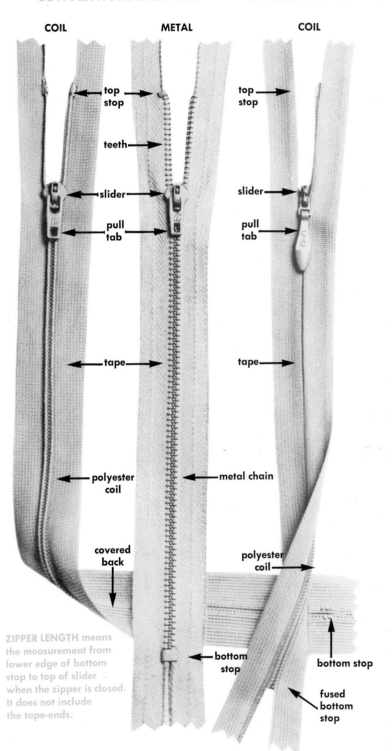

CONVENTIONAL ZIPPERS   INVISIBLE ZIPPER

COIL   METAL   COIL

top stop
teeth
slider
pull tab
tape
polyester coil
covered back

top stop
slider
pull tab
tape
metal chain
bottom stop

top stop
slider
pull tab
tape
polyester coil
bottom stop
fused bottom stop

ZIPPER LENGTH means the measurement from lower edge of bottom stop to top of slider when the zipper is closed. It does not include the tape-ends.

THINGS YOU NEED TO KNOW

ABOUT THE ZIPPER

To select the kind of zipper best suited to your garment, see THE BASIC ZIPPERS on the preceding page and the listing, page 186. Decide according to garment design, fabric weight, and your preference.

The zipper length required is given on the pattern envelope. You may wish to use a different length because of your body proportions or for convenience —a longer zipper opening lessens the strain on the zipper as you get in and out of the garment.

Any zipper can be shortened if necessary. Scissors will cut, without damage, across a coil or between teeth. When stitching across a shortened metal zipper, do so slowly, guiding needle between teeth.

A conventional zipper in a garment with a waistband or a stand-up collar is shortened at the top, **after** insertion. Insert the zipper before applying waistband or collar, as usual, letting excess length extend at the top. Open zipper and stitch across each tape at seam line. Cut off ends even with raw fabric edge (4).

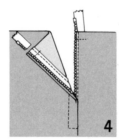

4

A conventional zipper in other garments is shortened at the bottom, **before** insertion. Measure and mark the desired length. Using thread doubled, whipstitch tightly 8 to 10 times across coil or teeth at marked point (5). Cut the zipper ½″ below.

An invisible zipper in any garment is shortened at the bottom, **before** insertion. Measure desired length **plus 1″**; mark. Using thread doubled, whipstitch tightly 8 to 10 times across coil at marked point (6). Cut the zipper ½″ below.

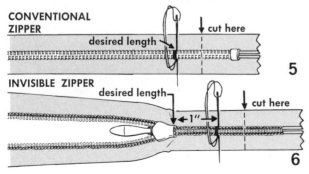

CONVENTIONAL ZIPPER
desired length
cut here
5

INVISIBLE ZIPPER
desired length
1″
cut here
6

For a zipper in a side opening of a dress, fasten zipper tapes together with a bar tack above the top stop (7). This will protect the seam above the zipper from strain.

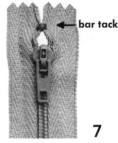

bar tack

7

If zipper tape is not 100% polyester, pre-shrink it if it is to be used in a washable garment. Immerse in hot water and let dry.

Any creases in zipper tapes should be pressed out. Do it from the wrong side.

ABOUT THE ZIPPER FOOT

Do not attempt to sew in a zipper without a zipper foot, which allows you to stitch close to the coil or teeth. There are two types:

For a conventional zipper, use the regular zipper foot (8). It can be adjusted to the right or the left of the needle. Be careful to have the needle centered in the notch of the foot.

For the invisible zipper, buy the special foot designed for it (9). Since coil sizes vary, get the one made for the brand of zipper you are using. Several shanks, to fit various sewing machines, come with the foot. Be sure the needle is aligned properly.

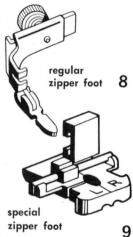

regular zipper foot 8

special zipper foot 9

ABOUT THE ZIPPER OPENING

If the fabric is stretchy, loosely woven or the edges are not cut on the straight grain, stay-stitch the zipper opening ¼″ from the edges.

Widen and reinforce the seam allowance by topstitching a strip of seam binding to it, if the fabric is ravelly, if seam allowance at opening is less than ⅝″ wide, or if the zipper has an extra large slider (10).

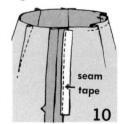

seam tape

10

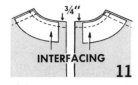

INTERFACING **11**

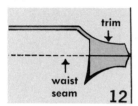

trim

waist
seam **12**

Where there is an inter-facing, trim it back ¾'' at zipper opening (11).

If the zipper opening crosses a seam, reduce bulk by trimming seam allowances, then clip through one seam allowance and press trimmed ends open as shown (12).

If a waistline is corded, pull back the cord covering at zipper opening and trim off ¾'' of cord.

GENERAL

Your pattern guide sheet will tell you at what point in the work to insert the zipper. If you are sure of the pattern fit, remember it is always easier to stitch in a zipper while the garment section is still flat (not yet joined to other sections). However, if the garment needs trying on and fitting, the zipper may have to be inserted quite late.

Pinning or hand-basting are not specified in any of the directions that follow. While they can be dispensed with, there is no reason why you should not pin or hand-baste if your fabric is hard to handle, or if you just feel safer doing so.

PREPARATION OF OPENING
FOR CONVENTIONAL ZIPPERS ONLY

(For an invisible zipper, turn directly to page 270.)

Length of opening—In a finished zipper application, the zipper opening should always extend a little beyond the top of slider when zipper is closed. Measure the zipper, then add the following:

• At a neckline opening, add ½'' plus ⅝'' seam allowance if neck is unfinished.
• At a dress side opening, add ⅜''.
• At a skirt or pants opening, add ⅜'' plus ⅝'' seam allowance.

Basting the opening—Conventional zippers, in basic applications, are inserted with the garment opening basted together.

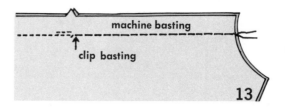

machine basting

clip basting **13**

• **If the garment sections are not yet joined,** the seam that will contain the zipper can be stitched and the opening basted in one operation. Using regular stitch length, stitch seam from hem to bottom of opening; back-tack. Change to longest stitch and baste-stitch the opening. Clip basting at bottom of opening (13). Press entire seam open.

• **If the garment sections have already been joined,** machine-baste the opening together on seam line from bottom to top. Press basted seam open.

NOTE: In some fabrics, the basting thread may be hard to locate and remove after a lapped application. Using contrasting bobbin thread will help.

To insure straight topstitching, use one of the following methods:

• **A guide-line of machine-basting** can be made before zipper is inserted but after zipper opening has been basted and pressed. Working on wrong side and avoiding the seam allowance, baste-stitch from bottom to top, close to planned line of topstitching—

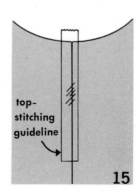

basted seam

basted topstitching guideline **14**

top-stitching guideline **15**

one line for a lapped, two lines for a centered application (14). When doing step **3**, topstitch alongside the basting line through all thicknesses. Remove basting stitches.

• **Magic transparent tape,** or some other tape designed for the purpose, can be used after step **2**, before the zipper is topstitched. On right side place a strip of the tape over the opening (still basted), one edge of tape along planned line of topstitching (15). Stitch along the tape, not through it.

NECK

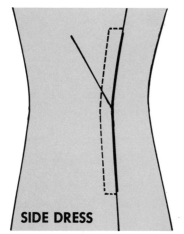

SKIRT

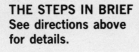

SIDE DRESS

LAPPED APPLICATION

This is for conventional zippers only. On the two preceding pages, you will have carefully checked over THINGS YOU NEED TO KNOW for whatever applies to your work. You have also followed the directions under PREPARATION OF OPENING. Your zipper opening is basted together and the seam is pressed open.

- Use a zipper foot throughout.
- Always stitch from bottom to top of zipper opening.
- Keep zipper pull-tab turned **up** for a skirt or neck application; turned **down** for a side dress application.
- Facings may be applied before or after the zipper.

1. Do this step very precisely, because it places the zipper in position for the rest of the application. Set machine for the longest stitch. Work on the inside of the garment. With bottom of zipper opening away from you and the bulk of the work to the left, extend the right-hand seam allowance as shown. Lay closed zipper on it face-down, with bottom stop at bottom-of-opening mark. Place zipper so that the coil or chain lies with its **full width** on the extended seam allowance and its edge exactly along the seam.

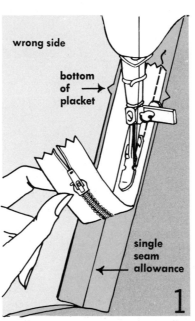

wrong side

bottom of placket

single seam allowance

1

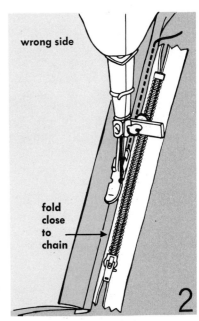

wrong side

fold close to chain

2

THE STEPS IN BRIEF
See directions above for details.

Machine-baste one zipper tape to one extended seam allowance.

Turn zipper face up and stitch folded seam allowance to zipper tape.

Starting at bottom of zipper, machine-baste along edge of tape, checking position of coil or chain, as shown, about every two inches. The stitching may curve out slightly around slider.

2. Change to regular stitch length. Turn zipper face-up, forming a fold in the seam allowance (not in tape). Bring the fold close to coil or chain, not quite touching it; starting again at the bottom, stitch fold to zipper tape, as shown, the full length of the tape.

3. Spread the garment flat. Turn zipper face-down over the free seam allowance, forming a pleat at each end of zipper in the seam allowance to which zipper is attached. At both ends, secure pleat and tapes with a pin (also marking bottom of zipper). Turn garment to right side. Put pins through at the same places from the outside, and remove the ones on the inside, where they would catch in the feed dog (3a).

The final topstitching is done from the outside. Move zipper foot to the other side of needle. At pin-marked bottom of zipper, put the needle in at the seam and stitch across bottom end of zipper. Pivot, and stitch along marked topstitching line, as follows:

- Where there will be a waistband or stand-up collar, stitch to end of tape.
- At an edge to be faced, stop one inch from edge. Cut off tape-end at seam line and continue stitching to raw edge (3b).
- In a dress with a side opening (3c), stitch beyond bar tack on zipper, pivot, and stitch across top of zipper to seam line.

NOTE: To do step **3** by hand, see page 276.

4. To finish, bring thread-ends to inside and tie. On inside, clip the machine-basting that holds the opening together and remove the threads. Press finished zipper opening and carefully press out the crease under the lap.

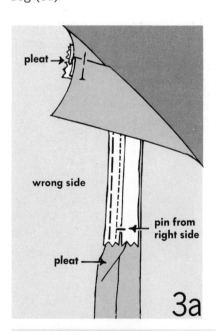

pleat

wrong side

pin from right side

pleat

3a

Topstitch garment to other zipper tape through all layers.

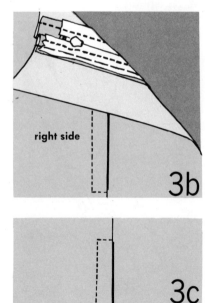

right side

3b

3c

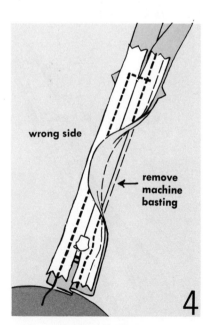

wrong side

remove machine basting

4

Clip and remove machine-basting.

CENTERED APPLICATION

This is for conventional zippers only. On pages 264 and 265, you will have carefully checked over THINGS YOU NEED TO KNOW for whatever applies to your work. You have also followed the directions under PREPARATION OF OPENING. Your zipper opening is basted together and the seam pressed open.

- Clip the basting every two inches for easy removal later.
- Use a zipper foot throughout.
- Always stitch from bottom to top of zipper opening.
- Keep zipper pull-tab turned **up** for a skirt or neck application; turned **down** for a side dress application.
- Facings may be applied before or after the zipper.

1. Set machine for longest stitch. Work on the inside of garment. With bottom of zipper opening away from you and the bulk of the work to the left, extend right-hand seam allowance, as shown.

Open the zipper. Place right-hand zipper tape face-down on seam allowance, with bottom stop at bottom-of-opening mark and coil or teeth along seam.

Starting at bottom of zipper tape, machine-baste that tape to seam allowance, as shown.

2. Close the zipper. Move bulk of work to the right, and extend the left-hand seam allowance. Machine-baste second zipper tape to seam allowance.

3. Change to regular stitch length. Turn the garment to right side and spread it flat. Mark bottom end of zipper with a pin. Do the topstitching in two steps, each time starting at seam at bottom of zipper. Stitch across bottom to the guide-line for top-stitching, pivot, and continue along line to garment edge. For the second line of stitching, move zipper foot to the other side of the needle.

NOTE: To do step **3** by hand, see page 276.

4. To finish, bring thread-ends to inside and tie. Working from outside, remove basting. Press finished opening.

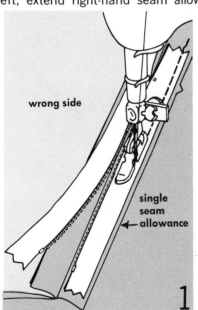

wrong side

single seam allowance

1

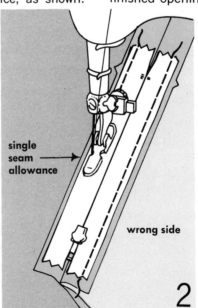

single seam allowance

wrong side

2

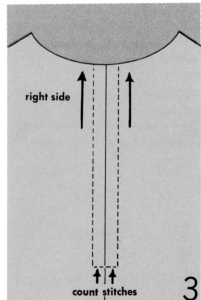

right side

count stitches

3

THE STEPS IN BRIEF—See directions above for details.

Machine-baste one zipper tape to one extended seam allowance.

Machine-baste the other zipper tape to the other extended seam allowance.

Topstitch garment to zipper through all layers. Remove basting.

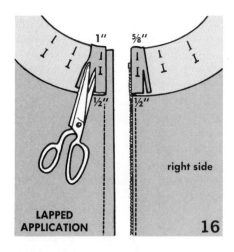

LAPPED APPLICATION **16**

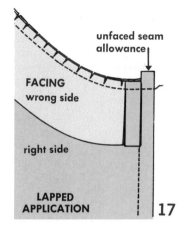

LAPPED APPLICATION **17**

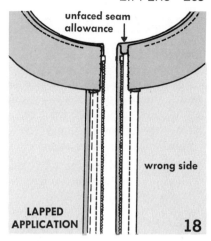

LAPPED APPLICATION **18**

FACING FINISH
WITH CONVENTIONAL ZIPPERS

A facing is usually applied after the zipper is in.

WITH A LAPPED APPLICATION

a. Pin facing to garment edge, right sides together. Fold right-hand end of facing back ⅝'' and left-hand end back 1''. Pin. Trim both ends to ½'' (16).

b. Stitch facing to garment, including folded ends. Grade and clip seam allowances, **except** for the unfaced portion at left-hand garment edge (17). Understitch.

c. Press facing to inside, including the portion of seam allowance just mentioned. Unless the fabric is a knit, which does not ravel, turn edge of seam allowance ⅛'' under. Slipstitch seam allowance and facing ends in place over zipper tape (18).

WITH A CENTERED APPLICATION

a. Pin facing to garment edge, right sides together. Fold both ends of facing back, even with edges of opening. Trim to ½'' (19).

b. Stitch facing to garment. Grade, clip, and understitch.

c. Press facing to inside and slipstitch ends in place over zipper tapes (20).

NECK FASTENERS—at conventional zippers

See FASTENERS, page 99. With fabrics that do not snag, a hook with a straight metal eye or a thread eye is most often used. Otherwise, use an extended snap (21) or a hanging snap (22).

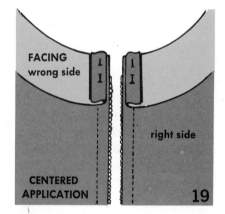

CENTERED APPLICATION **19**

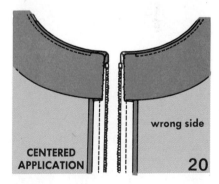

CENTERED APPLICATION **20**

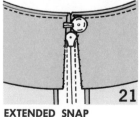

EXTENDED SNAP **21**

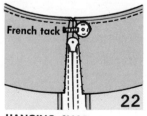

HANGING SNAP **22**

INVISIBLE ZIPPER APPLICATION

An invisible zipper is inserted in an entirely open seam; the rest of the seam is stitched after the application is completed. On pages 264 and 265, you have checked over THINGS YOU NEED TO KNOW for whatever applies to your work.

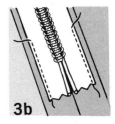

- Use the foot designed for the zipper brand you are using, because coil sizes of zippers vary.
- Stitch from top to bottom of zipper.
- Apply any facing after the zipper has been sewn in.
- Before starting, press the zipper as follows, using a synthetic setting: Open zipper; from wrong side, press zipper flat, using point of iron to push coil over so that the two rows of stitching show.

1. Attach the invisible zipper foot to the machine, with the needle lined up with center mark. Place open zipper face-down on right side of fabric as shown. Pin in place with coil on seam line (⅝″ in) and top stop ¾″ below raw edge of garment (1a). With right-hand groove of foot over coil, stitch zipper until the foot hits the slider (remove pins as you come to them). Back-tack.

2. To attach the other half of the zipper, pin tape face-down with coil on seam line (⅝″ in) and top stop ¾″ below raw edge of garment, as before. Make sure that the zipper is not twisted at the bottom. Use the left-hand groove of foot, making sure that the center marking is still lined up with the needle and stitch, as before.

3. Close zipper. Slide zipper foot to the left so that needle is in the outer notch. Pin the seam together below zipper opening. Fold end of zipper out of the way and lower the needle by hand slightly above and to the left of the last stitch (3a).

Stitch seam for about 2″, as shown. Pull thread through to one side and tie. Change to regular presser foot and complete the seam.

At zipper end, stitch about 1″ of each zipper tape to **seam allowance only** (3b).

3b

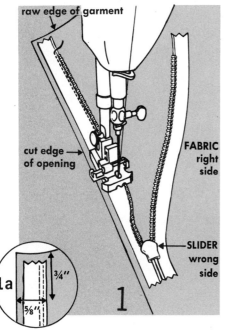

raw edge of garment

cut edge of opening

FABRIC right side

SLIDER wrong side

1a ¾″ ⅝″

1

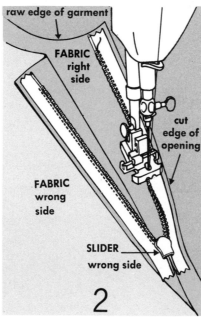

raw edge of garment

FABRIC right side

FABRIC wrong side

cut edge of opening

SLIDER wrong side

2

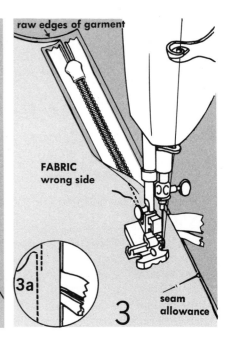

raw edges of garment

FABRIC wrong side

3a

seam allowance

3

MATCHING DESIGNS AND SEAMS
WITH INVISIBLE ZIPPERS

Since the two zipper tapes are attached independently to the two garment sections, special attention must be given to any lines (fabric design, waistline, etc.) that need to be matched.

a. Stitch one zipper tape in place. Close zipper.

To match horizontal lines, mark zipper tape at each line (23). Open zipper. Re-press coil of free zipper tape to flatten it as before. Pin tape to second garment section, matching marks to lines.

For diagonal stripes and for prints, fold stitched section on seam line. On the second garment section, fold the seam allowance under (press, if necessary). Match the two sections and hold in place with short strips of Magic transparent tape (24). On inside, pin the free zipper tape to the free seam allowance. Remove the tape and open the zipper.

b. Stitch pinned zipper tape and complete the seam below the zipper.

FACING FINISH
WITH INVISIBLE ZIPPERS

This method of finishing the ends of a facing at the zipper opening, shown here at a neckline, is just as suitable for skirts or pants that have a waistline facing instead of a waistband.

After you have inserted the zipper, stitched the garment shoulder seams and joined the facing pieces, open the zipper and proceed as follows:

a. Trim off the ⅝″ seam allowance on the two ends of the facing.

b. Place facing on garment right sides together (do not pin). Match the two trimmed ends to the garment seam allowances at zipper; pin. Using the regular zipper foot, stitch ⅜″ from edge through facing, zipper tape and garment (25).

c. Match facing and garment at shoulder seams; pin neck edge. At zipper, fold seam allowances away from zipper edge (26).

d. Stitch facing to garment (27). Grade and clip. Understitch, starting and stopping ⅝″ from zipper. Turn facing to inside and press (28).

Use a hanging snap, if desired (see p. 99).

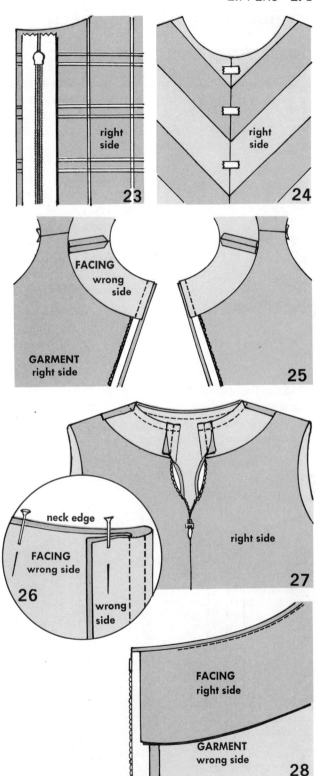

EXPOSED ZIPPER IN A SLASH

In this application, used where there is no seam, the two edges of the zipper opening just reach the coil, leaving it exposed. With the standard size zipper shown here, allowing only very narrow seam allowances, the application is suitable only in knits (and might be a little difficult for a beginning sewer to handle).

• The neck is finished before the zipper is inserted.

1. From outside of garment, mark zipper opening with a line of machine-basting, the length of zipper (top of slider to lower edge of bottom stop). Outline the opening with stay-stitching: For a regular coil zipper, make the two lines of stitching at least ¼″ apart; for a ring-pull zipper, at least ⅜″ apart. At bottom of opening, shorten stitches for reinforcement.

2. Change to zipper foot. Place zipper on garment as shown: lying face-down away from opening, with bottom stop just below bottom end of stay-stitching. At that point, using short stitches, stitch several times back and forth the exact width of stay-stitching outline.

3. Cut along basted center line from neck edge to just short of stitching. Lift zipper, bring tape-ends through opening to inside.

4. Working on inside of garment and with zipper flat, as shown, pin or baste one opening edge to one zipper tape, right side to right side, stay-stitching along edge of coil. Starting at bottom of zipper, stitch fabric to tape, close to coil. Back-tack. Repeat on other edge, carefully lining up sides at neck edge.

At neck edge, turn tape-ends under and whipstitch.

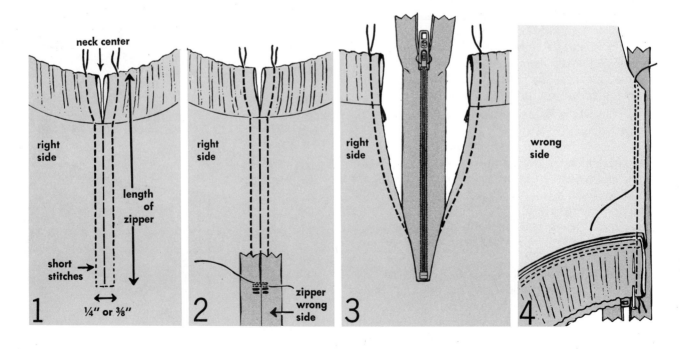

EXPOSED ZIPPER WITH TRIM

An easy application, in which the zipper opening is featured as decoration. It can be used in either a seam or a slash. The trimming shown here is decorative ribbon, ⅝″ to ¾″ wide, but almost any trimming will do if it is not too thick to miter at corners.

● Attach the trim to the zipper before insertion. Using a zipper foot, topstitch one edge of the trimming to the zipper tape, close to coil. At the bottom, miter the trim to form a point or a square, as shown (either one can be used for either kind of opening).

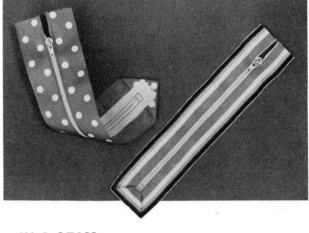

IN A SLASH

1. Mark zipper opening with a line of machine-basting the length of zipper plus 1″. Outline the opening with stay-stitching, ¼″ from basting.

2. Pin the trimmed zipper to the outside of the garment, coil even with basted center line. Stitch outer edge of trim to garment. Open the zipper. Cut through center line from top almost to bottom. Clip into corners.

On inside, fold the edges of the opening under and slipstitch to zipper tapes.

IN A SEAM

1. The seam below the zipper opening has been stitched. At bottom of zipper opening, clip seam allowances diagonally as shown. Press opening seam allowances to outside, as shown, and trim to ½″ (less for a narrow trim).

2. Pin the trimmed zipper to the outside of the garment. Machine-stitch outer edge of trim to garment. On inside, slipstitch folds of opening to zipper tapes.

IN A SLASH

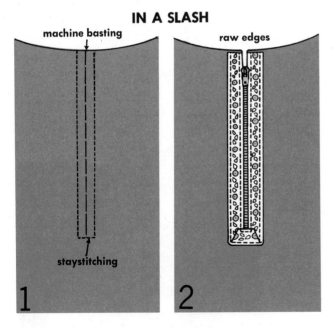

IN A SEAM

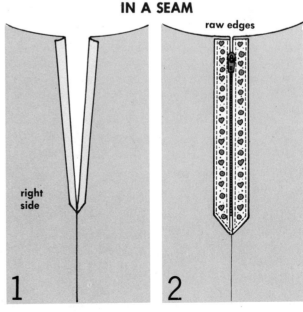

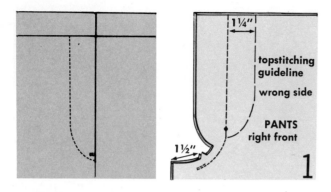

ZIPPER IN A FLY FRONT

The directions that follow are for a woman's fly front, lapping from right to left. For a man's fly front, lapping from left to right, either adapt the directions accordingly, or see page 176 in MENSWEAR.

On most women's patterns, a fly front has extended facings. In the application below, one such facing acts as a fly shield under the zipper.

It may be difficult to find a zipper of the exact length required in a fly opening. In such a case, buy a longer zipper and shorten it at the end of the application, as described below.

• The line of topstitching on the fly should be 1¼″ from edge of fly (center front); before cutting out the garment, check the pattern and make any adjustment necessary. On right front, mark the line of topstitching with hand-basting. Bottom end will be bottom of zipper opening.
• Do the zipper application before the front sections are joined to the back sections.
• Do all stitching from bottom to top of opening.
• If fabric tends to ravel, finish the curved edge of extended facings.

1. Join the two sections as follows: Starting 1½″ from inner leg seam, stitch to bottom of zipper opening. Back-tack. Machine-baste remainder of opening. Clip the basting every 2″. Press open.

2. With bottom of opening away from you and bulk of work to the left, extend right-hand facing. Place closed zipper face-down on facing with edge of tape along basted seam and bottom stop ¼″ above bottom of opening. Machine-baste right-hand edge of zipper to facing, as shown.

3. Turn zipper face-up, folding the zipper tape on basted line, and pin free tape to facing. Edge-stitch the fold in the stitched tape. Remove pins.

4. Move bulk of work to the right, and extend left-hand facing. Have zipper lie face-down on this facing. Fold and pin back the right-hand facing to keep it out of the way. Machine-baste edge of free tape to left-hand facing.

5. Spread work flat, right side up. From outside, pin zipper in place along topstitching line. Topstitch, removing pins as you go along. On inside, unpin folded-back facing. Bring thread-ends to inside and tie. Remove basting at fly edge. Press.

6. On outside, make a bar tack at bottom of opening, making sure to catch in all thicknesses, including facing. If zipper is longer than opening, **open** zipper and stitch across each tape at waist. Cut off excess length.

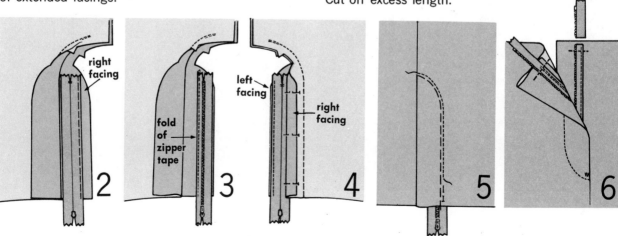

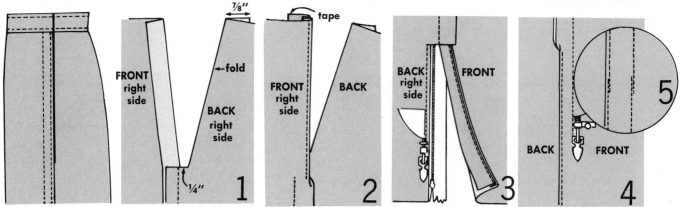

ZIPPER IN A FLAT-FELL SEAM

This lapped application that looks like the continuation of a flat-felled seam is used in sportswear where such seams are part of the style, and is usually in a side closure. The zipper is inserted before the seam is completely finished.

- With **wrong** sides of fabric together, stitch a ⅝″ seam from hem to bottom of zipper opening.

1. **Back seam allowance**—At bottom of zipper opening, clip through back seam allowance to ¼″ beyond seam line. Press seam allowance (now ⅞″) to wrong side, as shown.

2. **Front seam allowance**—Cut a piece of single fold bias tape the length of zipper opening and press folded edges open. Pin bias tape to seam allowance, right sides together, edges even. Stitch a ¼″ seam. Press tape to wrong side; edge-stitch on right side, as shown.

3. To position zipper, place fold of back seam allowance along zipper coil; pin. Using zipper foot, edge-stitch fold close to coil.

4. Lap front edge over zipper as shown. Pin. Starting at seam line at bottom of zipper (overlap a few stitches), stitch on seam line through lap and zipper to top of opening.

5. When completing the seam below the zipper, overlap stitches slightly, as shown.

ZIPPER IN A KNITTED JACKET

A zipper in a knitted garment is always applied by hand. The zipper shown here is a separating zipper.

- Finish edges of opening on wrong side with 1″ wide grosgrain ribbon. Press.
- Measure length of opening; zipper should be the same length or slightly shorter.
- Slip-baste edges of opening together.

1. Work on inside of jacket, with zipper facedown. Open the zipper, **but do not separate it.** Fold one tape under at top and place top stop at desired point. Pin. Baste that half of zipper to jacket, with teeth against basted edge. Close the zipper.

Baste the free zipper tape in place, folding top end under, in line with first one.

2. Working on outside of jacket, attach each tape with a line of pick-stitching (see the next page) about ¼″ from zipper teeth. Remove slip-basting.

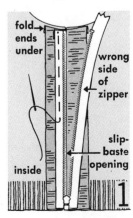

FINISHING DETAILS AND CARE

Most of the following details apply to both conventional and invisible zippers.

HAND-FINISH and SIMULATED HAND-FINISH

This is for conventional zippers only.

Hand-finish—The final, visible stitching done by hand is the most elegant, inconspicuous finish, usually seen only in expensive custom-made garments. It may be the only possible one in fabrics that are too delicate for topstitching, or that tend to pucker.

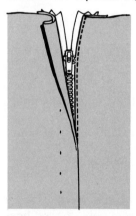

In either the lapped or the centered application, follow directions until you are ready to topstitch. Hand-stitching is easier to do with the zipper open: Pin or baste the zipper in place from the right side, remove basting in opening and open the zipper.

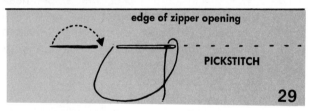

edge of zipper opening

PICKSTITCH

29

Use a single length of buttonhole twist or polyester core thread. Starting at top, follow the topstitching marking or guide with half-backstitch or pickstitch (29) through all thicknesses, placing stitches about ¼″ apart.

Simulated hand-finish—A hand-finish can be simulated if you have a zigzag machine that can be set for blind-hemming. This is done with the zipper foot. If the seam allowance is at all scanty, widen it with seam binding.

When doing the PREPARATION, omit marking for topstitching. Do the application through step 2. Then proceed as follows:

● In a lapped application, spread work flat, still wrong side up. Turn zipper face-down over free seam allowance, forming a pleat at each zipper-end, in the seam allowance to which zipper is attached. Pin the two ends of free tape in place to maintain pleats. Then hand-baste the tape to garment **through all thicknesses** in a very straight line, quite close to zipper coil or chain.

● In a centered application, spread work flat, wrong side up. Hand-baste each tape to garment **through all thicknesses** in two very straight lines, quite close to zipper coil or chain.

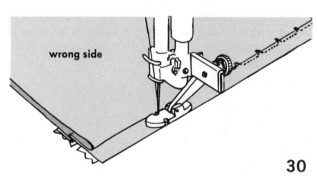

wrong side

30

● In both applications after the above step, set machine for blind-hemming, following instructions in your sewing machine manual. Fold garment back on basted line (30). Place it on the machine with bottom of opening away from you and zipper underneath, as shown.

Finish with step **4** of regular application.

LINING FINISH AT ZIPPER

After a lining has been placed in a garment, turn the raw edges under at zipper opening and slip-stitch to tapes, a scant ¼″ from coil or chain. To keep the lining away from the zipper, make a line of running stitches, catching the lining to garment seam allowances (31).

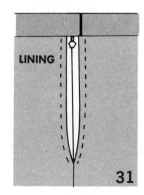

LINING

31

WAISTLINE STAY

In a close-fitting dress, a waistline stay lessens the strain on the zipper, making it easier to open and close. Such a stay is recommended when the fabric is stretchy, when there is waistline gathering or when the skirt is heavier than the bodice.

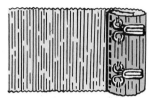

32

a. Cut a length of 1″ grosgrain ribbon to your waist measurement plus 2″. Turn ends under ½″ twice and stitch down firmly. Sew two hooks at one end and two eyes at the other (32).

b. With garment wrong side out and zipper closed, place the stay around the waist with hooks and eyes facing the zipper but positioned to one side of it to avoid bulk. Measure 1½″ to each side from center of zipper. With stay-ends about ¼″ apart (so the stay will be a little tighter than the garment), pin the stay to waist seam allowance at those two points. Pin the rest of the stay all around, easing the seam allowance to it as necessary.

c. Stitch stay to **seam allowance only,** through center of stay, leaving 1½″ of the stay unattached on each side of zipper (33).

In a dress of princess style, tack the stay to darts and seams.

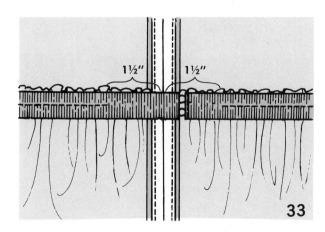

33

ZIPPER CARE

● **When pressing a zipper,** use a press cloth. This will protect the zipper and the iron, and will prevent an impression on the outside of the garment. If zipper is in a curved seam, use a pressing ham.

● **When putting on or taking off a garment,** open zipper all the way to prevent strain and breakage.

● **Keep zipper closed** as much as possible: during washing or dry-cleaning to avoid distortion of zipper; while garment is not being worn in order to maintain garment shape.

● **If zipper has become stiff** or difficult to operate after dry-cleaning, rub coil or teeth with beeswax or a zipper lubricant.

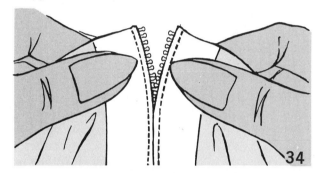

34

● **If fabric or thread gets caught** in a coil zipper, it can easily be removed (a coil zipper is "self-healing"). Fold zipper tape, pinch coil and pull apart (34). Then pull the slider to the bottom stop and up again to close the zipper.

● **When closing a separating zipper,** be sure to have the slider all the way down and to insert the pin **through** the slider and **firmly down** into the "box" (35).

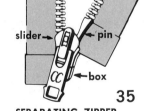

35
SEPARATING ZIPPER

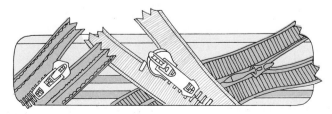

REPLACING A ZIPPER
SKIRT, NECK, or
DRESS SIDE OPENING

Before replacing a zipper, examine the opening to see if the stitching and the folded edges have left permanent marks.

If marks are not permanent—that is, if they can be entirely removed by pressing and steaming—you are free to use any method of application (lapped, centered, or invisible zipper), regardless of what was used before. For a lapped or a centered application, follow Method I below.

If marks are permanent, you will have to use the same zipper type and application as was used before, and the same folds and stitching lines. As you remove the old zipper, note exactly how it was put in. Follow Method II below, adapting directions to variations in construction as necessary.

PREPARATION

Take out the old zipper by removing the stitching. Where there is a waistband or a facing, remove enough stitching to open out the fabric attached to the zipper. Since seam allowance at a neck or waist will probably have been trimmed to less than ⅝″, be sure to mark the actual seam line if it is not plain. If the seam allowance is too narrow to restitch the waistband or facing on, mark the seam line slightly down, tapering back to old seam line.

LAPPED or CENTERED APPLICATION

Method I—Mark position for bottom stop of zipper so that top stop will be ⅜″ below a waist seam line or ½″ below a neck seam line. Press out folds of seam allowances. Machine-baste the opening together on seam line and insert the zipper according to instructions on page 266 or page 268.

Method II—**Do not** press out folds of seam allowances. Use a zipper foot and work on outside of garment. **For a lapped application,** pin or baste the underlap of the opening to the zipper, close to the coil or chain, and stitch close to fold. Baste the overlap to the zipper tape just outside of the old stitching line; make sure that the edge covers the stitching on the underlap and is in line with the garment

seam. Stitch, following the old stitching line. For a **centered application,** pin or baste each side of opening to the zipper so that the edges meet at center of coil or chain. Stitch each side from bottom to top, following the old stitching lines.

On both applications, bring thread-ends to inside and tie. Press.

INVISIBLE ZIPPER APPLICATION

Mark ⅛″ to ¼″ down from waist or neck seam line for positioning of top stops. Open the seam below the zipper opening for about 4″. Press out folds of seam allowances. Placing top stops at markings, insert zipper according to instructions on page 270.

REPLACING A JACKET ZIPPER

● Measure the old zipper. The new one should be the same length or slightly shorter.

● Examine the jacket to see how the zipper is put in. If necessary, adapt the instructions below so as to use the old stitching lines and folded edges.

● Take out the zipper by removing stitching.

● Separate the zipper and work with one side at a time.

36

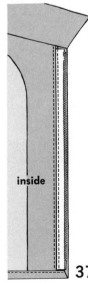

a. Work on inside of jacket with zipper face-down. Bring top stop of zipper as close to the collar as possible. Fold down the tape-end or tuck it under the collar. Pin and baste folded edge of facing to zipper tape, ¼″ from teeth (36). Keeping jacket body out of the way, stitch edge of facing to zipper tape only.

b. Work on outside of jacket. Pin folded edge of jacket over teeth so that teeth are covered. Stitch, following old stitching line (ill. 37 shows finished work from the inside).

37

If the tape-end has been tucked under the collar, sew up collar seam by hand. If the tape-end has been folded under, machine-stitch across the folded end, as shown (38).

c. Zip second half of zipper to attached zipper half. Turn jacket wrong side out. Line up the collar seam and pin the fold at edge of facing in position over free zipper tape (39). Separate the zipper and complete the application, repeating procedure for first side.

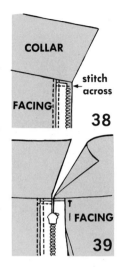

REPLACING A MAN'S TROUSER ZIPPER

Men's trouser zippers come in 9″ and 11″ lengths. In the 9″ length, there is a heavy metal zipper for work and play clothes that can, if necessary, be cut down for children's jeans. In other cases, any zipper long enough can be used and cut to fit the trouser opening (see p. 264). To do this, work with the full-length zipper following step **a** and letting the zipper extend at the top. Then cut as instructed below. Be sure not to close the zipper until the top end is secured, or covered by the waistband.

a. Left front (fly edge)—Remove the topstitching that holds the facing and open out the facing. Place closed zipper on it face-down, trimmed tape-ends at bottom of opening. Easing fabric to zipper, pin tape to opened-out facing over old stitching line. Baste. Stitch with two lines of stitching, stopping at waist-band seam line. Fold facing in place and baste.

If the zipper is too long, open it and cut off the stitched half ¼″ above waistband seam line, as shown (40).

Tuck zipper-end under waistband. Topstitch waistband seam (40a). If zipper is being shortened, close it, cut the second half ¼″ above waistband seam line and open the zipper again.

b. Right front (with separate extension). Working on **outside** of garment and beginning at bottom of opening, pin edge of opening (not edge of extension, see ill. 41) over the zipper tape close to teeth or coil. Tuck zipper-end under waistband. Baste the extension in place under zipper and stitch through all thicknesses, as shown. Topstitch waistband seam (41a), slowly stitching over coil or between teeth.

c. Left front—Change to regular presser foot. Keeping the other edge of the opening out of the way, stitch facing on outside as shown, over the old stitching line. On inside, at bottom, hand-sew raw tape-ends to facing, also edge of extension to edge of facing. Replace any extra stitching (bar tack or other) that you have taken out. Press (42).

• Examine the opening to see how the old zipper is put in.

If necessary, adapt the instructions below so as to use the old stitching lines and folded edges.

• Take out zipper by removing stitching.

• On the new zipper, trim tapes ¼″ below bottom stop.

• Use the zipper foot on your machine.

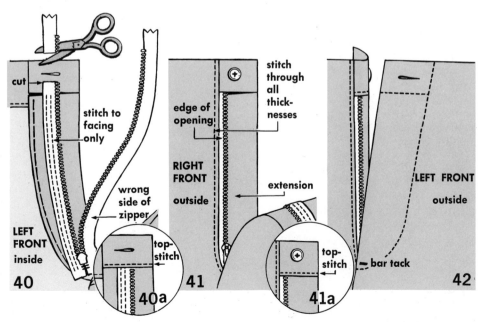

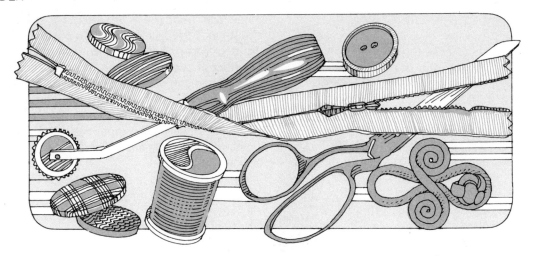

Index